*Respectfully dedicated to the officers and men of the
Fast Carrier Task Force and Logistic Support Group:
those who came home and their shipmates who
remain on watch.*

Contents

Author's Note

Many accounts exist of the late Pacific War in 1944–1945. Most cover the Pacific Theater of Operations as a whole, comprehensive in arc, some focusing on Marines, Army, or Navy. Others contain the memoir of a single serviceman and his individual perspective. The account that follows differs in scope and intent: it follows men of a single ship as an ensemble crew in the final year of the war. What you read is what they experienced, witnessed, and knew at the time, and nothing more.

If many noteworthy events from the Pacific are not present, this is an intentional approach to the narrative. Like every other ship serving in the Pacific Fleet, the men of USS *Astoria* were limited to what they learned at the time—sketchy Pacific War News Service reports in the ship's morning press and PA announcements from their captain. Beyond that, any "news" was rumor, "scuttlebutt," something shouted from the nearest ship when close enough. In many ways, civilian America spent this final year far better informed about the war than the men actually fighting it on the front lines.

Where practicable the terminology and slang is written as that of the period, although US Navy jargon has been minimized for accessibility to the reader. The events depicted within are all factual, from firsthand interviews and personal journals vetted completely against US Navy deck logs, war diaries, and action reports accessed from the National Archives. There are no exaggerated or uncorroborated "sea stories," but instead an insight into American men at war, their thoughts and experiences at the time.

If the readers find themselves understanding the limited perspective of the sailor and Marine aboard ship in a time of desperate warfare, this endeavor will have been a success.

—*Brent E. Jones*

Introduction

The Silence

Austin, Texas
Fall 2006

T he old man thumbed slowly through the photographs, both he and the images showing the ravages of time. For my grandfather, age brought weathered flesh and atrophied muscle, one hand covered in intravenous tubing and bandage tape. The photos he hadn't seen in decades showed age in their own way—black-and-white contrast faded into mottled shades of brown. He studied each image but said nothing; the only sounds in the room were rasps of breath punctuated by the rhythmic beeps of medical equipment and the IV drip.

Perhaps he has forgotten all of it. I felt myself slump on the inside. *Oh, Paw-paw...*

Image after image of youthful men—boys, really—all crisp uniforms and smiles surrounded by military trucks, government-issue tents, and palm trees...men of a different era, their thoughts and dreams only hinted at by snapshots in time. Paw-paw standing on his head in ocean surf, surrounded by his buddies, vibrant with their lives ahead of them.

So many years had passed. The old man finally paused at one photo, fixated on a face...and he began to chuckle. "I could write you a book about this guy!" he pointed. Memories unlocked and poured in. My grandfather spent the next hour relating vignettes from his time in the Pacific Theater during World War II. His stories always centered on humor, perhaps because that was the type of tale most accessible for those of us who hadn't been there.

As we walked through the parking garage on our way out of the hospital, Dad validated the decision to bring the stack of old photos to lift Paw-paw's spirits. "That was probably the best medicine he could have had." My grandfather hung on for a while longer, but his cancer ultimately took him from us. I secured his Good Conduct Medal lapel pin to his coat when I said goodbye to him; it felt right to bury him with it. And sadness aside, I was proud to see the American flag draped over his casket at the service.

His best friend had been one of the first American casualties of the war, killed in action aboard USS *West Virginia* in the attack on Pearl Harbor. Weeks later Paw-paw learned my grandmother was pregnant with their first child, and the following fall he had to leave her and his newborn son behind in Austin when his draft number was called. He didn't see his son again for more than three years.

When he stepped off the train just before Thanksgiving in 1945, wearing his Army dress uniform with a "ruptured duck" Honorable Discharge patch, a little boy at the Third Street depot recognized him from photos mailed back home and came up to hug his legs. "Hi Daddy," were the first words my grandfather ever heard his son speak.

That little boy, my father, stood next to me some sixty years later at Paw-paw's graveside service. He pointed out the nearby VA marker for Lawrence Jones, my grandfather's older brother. "Uncle Lawrence—now he was the one who saw real action in the war...But he never talked about it."

He never talked about it. Those words resonated, filled me with intrigue and yet sadness. Where my grandfather Sonny Jones reveled in sharing his stories from the war, Lawrence Jones found ways to talk about anything else. Lawrence never had children, yet was always so grandfatherly to me. He was the oldest brother, married long before the war...How was he the one who ended up in combat? I never knew anything of his US Navy service and now could never ask. Dad knew very little beyond a ship name—USS *Astoria*. Something about them seeing *Kamikaze* attacks, but nothing to elaborate on that; Uncle Lawrence never talked about it. He did, however, tend to grow faint at the sight of blood. There was a story there somewhere.

Perhaps if I had found a book or website chronicling the wartime experiences of USS *Astoria*, that would have been the end of that. I set to work to learn more, and what began as a search about a dear family member's World War II experience quickly grew. I tracked down a reunion association muster roll and started making phone calls, interviewing shipmates. A few men even remembered Uncle Lawrence, "Jonesy" to them. Families and other surviving shipmates found me on-line and reached out to contribute; some sent money to help fund a modest web page I built. Stories poured in, along with photographs and original documents—artifacts tucked away in dresser drawers, in shoe boxes under beds, hidden from sight, long forgotten and neglected.

New contact with families each year picked up around the holidays, driven by gatherings where a grandfather or granduncle's name came up and someone started searching online. Emails also spiked around Memorial Day and Veterans Day. Most of these men had passed on, but the one thing most common in my correspondence with family members was the Silence. "Dad never spoke about his time in the Navy...," "We don't know much, would love to learn more...," and so on.

He never talked about it.

This book is intended to help break the Silence. Not just regarding the officers and men of the USS *Astoria*, but the hundreds of thousands of sailors and Marines who served in the late Pacific War. A number of them *did* talk about it in later years and agreed to be interviewed for this project. I was fortunate to record the vivid recollections of some scattered throughout the United States who served side by side. Many remained razor-sharp in their knowledge of important details, their memories prompted by photos, film, and reviews of primary documents.

Many depictions of the Pacific War conjure images of sailors suffering steaming tropical heat supporting jungle warfare. For the men in this narrative, there is a kernel of truth beneath the mythos. Yet the late war Navy in the western Pacific also endured a very different experience—often cold, usually wet ("It was always raining"), and typhoon after typhoon. They were closing on the enemy at his doorstep, an enemy determined to preserve his way of life against the largest military force ever assembled, equally determined to assert that of America and its allies.

For the Okinawa Campaign of 1945, the final major offensive operation of the war, the Navy again suffered ratios of men killed in action at sea versus Marines fighting on land as had occurred at Guadalcanal three years prior. The difference was the enemy threat no longer came from the surface, but instead from the sky. Young Japanese men and boys were tapped to fly to their deaths by crashing into the American ships bringing destruction to their shores. Neither side understood the mindset and values of the other, resulting in a prolonged and cataclysmic final year of warfare.

The fathers and grandfathers, brothers and uncles who never talked about it knew things; they had seen things. They knew the boredom of routine punctuated by moments of terror—days of nothing much to mention shattered by events where every second mattered. These men knew the smell of burning flesh mixed with fuel oil and melting steel. They often witnessed it up close and personal. Many knew the screams of desperate men spilling over the rail from another ship to their own via any available lifeline. They knew the sharp crack of .30-caliber rounds over a vast expanse of water as lifeless shapes were turned out overboard under American flags.

But such things were rarely discussed, even among one another. Perhaps the most deafening sound from reunions I attended came in the silences between stories. Men looked down at their drinks and they remembered. They would scoff at any attempt to label them heroes. The other guy always had it rougher, and the heroes were the ones who didn't come home.

Much of what follows came from private collections and family holdings. Crafting this story could not have been possible without the efforts of many dozens of sailors, Marines, and their families. Individually their contributions might be limited in scope, but as this sprawling jigsaw puzzle was assembled a remarkably clear picture began to emerge. Their artifacts and recollections came together to breathe life into a perspective on the Pacific War that has been largely obscured by time, a story of regular people living through extraordinary events.

I will never know the full nature of my granduncle's experience, nor will so many others whose family members adhered to the Silence and have left us. But in every possible way, this account has been written from the perspective of its participants who served with them in the final year of the Pacific War—the year of the *Kamikaze.*

PART ONE

THE VENGEANCE
SHIP

1

The Old Man and the Sea

"You made your reputation at sea."

-Retired Vice Admiral George C. Dyer

Bethesda Naval Hospital, Maryland
January 1944

He couldn't wait to get back out there. Closing on five months since being wounded in the leg by an attacking German plane at Salerno, Italy, US Navy Captain George Carroll Dyer grew more and more restless. The wound had been severe when he was struck by enemy gunfire while aboard command ship USS *Biscayne*, badly damaging bone and requiring multiple surgeries. He had argued for weeks with the Washington detailer, a Naval Academy classmate and friend, insisting he not be confined to shore duty. Their latest telephone call held promise of a strong sea billet—provided he could be discharged from the naval hospital within fourteen days. Dyer left a small phone booth and struggled his way down the hospital ward hallway to his doctor's office.

"The answer is no," the doctor declared as soon as Dyer entered the doorway. "I know by the look on your face that you've just been offered a good sea detail…If you think I'm going to let you leave this hospital and go onboard ship, when you're still limping and have them all call you 'Gimpy' Dyer, you've got another thought coming." This preemptive response flattened him. He'd been offered command of the venerable heavy cruiser *Augusta*, certain to be a flagship in the invasion of Europe.

Shorter in stature than most officers, Captain Dyer's thick eyebrows, dark slicked-back hair, and prominent facial features gave him a grandfatherly look beyond his forty-five years. He never smoked, didn't drink coffee, and rarely resorted to even the softest of oaths—not easy accomplishments in the Navy. Yet all three practices had been tempting at Salerno when invasion progress stalled and then he was hit by an enemy plane.

For George Dyer the sea was a calling. Equally important, sea duty ensured rapid promotion and career advancement as a Navy line officer. This ambition was impressed upon him from an early age growing up in Minnesota by his father, a man who regretted his own choices. Despite his eagerness and drive, Dyer had proved to be an average student at the Academy. He excelled in the most nautical subjects, seamanship and navigation, while engineering and mathematics proved more difficult. Playing poker emerged as his only vice.

Due to America's entry into the Great War, George Dyer's Class of '19 was rushed through the Academy and graduated a year early in 1918. He had aspired to the Marine Corps like his uncle, but a presentation on the effectiveness of German U-boats changed his mind. Subs were "the hot thing, the future!" George Dyer began his naval career in submarines, and subsequently advanced from ensign to lieutenant junior grade in three months as opposed to the three-year standard before the war. He spent the final months of the war in antisubmarine patrols off the east coast. Almost ten years in submarines would follow.

His 1921 marriage to sweetheart Mary Adaline Shick also came on a Navy schedule, and Adaline and their three daughters were living near Pearl Harbor on Oahu when the Japanese attacked in December 1941. Dyer was predictably at sea, serving as executive officer aboard the heavy cruiser USS *Indianapolis* when war came to the US for the second time in his career. But promotions arrived regularly and ahead of schedule as George Dyer accepted every sea assignment he could. Though he had finished in the middle of his class at Annapolis, Dyer emerged charismatic and driven, precise and polished.

You made your reputation at sea.

A major surface ship, a man o' war, the "biggest thing he could command." Throughout Dyer's confinement the detail officer checked in, always with a list of "fine shore jobs he had lined up." Dyer's reply never wavered: "I'm going back to sea."

By the end of January 1944, the Bethesda staff had worked out his limp. After more than five months the captain could match stride with the best of them. The detail officer called with news of two upcoming command opportunities in a new cruiser division forming under Rear Admiral J. Cary Jones: USS *Pasadena*, to be Jones's flagship, and USS *Astoria*, one of several "vengeance ships" named for predecessors sunk in action. Both were *Cleveland*-class light cruisers completing construction up east, vessels that would be tasked with protecting aircraft carriers in the Pacific.

Dyer weighed his options. *Pasadena* was a cruiser name new to the burgeoning Navy, a name without heritage. He knew Cary Jones and got along well with him, especially after they had bonded after learning each other collected stamps. However, no matter the man in question he would still have an admiral looking over his shoulder the whole time if he took this command.

On the other hand, the name *Astoria* brought legacy—lead ship of her class, famed Admiral Kelly Turner's old command, Hollywood movie star before the war. She had been hand-selected by President Franklin Delano Roosevelt to return the ashes of Japanese ambassador Hirosi Saito to his homeland after he died in Washington. Great pomp and circumstance surrounding the ensuing 1939 Yokohama port call made front-page news worldwide. She had been the last American warship to visit Imperial Japan before war broke out between the two nations.

In May 1942, *Astoria* had seen action in the Coral Sea. Weeks later she fought at Midway, bringing down enemy planes attacking her task force. In early August, her big guns thundered at Guadalcanal during America's first offensive action of the war after the bombing of Pearl Harbor. Yet two short nights later she paid the butcher's bill for the successful Marine landing, one of three American heavy cruisers ravaged and sunk by the responding Imperial Japanese Navy.

Dyer made up his mind immediately; to the hungry captain, the choice was no choice at all. America needed an *Astoria* in action. The sunken cruiser deserved payback against the enemy, just as he sought for himself. Taking her namesake into war would make for a fine command indeed.

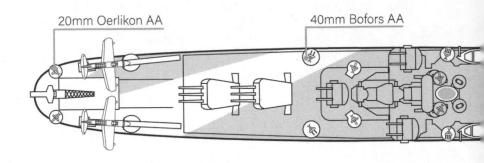

20mm Oerlikon AA

40mm Bofors AA

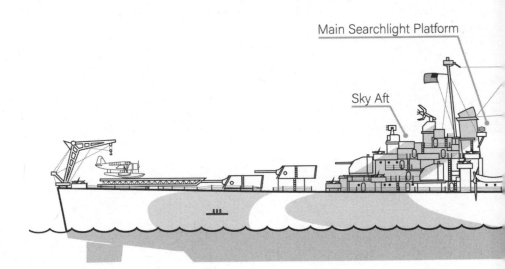

Main Searchlight Platform

Sky Aft

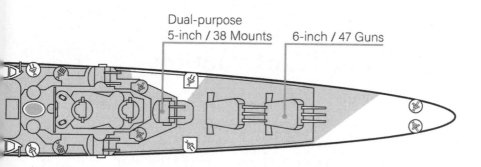

Dual-purpose
5-inch / 38 Mounts   6-inch / 47 Guns

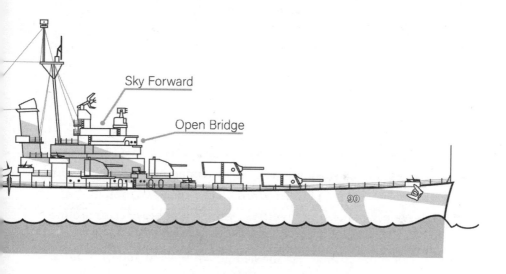

Sky Forward

Open Bridge

USS ASTORIA CL-90
'MIGHTY NINETY'
—1945 Configuration—

2

New Construction

Oh, take me back to New Construction, that's
the place I wanna be—
I wanna be a heel and lay the keel of a ship that
won't be ready 'til '63 . . .
—Anonymous, World War II cruiser
sailor song

Cramp Shipyard, Philadelphia, Pennsylvania
February 20, 1944

The trusses of the shipyard gantry towered above George Dyer in the crowd, casting no shadows in the thick winter overcast. Beside him stood a line of enlisted men in their dress blues. Some two thousand yard workers, Navy personnel, and dignitaries gathered in heavy coats around the mammoth iron frame. Contained within, the hull of a great ship rose six stories. For more than a year she had grown upward and outward as builders swarmed about her plates and frames, drilling, shaping, welding, and chipping. Now came her big launching day. Patriotic bunting draped her prow, flanked on both sides by anchors and gathered chain.

Sailors, shipyard officials, and guests lined the rail of her main deck. Others watched from the base of the surrounding gantry, down her length, with the heart of the throng amassed near a platform at the head of the builders' shipway. All eyes focused on the stem of the ship where a lone woman stood in her best hat and fur with bottle in hand, dwarfed by the colossus.

On cue the woman struck the stem in a burst of champagne mist. A cheer arose and the last captive keel blocks where the ship had been resting during construction were released. The shipyard's band, in matching overalls and construction helmets, struck up "Anchors Aweigh," the official march of the US Navy. The great hull slid down the greased 5 percent grade of the shipway, gathering speed. Flashbulbs popped as newspaper cameramen ran onto the wooden planking of the vacated way to get their shot. After a journey of just over six hundred feet, the hull settled into the Delaware River. She floated on an even keel; the new vessel found her home in the icy water. Nearby merchant ships contributed their traditional role for a launching by sounding their horns across the river.

Attending senior officers posed for photographs with the ship's sponsor. Her swing of a bottle had christened the latest warship launched for the US Navy: the future light cruiser CL-91, USS *Oklahoma City*. The Cramp band led a singing of "The Star-Spangled Banner" to conclude the event. More than a year of work by the yard, almost ten million labor hours, culminated in a fifty-five-second journey into the Delaware. Immediately afterward and without ceremony, a fresh keel for the next hull was lowered by crane into the vacated Shipway F. Such was the urgency and nature of New Construction; launching and keel laying went hand in glove. Time was money, and not a workday hour could be lost.

Ceremony aside, the ship was far from complete. Officially, *Oklahoma City* remained Hull 534 for the Cramp Shipbuilding Company. Though the hull was watertight with most decks and bulkheads in place, months of construction remained before she could be delivered to the Navy as a completed contract. Still ahead lay the buildout of her upper superstructure and the lowering into place of main battery turrets and secondary gun mounts. Hull 534/*Oklahoma City* cleared the second of three milestones and ceremonies: keel laying and launching. What remained was her commissioning as a United States Ship.

Cramp's press release for the event welcomed Captain Dyer's assembled contingent of sailormen: "They will man a sister ship, the USS *Astoria*, which is nearing completion in the adjacent wet dock." The release declared the core group of veterans "impatient to return to the firing line," closing with "our hearts, our hopes, and our prayers go with them."

Dyer's hopes and prayers lay elsewhere, at least for the moment. Characterizing *Astoria* as "nearing completion" might make for good copy in the papers, but he and his small precommissioning crew weren't going back "to the firing line" or anywhere else for a while based on the state of things at the yard.

Past the swarm of activity across the massive shipway gantries, beyond the crowds, he laid eyes on his prospective command floating idly in a nearby wet basin. Far from draped in bunting, his "vengeance ship" *Astoria* appeared months from completion, a tangle of pneumatic hoses, a smudge of construction filth stretching the length of two football fields. Her masts had yet to be set in place. The deafening sounds of ship construction might be throbbing around the clock as the yard fought to meet their workload, but precious little of that effort seemed to center on Dyer's *Astoria*.

In any case, the *Oklahoma City* launching gave Cramp some desperately needed positive press. Just weeks before, Philadelphia readers followed the much larger story portraying "Cramp City" as a ghost town, its workforce striking in defiance of management, the Navy, and even their own national union. Such strikes and news stories grew commonplace in the local newspapers.

Few if any names in Philadelphia carried such legacy and prestige as Cramp. William Cramp & Sons Shipbuilding bore the standard for American shipyards through four wars spanning a century—Mexican, Civil, Spanish-American, and the Great War. Its construction ways produced America's first battleship and most of the American belligerents that fought in the 1898 Battle of Santiago. Cramp & Sons built ships for both sides involved in the Russo-Japanese War, and served as a powerhouse of construction for American destroyers during the Great War. Their destroyer deliveries were so strong that the company literally built themselves out of business even before the naval limitations treaty of 1922 took effect. With no further government contracts to fulfill, the yard shuttered in bankruptcy.

Two decades later, resurrected by the Navy and the city of Philadelphia for the latest war effort, a newly formed Cramp Shipbuilding Company promised an economic boon for the Kensington neighborhood on its Delaware River bank. Beginning in 1940, from a rusting wasteland of abandoned buildings and dilapidated shipways arose a modern railhead, the nation's first fully electric shipyard, and a large dry dock basin. The old Cramp slipways would be deep enough to accommodate cruiser construction, and expansion along the waterfront further allowed for building submarines. The Navy was hard-pressed for more of both, and contracts flowed to the yard. Thousands of jobs poured into the economically depressed area. Kensington residents and businesses alike celebrated the revival. "More than a century of building stout ships for stout-hearted fighting men," boasted Cramp advertising, capitalizing on the name and prestige of its predecessor company.

George Dyer expected to walk into a manufacturing enterprise worthy of such heritage. Yet beyond the public facade, his February 1944 arrival at the sprawling Philadelphia yard brought him to a scene of abject disarray, culminating in his unfinished command—*Astoria*, Hull 533, draped not in bunting but the shipyard tools of incomplete work.

Beneath the cheers and bunting of the day lay a dark reality. Cramp Shipbuilding was in real trouble, not even four years after reopening. Incomplete submarine hulls packed the slipways and finishing basins. Heavy pressure from the Navy Bureau of Ships for submarines meant workers diverted to focus on the subs, leaving *Astoria* to languish in her wet basin. She had missed her target delivery date by months and counting. The truth was, beyond a few floating workshops and fleet tugs, Cramp had completed exactly one warship to date. The company had yet to deliver a single submarine, and the new Cramp Shipbuilding Company spent many months on the front pages of local newspapers before they launched their first ship.

The war's exploding demand for men in uniform brought further challenges. Despite management's best efforts to secure deferments and preserve their workforce, a burgeoning military continuously bled away skilled, experienced labor. Thousands of workers were called to the colors, whether by enlistment or induction, requiring training of replacements. Already fully racially integrated, Cramp took action in step with manufacturers across industry, training women for the first time as machine operators, shipfitters, and welders over the grumbling of naysayers. Cramp ultimately bit off more than it could chew in the interest of sating the voracious appetites of the Navy and investors. Work quickly fell behind schedule.

By late 1942, a supply backlog caused flares of community rage. The shipyard parking lot grew so packed with raw materials from contracts behind schedule that workers were forced to park on the narrow Kensington neighborhood streets. Once-elated Kensington residents took to vandalizing hundreds of Cramp workers' vehicles. They stuffed chewing gum in keyholes, scratched paint with keys, and poured water in gas tanks.

While *Astoria*'s launching on March 6, 1943, brought a momentary bright spot for the beleaguered yard, through the year relations between labor and management grew steadily toxic. A vicious cycle developed as costs soared and progress lagged. Management manipulated wages to control costs, and labor manipulated work delivery to preserve pay. The yard's motto of "No absentee in '43!" fell on deaf ears. Even as overtime spiraled out of control, so did absenteeism from work, the "Friday flu." A simmer became a boil when yard workers first walked off the job in January 1943 in protest of management practices. Cramp's response pointed to their "no strike, no lockout" labor agreement with the Maritime Workers' Union. "Is an Agreement a Mere Scrap of Paper?" blared the headline of the *Cramp News*. "Do you know what the Navy thinks about work stoppages and quitters on the home front?"

Navy Secretary Frank Knox entered the fray, demanding *Astoria's* completion and delivery to the Navy for the latter half of December 1943. Knox's date proved to be a pipe dream. An October strike of seventeen thousand employees, almost the yard's entire labor force, prompted Navy-sponsored changes in Cramp leadership to little avail. Locals took sides in letters to the editor, trading barbs of "unfair labor practices," declaring strikers "traitors to your country." A January 1944 walkout, just before George Dyer arrived, resulted in threats from local draft boards to cancel deferments. An editorial in the *Philadelphia Inquirer* declared, "The only thing the four-day strike at the Cramp Shipbuilding Company accomplished was to help the enemies of this country by halting construction of ships of the U.S. Navy.... It should mean something to them as Americans that every day they hold up war production by unjustified strikes prolongs the war and makes certain the killing of more of our boys."

Upon Dyer's arrival, it didn't take long for him to reach the conclusion that Cramp management was in over their heads. He saw anti-absentee slogans posted everywhere. "Don't slow up the ship!" "Remember—when you're absent from your job, you not only lose your pay for the absent period but our production on vital Navy contracts takes a severe boot in the pants. Keep on the job—defeat absenteeism!" To a disgruntled workforce, the posters served as mere wallpaper. The kindest thing Dyer could write about the yard was "things are going ahead slowly but surely." No one could give him a firm delivery date for *Astoria*, even as the Navy towed incomplete submarine hulls away to another shipyard for completion.

Perhaps it was in her name. All American heavy and light cruisers carried the names of US cities, but the *Astoria* hull began her life back in September 1941 representing another community, Wilkes-Barre, Pennsylvania. Her pre-war keel-laying ceremony came complete with songs from the anthracite coal city miners' choir to celebrate USS *Wilkes-Barre*, first ship of the name, and a grand parade through Kensington for the official reopening of the yard. She was rechristened *Astoria* more than a year later, after the sinking of her namesake had been made public, upon order of Knox's vengeance ships program. Renaming an existing ship under construction was no trivial matter to sailormen; traditional maritime superstition held the practice as bad luck, even a curse upon the ship.

As if by some decree of Neptune, just such a curse appeared to take hold for the new *Astoria*. Newspapers in Wilkes-Barre, Pennsylvania, cried foul immediately. "There will be other cruisers and why could not one of them been named the *Astoria*?" Nevertheless Knox kept the *Astoria* name in place and a newsreel went on to hail her as "named for the old *Astoria*, which dealt death to the Japs in battles off the Solomon Islands," "one of the most powerfully armored cruisers afloat. American sea power! Striking never-ending blows at the Axis."

Yet George Dyer had his command. He had made his choice of ship, and there was no going back. At the mercy of a slipping builder schedule, frustrated certainly, Dyer decided to make the best of the delays. Given the extra time, he sought to extend the vengeance ship concept into his crew. The proud *Astoria* name deserved legacy aboard ship. Perhaps a few men of the old *Astoria* could be located, veteran sailors to connect the two cruisers, provide leadership, and instill a fighting spirit. "With a desire to pay back these so and sos for what they'd done to me, I thought the ordinary sailorman would have the same idea," he reasoned. He requested the bureau locate any available men who had served aboard *Astoria*'s sunken predecessor to report for assignment under his new command.

One man proved quite easy to locate, for he surprisingly worked in the Cramp yard: Chief Machinist's Mate James Phipps. Wounded in the Battle of Savo Island where the heavy cruiser *Astoria* was lost, Phipps had reluctantly come forward for a Cramp newspaper feature as he was awarded a Purple Heart in August 1943 on the anniversary of the sinking. The chief would go back out with the new ship he was working to build and test, even if none too happy about the prospect.

The Navy Bureau of Personnel located five other available former *Astoria* men and ordered them to report to Newport, Rhode Island, where the large majority of the crew was being mustered. Four of the five were ship's cooks, all rated men, petty officers—the Navy's version of noncommissioned officers who led other enlisted men. The fifth and final was a deck division man, a gunner: Boatswain's Mate 2nd Class Rousseau Lemon from down at Key West. The captain held confidence and high hopes for this avenging nucleus to motivate his new crew, even in the months before the ship was complete.

Best of intentions aside, George Dyer would come to view the decision to locate men from *Astoria*'s sunken predecessor, particularly Rousseau Lemon, as one of the worst of his career. He would learn that not everyone wanted back out there.

3

Man o' War's Men

Elimination of the cuss words would have cut our
training time in half.
                    —*USS* Astoria *Fire Controlman Fred Lind, on*
                                    Navy Boot Camp in early 1944

Naval Training Station Newport, Rhode Island
March 1944

Three hundred miles up the coast, Dyer's newly assigned executive
officer, Erasmus W. "Army" Armentrout, faced his own set of delays. As his skipper babysat the ship's slog toward completion, *Astoria's*
"exec" directed a parallel effort from his desk, that of assembling a reasonably competent crew from scratch. A New Construction light cruiser
complement required almost 100 officers and 1,200 men, four times
what he was accustomed to dealing with on a destroyer. The billet proved
a far cry from the Academy grad's early war South Pacific convoy duty
aboard destroyers.

Reporting to Newport, the veteran officer now encountered an ocean
of paperwork and bureaucracy. The training station staff bogged down
progress at every turn. He wrote to Dyer of what he called "the inertia
of the place...too many desks to be crossed to get immediate action
on anything." The administrative red tape brought frustration, but the

decorous, polished commander could apply the necessary diplomacy well enough. He faced far more serious challenges.

Armentrout had a floating city to populate and precious little time to do so. He needed to locate men to keep her guns in action, her engines running, and her men fed and healthy. Mail clerks, ship's servicemen, cooks, storekeepers, electricians, steam and diesel engine operators—many specialties played a role aboard a light cruiser.

Filling allowances for chiefs and lower petty officer rates within each specialty made for a serious problem. Three years of expanding warfare left scant resources of qualified personnel within reach. A few available transfers could come from ships moored in East Coast ports, and other rated men could be pulled from shore assignments. Maybe some had convoy experience as he did, perhaps a few even had seen combat from the North Africa and Italy campaigns. But there was no getting around the reality that most of his crew would be green, neophytes at sea, fresh from recruit training and subsequent service schools.

The Navy was exploding in size even as America's coffers of the young and able-bodied grew thin. This manpower crisis forced the service to lower its acceptance criteria. By 1944 education level and literacy lost a degree of importance. The US Navy simply needed more bodies to stand watch and man the guns. The Selective Service System brought most of them to the colors through the draft.

The majority of *Astoria's* commissioning crew arrived from Naval Training Station Sampson, a wartime factory of extraordinary manu-facturing power in upstate New York. Sampson's raw materials were masses of boys and men from the nine northeast-most states, its finished product intended as smartly postured seamen for Uncle Sam's Navy. At a minimum, Army Armentrout expected to receive recruits who showed specific levels of proficiency on their "Q-cards," the results of their induction qualification exam. These men could be assigned to "strike" for a petty officer rate by training and learning within their specialties. There were so many needs to fill.

Instead the Bureau of Personnel sent him seamen alphabetically, with whole pages of the enlisted men and officers, the muster rolls from recruit training preserved intact. The first draft of men he received held surnames heavily concentrated around the first letters B, C, P, S, and W. He noted inductees like Schreiber and Schroeder from New York City, kids who had perhaps moved about alphabetically since homeroom in grammar school. The two had reported for Navy induction on December 3, 1943, in line one after the other, assigned sequential service numbers. Each wore a red fireman's shoulder stripe, so he could without much thought assign Schreiber and Schroeder to the ship's boiler rooms to strike as water tenders.

Such exceptions aside, this quirk of Navy administrivia crippled Armentrout's efforts. Receiving men alphabetically instead of by specialty left him desperately short on vital fire controlmen and gunner's mate candidates. Not one man in the muster made for a suitable tailor, cobbler, or laundryman. Armentrout set to work sending men to local civilian shops for crash courses in service trades. Again his efforts ran afoul of Newport, as he wrote Dyer of his superiors, "These people are not very receptive to requests for outside schools."

Responses from Dyer made it clear the "old man" was already plenty hot under the collar. Dyer rode his new exec hard, for Dyer had placed three New Construction submarines into commission over his career and knew the tremendous organizational challenges involved. A stream of letters from the captain requesting updates and actions kept the commander jumping with replies regarding training schools, officer billets, and ship's organization. An early list of requests from the skipper disappeared in the mail, causing Dyer to assume his exec was dragging his feet until the matter was cleared up. The old man was hell-bent on getting back out to sea.

There was a "large foreign extraction group" among recruits, first- or second-generation immigrants, which was a Navy concern for potential disloyalty to the American cause. Armentrout was more sympathetic; immigrants and children of immigrants shouldn't be automatically cause for suspicion. The forty-year-old's wife was of Latvian extraction, having entered the United States at the port of New York in 1933 as a Russian national fleeing rising anti-Jewish sentiment. They married before she obtained her citizenship, and now had a six-year-old son born in 1937 at their home port of Los Angeles.

His shortages left him far more concerned with qualifications than ancestry, even regarding officers. Underqualified, Armentrout's assigned navigator required an intensive course in plotting. No acceptable engineering officer appeared available. The exec identified enough men with 20/20 vision to fill his quota for lookouts, but his five-inch gunners would have to do at 18/20. With no proper training equipment available at Newport, these gunners would go down to Norfolk for temporary duty aboard USS *Wyoming*, a pre–World War I battlewagon being modernized for gunnery school. The window between *Wyoming's* return to service and *Astoria's* projected commissioning would be very tight, giving the men little time to train. His main battery gunners would be at further disadvantage with no available equipment to train on anywhere; they would have no hands-on experience with the main six-inch guns until after reporting aboard *Astoria*.

Every officer and man would require a two-day firefighting school, as hard experience in battle had demonstrated the need to the Navy. Armentrout himself needed to find time to attend training in firefighting and in the ship's Combat Information Center (CIC), which would pull him in two directions—Boston and Little Creek, Virginia. Yet leaving Newport even for a few days would cause further complication and delay. As it stood, his paperwork showed prospective *Astoria* officers and men scattered all along the East Coast—a precommissioning detail with the captain in Philadelphia, his aviation unit at Floyd Bennett Field in Brooklyn, his Marines at Sea School down in Quantico, Virginia. And they had yet to produce a commanding officer for the Marine detail.

In early April Captain Dyer sent an urgent request for more qualified fire controlmen. *Astoria's* completion required certain specialties within his veteran nucleus crew down at the shipyard for testing. Cramp was starting to point fingers at the Navy for delays. With a second draft of five hundred more men supposedly headed Armentrout's way from Sampson (no one in Newport could tell him exactly when that might be), he hoped he would find more suitable candidates. At least so far most men had some amount of high school as well as acceptable eyes and teeth. He had also managed to identify additional men from radar school that Captain Dyer had requested.

In between rushing arrivals through training courses and waiting on more recruits from Sampson, the exec reinforced haircuts, uniforms, and hygiene, and lectured on military etiquette. One week he had the barracks cleaned and painted just "to give the proper impression." Army Armentrout remained positive, at least regarding discipline. He wrote to Dyer, "We have had only two mast reports since I arrived." The low number of incidents requiring Captain's Mast, the standard form of nonjudicial punishment for enlisted men, suggested little dissention in the ranks from men forced into service.

Now if he only had more men whose Q-cards reflected potential for fire control. Hopefully the next draft from Sampson would come through. Experienced fire controlmen simply weren't available, and training even the brightest recruits would take time.

* * *

Naval Training Station Sampson, New York

The one thing Seaman 1st Class John Frederick Lind certainly knew how to control was a baseball. The full-faced, stocky recruit had graduated high school in Rochester as an all-star pitcher. When he learned his Navy induction Q-card qualified him for Fire Control School, Lind thought he would end up "on the end of a fire hose." Far from it: directional control of a large ship's guns at sea was a complex science, requiring men of high mathematical aptitude. Realizing he would be expected to put massive naval weaponry on target, Fred Lind immediately thought of his brother Paul. Two years his elder, Paul teased Fred growing up that he "couldn't hit the broadside of a bull" with a BB gun.

How did he end up here, at US Naval Training Station Sampson, geographically close to home yet so far from everything he knew?

Fred Lind never desired military service; that was Paul's calling. The youngest of eight children, born of Swedish immigrants, Fred lived at home fresh out of high school when his brother enlisted in the Marines in August 1940. Paul joined a light tank company, which sent him to stations in Puerto Rico and Guantanamo Bay, Cuba. If Fred held any ambitions of pursuing his baseball career further than high school, they were put on hold by the need to provide additional income for his parents, his sister, and her husband and daughter, all living under one roof in Rochester. The Lind family needed to rebuild their finances after enduring near-poverty through the Great Depression.

Fred found employment in 1940 at the Kodak Hawk-Eye Works, a vast production facility atop a cliff overlooking the Genesee River Gorge. The government contract work brought long days of wading through red tape and allocation issues in producing camera equipment for military defense. The war exploding in Europe weighed on everyone's mind, but it was still half a world away. On the positive side, Fred managed some spare pay for social events, especially the early shift so he could go bowling after work—"an extremely imperative non-violable commitment." *Work overtime a little to make sure those parts get to the lathe department? Can't today—we bowl on the first shift! I'll call the stockroom and maybe they can take care of it.*

Along with the rest of his community, Fred's status quo shattered on a Sunday afternoon, the seventh of December, 1941. He overheard someone ask, "Where the hell is Pearl Harbor?" Everyone scrambled to find a radio. The disposition of those around him turned rabid overnight, as Congress granted President Franklin Roosevelt a declaration of war against Japan. Not prone to cursing, Fred realized "suddenly there seemed to be a real need for expletives." Civil words were simply inadequate. The Japanese attack on American bases galvanized his friends and coworkers with "vehement hatred." *The bastards would pay for this.*

At home the immediate worry turned to his brother in service. Letters to Paul grew into a daily task for everyone. Fred also noticed his parents expressing a concern toward him he had never before experienced. With an expanding national draft, Fred represented at his age the lone remaining ripe target in the family for the draft board. Alarmed and cautious, his letters to his brother asked for any inklings of what military service might be like.

At the Kodak plant, routine changed as well. Secrecy replaced trust, with insistence to "report any suspicious activity or irregular occurrence," lest there be a saboteur. Local draft board classifications and employment deferments became a hot discussion topic among supervisors. Extra hours of work replaced the bowling leagues. Gasoline rationing perhaps impacted Fred's life the most as wartime requirements spread across the home front, resulting in reliance on mass transit and carpooling. *Six to a car? Damn Japs!*

Fred spent his evenings at the family radio listening to news updates from familiar voices of broadcasters with their signature openings: Lowell Thomas—"Good evening, everybody," and Gabriel Heatter—"There is good news tonight." Yet much early news of action in the Pacific remained "limited to the defensive...grim and depressing." A June 1942 victory at Midway brought an uptick in morale and spirit, which plummeted again to uncertainty with the August announcement of America's first offensive of the war raging in the Solomon Islands. Throughout, Fred wrote letters to his brother, although Paul's censored replies never gave an indication of where he was stationed or headed. As Guadalcanal became a daily front page and household word, Paul's response letters stopped. Weeks of waiting stretched into long months. The mid-October revelation of three American cruisers lost in the Solomons back in August—*Vincennes, Quincy,* and *Astoria*—certainly didn't help.

Despite Gabriel Heatter's encouraging broadcast sign-on, there was no good news to be had for the Lind family on a chilly day two weeks later, in late October 1942. Fred's mother Mary shrieked "like a stricken animal" when she read the War Department telegram: Corporal Paul Joseph Lind, killed in action. In the cruelest of coincidences, the evening's new issue of *LIFE* magazine included a photograph of Marine dead buried on Guadalcanal under fresh mounds of dirt covered with palm fronds. In the foreground of the photo a Christian cross bore the name of Paul Lind.

Fred wrote, "The dreaded news crushed the entire family. I didn't know much about grief until then, and I felt like I had swallowed a bucket of cement that had set up in my throat…How Mom and Pop were able to bear up under this is a marvel." Fred's rage toward Japan "deepened immeasurably." His brother had also been his best friend. The family would eventually learn that Paul lasted just five weeks into the invasion of Guadalcanal, killed with his tank crew on a ridge while protecting the island's vital and contested airfield on September 14. With their light tanks knocked out by Japanese guns, the Marine tankers were burned, bayoneted, and drowned.

All eyes in the family turned to Fred with fear, for it was likely only a matter of time before his draft lottery number was called. He focused on his work, putting in more time and effort than ever before, every day waiting for the War Department to come grab him by the scruff of his neck. He purchased his share of war bonds and devoted his efforts to "shooting down Japs with our invincible products." Evening and weekend shifts layered on as the plant further ramped up production. Fred and his coworkers at Kodak Hawk-Eye rose to the occasion, as at the close of 1942 the plant was awarded the US Army-Navy "E" for excellence in war effort production.

A full year passed before his number was called and his parents' worst fear was realized. In December 1943 a new blue service star joined the gold star for his fallen brother in the Lind home's front window. Like so many thousands of other Northeast American boys, Lind headed off to report in at Naval Training Station Sampson.

* * *

They came from all walks of life, the men and boys who stepped off the train with Fred Lind at Sampson in January 1944. A multitude of draftees shuffled into ranks alongside fresh-faced boys newly eligible and eager to enlist. The assembled recruits filled the growing needs of a Navy that entered the war with a scant three hundred thousand men across the globe; the number of Navy bluejackets now in service passed two million at year's end with another million more slated for induction through 1944. They reflected the scale of worldwide warfare: seventeen-year-old kids who lied about their age assembled shoulder to shoulder with men of thirty-odd years forced to leave behind wives, children, and the best-paying work they had seen in more than a decade.

Not all came willingly as Lind did. Even for him, at a Navy recruit camp an hour from his front door, the culture shock permeated from the start. He wrote, "None of us had been away from home too much, and suddenly we were thrown into a group, with absolutely no choice in the matter. We met and lived with characters that we never would have selected in civilian life, and all of that was part of our indoctrination."

Each trainload brought high school letterman jackets alongside business suit coats. In any case attire didn't matter; it would be promptly mailed back to family members and replaced with Navy-issue clothing from head to toe. The hairstyles and facial hair reflecting personal identity were likewise shorn away. "You'll be sorry!" came the taunt from other men who had themselves just gone through the process.

Located two-thirds up the eastern shore of Seneca Lake, largest of the glacial Finger Lakes, Naval Training Station Sampson stretched from a rail stop down to the water's edge. In its second year of full-scale operation, the facility sprawled along the lakeshore, a sea of vast training halls surrounded by barracks buildings. Officially named New Recruit Training by the US Navy, Sampson's indoctrination process was universally known to the men as "boot camp."

A new Navy "Boot" was called such for the leggings he wore as part of his uniform. Khaki canvas gaiters laced up the trouser seam to mid-calf and strapped under the sole of the shoe. These leggings identified the man as a recruit in training, separate from other sailors stationed at Sampson. The only uniform Fred Lind was accustomed to was a wool baseball jersey with "East High" emblazoned on the front, not "goofy looking" thirteen-button bell-bottom trousers and a flat "Donald Duck" hat.

Fred Lind's drill petty officer made an impression on him from the first day. The young man wrote, "We were given to understand that we were naval reserves, something other than human, and were strictly temporary, totally insignificant as compared to the regular Navy personnel. The drill non-com professed to be our mother, our father, our minister, our teacher, our boss, and our God, all rolled into one. He didn't look anything like my mother! And our minister never talked like he did!" Lind and most of his fellow recruits were "sensible enough to keep our traps shut and let them carry on any which way they preferred."

Lind and his fellow Boots learned to speak a new language. Gone were familiar terms such as floor, ceiling, and wall, replaced by their nautical counterparts—deck, overhead, and bulkhead. The terms applied even in Sampson's barracks buildings ("ships" to the men) and vast training halls. One climbed a ladder, not stairs. They conducted personal business in a head, not a bathroom. They slept in a bunk, not a bed, which during training meant a canvas hammock suspended from the second deck of their barracks over the stretch of planking where they lined up for daily inspection.

Each man was issued a seabag which held the entirety of his new life's possessions—bathing trunks, underwear shorts, undershirts, socks, jumpers, trousers, caps, and an overcoat. All were stamped with the recruit's last name, followed by first and middle initials. Each article held a specific place on the deck alongside issued personal toiletries when seabags were laid out for inspection. The most a man could retain from home was a small book or a pack of playing cards. Marching four circuits around the station with this full ninety-pound seabag made for powerful reinforcement to keep noses clean and obey the drill petty officer.

Divided alphabetically into regiments, battalions, and companies, Boots assembled daily for Morning Colors and Evening Retreat. Up at 4 a.m., they ran what they called "the grinder," covering vast camp parade grounds while trying not to slip on icy ground. Next they drilled in formation, learned basic seamanship, and rotated through mess detail. Everyone scrubbed pots. They learned to handle dummy rifles and swab decks.

The strict authoritarian nature of the Navy pervaded every menial task. Fred Lind learned firsthand what it meant to "salute anything that moved, and paint anything that didn't." Life became a daily exercise in rigorous routine, the goals—as stated in the Sampson literature—to teach the recruit to "become self-reliant, responsive to commands, and indoctrinated to the ways of the Navy."

In whipping wind over frigid Seneca Lake, Lind shivered in his pea-coat as they lowered boats from davits into the water. They learned small boat handling, pulling oars in unison as a coxswain called the stroke. Classes in marlinspike seamanship taught eighteen basic knots as well as rigging and splicing of hemp and wire rope. Swimming instruction in the station's vast drill halls included going over the side, improvising flotation from clothing, and climbing aboard rafts. Lind's class was even directed in personal hygiene and proper washing of clothing.

The duration of training that winter varied from three to eight weeks, more a function of urgent Bureau of Personnel need than the progress of recruits themselves. Some who demonstrated specific aptitude headed off to service schools such as radio or electrical, while others reported directly for active duty. Virtually all left Sampson with a rating of seaman second-class, one step up from apprentice seaman. And in the early months of 1944, the vast majority of Sampson seamen second-class were sent to fill out New Construction crew complements at east coast shipyards. They averaged six weeks in training, and whatever got missed would have to be taught and enforced later, perhaps even at sea.

From January through April 1944, Sampson transferred hundreds of men to muster in Newport, Rhode Island, most based on the alphabet.

They would report as the commissioning crew of a new light cruiser approaching completion in Philadelphia named USS *Astoria*. Destined for duty aboard a ship of the line, they would become "Man o' War's Men," headed for battle. Fred Lind joined a draft of some five hundred newly graduated Sampson men headed for Newport and ultimately *Astoria*, but his orders differed. With a handful of others of similar technical aptitude, he would report to Fire Control School for an intensive training course. The group would miss *Astoria*'s commissioning and shakedown cruise, but their skill set was urgently needed before the ship steamed into war. The Navy would make sure the twenty-one-year old Swedish son learned how to control more than a baseball; instead he would direct and fire the most modern of naval weapons at an enemy who had taken his best friend—his big brother.

* * *

Cramp Shipyard, Philadelphia, Pennsylvania

Motor Machinist's Mate 3rd Class Herbert Munroe Blodgett also loved to play baseball. Far from a stocky pitcher like Fred Lind, he carried the lean physique of a scrambling outfielder. Growing up a Boston Braves fan, he cheered Babe Ruth in his final season. Blodgett admired sluggers, and as a result the young man from West Concord, Massachusetts, swung a very big bat. Reporting to Captain Dyer at the Cramp Shipyard for the *Astoria* precommissioning crew, Blodgett made sure to bring his glove along with his seabag. Baseball season was right around the corner.

He also brought aboard a campaign ribbon with three bronze service stars, the result of action aboard the light cruiser USS *Boise*. At Sicily his ship provided fire support for Dyer's landing force. As Dyer was wounded two months later at Salerno, *Boise* conducted a secret mission ferrying British commandos around Italy's "boot" to Taranto. *Boise* returned to the East Coast months later, and Blodgett received orders for transfer. On paper he was exactly the type of sailor Dyer and Armentrout desired to lead and teach their shipload of Boots—experience at sea, a petty officer rate, and a clean service record. They needed such men to work on the ship's engineering plant in the runup to commissioning. Yet the slugger had to chuckle to himself at the very thought of it. Aboard *Boise* he had considered himself "the least important man in the engine room."

His entire Navy career could be viewed as what sailormen called a SNAFU—the polite version meaning "Situation Normal, All Fouled Up." Voluntarily enlisting in November 1942, a Navy recruiter assured the eighteen-year-old kid he would receive a service school of his choice. He requested in preferential order: storekeeper, yeoman, and for lack of a third interest, diesel engines. Following boot camp and perhaps predictably, the Navy assigned him to a seven-week diesel engine school in Richmond, Virginia.

Not that the schooling mattered much. When he had reported aboard USS *Boise* in April 1943, the A (Auxiliary) Division, which operated the ship's diesel generators, didn't need any more hands. He was placed in M (Main Engine) Division, assigned to regulate steam for one of the ship's four geared turbine engines. Herb Blodgett didn't know anything about steam. He found himself instantly out of his training, with precious little to do on watch but hope to learn on the job.

In lieu of proficiency, the men took to him for his bat and his glove. Once *Boise* arrived in the Mediterranean, the crew created a makeshift ballfield in port while awaiting the Sicily invasion. Blodgett averaged .500 in the so-called North African League, as his division team dominated their opponents. He might have been the least valuable man in the forward engine room, but Blodgett anchored the M Division lineup in Babe Ruth fashion.

He had to laugh and shake his head. So superfluous to *Boise* that they detached him upon return to New York, he became apparently so "vital" to *Astoria* that he reported aboard in January 1944 as one of the first few down in the engineering spaces. He carried a diesel man's rate, motor machinist's mate, yet he had never once operated a diesel engine at sea. Nine months removed from his training, rated for a role he had never performed, Blodgett was again assigned to M Division—steam. *SNAFU*. He hoped the *Astoria* crew would at least play some baseball.

Living in a barracks near the Cramp Shipyard, Blodgett went aboard ship each day and below into the engine rooms, ready to assist with whatever the shipbuilders required. Even without the engines ready and running, climbing spring temperatures and lack of air circulation brought the claustrophobic compartments to an uncomfortable wilt. He knew full well the swelter they would reach once fires were lit under the boilers and the ship was underway.

Blodgett didn't mind the construction delays. He earned liberty to go into town almost nightly, which he used to telephone his girlfriend Betty up in West Concord. Weekend passes allowed him to take a train home to visit her in person, as well as his mother and friends. Through the end of winter and early spring, Blodgett also took in as many hockey games as he could. He watched the Philadelphia Falcons of the Eastern Hockey League play the Boston Olympics, the Brooklyn Crescents, and the brawling US Coast Guard Cutters. The Coast Guard team had a special reputation in Philadelphia after a memorable fight that pulled in the fans and eventually a police riot squad. He just hoped *Astoria* wouldn't leave Philadelphia before the spring start of the major-league season. He might get a chance to watch his beloved Braves play an away game in Philly.

Herb Blodgett wasn't alone in finding himself out of his element in training. His friend and fellow engineer, Electrician's Mate 2nd Class Jim Peddie, also detached from *Boise* for the *Astoria* precommissioning crew. A talented electrician also hailing from Massachusetts, Peddie knew *Boise*'s power plant inside and out. Peddie quickly discovered the main electrical systems built into *Astoria* reflected a different beast altogether. Nonrated men, "strikers" fresh from Electrical School and with experience from other New Construction builds, held far more knowledge than he did. Peddie might be a veteran with plenty of sea experience, but his expertise covered obsolescent systems not present in *Astoria*.

When asked to manage circuit breakers aboard ship, he knew there were more qualified men. He graciously volunteered himself to move into lighting, where not much had changed and he could lead men effectively. He landed his own shop in charge of topside lighting and would have twelve men under him. Blodgett's work brought more time than responsibility, but Peddie found plenty to do in testing lighting systems.

While Blodgett found the local hockey rink, Peddie spent his liberty at a barroom near Cramp called The Tin Roof. The barroom backed up against train tracks bringing materials to the shipyard. Enjoying glasses of beer over frankfurters with hot mustard, Peddie could reach his arm out the window and touch the moving trains.

So went the hodge-podge of New Construction—green Boots and unproven transfers. Once a ship had been to sea, sailors came aboard and transferred out in small numbers on a regular schedule. This ensured a smooth transfer of knowledge and a core group in each division that knew one another and functioned as a team. For Dyer and Armentrout, no such luxury existed with *Astoria*. While Armentrout mustered untested men learning new skill sets in Newport, Dyer's precommissioning crew at Cramp brought an even greater unknown.

Expected to immediately settle in as proficient leaders, the arriving men detached from other stations tended to be castoffs for a variety of reasons. Some like Blodgett possessed training outside their assigned specialties. Others like Peddie possessed training and proficiency in old equipment. Some might even be disciplinary trouble, with their previous command only too happy to push the problem to someone else. Most were available for a reason, and precious few had ever worked together.

The final critical component was an area where neither Dyer nor Armentrout could exercise much control: assignment of the ship's officer complement. The Bureau of Personnel detailed all regular Navy officers and reservists. Seven lieutenant commanders were assigned as heads of departments—Engineering, Gunnery, Medical, Communications, Supply, Navigation, and the First Lieutenant, responsible for the deck divisions. Neither the skipper nor exec had ever been to sea with any of them.

The remainder of the *Astoria* officer complement, all junior, brought scant experience. Beyond a handful of combat veterans, many were "90-day wonders," a derisive slang term applied to wartime additions rushed through three-month officer candidate schools at colleges. A few men with special skills—a lawyer, doctor, dentist, and chaplain—received commissions at higher ranks directly from civilian life. Much like the other branches of service, the Navy largely utilized its senior noncoms, the chief petty officers, to educate both "fresh-caught" officers and enlisted men. Dyer's nucleus of veterans would have their work cut out for them with such a green crew in a new ship. The skipper held hope that at a minimum his six old *Astoria* men, each a petty officer and combat veteran, would lead in fostering fighting spirit aboard the new *Astoria*.

* * *

On April 17, a fuming Rousseau Lemon arrived with his seabag at the Cramp yard, sailors fresh from boot camp in tow. The ruddy, freckled twenty-four-year-old petty officer had said goodbye to his pregnant wife and reported up to Newport to lead and train men, just as the Navy expected. His qualifications included the loading and firing of big Bofors 40mm antiaircraft guns, and the new *Astoria* would carry plenty of them. His men would outfit the ship's 5th and 6th Divisions, starboard and port 40mm mounts respectively. Now he joined the likes of Blodgett and Peddie at the shipyard for precommissioning detail. Veteran of the sinking of heavy cruiser *Astoria*, bitter at the Navy, bitter at the irony of this new assignment, Lemon even held reason to be bitter about his seabag. Just getting a replacement after his first *Astoria* had been shot out from under him off Guadalcanal brought plenty of red tape.

Lemon had enlisted in June 1941, before the war. He hailed from San Antonio, Texas, where his father had relocated the family from Indiana following the untimely death of his mother. At seventeen and with five younger siblings, he had dropped out of high school to help his father make ends meet. His uncle ran a Venetian blind company, and Rousseau Lemon worked in the Alamo City alongside his cousins as an installer making $45 per month. After some trouble with the local law—"disturbing the peace" was the arresting charge—the US Navy became an attractive option.

His stated reason for voluntary enlistment was "to learn a trade," and pure chance put him aboard a heavy cruiser named *Astoria* in late 1941. A proud, storied ship to others, *Astoria* was just a name to Lemon. He joined the Navy for work, pay, and an insurance policy he kept up to date for his family. He certainly didn't sign up for a war.

Yet war arrived with a fury. At sea when Imperial Japan struck on December 7, Lemon and his *Astoria* shipmates returned to their home port of Pearl Harbor days later to find American battleships strewn like children's toys, men and parts of men floating in a sludge of fuel oil and debris. Lemon's deck division was assigned the terrible, nauseating task of lowering boats and fishing human remains from the morass, recovering what they could for identification and burial.

Lemon spent his first Christmas away from home standing watch at his 1.1-inch antiaircraft gun mount. Wake Island had just fallen to the Japanese after a gallant stand by US Marines, bringing a further setback to America in the fledgling war. *Astoria* men seethed at the news, for they had sortied out to the Wake siege as part of a reinforcing task force, only to be recalled as they drew near enough to make a difference. Their war would have to wait for the new year of 1942 even as the surviving Marines were taken prisoner.

The patrols in the months that followed proved fruitless and discouraging. Further Japanese advances drew the US Navy south of the equator to protect shipping lanes to vital allies Australia and New Zealand. A ninety-nine-day foray of aircraft carrier escort duty across the equator left the ship short on supplies. Lemon and his shipmates endured weeks of food and water rationing.

In May 1942, Rousseau Lemon and *Astoria* first saw action while guarding the aircraft carrier *Yorktown* in the Coral Sea. While *Yorktown* survived multiple attacks, another American carrier, USS *Lexington*, was sunk. More direct combat followed shortly; a month later Lemon's antiaircraft guns spit fire at enemy planes off Midway in a desperate bid to protect *Yorktown* from a similar fate. Despite their best efforts, *Yorktown* was bombed, torpedoed, and ultimately also sacrificed to the Pacific Ocean's depths. Considered American victories despite the precious carrier losses, the battles sent the Imperial Japanese Navy reeling. Lemon earned two bronze service stars for his Asiatic-Pacific Campaign ribbon.

In August 1942, America went on the offensive. *Astoria* covered the Guadalcanal invasion with her thunderous main battery as eleven thousand Marines made their way ashore. Lemon fought off aerial attacks from responding Japanese bombers for the two days that followed as a pointer for his quad 1.1-inch mount. Over those days the smell and taste of war merged with now familiar sounds.

He'd learned what war was, or so he thought.

Then came the night patrol off nearby Savo Island, where the young man witnessed wholesale slaughter. Fewer than forty-eight hours into the invasion, responding Japanese warships preyed upon Lemon's column of ships. They struck with surprise and accuracy, raining steel the length of *Astoria* and two other American cruisers. Salvo after salvo aggressively sent glowing shapes slamming into *Astoria*, crashing through her decks and hull, igniting massive fires. With precious little shielding at his fantail mount, Rousseau Lemon watched in horror as his friends were blown apart, the screams of the dying swirling around him as they fell in the storm of naval gunfire. The surviving gunners managed precious few return shots before seeking cover behind anything not burning, anything that put some steel plating between their flesh and the onslaught.

Following fifteen minutes of hellish pounding, the attack ended as abruptly as it had begun, with the enemy ships departing at high speed. The burning silhouettes of *Astoria*'s sister cruisers *Vincennes* and *Quincy* were also gone, lost to the depths of Savo Sound. *Astoria* lay dead in the water, fires raging amidships. A sickening miasma of burning fuel oil, aviation gasoline, paint, and flesh hung over the deck as Lemon rose from cover. He felt pain in his leg, but it didn't appear to be bleeding. A survivor by fate, he helped treat wounded on a deck slick with their blood. All the survivors could do was hold on, fight back the flames, and wait for support from other American ships. Hours passed.

Dawn broke before a destroyer came alongside to unload more men astern to help fight fires. Their efforts lasted until almost noon, when a dull thump below the surface suggested an exploded magazine had ruptured the hull. The stricken cruiser careened to port, creaking, popping, and growling. Lemon and his fellow survivors slipped over the side as she rolled, splashing into water thick with oil and brimming with sharks. *Astoria*'s bow lifted in a final fighting gesture, then slid below the surface. Rosseau Lemon's home of the past year was gone, plunged into what would become known as Ironbottom Sound for the sheer number of sunken ships in its waters. There was nothing for the gunner's mate to do but tread water until another responding destroyer could pull him and his fellow survivors aboard, away from the sharks.

The odyssey home brought a blur of horror and pain. Hundreds of shipmates had been killed, wounded, or were missing. Lemon and his surviving shipmates came to learn the screams of improvised amputation, the stench of infected wounds, and the heavy rasp of bodies sliding from canvas cots into the ocean under American flags. He wasn't even eligible for a Purple Heart, as no blood had spilled from the leg, just deep bruising sustained during the battle. Days turned into weeks as the ache in his leg healed from the action. Adding to the indignity was the expectation of transport crews that the survivors stand watches in the sweltering engineering spaces belowdecks.

After a long journey from Nouméa, New Caledonia, back to Pearl Harbor, then aboard another transport to San Francisco, the survivors of the three sunken American cruisers were herded and locked up at the Treasure Island Navy complex. Leave and liberty were denied to ensure the press didn't learn of the losses. The sequestration resulted in a "chair-flinging riot" as the men protested their imprisonment.

Almost another month passed before the Navy divulged its secret to the public, when there was encouraging progress from Guadalcanal to offset the devastating announcement. The news sent a nation reeling.

Survivor stories from USS *Vincennes*, *Quincy*, and *Astoria* plastered the front pages of newspapers for weeks. Unlike some of the men, Lemon did not speak to the press about the Savo battle.

Navy bureaucracy further embittered the boatswain's mate. Even replacing the contents of his lost seabag, a requirement for taking a thirty-day "survivor's leave," had to come from his own pocket. The $125 reimbursement claim for "personal property lost in a marine disaster," "without fault or negligence," due to "the operations of war," took four months to process.

The year 1943 brought respite. Although still technically assigned to sea duty, it couldn't get much better than Naval Operating Base Key West, Florida. Far removed from combat, he at last enjoyed one of the most plumb assignments in the US Navy. As a gun captain on a boxy World War I–era patrol craft plying balmy waters in the sunshine of the Florida Keys, his days looked pretty much the same. Each morning his aging USS *Eagle-48* put to sea with an equally outdated submarine to train officers and men in sonar operation. Save for the occasional harbor patrol, his small vessel returned every night to Pier 8 at the East Coast Fleet Sound School. The work grew so routine that one day's deck logs could substitute for another. That was perfectly fine with him. It was, thankfully, a far cry from the hell of that night where everyone around him fell amid the exploding impact of Japanese naval shells.

Lemon earned quick promotion and more pay than ever before. Back to back promotions brought him to a boatswain's mate second-class rate. As a member of a small crew, he had few officers to deal with. He manned his four-inch gun, kept his nose out of trouble, and used his backlog of leave to visit his new bride. Regarding *Astoria*, lost with half her crew of a thousand killed or wounded, he had spent the year and a half that followed the battle working to put it all out of mind.

Once safe at Key West, Lemon could see the finish line. He held every intention of riding out the remaining eighteen months of his Navy enlistment stateside, and then the order came: report to a new cruiser carrying forward the proud name of a man o' war sunk in battle. He would be expected to represent the legacy and fighting spirit of the lost *Astoria* as a combat veteran leader of men fresh to the service. Lemon processed the orders in disbelief. A name he knew all too well, and one that brought the awful memories with it: USS *Astoria.*

Not again. The orders read as a death sentence, bringing it all back. The swirling chaos in the dark, the flashes of naval gunfire, enemy shells exploding across the full length of his ship. The sailors surrounding him, many of them friends, screaming and falling. Dead men and their component parts strewn across a teakwood deck stained with lifeblood, illuminated by fires raging in the night. Rousseau Lemon knew all too well he had emerged a survivor by chance and chance alone. The new ship would certainly be headed into battle.

No. He had done his part. He knew the realities of war, knew what hurtling steel did to the bodies of young men. *It was someone else's turn.*

The transfer order came with a few days' leave, which he used to meet his wife in a Louisville, Kentucky, hotel to break the news. Traveling to meet from their rural central Texas home, she brought news of her own: she was two months pregnant with their first child.

The boatswain's mate made up his mind right there with his bride. She need not worry. A lone sailor could get lost in the vast bureaucracy of the US Navy. A man could game the system if he played his cards right. There were tricks, and Lemon knew them. There was no way in hell he was going back out there with that ship. Not again.

Up at Newport, now down at Cramp, Lemon performed his role. He led his cadre of green seamen and trained them on the "forties," as their antiaircraft mounts were called. It might be a slow process—the slower the better—but ultimately his second *Astoria* would put to sea. He knew what he had to do.

* * *

By late April 1944, a single ray of light shone through the gloom at Cramp: the pending delivery of Hull 533, the light cruiser USS *Astoria.*

Towed submarine hulls, canceled contracts, and diverted labor permitted a concerted push by the beleaguered yard to complete the ship. Following final inspection, she would be the second warship delivered by Cramp. The Navy and Cramp agreed on a delivery date of May 17, 1944, almost one thousand days after her keel was laid. No cruiser built during the war had taken longer to deliver. The new *Astoria* also reigned as the most expensive and overbudget cruiser ever built.

The Cramp Shipbuilding Company faced investigation by Congress and the Navy into their work management, their labor relations, their overtime practices, and indeed their basic competence. Even with leadership changes from both sides, strife between labor and management flared again and ran rampant. Contracts for two future cruisers and eight submarines recently canceled, the future of the yard lay in question at best. Investors had yet to see a dime of return.

But those were problems for Congress, for the Navy, and for Cramp. George Dyer had his ship on its way, the major surface command he saw as a path to flag rank. Army Armentrout had also delivered, first with the additional specialists for the precommissioning crew and then the final draft of men headed down to Philadelphia from Newport. Not that the exec was breathing any easier. Little things still required attention with limited time before the ship was delivered. Invitations for the commissioning ceremony—how many guests should each officer, warrant officer, and chief petty officer be allowed? Should the ship's organization books be printed or mimeographed? Cramp raised a $300 fund as a gift to the crew, and the old man wished to use it to purchase phonograph records for them to enjoy at sea, not cigarettes like the last ship put into commission. "While they won't last forever, they will last longer than three or four packages of cigarettes," Dyer instructed.

As for the crew, the pair of officers had done their best. Precious few were combat veterans, even fewer cruiser men. Eighty percent of both officers and men had never even been to sea. The upcoming trial runs and shakedown cruise would be aptly named: tests of craftsmanship, equipment, mettle, and character. Petty officers like Rousseau Lemon,

Herb Blodgett, and Jim Peddie would be expected to lead, surrounded by rookies. Much remained to be done before the old man could return to the war, and when he did so he would take an assemblage of neophytes under his leadership. As for *Astoria*, born of questionable craftsmanship, née *Wilkes-Barre*, the superstitious question remained whether and for how long Neptune's curse might hold.

4

Commissioning

Individually each officer and man must always
consider himself a representative of the best of the
Navy, and so conduct himself ashore and afloat
that the Navy can be proud of him, his family and
friends can be proud of him, he can be proud of
himself.
>—*US Navy Captain George C. Dyer to his new*
>*Astoria crew, May 17, 1944*

Philadelphia Navy Yard
May 16, 1944

Cloudless sun brought near-record temperatures as US Marine
Corps Captain Gerard Thomas Armitage marched his men
through the Philadelphia Navy Yard. Heat reflected from the pavement
upon the forty-two-man detail in ranks behind him, all fresh from Marine Sea School in Quantico. The unusual warmth didn't bother him in
the slightest; he was focused on the day ahead. First impressions would
be lasting ones, and the twenty-three-year-old combat veteran expected a
good showing from his Marines. Over a thousand Navy men would respond to how they presented themselves.

He took in the surrounding brick buildings, so familiar to him. More specifically, he thought of the memories locked inside, for the colonial-style barracks had served as his home during Special Basic Training upon an early college graduation in January 1942. Five months of training in these Marine barracks followed, where tactics, weapons, and leadership courses replaced history, geography, and literature. *Now this is school*, he had thought. While his father accepted the young man's diploma from Boston College the following June, the then second lieutenant stood watch aboard a transport headed for America's first offensive of the war: the invasion of Guadalcanal.

The barracks sergeant major had been all too pleased to inform the enlisted men of the detachment that their commanding officer (CO) had come through this duty station when first commissioned as an officer. Armitage shrugged off what was meant to impress his men. All he could think of were seven bunkmates, "maimed, missing, and left on Guadalcanal under the white crosses." He could still see their faces, along with so many others. He had visited their graves in the temporary Marine cemetery on the island after living the horrors of war for months, witnessing youthful friends cut down around him.

They had been so eager for action when they hit the beach, the men of the 5th Marines, 1st Marine Division. Their objective, the Japanese airfield under construction, was captured by sundown. Yet harsh reality set in soon enough. By the time Armitage's regiment was evacuated to Australia almost five months later, the remaining 5th Marines rated as combat ineffective, decimated by casualties and racked by starvation and disease.

Today held far more pleasant events in store despite the heat. Captain Armitage and his detachment marched through the Philadelphia Navy Yard toward Pier 1 on the Delaware River to greet their new ship, and home, for the foreseeable future—the latest man o' war to enter service and take the fight to the Axis powers. She was to be put into commission tomorrow, her first watch set as a United States Ship, USS *Astoria* (CL-90). CL denoted a light cruiser, 90 the ninetieth such man o' war to serve the US Navy. And she would carry the name *Astoria* in honor of a ship Armitage witnessed battered by Japanese gunfire in the night, burned and sunk off Guadalcanal while he stood watching helplessly from the beach.

The Marine captain swelled with pride at the thought. Assuming command of her Marine detachment brought satisfaction along with honor. It meant taking the fight back to the Japanese, payback for friends lost in combat, and doing so aboard a vengeance ship whose namesake was destroyed in the fray. Most importantly, it meant he was going back into frontline service for the first time since a devastating injury. His part in the war and his Marine career weren't at an end, a question that had hung in the balance for more than a year.

Hailing from a large Massachusetts family of Irish descent, Gerard Armitage cut an impressive figure. With dark trimmed hair, pronounced widow's peak, regulation mustache, piercing eyes, and a solid jaw, the man simply carried the look of a Marine officer. He had aspired to be such since as far back as he could remember, from drawing pictures with "USMC" all over them on book covers in Catholic grammar school. In early 1942, after two years of reserve training on weekends while at university, he became the first man of his class from Boston College to transition from an enlisted platoon leader program to become an officer. Guadalcanal intervened, and his carriage as the prototypical Marine officer did not survive the year.

Armitage had set foot on Guadalcanal at H hour plus two minutes on August 7, 1942, from a landing craft off his transport ship USS *American Legion*. Navy planes raced overhead, support ships thundered, and deep thumps of ordnance exploding inland echoed to the beach through thick foliage. Just his first step into combat left him wincing in pain. He nursed a foot tied tight into his boot after breaking it on coral during a rehearsal days before, but determination kept his mind from the searing hurt. He would not be placed on the casualty list. Armitage had planned his battalion's assault on Red Beach and was determined that the operation come off without a hitch. It did, as the landings went largely unopposed after a withering shore bombardment. Preparation shelling by the heavy cruiser *Astoria* and other Allied cruisers and destroyers forced the Japanese from their camps and into the jungle. Armitage's Marines seized their first day objectives with little resistance.

The next night, the Marines were unloading equipment and supplies from their transports when a responding column of Japanese cruisers blasted the Allied support ships patrolling off nearby Savo Island. From the beachhead Armitage watched brilliant flash after flash of naval gunfire pierce the darkness, heard the manmade thunderclaps roll across the sound. Men cheered in assumption of Allied might as first the Australian *Canberra*, then American cruisers *Vincennes*, *Quincy*, and *Astoria*, burned instead of the Japanese attackers. The Marines ashore had no idea what they were witnessing at the time.

What they knew for certain the next morning was that the Navy was pulling out, taking their transports with them by sundown. Much of the Marines' gear and supplies remained aboard, including vital ammunition and rations. Just two days into the offensive, eleven thousand American men were left to fend for themselves on Guadalcanal. Armitage's Marines grew bitter and resentful of the Navy's actions even before the Japanese attacked and reinforced. With the enemy coming, they were left on their own.

The men hunkered down in a defensive perimeter of the vital airfield and fought a contest that stretched into weeks. Beyond savage fighting with Japanese defenders and reinforcements, food and ammunition dwindled. C rations became a Sunday luxury. Marines learned to subsist on captured rice, seaweed, and dried fish, their bodies deteriorating even as the Japanese stepped up attacks. Exhaustion and disease preyed upon weakened immune systems, claiming men at a rate almost on par with the enemy.

The attrition of killed, wounded, and sick brought Armitage to serve as headquarters company commander while still a second lieutenant, a role typically held by a captain. He also performed double-duty as the battalion adjutant, an administrative role he loathed. Casualty reports, letters of condolence, and personal effects inventories flowed "steady as a river." The aggressive young officer longed to lead a rifle platoon instead and take the war to the enemy. His wish was granted soon enough, when one company was badly chewed up on November 1. Two officers were killed and one wounded, all friends of his.

Armitage spent the next two weeks as the only officer in the line company under the CO and exec. There were simply no others available. Across the regiment three company commanders and one in three platoon leaders lay either dead, wounded, or out of action due to dysentery, malaria, and a variety of jungle diseases.

Four months to the day of the landing, on December 7, 1942, the first anniversary of Pearl Harbor, relief finally arrived in the form of a fresh Army division. By that time Armitage's platoon of thirty-nine enlisted men could only scrounge ten capable of conducting a patrol. The second lieutenant himself had developed malaria and amoebic dysentery, and for him the worst remained to come. Prior to loading the remnants of his platoon for evacuation, Armitage was tasked with overseeing the unloading of a Liberty ship that had beached after a Japanese torpedo hit. As he stood atop an I beam spanning the aft cargo hold, the ship lurched and sent him tumbling almost twenty feet below. The withered officer crashed down onto ammunition crates, landing on his back and rendering him unconscious.

The days that followed brought excruciating back pain. Counting the hours and minutes until departure, Armitage spent much of his time with his spine against a tree to alleviate pressure. When the 5th Marines embarked USS *Crescent City* for transport off the line to Australia, the lieutenant wasn't alone in having to be helped up the rope nets. Sailors with tears in their eyes lifted the gaunt, pitiful Marines of Guadalcanal aboard. Back home the 1st Marine Division had grown famous in the press; they had held the airfield against all odds.

While curing the dysentery and malaria took long enough, Gerard Armitage endured a 1943 odyssey of pain from Australian to stateside hospitals addressing the chronic torment of his back. His diagnosis included "at least one ruptured intervertebral disc" and spondylitis, but very likely he had simply broken his back in the fall. "Weeks were lost to testing, probing, immobilization, traction, and therapy," he wrote. Refusing a new procedure of spinal fusion which would have ended his service, he instead spent months in a body cast, then more making "countless laps daily in a heated pool." While George Dyer faced his therapy in Washington resolved to return to duty, Gerard Armitage performed his own daily routines in Boston with equal determination.

In December 1943, a full year after his fall, a Boston orthopedist declared Armitage fit for duty and released him back to service. The surgeon, a friend of his father, told Armitage, "You are the first young man I know of trying to get back to the war—everyone else seems to want out." Promoted twice in the interim, Captain Armitage reported to Camp Lejeune in January 1944 to establish a hand-to-hand-combat instruction center. So physically fit had he again become that he taught future in-structors in "unarmed combat, club, knife, and bayonet fighting." While establishing the school brought him pride in accomplishment, Armitage placed repeated requests to return to the war, and by April his desire was granted. The new light cruiser USS *Astoria* desperately needed a Marine CO, and Captain Gerard Armitage fit the bill. Armitage reported to Sea School in Quantico to lead a detail of Marines aboard a man o' war. He could return to the fray.

Sea service would bring its own set of new challenges, but Armitage understood them. The manifold duties of a small Marine detachment aboard a Navy ship of the line was rooted in long military seafaring tradition. The detail protected the skipper at all times, kept watch over the brig, and provided general security aboard the vessel. At general quarters they would man the ship's light antiaircraft battery, the 20mm Oerlikon machine cannons. They also provided security for the captain ashore and could even detach as an independent unit on land if a situation required. Their presence further required civil coexistence with a Navy crew thirty times their number, an arrangement strained by the resentment of perceived abandonment at Guadalcanal.

The composition of Armitage's men differed very little from the overall ship's complement. His top sergeant had also served in the brutal Solomons campaign, along with a couple of other Marines. The remainder of the unit were green reservists from stateside assignments and boot camp. Armitage wasted no time in assessing and prepping his men for sea service as time grew short. At Dam Neck, Virginia, he put them through a full course of live-fire on 20mm and 40mm guns. Even the detachment's cook and field musician qualified on the weapons, for Armitage believed strongly in the tenet that every Marine should be a rifleman first with a specialty second. The unit carried their own cook in case of disembarking independently as a landing force, but even the cook would man a gun mount at sea. For the same eventuality, Armitage loaded his *Astoria* detail with every weapon they might need ashore—even Browning automatic rifles, light machine guns, and bazookas. In the evenings they familiarized themselves with the ship from detailed plans of her construction, studying for hours. Despite the tight timeframe, they would be ready.

* * *

In the afternoon swelter of May 16, 1944, a ship rounded the turn from the east and headed toward Captain Armitage and his men waiting at Pier 1 of the Philadelphia Navy Yard. Brilliant sunshine cast crisp shadows as the detachment lined the pier at attention. A polished impression—the young Marine officer expected nothing less.

Not yet ready to steam under her own power, the ship was towed by a tugboat with other tugs alongside to maneuver her toward the dock. Hours before, she had pushed out from Cramp Shipyard toward opposing Petty Island nine miles down the river. Her tugs shepherded the newborn giant south under Delaware River Bridge past the skyline of downtown Philadelphia, following a sweeping S to the mouth of the Schuylkill tributary and the Navy yard.

As she approached the pier, Armitage took measure of the ship's lines. There could be no doubt this was his light cruiser. A far cry from Navy

Captain Dyer's first impression back at Cramp four months before, she struck Armitage as an instrument of war far beyond the blueprints he had studied. Sleek and predatory, her hull ran ten times the length of her beam, her bow drawing to the stem of a seafaring bayonet designed to part the water cleanly at flank speed. Six hundred feet of armor and guns, her main deck and superstructure bristled with weaponry, gunfire directors, and the recently developed Allied superweapon—radar for acquiring and ranging threats from the surface and the air. From stem to stern, USS *Astoria* brought the latest in US Navy technology and lethality.

Massive geometric shapes of camouflage paint rendered her a floating work of Cubist art. Officially referred to by the Navy as Measure 33 Design 24d, the resulting light- and medium-gray livery crossed every surface. The two-tone geometry extended across her teakwood decks, with white paint applied under overhangs to offset shadows. At a distance this camouflage would disrupt her shape, confounding her class of ship, range, and heading to the enemy. It could even conceal the ship altogether against submarines and surface threats in the right conditions. Her sole identifying mark was a small "90" on each side of her hull, halfway between the stem and forward gun turret.

Down her length sailors stood at the lifelines, both watching the approach to the dock and studying the Marines who sized them up right back. Effective security at sea aboard a man o' war would require respect and a degree of distance between Marines and sailors. Well aware of the nature of interservice rivalries, Armitage fully expected to encounter some "Navy games" as his detail moved aboard their new home. He wouldn't have long to wait.

The Marines presented arms as the ship's brow, the gangway leading to the quarterdeck amidships, was lowered. Saluting the national ensign fluttering from the stern, then the waiting officer of the deck, the Marine CO reported his detachment assembled and requested permission to come aboard. A nearby lieutenant approached and loudly proclaimed, "If you'll follow me, I'll lead you to the Marine Compartment—we wouldn't want the Jarheads to get lost." *Navy games.*

As the man's equal in rank, Armitage didn't miss a beat in response. He and his Marines had thoroughly studied *Astoria*'s deck plans. "Thank you, Lieutenant, we all know the ship." *Top to bottom, inside and out, actually.* He turned to his first sergeant. "Top, kindly move out, shake down, and be prepared for the first formation in one hour." His top sergeant moved past the surprised Navy officer, who introduced himself in a more accommodating tone as *Astoria*'s assistant first lieutenant. The junior officer carried responsibility for maintaining the ship's sundry spaces and compartments, the right man to speak with to ensure getting the Marine detachment settled. Two could play his game.

"Then you will have assigned billets in the Chief's Quarters for my first sergeant and gunnery sergeant, correct?"

"No, we haven't, Captain. There are two bunks in the Marine Office—and the Chief's Mess is pretty full." *Unacceptable.*

Armitage spent the next several hours taking up concerns for his men. He had fought too hard to return from suffering and loss to put up with petty rivalries. He might report under the ship's gunnery officer and ultimately Captain Dyer, but *Astoria*'s Marine detachment was his to look out for. Armitage had no problem taking his grievances to Captain Dyer if necessary. Ultimately no such action was necessary. Apart from moments of friction against a couple of peer junior officers, Armitage was pleased to find the senior Navy men aboard ship quite amenable and accommodating.

By evening his senior NCOs had received appropriate berthing arrangements with the ship's chief petty officers. His detachment booted eight "swabbies" from their berthing compartment—the one with "Marine Detachment" emblazoned over the door, he reminded—an area *not* for sailors to access. He secured separate space for instruction, weightlifting, and weapons and equipment storage. The ship's engineering stores had been stashed in the Marine armory, but he addressed that too. By late afternoon deck sailors were even pitching in alongside the Marines to bring aboard their ammunition crates.

As the sun set on the eve of commissioning, Armitage had established himself to the *Astoria* Navy officer cadre as a competent, professional warrior ready to go to sea. His men and equipment were situated in their appropriate and segregated manner. Captain Armitage had met Captain Dyer. Although the two men shared a rank in name, a Navy captain reflected some twenty years in service as opposed to a Marine captain's three. Dyer respected his Marines, having so much sea experience with them. Noting the day as "most challenging and interesting," Armitage couldn't be more pleased with the outcome. He wrote in his personal journal, "I think I'm going to like going to war on this ship."

* * *

The next morning, Wednesday, May 17, 1944, dawned as just another day for a world at war. News reports spoke of fresh Allied attacks launched in Italy as the German Wehrmacht withdrew from the ruined abbey of Monte Cassino. Out of the press and far across the Pacific, USS *Biloxi* and other American cruisers resupplied at anchorage, back from gunfire support for American forces advancing in New Guinea. Next in their steady march toward Japan would be the Marianas—Guam, Saipan, and Tinian.

Biloxi was far from the only cruiser built, commissioned, and participating in the fray in less time than *Astoria*. Also on station were fellow Savo Island vengeance ships USS *Quincy*—at Belfast Lough preparing to provide shore bombardment in the invasion of Europe—and USS *Vincennes*—moored at Pearl Harbor in final preparation to join the Pacific Fleet. Even an American cruiser honoring the Australian *Canberra*, also lost in the battle, had joined her task force in the Pacific. Of the cruisers lost at Savo in August 1942, only *Astoria*, named for a ship that clung to life, stubborn to sink, remained to enter service.

Today would be her day. *Astoria* was moored to Pier 2 by six lines, four fabricated of wire and two of manila rope. A single boiler provided steam to power auxiliary functions. Her fresh water, electrical power, and telephone service came via cables and hoses stretched across the dock.

Yet the fledgling cruiser at last approached independence after three and a half years of construction.

The senior officer present afloat (SOPA) commanded the giant battleship *Wisconsin*, a month into her own commission but yet to leave her nearby berth at Pier 4. Also surrounding the newest ship to join the US Navy were destroyer escorts, submarines, test ships, and even French vessels. Yet all eyes were on the darling of the moment.

Three hundred honored guests filed into the Philadelphia Navy Yard to stand dockside as her crew of 1,300 packed her fantail at attention between the number four main battery turret and the aircraft catapults. At 3 p.m. Captain George Carroll Dyer, USN, took center stage before his crew. Resplendent in dress whites, the "dolphins" of a submariner pinned above his service ribbons, the captain strode confidently and without a limp. The sailors assembled before him would never know of his wounding at Salerno or lengthy recovery, beyond perhaps noticing the Purple Heart ribbon on his breast.

Mindful of the recent USS *Wisconsin* commissioning ceremony, which he attended and felt was overwrought, Dyer kept his address short and to the point. He referred to his new ship as "a mass of metal and machinery, without life, without spirit, without character, and without reputation. What she becomes depends upon our efforts." He spoke of maintaining "maximum fighting efficiency," personal conduct, discipline, teamwork, and responsibility. His close was meant to persuade and linger: "All this cannot be accomplished without hard work and unfailing devotion to duty, but to this end I pledge my utmost efforts. I can demand no more of you. I shall be satisfied with no less." *Astoria*'s commissioning pennant hoisted, her first watch set, she became a ship of the United States Navy.

The first day in commission brought the tedium of daily deck log entries, broken into four-hour watches. "Number two boiler steaming for auxiliary purposes... Received 65 gallons of fresh milk, 462 pounds of bread... Tested steering gear. Lighted off number one boiler, secured number two boiler. Still receiving men aboard."

Army Armentrout had delivered. Of the men standing in crisp ranks for the ceremony, 1,144 were enlisted sailors, most from Sampson and the Northeast states the training station represented. Fully 70 percent were unrated seamen and firemen first- and second-class, blue or red stripes on one shoulder seam. Not one man in five had ever been to sea before, and many had never even seen the ocean. A handful of strictly segregated black steward's mates came from southern states—Alabama, Mississippi, the Carolinas, and Florida. They would serve meals in the officers' wardroom.

Dyer held confidence in his veteran nucleus to inspire and to motivate. His men from the previous *Astoria* would carry on the legacy of their storied ship. But rated men drew liberties right away, and largely their minds were elsewhere—enjoying their time stateside before the ship got underway for war. There were families to visit and sweethearts to call. Herb Blodgett celebrated the evening of commissioning with an annual rite of spring: his first baseball game of the season. He took a bus to Shibe Park, where the visiting Detroit Tigers beat the Philadelphia Athletics in a pitcher's duel with Dizzy Trout outlasting Bobo Newsom 2–1. The war could wait one more day.

5

Rocks and Shoals

Get up with a smile and never refute him
For none of us particularly care to salute him
Let's wait for our chance, we may get to shoot
him—
The reveille P.O.
—Anonymous, from a poem published in USS
Astoria *ship's news*

Philadelphia Navy Yard, Late May 1944

T here was far more to whipping a green crew into a fighting unit than expecting boot camp training and service schools to do the trick. A captain might set expectations in a commissioning speech or other such address, but having the message take hold required much harder, more extensive effort—repetition and drilling, reinforcement of training. Captain Dyer learned this lesson early, leading to his last billet aboard a man o' war as executive officer of USS *Indianapolis* in 1941.

Stationed at Pearl Harbor, the assignment aligned with his career progression. Yet his years of sea experience against a backdrop of rising tensions in the Pacific led him to feel all was not right aboard the heavy cruiser. Complacent port routine troubled him. In August 1941 Dyer took the matter to his skipper and declared his opinion that "we are not maintaining the proper state of readiness in this ship for what very well may happen." The ship's captain agreed, and the pair put the *Indianapolis* on a stringent watch and training schedule over the protests of even their own department heads.

Within days Dyer was approached ashore by Adaline. "All the wives have been calling me, asking me, what's the *Indianapolis* trying to do? Fight a war that doesn't exist? Their husbands aren't coming home and they're upset." Dyer replied, "I'm sorry, but that's the way it is in the good ship *Indianapolis*." Stepped-up watches continued, above and beyond those required of the fleet at Pearl.

The grumbling went on for four months, even as the ship grew tauter and more efficient. *Indianapolis* was at sea when the December 7 attack came. When Dyer handed his skipper the dispatch announcing "air raid Pearl Harbor," the captain looked at his exec and said, "You and I are lucky this dispatch came. In another week the crew would have thrown us overboard." *Indianapolis* entered the war with the advantage of heightened training and readiness while other ships scrambled.

George Dyer set out to establish a similar level of proficiency and readiness in his *Astoria* crew. His experience aboard *Indianapolis* had been with a veteran complement; even more effort would be required aboard *Astoria*. Dyer tasked Armentrout with executing a strict ship's table of organization and procedures: damage control, drills, standing orders, and operating procedures. Each department would be well rehearsed for every contingency.

Yet Dyer's own exec countered with another urgent matter that had raised its head: discipline. Despite the captain's commissioning speech, problems had arisen immediately. Before men could be relied upon to fight and execute their duties, even to train effectively, they had to be present, accountable, and obedient. The first days in *Astoria*'s commission were proving the crew as a whole to be anything but.

Packing 1,300 men into a six-hundred-foot long floating home, expecting them to sleep in cramped berthing compartments in bunks four tiers high, was no small matter. Such proximity and monotony could cause tensions in any crew. Taking some one thousand men from civilian life, many unwillingly, and placing them into such close confines required an even higher degree of indoctrination.

Irish, Italian, and Czech, farm boys and city dwellers, Catholic, Protestant, and Jewish: all brought their own prejudices and conflicts aboard along with their seabags. "Colored," "Mexican," and "Indian" were the most charitable terms for minority groups. Just about anything could start a fight, including the collision of Billy Yank and Johnny Reb from men who grew up provincially among relatives within living memory of the Civil War. The hodgepodge of North and South, young and old, blue bloods and immigrants, Breen and Bullard, Dargiewicz and DeScisciolo, Dolci and DuBose, Moccia and Migliorisi, Tackett and Theaker, all moved into roles that began alphabetically.

Fighting and disrespecting the authority of rank arose quickly as problems, but the biggest disciplinary issue by far was absenteeism. From the time a man left ship, the clock was running, his return expected down to the precise minute. Reporting back aboard beyond that time constituted "absent over liberty." Many men returned from liberty hours overdue, some days, some even weeks. A handful had never reported to commissioning muster at all and chose to go AWOL—absent without leave. Time would tell if they were merely "stragglers" (a serious enough military crime) or outright deserters from the service. Such men assigned to *Astoria*'s commissioning, or "plankowner," crew would be hunted down and ultimately serve time in disciplinary barracks if apprehended.

These problems were nothing new to the Navy Department. A ship at sea required strict adherence to order and authority, and testing that authority was a time-honored practice by young men. Hundreds of years of nautical experience sculpted the modern Articles for the Government of the United States Navy. Colloquially and universally referred to as "Rocks and Shoals," the articles mapped out the conduct and expectations of all officers and men in American naval service.

The articles covered a wide range of infractions—disobeying lawful orders, striking a superior, sleeping on watch, abandoning post without relief, swearing, drunkenness, gambling, or "any other scandalous conduct tending to the destruction of good morals." High crimes such as mutiny and sedition received due coverage, and Rocks and Shoals even retained such arcane concepts as challenging another man to a duel or acting as a second for such.

Dyer had ordered his division officers to read Rocks and Shoals to their men at commissioning. As stated within the articles themselves, they would be posted and read again to the crew monthly. Navy practice drilled the laws into a sailor through repetition, yet some men soon appeared to be on a quest to treat Rocks and Shoals as a personal checklist. While such matters came part and parcel with leading sailormen, the sheer volume of incidents alarmed Armentrout. Rocks and Shoals had never been tested to the degree of the 1944 Navy in a fourth year of national compulsory service.

Despite wrathful language of punishments up to loss of citizenship or death, Article 30 of Rocks and Shoals dictated the limits of punishment that could be doled out for most offenses. The desperate wartime need for manpower mitigated things; court-martial judgments recommending bad-conduct discharge from the service were almost always remitted upon review. The 1944 situation was simply so strained that otherwise undesirables had to be retained on board to perform menial duties.

Dyer and Armentrout set to work doling out strict punishment for infractions, especially for cases of insubordination and absenteeism. Through Captain's Mast, the man on report would appear before the captain or executive officer for a preliminary review of their actions and to plead their case. The skipper or exec might dole out punishment on the spot for something minor, or send them to deck court to render judgment, a process that pulled in other officers. More serious crimes would be set for court-martial proceedings.

From the first days following commissioning, sailors and Marines lost liberties, lost pay, and received extra duty. Many were confined to the ship for extended periods or worked as prisoners-at-large, standing watch while awaiting adjudication. In severe cases, a man could be confined to the brig for five or more days on a diet of nothing but bread and water, with a full ration served every third day. Yet there was only so much one could do to punish and motivate a lowly seaman second-class, especially a man who had no desire to serve. Just being dockside in Philadelphia raised temptation with the pull of family and sweethearts nearby for a largely northeastern crew.

Petty officers were easier to motivate, and in theory should have been more disciplined men to begin with due to their tenure. To earn a noncommissioned officer's rate, they would have spent a year or more in wartime service, learned to adhere to Rocks and Shoals, and demonstrated proficiency in their rating, or area of specialty. Earning a place on report for bad conduct put a petty officer's rate at risk, and with it the permanent loss of additional pay plus the stigma of lost authority such a rate reduction carried.

The first ten days in commission entailed mustering men at quarters, learning routines, and running tests on the electrical and propulsion systems. Over that period fully one hundred of *Astoria's* men either stood at Captain's Mast or were missing—absent over liberty, absent over leave, or AWOL. From brief liberty ashore, men tended to return in pairs or threes, often in similar condition. Reporting aboard overdue was one thing, but doing so drunk and incapacitated escalated the punishment. Other men had a different motivation than Philadelphia bars and clubs; they were more than willing to accept standard Navy punishment for a little more time with their girl.

The solution was to get out to sea, and Captain Dyer's *Astoria* would stretch her legs for the first time in the morning. It would all take time to come together, and a skipper went to sea with the crew he had.

* * *

Lower Delaware River
May 28, 1944

Cool breeze carried across the bow, over the forward guns, and found Herman Schnipper's face. His wavy hair, pushing the lengths of regulation, barely kept his "dixie cup" hat in place as flags whipped overhead. *Astoria* approached 15 knots, standard speed, adding strength to the headwind. Men in similar undress white uniforms and hats bustled across decks and ladders above and below his position on the navigation bridge. Morning sun peeked over the horizon astern, casting light across the Philadelphia skyline growing distant in *Astoria*'s wake. These new sensations swirling about the seaman second-class brought his slight curl of a smile. Officers and petty officers might be calling out orders to others from all directions, but for the moment the young man had no responsibilities than to take it all in.

A football field's length of steel stretched from his vantage point in either direction. The shorelines—Pennsylvania to starboard, New Jersey to port—gradually opened distance as the river grew wider. *Astoria*'s first day cruise would be a "river run," taking her fifty miles down into Delaware Bay as an engine trial. She would return the same evening, with observers aboard from propulsion system manufacturers General Electric and Western Electric monitoring throughout.

Once he had enough daylight to work with, Herman Schnipper would begin his task. He may have been one of seventeen men aboard whose last name started with "Sch," almost all out of Sampson, but he was the only one to have full run of the ship. Far from standing watches in the sweltering engineering compartments down below (Schreiber, Schroeder, and Schuler could have those) or handling lines in the deck divisions (Scherer, Schleifer, and Schneider), Schnipper was given a singular task aboard ship. Executive officer Armentrout had assigned him to be a photographer.

Schnipper grew up within sight of east coast shipbuilding. He hailed from Bayonne, New Jersey, just south of "Liberty Enlightening the World" atop her perch in New York Harbor. The Statue of Liberty held special meaning for his family, as his parents had passed through Ellis Island in 1905. Emigrating from Minsk, they naturalized and gave birth to six children. Schnipper already had two older brothers in the service. His father, Jacob, supported the war effort building patrol torpedo (PT) boats in Bayonne for the Elco Naval Division of Electric Launch.

As the youngest son, Herman Schnipper arrived at NTS Sampson at the age of twenty. A high school track athlete and Eagle Scout, he excelled in the physical fitness regimen and knotwork. Beyond the frigid weather, boot camp was a breeze. He could have ended up in any of several training schools as Fred Lind had, but one thing stood out to Armentrout on Schnipper's Q-card: The young man had taken an interest in photography. He knew how to work a camera and develop film. With just weeks to commissioning, *Astoria* still lacked a photographer. Armentrout took a chance with the fresh Boot.

Although the Navy operated photography schools, the tight turnaround upon graduating from Sampson wouldn't allow for that. If Schnipper proved proficient, he could strike for a photographer's mate rate aboard ship while at sea. Assigned to the N (Navigation) Division, he was surrounded by quartermasters and buglers. He held a singular role, found himself lightly supervised, and quickly learned he had run of most of the ship. The only school he attended was the two-day firefighting school, where he learned damage control in mock-up cross-sections of a ship. He jokingly wrote his mother that he had gained weight from all the smoke he inhaled.

What he didn't have was a Navy-issue camera or developing materials. The chief storekeeper in Supply Division assured him they were on order. Schnipper solved the problem for the river run by bringing out his personal 35mm. The images wouldn't have the clarity of the larger Navy cameras, but at least he could shoot. As *Astoria* followed the course of the river through the morning, "conforming to the channel" as the quartermasters called it, Schnipper began to snap images.

His subjects differed little from back in Bayonne: barge traffic, merchantmen, and ferries. With no real instruction or orders, no issued equipment, the work was practice. Capturing clear images from a moving ship brought challenges not present from shore. What he didn't expect was immediate interest from the other men in the division—pictures they could obtain copies of as souvenirs. Schnipper obliged, capturing sailors learning to take bearings from an optical pelorus, the buglers laughing and hamming it up. He even took a request from one division petty officer in particular, lest the request become an order. The man might have smiled for the photo, but he had already taken to referring to Schnipper as a "dirty Jew." Schnipper despised such open prejudice on display, yet had no recourse other than to work around such prevalent anti-Semitism. The fledgling Navy "photog" thought of home. *Liberty Enlightening the World, indeed.*

* * *

Moored once again at the Philadelphia Navy Yard that evening, Captain Dyer reviewed the day. Overall, he was pleased. His men down in the engine and boiler rooms had executed well in bringing *Astoria* to life. Her power plant performed superbly and she handled well. The Cramp-built cruiser executed a sweeping maneuver around Miah Maull lighthouse at the mouth of Delaware Bay, then returned without mechanical issue. A twelve-hour excursion, one hundred miles round trip. The only mishap of the day had been a sailor losing the tip of his right index finger in a six-inch ammunition hoist.

The week that followed brought a bustle of final preparations for *Astoria*'s shakedown cruise. Standard practice for "shaking down" East Coast ships, which tested man and machine in open seas, sent each cruiser, battleship, and aircraft carrier under escort south in the Atlantic to Trinidad, British West Indies. Staging from there, the ship would drill day and night, live gunnery fire, aerial spotting, refueling, and countless other exercises. The purpose was two-fold: to train until men obeyed and executed orders as second nature, and to stress-test the ship to identify construction imperfections. The ship would then return to Naval Operating Base Norfolk for final inspection before joining the fleet.

Astoria received her aviation unit aboard. Twin OS2N-1 Kingfisher floatplanes were hoisted onto catapults at either side of her stern, surrounding a large recovery crane. Seven thousand gallons of aviation gasoline were pumped into the "avgas" reservoir atop her hangar. Captain

Armitage led a large contingent to nearby Fort Mifflin, where they met the ship to load thousands of rounds of ammunition into her magazines: 6-inch for the main guns, 5-inch for secondary, and 40mm and 20mm for the smaller antiaircraft batteries. With the magazines live, *Astoria* truly could be considered a warship. One final step required degaussing the ship, a demagnetization of the hull to ensure she would not detonate enemy magnetic mines. Fully loaded on June 5, she was ready for her shakedown cruise and would get underway in the morning.

The only headache for Dyer and Armentrout remained Captain's Mast, a daily occurrence. More absenteeism, with many men already confined to the ship. Insolence to an officer. Kicking at the reveille petty officer and refusing to muster at quarters. Shirking duty. All told, *Astoria's* crew was saving the War Department quite a bit through lost pay.

Dyer mustered the crew and addressed the absentee problem, laying down his expectation in no uncertain terms. Every man was to be aboard for sailing or face harsh punishment. Anyone missing would demonstrate to his shipmates what a "pantywaist" he was. "You're not even sailing for a war zone. You're sailing in the safe Atlantic." Yet for some, the pep talk fell on deaf ears. By evening two more men were AWOL and all signs indicated they would miss the morning sailing, bringing the latest total to fourteen.

Gerard Armitage walked the weather deck as night fell. He noted men crowding topside spaces, mostly the teenagers: "Too excited to sleep…fresh from recruit training or Naval technical schools, off on their first adventure away from home." Getting underway as CO of the Marine detachment of *Astoria* brought him a first step toward closure with Savo and Guadalcanal. So many fine ships and fighting men left behind that they must avenge. June 5 also brought closure of a chapter for Dyer, Blodgett, Peddie, and others who served in the Italy campaign. The daily newswire reported that Allied troops had liberated Rome. What it could not report that evening was that Allied paratroopers were also dropping into Normandy to begin the liberation of Europe.

6

Breakdown Cruise

> They told us we were not supposed to keep a diary,
> because if the ship was ever sunk and stuff was
> floating around in the water somebody, the
> Japanese, might pick up our diaries and maybe
> learn something...I know a lot of the fellows kept
> records. Like I showed every time I got payday.
> Forty-two dollars payday, thirty dollars
> payday...[laughs] week to week.
> —*USS* Astoria *Motor Machinist's Mate*
> *Herb Blodgett*

Ninety miles out of Naval Operating Base Norfolk
June 20, 1944

Beginning at Sampson, Seaman 2nd Class Herman Schnipper had been instructed that leaning against a ship's perimeter lifelines was a lubberly practice, just as lubberly as calling a block a pulley. At the moment he couldn't have cared less. He gripped the lifeline, leaned over the side of the ship and retched again. And again. Far from alone, other Boots joined him throughout the morning. The Navy maintained a third unspoken purpose of a shakedown cruise, he realized. Exposing men to rough, open water on a pitching and rolling ship would shake the landlubber out of the man and provide his sea legs. Overcoming *mal de mer* was a necessary naval rite of passage. The H Division medical men, pharmacist's mates, walked about and joked that *Astoria* was the best fed ship in the Navy: "Six meals a day, three going down and three coming up!" *Damned pill rollers.* Food was the last thing he could think about.

The past few days had brought plenty of opportunities for meaningful photographs, but the Supply Division chief hadn't managed (or bothered) to procure a Navy-issue camera for Schnipper until the last minute before leaving Norfolk this morning. The camera was locked away in the ship's darkroom two decks below astern, and he wasn't about to go down there and get it in this condition. Just five hours into the Atlantic, *Astoria's* geometric camouflage hull was receiving a coat of vomit from her green crew. A Navy blimp passed overhead on antisubmarine patrol—*would have made a nice shot*—but Schnipper had more pressing matters at the moment.

The past few days brought many missed photo opportunities, beginning with exercises off Brandywine Shoal in Delaware Bay. *Astoria's* aviation unit launched her Kingfisher floatplanes for the first time. Her twelve 6-inch rifled guns thundered with their first test rounds, followed by the twelve lighter 5-inch counterparts. After a night anchored in the bay, the next day it was the antiaircraft gunners' turn. Exercising nearby in the bay was the mammoth USS *Wisconsin*, an *Iowa*-class battleship also headed for shakedown at Trinidad. Through man-overboard drills and fire drills, Schnipper made mental notes of future images to capture. He had precious little else to do.

Throughout the tests and drills, small Coast Guard craft shuttled absentees back to the ship, most under Military Police (MP) escort. With nowhere to go but overboard, the men were made prisoners-at-large by the master at arms. They would soon face the captain at mast followed by punishment. The first mishap of the cruise also occurred, as a 5-inch mount door was left open as the guns were trained. The open mount door was wrenched off its hinges as it rotated into the ship's superstructure.

With most stragglers back aboard, the training location shifted south to Chesapeake Bay. General quarters drills followed from various states of readiness, with men learning to use ladders and companionways efficiently. The naval equivalent of kicking over an ant mound, the goal was to get them to their GQ stations as quickly as possible without log-jams and collisions—up and forward to starboard, down and aft to port. Live-fire gunnery ensued, with the 6-inch main battery gunners at long last getting much needed practice. For night firing practice, star shells burst and fell to illuminate target floats. Other ships practiced firing nearby—*Wisconsin* and the latest fleet aircraft carrier, *Ticonderoga*. The ever-present obsolete battleship *Wyoming*, the training ship where *Astoria* gunners fresh from Newport had cut their teeth in April, rounded out the group. Again Schnipper lamented his lack of equipment.

For a final operation before heading into Hampton Roads on June 18, Schnipper broke out his personal 35mm again. Refueling while underway at sea provided quite the spectacle. For fleet operations, *Astoria* would have to become proficient in coming alongside an oiler, matching speed, and maintaining position while sending across hoses to pump fuel oil into her reservoirs. All in the shortest possible time to clear the oiler for the next ship in the fuel line. For the first run in the confines of Chesapeake Bay, *Astoria* paired with USS *Aucilla*, a fleet oiler fresh back from North Atlantic convoy duty. Before she put back to sea, *Aucilla* offered a brief window of opportunity for fuel runs with the three New Construction ships—*Astoria*, *Wisconsin*, and *Ticonderoga*.

Schnipper climbed high in the superstructure to photograph the lead lines as they went across, snaking long fueling hoses in return fore and aft. This was by far the closest he had ever been to another ship (mere feet!) and underway at that. Captain Dyer set a goal of one hour from first line across to casting off. His crew missed the goal by ten minutes. More to his chagrin, his ship banged into the port side of the oiler both coming and going. *Aucilla* wasn't damaged, but the incident bent *Astoria*'s starboard propeller guard.

Arrival at NOB Norfolk had been a sight to see. The central base of US Atlantic operations, Norfolk appeared a seafaring highway of ships coming in and standing out. Allied ships filled the base to near capacity—transports, escort carriers, destroyers, and small craft.

The two days at Norfolk as final stopover before heading out for Trinidad brought the familiar bustle of port activity: men coming aboard for temporary duty, as well as trainers and observers. The brief respite also brought fresh food to the galley and supplies to the storerooms. Most importantly to Schnipper, his camera and photographic materials had arrived.

Now at sea, ninety miles out from Norfolk, clinging to *Astoria's* perimeter lifeline, Herman Schnipper only wished he were well enough to use them.

* * *

Herb Blodgett came off watch at noon, but he was hungry. Thankfully he was relieved a few minutes early. Any opportunity to get topside and breathe fresh air was the goal for a member of the "black gang," the engineers who stood watch belowdecks. Plus it was time for some lunch. Far from the poor new guys he passed hunched over the side, Blodgett had lost any feeling of seasickness aboard *Boise* a year before, headed to the Italy Campaign.

Open water, out from the continental US and the safe confines of Delaware or Chesapeake Bays, brought familiar territory for him. Standing in the chow line, Blodgett could see *Astoria's* destroyer escort, USS *Mayrant*, ahead. The escort had been severely damaged by dive-bombing at Palermo in July 1943, days after Blodgett's *Boise* provided fire support for the Sicily island invasion. Patched up and put back into service, *Mayrant* would screen *Astoria* against submarines all the way to Trinidad. Sub attacks in Atlantic waters may have diminished, but the Navy remained careful with New Construction ships.

Blodgett felt satisfied his new ship was ready for her flank speed run. The propulsion stress test would take *Astoria* up over 30 knots for her first time. Despite being a diesel man in a steam man's job, he had become proficient at taking readings from the twenty-plus gauges across the system for temperature and pressure. He would move from one to the next, reading each gauge three to four times an hour. All read normal throughout his watch. She was ready.

Now topside, he listened as *Astoria* came up to flank speed. The engines ran up briefly, right on schedule, then abruptly backed down. *Astoria* bucked and slowed, her wake calming. Blodgett could feel a drive shaft shudder under his feet through the deck, one of four that propelled the ship's four screws. *That's my engine*, he realized. *Number two.* He abandoned his tray and rushed back down to the aft engine compartment.

The number two steam turbine had ground to a halt by the time he arrived. Men clambered about in the crowded space to remove the turbine housing. The main shaft had only dropped a sixteenth of an inch or so, but the tips of the turbine blades were ruined. More damage assuredly would lie deeper inside. No expert on the engine, he only knew his readings had been within bounds.

It had given us no hint. The turbine engine had instantly failed.

* * *

Neptune's curse struck with a fury, mere hours into the shakedown cruise. A wiped bearing, came the report to the bridge. The aft bearing in the number two low-pressure turbine had abruptly failed, wrecking the entire engine. Captain Dyer's frustration began at the top with his engineering officer. The man was simply too old and out of shape for his role. With bad knees and unable to stand effective watches, he hadn't properly trained his division on handling a bearing failure. Slow to respond, unaware of how to handle such a contingency, the men on watch had let the turbine grind metal as it turned. The chief engineer should have already been retired by the bureau in Dyer's opinion, not placed aboard a man o' war. He had been all the Navy could scrounge.

Dyer's ire carried to what he knew lay ahead. After informing the Navy immediately, the first dispatch he received in reply directed him to reverse course back to the Philadelphia Navy Yard. *No.* He replied with a request to continue on three engines to keep the shakedown on schedule. This would also enable the Navy to prepare parts and material for a turbine replacement. His request granted, *Astoria* limped south. They would return to Norfolk for inspection after the Trinidad exercises, but that would be where adherence to their timeline would have to stop. Weeks of repair at a Navy yard were a certain outcome as the engine would be cut out through the hull and replaced.

By this time, Europe had been invaded by the Allies in what was universally being called D-Day. The successful invasion took place even as *Astoria* put to sea without fanfare; Adaline Dyer and the other shipmate families received no notice their loved ones had left the continental US. A week later the ship's morning press brought news of an even bigger invasion, all American, that seized the Marianas in the Pacific. Guam, Saipan, and Tinian would provide bases of operation one step closer to Japan. Yet *Astoria* would mark more time stateside. More time spent as the war progressed without the bellicose captain in action, and plenty more opportunity for his crew to go missing ashore.

* * *

Herman Schnipper tried to convince himself he wasn't dying. As he lay flat on the aft engine room decking, the room spun and his insides churned. Acute seasickness was bad enough, but the pervasive smell of fuel oil and engine lubricants in the tight space made things much worse. Sent down to photograph the bearing casualty for an official Navy report, he managed a picture or two in between having to lie down every few minutes. What a way to break in his issued equipment—not with photos of shakedown exercises that might hold promise for a feature in *All Hands* magazine or another Navy publication, but of ruined engine parts.

On the upside, the camera sure was a beauty—a Graflex Anniversary Speed Graphic. Boxy, leather-coated, and somewhat cumbersome, the medium-format camera produced stunning detail in four-by-five-inch

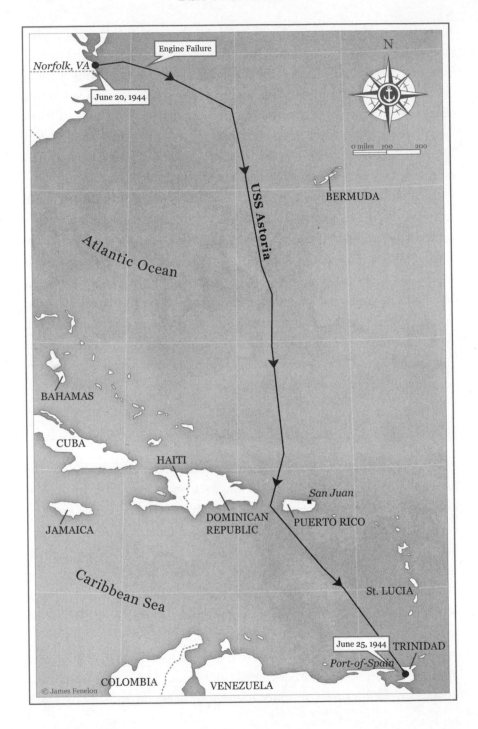

images. A very popular press camera, his military-issue version came with many metal parts blackened to prevent light reflection. Unpacking the boxes in the ship's darkroom had brought more vomit—two decks down, no rail to lean over—but Schnipper picked up the camera's operation right away.

The darkroom brought its own discomfort in the days that followed. The overall black paint that coated the compartment bulkheads kept him queasy at times, even after he overcame the early seasickness. He pledged to do something about that when he could—who cared what color the bulkheads were when the room was darkened?

While *Astoria* steamed into the Caribbean, his photographic tasks proved mundane at best. Navy ID photos followed the burned-out bearing, along with reproduction of training materials. Schnipper tried his hand in down periods at capturing sunsets on the open sea, with nothing else to photograph except expanses of ocean. Yet he also noticed certain trends aboard ship. Still no one really watched over him, and when he walked around with a camera officers assumed he was on a job. Further, no one else seemed to set foot in the ship's darkroom. He tested the waters in sleeping there as opposed to his rack in the division berthing compartment. Not a soul noticed.

Perhaps the most important lesson for the young photographer wasn't in any manual. Schnipper realized that he alone possessed the single most powerful currency on the ship—the ability to take and develop photographs. For the men it became a magnet. Beyond cigarettes and gum from the ship's store, sailors had little use for money at sea; some chose not to even draw their pay. But a photograph a man could take home to his wife or sweetheart? That had true value.

This proved to be both a blessing and a curse. Men flocked to him when they saw the camera. *Picture for my girl, Schnip?* Some of the same men were those who openly slandered Jews and had no problem spouting racial epithets within earshot. On the one hand, he could get his uniforms pressed for him in exchange for a few photos of the guys in the laundry. A souvenir 40mm dummy round from the gunners in trade for a couple of snapshots was no problem. Schnipper never ran short on free smokes. On the other hand, he found himself consistently pestered when trying to perform his official duties. "Men were always hounding me for pictures," he would write. "Sometimes I just tried to avoid them altogether."

The darkroom became a refuge. Smoking on deck was strictly forbidden after "darken ship" at sunset, as a single lit cigarette at sea was visible for miles. He just shrugged; he could smoke all he wanted in the darkroom belowdecks instead. There he could stretch out in relative privacy, free from the constant movement of men and the rattle of tricing chains supporting tiered sleeping racks. If the solitude furthered the distance between him and the other men, it also provided a respite from the dreaded "three Fs" of the berthing compartments that men joked about—feet, farts, and fannies. Schnipper gladly traded the reek of unwashed bodies for a small degree of alienation from the crew. And he could still hear the phonograph records the exec had procured that piped through the ship on occasion.

* * *

The primary purpose of a shakedown cruise was to identify problems. The turbine casualty proved that within hours. Other, more correctible issues quickly emerged. For one, men from the Deep South could not be utilized as "talkers" for the ship's wired internal communications system. The bulk of the men from the Northeast simply could not understand them when relaying messages over the sound-powered telephone headsets. Their regional accents were too pronounced. Herb Blodgett had to laugh about his own reassignment to the telephone set in his engine room as a result. Men from Concord, Massachusetts, brought their own highly unique accent, "a variation of the Harvard accent." Fellow sailors always told him, "You talk funny." The diesel man welcomed the new assignment in his steam world.

Blodgett grew further shocked as *Astoria* put in at Port of Spain,

Trinidad, just in time for the Fourth of July. Executive officer Armentrout tapped him as one of twenty rated men assigned for shore patrol when the first liberty party went ashore. He had never served in the capacity aboard USS *Boise* or even been trained for it. Such was the state of affairs; with *Astoria*'s limited number of rated men, so many had been placed on report that Blodgett remained one of the few choices with a clean record. Temperance also made him a perfect choice; he came from a family of teetotalers and had never taken a drink in his life. The skinny motor machinist's mate laced on khaki canvas leggings for the first time since boot camp, strapped a brassard marked "SP" on his arm, and stepped over the rail with a billy club swinging from his web belt. At five foot seven, he didn't feel terribly intimidating.

Pharmacist's mates lined up to distribute "personal hygiene kits" to men going over the side, leaving empty boxes scattered on the deck. The Navy didn't issue prophylactic kits based on any moral grounds; they did so because they needed men healthy and able to report for watch. Blodgett had seen it all before and looked down on such matters. Perhaps some were just teenagers on a perceived path to manhood, but his faith in some of the senior men inevitably fell. Some of the men in their thirties or even forties, with a wife and children at home, would "be the first in line to rush into the brothels when you'd hit a port." For Blodgett, behavior on liberty became the measure of a man. To him Port of Spain was just a lousy liberty town—dirt streets, horse-drawn carts, and the ubiquitous brothels.

Liberty at Port of Spain inevitably caused its share of casualties, as a few men returned to be placed on venereal watch despite the Navy's best efforts to issue protective kits and regulate the local houses. For Herman Schnipper, no one paid attention to him snapping pictures of the prophylactic distribution from the deck above. He had time to kill, a sense of humor, and he held a camera. As for Blodgett, his foray into shore patrol ended successfully. Regardless of condition, all men were back aboard ship before midnight.

* * *

If there were a dozen things that could cause friction or start a fight, there were also a few that could draw men together. The most potent was the hometown. Even if you didn't know a guy, he was as close as you were going to get to the kids from the old neighborhood. For Herman Schnipper this meant some fellows from Bayonne, scattered across the ship. But he occupied a unique role to even discover such; most sailors only knew a few other men with whom they stood watch. The rest of the crew and even their own division mates mostly comprised just faces one learned to recognize. The ones that did work closely referred to one another by last name only, at least at first. If they bonded it might be for something else. Such became the case for 4th Division gunners Tom Kane and John Snyder.

Kane and Snyder grew up hundreds of miles apart and held no background in common. The aft 5-inch gunners of the 4th Division took to calling Kane "Pappy" from the start, given his thirty-four years, exceptionally old for a seaman first-class. Despite only an eighth-grade formal education, his life experience and resulting wisdom made him a natural leader among young men. Snyder on the other hand brought the typical youth, nineteen years of age and also fresh out of Sampson. Thomas LeRoy Kane and John LeRoy Snyder shared a middle name, that was all, other than an absolute devotion to their wives.

Pappy Kane had driven for the Public Service Bus Line in Bergen County, New Jersey, since before the war. He detested the job, but it provided for his seven children. When he accepted a better opportunity at a machine-tooling factory in Hackensack in 1943, he was shortly informed by a local board that he had violated a wartime civilian job freeze law. He could likely expect to be inducted into the Army. Kane preemptively enlisted in the Navy in response. Leaving the recruiter's office, he promptly went home to inform his wife, Florence, nursing their months-old infant son, what he had done.

Tom Kane had married Flo on Valentine's Day 1928 at age eighteen.

His love for her ran inviolate, even as some other men flocked to the brothels in Port of Spain. Instead he stuck with John Snyder on liberty, a Pennsylvania son barely half his age but also a husband at eighteen and equally devoted at home. The pair had grown close during their training in Chesapeake Bay precommissioning, aboard the refit battleship USS *Wyoming*, last of her kind built by the original Cramp & Sons Shipbuilding back in 1912. The "Chesapeake Raider," as the converted battlewagon was affectionately known, was obsolete for combat, but the training ship with refit, modern 5-inch mounts taught plenty of late-war sailors like Kane and Snyder how to rapidly load and fire their projectiles before they reported to New Construction.

Now two months later Kane and Snyder looked out for one another on liberty far from home while their wives did the same back in the States. Alice Snyder wrote to Florence Kane with concerns put forth from a friend, a woman who had said disparaging things about the Navy. The woman called it "the dirtiest service," a concept that left Alice alone with thoughts that her young husband might be surrounded by bad influences, men of low moral standing. The older Flo Kane set her straight regarding the dedication of their husbands. Certainly neither of their men would weaken in their moral fiber.

In fact, the two men maintained unauthorized diaries, in which they elected to share daily entries together. Between them they would collect all the "scuttlebutt," latest news and rumors aboard ship. Alice Snyder need not have worried; her husband's diary carried her initials inside a heart on the cover. Pappy Kane cut a poem from a Navy publication and tucked it inside his, as a daily reminder about Flo. It stated in part:

> So, mates, when guns are blazing,
> And it seems you can't come through,
> Just stay right in there fighting
> For that wife who waits for you.
> And when this war is over,
> Big stories you can tell—

But remember, you had training—
It's the wife who caught the hell.

The official stance from the US Navy strictly forbade such diaries lest they fall into enemy hands. In reality, this regulation was scarcely enforced if at all. Men across the ship took up their own form of daily journaling. Even officers kept them, including Gerard Armitage long before he came aboard. Most men, Kane and Snyder included, found some sort of small discreet notebook, usually olive drab and nondescript to avoid notice, that they could tuck away in a seabag or a mattress cover.

Other men were less subtle with their journaling, such as Herb Blodgett. Given to him by a family friend, the bright blue and red cover of his diary blared, "My Life in the Service." Sections were dedicated to personal information, stations and assignments, "officers I have met," and so on. "Keep a diary!" it proclaimed. "If for any reason it becomes inadvisable for you to keep your diary with you, don't stop making entries! Send your diary home or to a friend for safekeeping. Then while you are away, send your entries home in letters—regularly." "This book, conscientiously kept, may prove to be the living record of your destiny five hundred years from now!" In reality, any such attempt would never have made it past the mail censoring officer. Most men new to the service such as Kane and Snyder weren't ready to be so bold; their little canvas notebooks would suffice.

The men in their gunnery division learned other lessons. Not all things could be covered explicitly by Rocks and Shoals; unwritten rules existed as well. Early on a fellow 4th Division man was approached by a senior petty officer. The word had spread regarding the petty officer—perceived homosexual tendencies. The young Boot jumped when pinched on the backside, as the PO winked after. *Testing the waters.* The young sailor whipped around and asserted to his senior, "If you ever do that again, I will whip your ass, you son of a bitch!" The incident of insolence to a superior rate went unreported; some matters were managed outside the chain of command.

* * *

While some matters could be handled among the sailormen off any official record, others fell well within the articles of Rocks and Shoals. Captain Dyer's senior officers spent time between training exercises working the backlog of deck courts and summary courts-martial. Men rotated through their stint in solitary confinement on bread and water; at one point the waiting line for *Astoria*'s two brig cells ran four men deep per cell. A sailor might be a prisoner at large confined to the ship for weeks before serving his punishment for something he did before *Astoria* even sailed for Trinidad.

It might be impossible to be absent over leave while underway at sea, but there were myriad other ways to end up at Captain's Mast. Most had to do with disrespecting and disobeying authority: lack of deference to senior men, not following orders to the letter in a timely manner, or not being in the right place when you were expected to be there. Such matters could make the difference in a critical moment, especially for a ship headed into war.

Dyer came to realize that many of the petty officers he relied on to lead sailormen were clearly castoffs from other commands, prone to misconduct or accustomed to lax discipline. One gunner's mate was promptly found incompetent in his rate to the point of permanent reduction to seaman first-class. Through repeated appearances at Captain's Mast, it also became clear who the prominent troublemakers were, as opposed to men who learned from their punishment and responded. A handful of men were simply chronic offenders, appearing at mast two, three, even four occasions. Dyer was soon fed up with these repeat men. Caught gambling? Deck court. Late for watch relief? Deck court. Several men were tried through deck court on one offense even while awaiting a second trial for another.

In general his combat veterans of the Italy Campaign, like Blodgett and Peddie from USS *Boise*, demonstrated the best conduct and never appeared on report. Their time in highly stressful situations, under danger of enemy fire, had hardened their resolve and impressed such need for discipline at sea. His six former *Astoria* men from the Savo battle showed similar leadership by example.

Dyer also brought enough experience in leadership to know what to overlook. Green men tended to pick up a second seafaring language. If boot camp had replaced words like "floor" and "ceiling" with "deck" and "overhead," these new experiences at sea reduced some vocabulary to four-letter words and profane adjectives, at least out of earshot of an officer. Dyer might not swear as a personal stance, but as long as a man did so among his fellows and not as an act of insolence, such was a matter not worthy of addressing. There were simply too many other proverbial fires to fight.

Throughout, the crew learned the practices of wartime: "darken ship" at sunset—all doors, hatches, and portholes closed, all lights doused— and her course disrupted by zigzagging. She trained with her destroyer escort on vessel recognition and identification protocols. Ship design problems emerged, as what looked fine on paper didn't always translate to real-world use. When the early *Cleveland*-class cruisers proved to be top-heavy in design, the thick armor of an enclosed bridge had been reduced. As a later *Cleveland*-class, *Astoria* was built with an open bridge forward of the pilothouse. But as a result, when the ship engaged in antiaircraft practice, the concussion of the elevated dual-purpose 5-inchers tore the open bridge plot table from its mounts and sent Captain Dyer flying onto his backside. He began a strongly worded letter-writing campaign against using the configuration in future ships.

Training deficiencies emerged among his young officer cadre. Most seriously, a "ninety-day wonder" ordered his antiaircraft gun crews to remain at their station on the main deck during live-fire exercises of the main battery on July 5. As the big 6-inch guns roared over their heads, the men of a portside 20mm crew were left reeling and scrambling for any form of cover. The blasts shook their very insides until gunnery officer Ken Meneke learned what was happening. He stopped the exercise and ran down personally to check on the men. Several lay huddled in shock, some vomiting blood, eardrums shattered. Meneke and Dyer subsequently established two sets of battle stations. For surface firing of the main battery, antiaircraft gunners near the big turrets would not man their smaller, exposed mounts. A second form of general quarters was designated "air emergency stations," in which a perceived aerial threat would send all antiaircraft gunners to their stations as the biggest guns would stay silent, useless against such an attack in any case.

Over the training weeks in Trinidad's Gulf of Paria, inexperienced officers learned what to enforce and how to lead. Certainly ordering men to stand directly under the main battery would not be a repeat mistake. Sleeping arrangements became another area where strict adherence to things could be eased off. In claustrophobic belowdecks berthing quarters, especially given the steamy equatorial climes, men suffered the stench of one another after long days. Further, the metal racks were placed so tightly atop one another that a man often had to slip out of his bunk and climb back in just to change his sleeping position. Instead, many men learned to carve out a space topside and gradually took to sleeping some nights on deck. The officer complement in turn learned to look the other way regarding the practice, as long as a man turned out for reveille and his watches. By the time the ship left the training area, Herman Schnipper's bunk stayed empty. He had effectively moved into his darkroom as a one-man apartment at sea, and no one noticed.

A related matter became protective flak suits Captain Dyer expected his gunners to wear topside during quarters. Before leaving Norfolk, Dyer had agreed to test a new type of experimental suit for the Bureau of Medicine and Surgery. With many men in the Pacific wounded or killed by shrapnel, the Navy attempted to address the issue by developing protective coveralls. Hooded to guard against flash burns, the suits carried heavy padding around the vital organs.

Intended to save lives, all the suits really did well in the tropical climate was stink to high heaven. Wearing them during exercises, men would sweat profusely. Combat and the prospect of shrapnel remained distant thoughts, so men quickly stopped wearing them. In the summer sun, the Navy work uniforms of blue chambray shirts and dungarees were plenty hot enough without donning what amounted to a winter layer. Dyer first directed his officers to always set the example, despite the suits being "hotter than all Harry." Practicality set in quickly enough. If he as captain and a man who had been wounded in war could scarcely tolerate them, he couldn't subject his crew to such misery.

Astoria departed the Trinidad area on July 16, 1944. By that point her crew had the phrase "this will be a dummy run" pounded into their heads: battle problems, tracking drills, man overboard, abandon ship, collision drills, firefighting—everything Dyer and the Navy could come up with to bring a New Construction ship online as a taut man o' war. She performed a final live-fire on the Navy gunnery range at Culebra, Puerto Rico, and headed back to Philadelphia.

The men were plenty salty. Herb Blodgett's engine room neophytes had earned the right to refer to their engineering space as "flareback college." Gerard Armitage's Marines knew how to fieldstrip a cigarette and leave not a trace. Men across the ship could measure the passage of time on their watches by how many cups of coffee they had gulped down. And Herman Schnipper had his sea legs in place along with a growing collection of photos for official US Navy use.

Ahead still lay the turbine repair. Whether there would be a war left for *Astoria* to fight grew into a real question and topic of discussion aboard ship. The invasion of Europe had brought the Allies a solid hold in France as they marched inland. Out in the Pacific, the US Navy had won a great battle in the Philippine Sea, decimating Japanese airpower and sinking three aircraft carriers. News stories in the *Astoria Morning Press* turned to more routine matters, such as the presidential election primaries.

Having no war left to fight sounded perfectly fine to Rousseau Lemon. He had done everything asked of him, shining as a model bluejacket from the day he reported aboard. He regaled shipmates with tales of battle, his time aboard *Astoria*'s namesake in the Coral Sea, Midway, and Guadalcanal. He backed up his bona fides with perfect 4.0 marks on his evaluation reports for proficiency and conduct. Yet Lemon never forgot a moment of the Savo horror. He had passed an important milestone: three years completed of his four-year enlistment.

He thought of his wife at home, now eight months pregnant. He wasn't going back out there again. His plan just required the right window of timing.

7

Golden Gate in '48

The Navy was having a tremendous "absent without leave" problem . . . there were just literally
thousands that didn't want to go fight in World
War II, and don't let anyone tell you otherwise.
— *Retired Vice Admiral George C. Dyer*

Philadelphia Navy Yard
July 31, 1944

Ninety-pound seabag over his shoulder, Fred Lind at long last reported aboard his new home, USS *Astoria* CL-90. Fresh from
completing Fire Control School at Newport, he brought a cohort of other
such men with him. They had missed the *Astoria* shakedown cruise, but
at least with their arrival executive officer Armentrout had completed his
required complement of men to direct the light cruiser's big guns.

While *Astoria* broke in most of her crew off Trinidad, Lind and his
new buddies received weeks of textbook education and hands-on training
ashore. Subjects ranged from math and electricity basics to advanced
courses covering airplane recognition and gunfire control. Ever the joker,
Lind found moments for practical jokes too, like wiring a toilet seat
to deliver an electric shock to men tending to personal business. The
electrical course had paid off.

The men had celebrated Fire Control School graduation by rigging a fifty-five-gallon drum of water to douse individuals coming up the barracks ladder. They spent that night drilling the Newport parade grounds from midnight to breakfast for that stunt. "The Navy didn't seem to have too good a sense of humor," he wrote in his secret diary, cryptic and undecipherable to any snooping officer, by using the loops and curves of Gregg shorthand.

The SNAFUs of Navy life followed him and his fellows when they went to catch the ship at Norfolk. Upon arrival at the receiving station in the late night, NOB Norfolk had no available quarters. The group spent the night sleeping outside on the grass, seabags for pillows. Still better than marching the Newport parade grounds. They woke the next morning to discover that *Astoria* wasn't even in port; she had sailed back for Philadelphia the day prior. The grubby men climbed on a train and headed back up the coast.

Now aboard ship, they learned that the spartan accommodations of training barracks had a further purpose for indoctrination: acclimating men to packing their seafaring lives in as small a space as possible. At least in port they could always choose to sleep on deck. Fred Lind swelled with excitement at a further revelation: his new ship wasn't going anywhere for a while due to extensive repair. Something with her turbine engines.

His excitement stemmed from two prospects. First, with little to do for the foreseeable future, even newer men were being granted their fourteen-day annual leave. Plenty of time to get home to Rochester and see family. With the second anniversary of his brother Paul's death approaching, it would be good to spend time with Mom and Pop.

The second blessing: plenty of liberty in a major-league city. Newport liberty had required a lengthy train ride north to Fenway in Boston, but Philly's Shibe Park was right there. And with the two Philadelphia teams sharing the same field, someone was always in town. In his Gregg shorthand he wrote, "Of course the service had gobbled up most of the stars, but baseball was baseball."

Herb Blodgett held similar plans, fourteen-day leave back to West

Concord for family and time with Betty. Otherwise baseball at Shibe. The arrival of new men meant other fellows to head down there with; the fresh fire controlmen apparently brought aboard a few ballpark fanatics. Both local teams might occupy the cellar of their leagues with losing records, but Shibe had lights—*night games*! And his beloved Boston Braves appeared on the Phillies' upcoming schedule. Before getting back underway, he also had plans to ask Betty to marry him.

If he could only stop scratching all over. For Blodgett, the trip up the coast from Norfolk to Philly brought a sea of fiberglass shards and asbestos dust. In preparation for repair to the turbine, his aft engine room force spent days tearing out surrounding insulation and components for the number two engine's removal. Blodgett called the fiberglass job "one hell of a mess. You get it in your clothes and you can't get it out...even after several laundries you'd still get pieces of fiberglass that would scratch your back."

General Electric and the Navy had decided not to replace the ruined turbine with a new one, but to extract it and haul it up to Schenectady for examination and rebuild. All at an estimated thirty to sixty days and $100,000. Just because of a bearing failure, a small yet critical component. The demolition job required insulation removal across the overhead and the full starboard side of the engine room. Such a turbine couldn't be lifted up through the deck: it had to be hoisted out sideways through a mammoth hole cut into *Astoria*'s hull.

Yet Blodgett wouldn't be around to see the turbine come out when the ship moved to dry dock for repair. He rated first leave. Two weeks at home, away from the Navy and the engine room mess.

* * *

Thirty to sixty days. Dyer had to shake his head at such a run of bad luck. By mid-August he had a turbine engine under repair at General Electric 250 miles north of the shipyard, leaving a huge hole in its place as it was rebuilt. Best projections put *Astoria* back underway in mid-September.

The invasion of southern France had just kicked off, buttressing the Allied drive toward Germany and effectively ensuring the Pacific as *Astoria*'s future theater of operations. Other *Cleveland*-class cruisers headed that way to protect the vital carrier task forces. Rear Admiral J. Cary Jones's flagship USS *Pasadena*—the command Dyer turned down in favor of *Astoria*—was now training in the Gulf of Paria. *Pasadena* had launched more than nine months after *Astoria*, built at the far more efficient Fore River Shipyard. *Astoria* had been planned to beat her into action by months, but now Dyer wondered if his Cruiser Division 17 commanding officer would reach the Pacific Fleet first.

Shipboard publications focused more attention on taking the fight to the Japanese, solidifying them as the enemy. Drumming up deep resentment toward Japan didn't require much for the American serviceman: everyone remembered Pearl Harbor. Derogatory names—"Japs" and "Nips"—filled headline stories in papers across the country, meant to dehumanize their foe. *LIFE* magazine even saw fit in a recent article to include a photo of a Japanese skull on the desk of a woman stateside, a present from her Navy boyfriend in the Pacific. She had named it "Tojo."

At least there were some positives to latch onto. The postshakedown inspection and subsequent battle training exercise received glowing reviews for the crew, declared "fit and ready for all action." With some experience and repetition, the Sampson Boots were growing into fighting sailormen. The Navy also utilized the delay to bolster *Astoria*'s antiaircraft guns, trading a number of 20mm Oerlikon mounts for the more potent Bofors 40mm. If he was headed for the brutal island invasions of the Pacific, Dyer took no issue with more and bigger guns. Besides, no fresh-caught junior officer could make the mistake of leaving men under the main battery during firing. One man from that incident had required a medical discharge from service as a result. Those small mounts were torn out.

Armentrout also informed Dyer of more turnover in experienced men. Some of his chiefs had only been on temporary duty, focused on preparing crews at sea shakedowns late in their careers or even brought out of retirement. Newly promoted first-class petty officers would move into their vacancies. Others, even Sampson men with just a shakedown cruise under their belts, transferred off to outfit other New Construction crews. Some *Astoria* sailors went to other emerging vengeance ships, such as USS *Chicago* and USS *Atlanta*. While all pre-war cruisers had been named for US cities; these new cruisers were named in honor of their predecessors to avenge them as combat losses. Former secretary of the navy Frank Knox didn't live to see it—he died of a heart attack in his office just days before *Astoria*'s commissioning—but his vengeance ship program lived on.

Captain Dyer held one stance adamantly about transfers to outfit new ships. With each new dispatch from the bureau, he instructed his executive officer to verify the names against his men with the worst conduct records. "Don't ever permit their names to be on these lists," he ordered. "They may be perfectly worthless, and they probably are so because of what they did, but they've got to stay in this ship as long as I'm in this ship." Other matters fell beyond his control. During this period the ship lost a chief to civilian morals court in Philadelphia on charges of "fornication."

The engineering officer remained a concern. The question of his competency nagged at Dyer, and for the time being he was stuck with a man he still felt should be retired. If they ever experienced another bearing failure, he wanted the engine room men ready to address it immediately. He directed Armentrout and the chief engineer to drill and practice bringing an engine down properly, rapidly, to address the bearings.

As the first rounds of men granted leave began to return, so did a sharp rise in absenteeism. Sailors grew savvy to the limits of Rocks and Shoals, and how the Navy was forced to handle adjudication given the national manpower crisis by mitigating consequences. Men talked, and scuttlebutt grew with methods learned for gaming the system. If the same punishment were handed out for seven days over leave as would be the case for just three days, why stop? More time with your girl or your family. Even as the refurbished turbine engine returned from Schenectady, many men did not. The mast reports again ballooned.

The skipper walked a tightrope between strict discipline and fairness. He would excuse an absence or send a man away with a warning if the situation merited. A black steward's mate was assessed on the same criteria as a white sailor. A drunken or fighting man kept overnight in a brig ashore, while still receiving punishment, was to be handled differently than a man gone the same amount of time through reason of intent. For each of these scenarios, Dyer ensured Armentrout doled out mast on similar terms. Neither man shied away from deck court or even summary court-martial as appropriate.

By now men should know better, so Dyer raised penalties as much as he could. If extra hours of duty or even loss of pay wouldn't do the trick, perhaps loss of future liberties would. Five liberties, ten, even confinement to the ship. One man proved such a flight risk to go overboard he received confinement to the brig until *Astoria* would get underway.

Dyer bristled when one of his old *Astoria* men reported aboard days late over leave. Chief Phipps, no less! Located and plucked from the Cramp Shipyard ranks during the new *Astoria*'s construction, he had been basically ordered to trade nights home with his family for extensive sea duty. Regardless, Dyer expected proper leadership from his chief, perhaps more than anyone. He was an *Astoria* man, a combat veteran to set every example.

Another of his six Savo survivors appeared at mast, this one for the first time: Rousseau Lemon. He had returned aboard on time following his leave, but was placed on report for wearing dungarees instead of whites when he did. Lemon pled his case to the captain. His wife had given birth to their baby daughter just that morning, and he scrambled back to beat the ticking clock at the quarterdeck. Lemon was no troublemaker and his marks were perfect. Captain Dyer let him off with a warning.

Standouts Herb Blodgett and Fred Lind both returned from leave with time to spare. If nothing else, lost liberties meant missed innings pitched. *Hey—the engine's back!* Blodgett could look forward to a second bout with the fiberglass insulation, while Lind could get settled into the fire control spaces. While at home, Blodgett had not been able to convince his mother he had nothing to do with the D-Day invasion. She had replied, "Oh, I understand, Navy rules, secrecy." Yet Blodgett returned walking on cloud nine for another reason. When he proposed to her back in West Concord, Betty had said yes.

* * *

Slowly but surely stragglers were apprehended in their hometown areas: Cincinnati, Buffalo, Indianapolis, Nashville. Dyer wanted every one of them back aboard. If the lengthy repair brought constant temptation, it also improved chances of their recovery and return under guard. By September 1 fully one man in four had stood at Captain's Mast for sentencing, many repeatedly. The absenteeism and other disciplinary problems had to be curbed, and discipline alone wasn't going to cut it. There were only so many things a skipper could dole out to get his sailors to respond. Putting to sea, the obvious solution, remained weeks away.

One method he adopted was keeping idle hands occupied through training. Dyer sent as many men as he could through training schools for firefighting, surface and aerial recognition, and gunnery. He also conducted every drill he could think of while dockside, especially focusing on the engineers. Yet a crew needed inspiration, things to galvanize and rally around, not just punishment or keeping their noses to the training grindstone.

One spark of inspiration came through the form of a book just published. *Through the Perilous Night* depicted a graphic firsthand account of a press correspondent stationed aboard the first *Astoria*. Taking the reader through the Guadalcanal invasion, the author gave his personal account of the Savo battle, including his being wounded in the maelstrom of casualties. Perhaps the vengeance ship concept wasn't fully the right approach. If Dyer's *Astoria* could benefit from the connective tissue of his Savo men, she might benefit even more from her own, unique identity. Something better than "CL-90." Something unique to her crew.

Astoria needed a nickname. Not something proclaimed by the Navy: she needed a sailorman's name. The first ship's crew had always called her "the Nasty Asty," but *Astoria* CL-90 needed distinction all her own— something not tied to the depths of Savo Sound in the South Pacific. Dyer approached Armentrout and the ship's chaplain about running a contest in the ship's newspaper for any man to enter. They placed a box out on deck for submissions and appointed a chief and two other senior petty officers as a selection board after a period of days had passed. Men responded well and placed many entries in the box.

When selection time came, the three enlisted men came back with a unanimous decision: their home would be christened "the Mighty Ninety." Men embraced the moniker, and it immediately rose into conversations across the ship. Captain George Dyer could not have been more pleased, and the men of the Mighty Ninety would never know why. Others might have come up with the same idea, but he had secretly submitted the name himself.

The ship's newspaper also brought a lift in morale. The ship's chaplain, Al Lusk, a Baptist pastor from Battle Creek, Michigan, served as editor. He brought two ideas to his captain. First was to go beyond the daily news, which focused on press dispatches and sports scores, and set up a biweekly magazine to circulate. He would need a small amount of support work from yeomen in the Communications Division, as well as a few volunteer "beat reporters," maybe one man from each division. They could submit funny stories and jokes, razz one another, even submit poetry and art. He would run the whole thing and include a "Chaplain's Page" to keep spirituality present of mind. Dyer embraced the concept warmly.

Lusk's second idea came about more or less by accident. He had discovered a talented sketch artist aboard ship named Joe Aman, an older Sampson man from Rochester. Aman served in the aft main battery division. Starting with sketches for the other guys he worked with, he proved to have a pronounced wit to match his drawing capability. Lusk and Aman had discussed including a comic strip at the top of each daily *Astoria Morning Press*, something he could whip up based on events aboard ship or general humor about Navy life. Again Dyer saw value, and he granted the chaplain permission to move forward with the idea.

It didn't take long for Dyer to summon the "Padre" back for a second discussion. Joe Aman had taken the idea and run wild with it. After a short experiment with nameless characters, he felt unsatisfied with the reactions of the men and so he had introduced a ship's mascot, a sketch alter-ego for himself. Scrawny with oversized glasses perched atop the nose of a lying Pinocchio, his foul-up apprentice seaman creation was named Joey Fubar. The Fubar character appeared each morning in some predicament, basically embodying everything the Navy did *not* want out of its bluejackets. Himself abstinent regarding foul language, the captain knew full well what the acronym FUBAR meant: Politely, "Fouled Up Beyond All Recognition." Yet his crew already provided anything but polite company. The pair debated whether to let Aman continue with the character.

The men of the Mighty Ninety gave them their answer. Joey Fubar became the talk of the ship, universally embraced out of the gate. Atop assembled wire reports from London, New York, even Axis radio, every morning brought an example of lollygagging, shirking duty and all the things that tended to land a man jack at Captain's Mast. He might be a foul-up sailor, but perhaps he brought the best out in *Astoria* men: *Don't be Joey Fubar.* Joe Aman's creative mind had managed to capture the essence of Rocks and Shoals.

Joey Fubar also provided a daily snapshot of the stratified Navy life through humor. Men of authority could smirk at a slacker they had all encountered, while the rest of the crew chuckled about what military men universally referred to as "chickenshit" from a superior. Dyer and Lusk decided to keep the "chief's problem child" strip running. The captain even began a personal file of his favorite Fubars.

* * *

Back from their surprise two-week leave, Fred Lind and his fellow fire control strikers settled in aboard the Mighty Ninety. It didn't take long to pick up on what life aboard ship meant: "Few frills and lots of drills." They found the F Division berthing compartment packed to capacity with some seventy men. Arriving so late in the game they also had to choose from the worst racks, typically at the top of a stack of four, requiring a climb. The bottom bunk brought first choice, for no one would poke you in the back and wake you as they rolled over. Middle racks were chosen next, although a man had to slide out to turn over. In addition to the climb, top bunks were least preferred for a reason that quickly became clear—the ship's public address loudspeakers in your ear.

On the other hand, Lind could not have been more pleased with his duty stations for watches and general quarters. Assigned to the antiaircraft battery, all would be topside and in fact just about as high up as a man could stand watch in the ship. With no decks above them, the open-air platforms were referred to as Sky Forward and Sky Aft. Sandwiched in between the main battery and AA fire director positions, seventy-some feet above the waterline, he would be able to see everything that was happening, unlike some other poor fellows in the division down in the bowels of combat plot. The downside might bring exposure to the elements, but at least he wouldn't spend all hours going blind on instruments.

The real problem proved to be efficiently getting from the F Division berthing compartment on the second deck all the way up to Sky Forward in the expected time during battle stations. The first lesson learned was don't be the last guy out—he had to dog down the watertight hatch. Nevertheless, Lind's path emphasized the "up" portion. For his first GQ drill, Captain Dyer had some choice words when the crew took more than two minutes to fully arrive in place. Next time Lind would focus on the vertical ladders.

Fire Control School wasn't the only experience that paid off for Fred Lind. His previous work as a civilian in Rochester at Kodak Hawk-Eye also brought opportunity. The plant had manufactured optical equipment now used aboard ship for star triangulation and stereo viewing. Quite familiar with such instruments, and their care and cleaning, he was placed in charge of cleaning and maintaining the ship's optical shop located directly below his battle station. Cleaning lenses would be no problem, especially for the ship's stereo training scopes. He knew those so well he was further made responsible for teaching F Division officers and men in their use. *Life could have its moments in the Navy.*

What the optical shop didn't have was a coffee pot, something he set out to rectify. He cut a deal with the machine shop to cut down and shape a spent 5-inch shell casing into a coffee pot. The machinists were welcome to their coffee anytime in exchange. With further creativity, Lind fashioned a hot plate and a coil to heat the coffee and make toast. "When I plugged them in, the ship's lights dimmed," he quipped.

Men gathered to grab a mug. The coffee tasted horrible, "jet black with sparkly things shining back." Scouring and polishing did nothing to improve the taste as days passed. But immediate access to coffee and toast was worth something, and Lind considered it "one act we could perform that was not dictated by someone else...a mysterious break to our routine." Perhaps the burnt smell alone would also be enough to limit junior officer visits.

One such ninety-day wonder took his role as F Division inspection officer with a bit too much importance. Lind took ownership of the optical shop quite seriously, ensuring everything looked spic-and-span for inspection. The inspection officer, in white gloves, went out of his way to trace some dust from the top of an overcounter cabinet. He put Lind on report, never even noticing the shell casing coffeepot. After that the F Division enlisted men referred to him as "Officer Wonderman." "Some of them were unbelievable," Lind would write of the junior officers, "and were obsessed by their sudden power and importance."

Aboard ship, rank wasn't everything. A man Fred Lind had looked up to immensely since Newport went by the name of James Hay Thomson.

Already thirty years of age, Jim Thomson shared Lind's post-boot-camp rate of seaman first-class. Both were striking for their fire controlman rating, but neither would be eligible for months despite school attendance. Already sharing a role and working in close quarters, Lind found another reason to look up to the older man: Jim's relationship with his little brother and baseball.

Plenty of Boots had passed through Sampson approaching age thirty or older. However, Jim Thomson had not started his life in the Northeast, nor even in the United States. He had been born in Glasgow, Scotland, in 1914. In search of opportunity, his father brought the family across in stages, settling them in Staten Island once he saved enough money as a cabinetmaker.

To help make ends meet, Jim began to work at an early age. He took a job at Sears, Roebuck, where the avid Brooklyn Dodgers fan bought a baseball glove for his little brother Bobby. Jim worked with Bobby in their backyard from the time he "was strong enough to hold a bat." Mentor and coach, he pushed his brother through youth leagues and high school. Upon graduation Bobby signed a professional contract for the New York Giants system.

While playing rookie ball that summer, Bobby wrote that he was struggling. Jim was adamant in his response: "Keep your chin up. Keep hustling. Get mad, hit somebody when sliding into second base." He closed the pep talk letter with the salutation, "Your severest critic and your most ardent admirer." That advice relit the proper fire. Yet war intervened, and now both Thomsons wore uniforms that had nothing to do with baseball.

Jim Thomson brought much to resonate with Fred Lind: the teamwork and humor, sharing responsibilities in a war neither man volunteered to fight. Both would certainly prefer to be elsewhere than a ship compartment drinking terrible coffee from a brass shell casing. Yet despite his junior enlisted rate, Thomson brought wisdom and coaching to other men. For Lind, perhaps the biggest void he filled was that of an older brother who would never come home.

It wasn't long before Thomson provided Lind with a new life lesson, offering "excellent advice to give." Fred had approached his friend lying in his bunk, looking terrible. "Do not ever call the mess cook a son of a bitch," Jim moaned. Earlier in the mess line, a huge cook had carelessly slopped gravy over Thomson's ice cream on his tray. Thomson's irritated reply caused the cook to remove his apron and waltz the new guy around the corner. "What did you call me?" A thorough beating in the stomach followed.

Thomson called uncle. "Look, I'm beaten."

The cook replied, "No, nobody calls me that." He continued pounding a little longer.

Later after his friend had recovered from the sailor's lesson, Lind took to his shorthand diary. "Know something? Gravy on ice cream didn't taste too bad after a while."

* * *

Herman Schnipper wrote to his mother shortly before the ship got underway. "It will now be impossible for me to come home because we are now on the way out. When I have a chance and the censor permits, I will tell you where I am. At present we are in the [redacted]. So until you hear from me again which will be soon, please do not worry about me." The censoring officer had torn the location of the ship out of the letter.

Could it really be a big Navy secret that *Astoria* was still in Philadelphia after so much time and so many leaves? Fellows created plenty of ways to alert family members where they were. Schnipper's location may have been redacted, but he knew of a man who kept his wife informed of his whereabouts with every letter he sent to her. The method was deceptively simple; he changed the middle initial of his name on the envelope anytime the ship moved. His wife could match the initial to a marked-up map at home, and the censors were none the wiser.

What a laugh—surely officers had better things to do. Just days earlier four more men had gone over the hill. All were apprehended by civilian authorities and brought back. The captain sure was serious about getting men back aboard. He had given another tough talk to the crew about expectations that every man be aboard for sailing or else. And this time they were headed for the Pacific Fleet, not the safe confines of the Atlantic training zone.

Schnipper had come to respect the skipper, and many other officers were proving to be decent as well. Armentrout had become especially beloved by the crew as a very kind gentleman, which was tough to pull off for an executive officer running the ship. Officers demonstrated their own humor also, something Schnipper was privier to than most. When a fresh-caught ensign, Jack Haasis, came aboard as the Electrical Division junior officer, he earned the dubious honor of "Boot Ensign," the junior-most officer aboard ship. His seniors had Schnipper photograph him for his ID card wearing enlisted dress blues as a joke.

Other than an occasional such chore, Schnipper found himself with lots of time on his hands. Men still hounded him for photos anytime they saw the camera; some were the same who talked down to him. Much that might have even been unspoken proved obvious in crew relations. He largely kept to himself, and when he did shoot pictures he had adopted the general practice of taking them from behind or from above, quiet and out of view. Beyond a few buddies from Bayonne, he did his best to blend into the background.

No one visited the darkroom. When he stripped the black paint down to the bare bulkheads, he eliminated any lingering source of his nausea. He slept in the small compartment, read in it, and smoked in it. The only aggravation would come when the engines went to high speed, as the shafts rattled and shook the space, but that certainly hadn't happened recently.

Schnipper had also taken to decorating the bulkheads with favorite photos he snapped. So far the best were seascapes and sunsets, none of ship activities. During the shakedown cruise he realized the need for better optics to get closer to his subjects, given the wide expanses at which the ships operated. When he placed the request, it was immediately denied. The chief storekeeper, who had been so slow to even procure the Speed Graphic camera, had said, "You don't need another toy." Then he smiled and stared.

* * *

Delaware Bay, off Brandywine Shoal
September 18, 1944

At last Captain Dyer could make an announcement that brought pride to his men. After weather conditions fouled the prior day's attempt at *Astoria's* high-speed test, today the Mighty Ninety cleared the hurdle. Zigzagging at full speed, the run up to flank speed proved successful— 30 knots, a design expectation of all modern cruisers, what she was designed to do. In spite of the extra weight of a full load and heavier gun mounts, she accomplished the test that had left her crippled three long months before. Atlantic Command signed off and released her to report for duty.

The past few days had proven fortunate indeed. The day before departure, Marine Captain Armitage had led a force in bringing aboard a full load of ammunition from the Fort Mifflin storage depot. The working party accomplished the task despite gale-force winds and soaking rain throughout the day. A strong Atlantic hurricane rolled past, just missing the Philadelphia area. As *Astoria* put to sea at midday on September 15, the hurricane moved ashore in Long Island. Soaked to the bone himself at Fort Mifflin, Joe Aman naturally seized on the event for the next morning's cartoon.

But not all could be humorous. In the two days prior, the powerful storm sunk a US Navy minesweeper, a destroyer, and two small Coast Guard cutters. Its sweep from the Bahamas to Cape Hatteras claimed some three hundred souls with these ships. As the beast bore down on them, Dyer and Armitage had agreed to load ammunition despite the weather. Getting the ship underway on schedule to meet her destroyer escort left them little choice. The Mighty Ninety showed some luck and now some pluck; she squeaked out and made her speed. September 15, one year to the day since he was wounded, Dyer was back at sea.

The one sour note for the captain: despite all efforts to enforce discipline, set expectations, and boost morale, *Astoria* did not put to sea with a full complement. Eight men missed the sailing. Once apprehended their punishments would include imprisonment in disciplinary barracks and bad-conduct discharge. After months of yo-yoing reluctant sailors back aboard, none of these men would be brought back to *Astoria*. She headed south, not to return to the East Coast. Her path to the Pacific would take her through the Panama Canal, plenty of exercise and gunnery along the way, and a final stop in San Diego. From there she would head to Pearl Harbor and report to the United States Pacific Fleet.

* * *

Fred Lind delighted to learn the latest new officer scheduled for his stereo optics training: Ensign "Wonderman," whom his fellows loved to poke fun at. The stereo trainer device taught an operator to observe two images of a moving target until they aligned through the stereo optics. Once they matched, the trainee would say "Mark" and press a button to report the target's range electrically for Lind to verify. The training assessed a man's ability to use range-finding equipment under quickly changing circumstances, such as an aerial attack.

Time for a little payback. For Wonderman, Lind had rigged an alligator clip to the device's ground wire. Lind let the machine perform as normal during the first few tests. "Mark." *Click.* "Mark." *Click.* Then he released the alligator clip, removing the electrical ground for the next test. "Mark." *Click-zap.* "Jesus!" Ensign Wonderman received an electrical jolt. After several such shocks, the officer abandoned the test. "I hate this instrument," he declared as he stomped away. Tipped-off fire controlmen in the passageway tried not to snicker. "Mark—Jesus!" became a private joke.

In contrast, Lind had developed tremendous respect for his watch officer in Sky Forward, Captain Armitage. The first time Lind encountered the Marine, he was performing one-armed pushups on the platform. It didn't take long for the subject of Guadalcanal to come up, and then of course Lind's brother Paul. Armitage found a way to bond with enlisted men, all while staying within bounds of authority. The memory of Guadalcanal brought just such an opportunity. He soon learned the skill set such men brought fresh from their Newport training, as *Astoria* and her destroyer escort conducted tracking and fire drills.

Accurate gunfire from a rolling, heaving ship against a target maneuvering to avoid it made for a complex equation. The fire control equipment in the sky platforms were designed to designate a target, then establish range, train the guns toward the target, and elevate. This data was passed down to the men operating the ship's analog computer equipment. While the men up top accounted for tracking the target's movement, the plot systems down below accounted for the ship's relative movement. Ship speed and relative course, parallax, wind, roll, pitch, the list went on. Such mathematical problems took forty-five minutes to solve by hand in Fire Control School, but that served merely to educate the trainee. The ship's analog computers could produce a firing solution to train and point with the proper shell fuse instantaneously.

Lind, Thomson, and the new fire controlmen practiced using the ship's Kingfishers as maneuvering aerial targets and their destroyer escort as a surface target. In exercise after exercise, the group demonstrated proficiency in ranging and tracking, which impressed Armitage. The Mighty Ninety might just be a swell-shooting ship. Through the days of exercises, Fred Lind learned other lessons. Focusing on the vertical ladders worked best, and he lowered his race time for his battle station to forty-five seconds. He also came to prefer his watches at Sky Forward over Sky Aft. The latter platform lay immediately aft of the smokestacks, and the fumes could be overpowering.

* * *

When *Astoria* passed through the Panama Canal, the fifty-mile wonder that connected the Atlantic Ocean to the Pacific, on September 24, men lined the rails to marvel at the engineering. Raising and lowering a ship in the water through a series of manmade locks to avoid having to go around the entirety of South America provided a wonder no boy could have imagined just looking at a globe. Others like Herb Blodgett never saw a thing. Over the six-hour process of moving through the locks, he spent the entire time on watch. He emerged disgusted to see he had missed the whole show. Men rating liberty waited with bated breath, for on the Pacific side of the Canal Zone lay a veritable Fiddler's Green on earth. *Astoria* would dock at Balboa, which opened up into Panama City.

Unlike Port of Spain, Panama City was very much a "liberty town," with plenty of places for a sailor to spend his money. Years of US "two-ocean Navy" activity brought economic boom once the canal went into service in 1914. Bars with American names like "Tom Brady's" lined the streets. Men set out on foot and hopped aboard buses. Each group found some senior man with experience to lead the way. Following the crowd, Fred Lind noticed more than just bars lining the streets.

Passing one house early on, an attractive teenage girl ran from the porch and grabbed Lind's arm, directing him inside. He shrugged her off and kept moving. After glaring at Lind, a couple who were presumably her parents chastised her. *I suppose the family income just took a downward turn*, he thought. *Oh, well, lots of other sailors coming down the street.*

One main street boasted no stores, no window displays, no signs. Just brick buildings with open doorways, each framing a woman surrounded by sailors. Lind stood in amazement observing the sales pitches and transactions in progress, never having seen anything of the sort. Curious to see one section barricaded off, he asked the shore patrol standing in front of it. In response he learned the same goods were sold there, but they were off limits. The houses open for business contained the women who had passed their weekly Navy-managed physicals. Lind kept on walking.

Electrician's Mate Jim Peddie always went ashore with the biggest guys he could find. Self-proclaimed as "115 pounds soaking wet," he and a few buddies set out on a different mission. The senior men knew an age-old trick of sailors and their bell-bottom trousers, that of using their socks to store things. The electricians took great care when returning from liberty to walk slightly bowlegged, to prevent the clinking of the half-pint whiskey bottles stuffed into their socks. They had discovered that certain fuse boxes perfectly fit such bottles—overboard went a few spare fuses, in went the whiskey. Rocks and Shoals explicitly forbade distilled spirits aboard ship for nonmedicinal purposes, but an occasional snort when off duty merited the risk. Rationed properly it would hold them over to Pearl.

Other men were not so calculating and focused on consumption. They returned to ship with their booze in their bellies instead. Jim Thomson noted some sorry sights returning to the F Division berth. Joe Aman seized the opportunity, as a liquored-up Joey Fubar held up between two other drunken sailors staggered back atop the *Morning Press*. The cartoon drew laughs, but there was truth to the matter, some quite serious. Two men assigned to shore patrol received summary courts-martial after being caught drinking in a bar instead of performing their duties. For his part, Rousseau Lemon remained on his best behavior. He never even left the ship.

By noon *Astoria* resumed course, escorted by her new Pacific-side destroyer, USS *Hyman*. More days of exercises lay ahead before the stop in San Diego per the ship's operational orders. Exiting the Panama isthmus, a Navy blimp performed overhead antisubmarine cover. *Hyman* promptly broke off to investigate a sound contact and drop a depth charge. It didn't take much effort for the crew to conclude that the Pacific side of the canal brought more danger than the Atlantic at this stage of the war. If a two-ocean American Navy could be crippled, the Canal Zone would be a good place for it, and not just through liberty at Balboa.

* * *

Fifty miles south of San Diego
October 3, 1944

Despite the early morning fog, Captain Dyer elected to proceed with a final firing exercise before putting into port. A second destroyer, USS *Boggs*, assumed station for the day's battle practice. The joint exercise called for standard speed at 20 knots. With men at stations and firing moments away, Neptune's curse struck yet again.

The aft engine room rang up—loss of oil pressure in number three. From Dyer's bridge and Blodgett's engine compartment, men scrambled to put their emergency protocols into place. The ship backed down to 10 knots and brought number three offline. Once secured, a quick inspection proved their worst fear. *Astoria* wiped a bearing in steam turbine engine number three.

Maintaining his composure, Dyer returned his attention to the firing drill. There were two other ships to consider, and his trained engineers would handle it. Surely this had to be a manufacturing problem, not one of crew competence, *yes?* He considered his engineering officer, whom the Navy scrounged and whom he felt unfit. He considered the Cramp Shipbuilding Company, their months of delays and the mad scramble that followed. He considered the report he would have to make with the senior officer present upon docking. Captain George Dyer returned his attention to the exercise, and ordered the guns to open up.

* * *

State Pier, San Diego
Hours later

We're coming in all wrong. Off watch, with no responsibility over number three, Herb Blodgett had joined some other men at the forecastle, the foremost bow deck of the ship. As they often did in shallow water, some harbor porpoises could be seen playing in the bow wake so he had gone

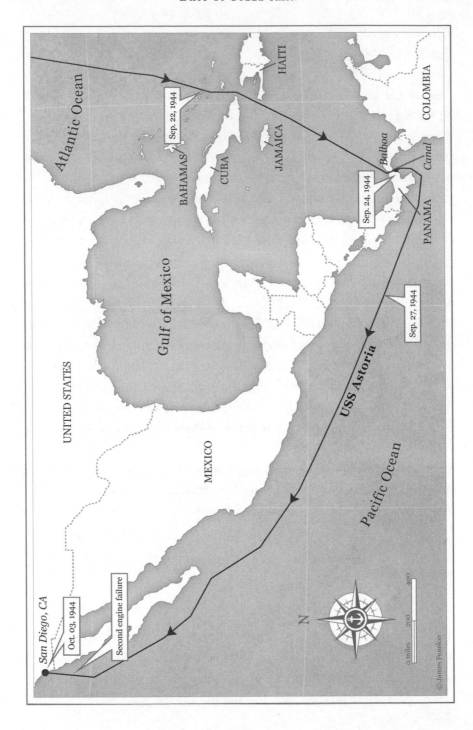

forward to watch. Blodgett looked up to see the pier approaching. Even with the slow speed of the maneuver, he instinctively thought, *Turn the ship to port! Something to counteract breeze and current pushing us to starboard*... Then out loud to nobody and everybody, "My God, we're gonna hit it!"

Astoria banged into the corner of the pier on her starboard bow. Blodgett and the men surrounding him stumbled to keep their feet. Looking across the dock, something else struck him odd. *Where are the men to handle our lines?* He shook his head over what he assumed was some junior officer at the helm of the ship.

* * *

The culprit had been the State Pier harbor pilot. Handling cruisers could be tricky business. Dyer knew how tricky such maneuvers could be from firsthand experience in his two stints aboard *Indianapolis*, as first lieutenant stationed on the forecastle and later as executive officer in the pilothouse, through all manner of wind and weather. This pilot appeared accustomed to handling ships of far less displacement than a *Cleveland*-class cruiser. He simply misread the current.

Men scrambled for lines to moor the ship. Once the brow was dropped, Dyer had his passengers detached along with a couple of hospital cases. No liberty passes yet. The captain sent his first lieutenant, Rodney Badger, to assess damage to the bow, then left the ship and sought out the harbormaster, furious.

Within an hour of phone calls, it all came clear. The senior officer present confirmed that *Astoria* received incorrect orders: Dyer had been sent to the wrong facility. The Bureau of Ships ordered *Astoria* to move down to the US Naval Repair Base San Diego for initial condition assessment. And the harbormaster expedited that request by informing the captain that remaining where he was would cost $1,000 per day.

* * *

Gerard Armitage had no more taken position on the quarterdeck as officer of the deck than Captain Dyer abruptly returned to the ship. Returning the Marine's salute, Dyer ordered, "Make all preparations to get the ship underway within thirty minutes. Advise me as soon as the pilot is aboard."

"Aye aye, sir." Armitage stood taken aback. He was not underway-qualified; Marine officers assumed watch as officer of the deck in port only. *Surely relief was coming.* However, Armitage was not about to correct the captain. Dyer and Armentrout had developed an outstanding ship's organization manual, "a bible of checklists, charts and instructions of most things nautical." Armitage began to run down the checklist for getting underway, notifying each appropriate department from the quarterdeck.

After-brow removed, harbor pilot received, captain informed. *No relief.* A turbine engine turning up, *check.* Lines singled up and watch set. Sentries recalled and forward brow hoisted, *check.* With no relief in sight, the Marine CO continued. "Now hear this. The officer of the deck is shifting his watch to the bridge."

Whether they realized one of them should have relieved him, or maybe they just recognized the voice of the "goddamn Marine," four underway-qualified officers scrambled to the bridge. With no expectation of getting underway anytime soon, they had retired to the wardroom for coffee and Parcheesi. Entering the pilothouse, they encountered Dyer and Armitage.

The Marine saluted and reported, "Sir, standing by to cast off."

"Very well, Soldier. Cast off." Dyer had taken to calling Armitage such, perhaps to distinguish the difference between their respective ranks of captain in different service branches, or perhaps just a nickname he latched onto. Either way, enough mutual respect had emerged between the two combat veterans for Dyer to get away with an Army term that tended to make Marines bristle.

Dyer turned the ship's conn over to the harbor pilot, then leaned in for a softer tone. "Soldier, nicely done, you may stand relieved when ready." Then he sized up his four full lieutenants, as he cut a glare at them and rumbled, "As for you, gentlemen, no bedroom slippers on my bridge, please."

As Armitage departed and *Astoria* pushed away, the ship's navigator replaced the Marine captain. Summoned to the bridge by Dyer, the navigator took up position next to the harbor pilot to watch his every move.

* * *

US Naval Repair Base San Diego
That evening

Once in the correct base, and unable to get underway for Pearl Harbor or anywhere known until damage was properly assessed, officers and men exercised liberty. Gunnery officer Ken Meneke seized the opportunity for a quick train ride up to Los Angeles to meet friends for a swanky dinner at Earl Carrol Theater. Fred Lind took in a movie and window-shopped. "It felt good just to be among civilians," he wrote. "Although sailors were not the optimum in the eyes of families who had to put up with their shenanigans. Wonder how we ever got that reputation—all the guys on the *Astoria* were impeccable in their demeanor."

Also ashore for liberty, Herman Schnipper decided to break a regulation. He remained determined to let his mother know where he was. "I just got into San Diego, California, after a very slow trip from Philadelphia," he wrote. "Still doing photography work on the ship. The photo work comes so far between that I have nothing to do, so I just take it easy." He signed using his Hebrew name, Sholem, as always. Then he added, "PS This letter is being sent off the ship. That is why it is not censored." Announcing a ship's movement would be a serious offense if Schnipper were caught, but ashore he elected the risk was worth it for his mother. Other men did the same all the time. He dropped the letter into a regular mailbox to avoid US Navy censorship.

Others with good-conduct records also rated liberty ashore and that included Rousseau Lemon. He had only nine more months left until discharge from the service but he had no intention of going to the Pacific. He saw this stop as his window of opportunity.

Lemon wasn't just familiar with gunnery drills; he knew this drill too. He had been here before. New Construction ships headed for the Pacific Fleet always made a final stop on the West Coast once through the Panama Canal. Short stops, just long enough to load passengers and materiel to shuttle out to Pearl Harbor. The port calls weren't long, but all he needed was a clean enough nose and one available liberty to set foot back on land.

The dungaree uniform incident had been a close call, but the captain understood given the circumstances of a birth and excused the infraction. Now Rosseau Lemon had that same wife and infant daughter in mind. The model boatswain's mate made his move, heading out on liberty along with a handful of other combat veterans he had befriended. Some were rated men, petty officers. Once ashore they quickly dispersed. Holding no intention of returning, their immediate priority was to get as far from San Diego as possible before they were missed. *Astoria* would sail west into the Pacific. Lemon would move east, first to visit his new family, then to New Orleans, where another stateside assignment and freedom awaited.

No more war.

Nine more months.

* * *

Astoria limped from San Diego in the morning of October 6, three days later. Dyer's first lieutenant and ship's divers had assessed the bow: plating damage at frame 44, third deck. A need for further assessment of structural repair.

The men from the aft engine room confirmed a second bearing failure. There was no engineering officer aboard to deliver the report, for he had left the ship with the authorized hospital cases. The beleaguered officer Dyer had already deemed incompetent complained of his crippled legs based on age, and received medical authorization to report in at the local Navy hospital.

The Bureau of Ships had elected to send *Astoria* up to Mare Island Navy Yard north of Oakland. The old shipyard had room to take her while executives from General Electric, Cramp, and inspectors from the Bureau of Ships could fly cross-country to see what was going on firsthand.

Army Armentrout delivered the crushing blow to his captain. When *Astoria* sailed from San Diego that morning, nine men were missing at muster. Four were rated men, boatswain's mates. Shipmates had already begun to fess up that the ringleader was Rousseau Lemon, the old *Astoria* man Dyer had personally requested. He had been hitting them up to jump ship with him once they reached the West Coast.

"Golden Gate in '48," a popular phrase among servicemen, referred to coming home from a lengthy war. *Astoria* now steamed toward an unplanned date with the famous landmark. *Might she still be there in '48 at this rate?* A cracked bow, a second dead engine, no engineering officer, and a date with civilian and Navy brass ahead. To top it off, after all Dyer's pep talks and strict handling of absentees, Lemon had just pulled off his little mutiny. Taken in full, it might just be enough for a skipper to consider going over the hill himself.

PART TWO

HERE BE DRAGONS

8

Into the Fray

Whether you are in the Naval Service of your own
free will or only because the hot breath of the draft
board was on the back of your neck, all of you
took the same oath of allegiance to the United
States of America.

—*Captain George Dyer to his* Astoria *crew on*
November 9, 1944

Pier 21, Mare Island Navy Yard
October 21, 1944

All the papers carried the story as headlines, including the stacks of
San Francisco *Examiner* morning editions delivered to the ship.
Men in line for chow read and learned that General Douglas MacArthur
had returned to the Philippines as promised, wading ashore from a landing craft in grand fashion. A few men sought solitude to write letters
home, while others worked the puzzles or chatted with their buddies. Just
another morning aboard a ship somehow magnetically attached to the
United States, while an entire Navy fleet cleared the way for MacArthur
at Leyte thousands of miles to the west. Shipyard cameras captured the
routine *Astoria* scene from an overhead crane, not for posterity or even
publication, but for practical reference of her configuration by the Bureau

of Ships. A nearby open-top dumpster overflowed with waste material from another engine rebuild. After two weeks in a repair berth, her days in refit grew short.

Another newspaper circulated the ship the same day, the inaugural issue of Chaplain Lusk's *Mighty Ninety* biweekly magazine. The front-page Joe Aman sketch depicted a baby *Astoria* in a diaper receiving a handshake from Uncle Sam, while a villainous Japanese caricature lurked across the ocean. Their headline for the "little paper with a big punch" read "Mighty Ninety Gets the Go-Ahead Sign." On one level that referenced the launch of the newspaper magazine of the same name, but given the drawing and surrounding copy it also informed the crew that *Astoria* would soon get underway.

The past two weeks had brought both stress and closure for George Dyer. Fortunately, it had also brought his beloved wife Adaline across country for much-needed support. The captain flew her out once he learned that lengthy delays would be expected. He needed her company. He could share with her things he could not with anyone else, above or below in the chain of command. Had the Navy not issued an incorrect operational order, an inexperienced harbor pilot might not have struck the pier. Had the bearing not failed, they wouldn't have put in at San Diego for three days' time. Lemon might not have been able to get so far away with his band of vital men who jumped ship. Had many things not happened in sequence, he might have been right there supporting MacArthur's first step into liberating the Philippines.

Regardless, such thoughts mattered little professionally. The engine discussion alone had gone as high as Admiral Ernest King, chief of naval operations. Despite Dyer's history of working closely with the top four-star, Ernie King carried a short memory for tolerating setbacks. Captains lost commands for such things. Dyer knew all too well: serving on King's Washington staff early in the war, he had once been ordered to toss two captains and a rear admiral out on their ear the same day— as a commander. "I want them out and you're going to do it," King had barked.

Fortunately Admiral King did not order Dyer relieved on the spot. What he did order was a special Board of Inspection and Survey to visit the ship at Mare Island, accompanied by the General Electric and Cramp experts. The board composition shocked Dyer—five engineering duty officers. He had never even heard of five engineering duty officers in one place before, all experts dedicated to naval engineering. Yet they were coming out to crawl through his engine rooms. Dyer had Schnipper crawl through the spaces first, not just to photograph the one failed engine this time, but all of them. All aft bearings lay placed on display, dismantled, and all betrayed some level of wear. Given time, each one would fail and clog the flow of oil. Clearly a problem existed with the component.

Upon arrival, the engineering duty board members had no choice but to agree. Despite their initial suspicion that a problem lay solely with *Astoria*, the same issue had just been reported aboard another ship. USS *Springfield*, twin sister in Cruiser Division 17 and fresh from the assembly line, experienced precisely the same failure in an aft low-pressure turbine bearing during her first speed run out of Boston on October 10, three days after *Astoria* arrived at Mare Island. Identical to *Astoria*'s mishap, *Springfield* would be laid up for weeks of repair following her own shakedown cruise.

Antimony—white metal composition in the bearings—became the word for the culprit. Based on all factors, the board quickly concluded the responsibility lay not with George Dyer and *Astoria*, not with Cramp Shipbuilding, not with any shipbuilder. It lay with a Bureau of Ships decision to change bearing specifications due to wartime material shortages. Further, the Mighty Ninety's engineers had saved another turbine loss when the second bearing failed, due to their experience and extensive training on the issue. "No fault is to be found in the ship's handling of this casualty," read the report. *Saving words*, as far as Dyer was concerned.

New bearings were on the way, manufactured to prior specification with no shortcuts. Spare replacements to boot. Even better, the bureau had located a new engineering officer for *Astoria*: Lieutenant Commander Sylvester "Tex" Simon, originally out of the merchant marine. To Dyer,

Simon immediately proved a "rugged individual," short and wiry, able to crawl into any space. Simon led from the front. Dyer promptly decided he was "ten times the engineer the other chap was," the absolute right man for *Astoria*. Now to get the blooming bearings and to get to sea. J. Cary Jones and USS *Pasadena* had leapfrogged them and were already out at Pearl.

Again, sidelined, Dyer's crew largely focused attention on other matters. *Astoria* men might be sailors, might have many differences, but they were also Americans first. Absentee "Official Election War Ballots" flowed from the ship for the pending presidential election that pitted two New Yorkers—Thomas Dewey versus Franklin Roosevelt. For the majority of the men, FDR had served as US president since their childhood. Men listened to the radio broadcast of the World Series playing out even as *Astoria* maneuvered under the Golden Gate bridge with Navy blimp protection overhead on October 7; the Cardinals topped the Browns 5–1 behind the bat of Stan Musial in game four. Now with an all–St. Louis World Series in the books with the Cardinals victorious over their cross-town rivals, the news reported even Musial was headed for the Navy.

Chaplain Lusk's *Mighty Ninety* magazine also worked. It brought the right degree of mirth and spirit for a crew stuck in the States. The magazine reminded men of the ship's library, which hosted a fine selection of mystery and adventure novels, educational manuals, and classic literature. "Whenever new books are received, a new list will be published on these pages," his article declared. Perhaps the most popular book aboard ship never made the shelves, an oft-mentioned yet rarely seen copy of the recently published *Forever Amber*. The scandalous and best-selling novel, banned as "pornography" in fourteen states, circulated through the crew.

Lusk's concept of allowing pages for men in each division to poke fun at one another also worked, giving sailors an outlet to express humor and build a bond. "Colgan is a free man again—congrats PAL!" read one entry (meaning prisoner-at-large, awaiting his next deck court). "A friendly tip to Frankel, Coxswain. The barber shop has not closed

First *Astoria* commanding officer
George Carroll Dyer *(US Navy photo
taken by Herman Schnipper)*

First *Astoria* executive officer E. W. "Army" Armentrout, swimming in paperwork *(US
Navy photo taken by Herman Schnipper)*

Marine commanding officer Gerard Armitage
(US Navy photo taken by Herman Schnipper)

Navy Chaplain Alpheus Lusk *(US Navy photo taken by Herman Schnipper)*

Senior Aviator Charles Tanner *(US Navy photo taken by Herman Schnipper)*

Aviator Jack Newman *(US Navy photo taken by Herman Schnipper)*

Aviator Donald Comb *(US Navy photo in shipmate family collection)*

Gunnery Officer Kenneth Meneke *(US Navy photo taken by Rudy Guttosch)*

Ship's Photographer Herman Schnipper
(US Navy photo taken by Herman Schnipper)

Fire Controlman Fred Lind *(US Navy photo in shipmate family collection)*

Fire Controlman Jim Thomson *(US Navy photo in shipmate family collection)*

Machinist's Mate Herb Blodgett *(US Navy photo in shipmate family collection)*

Electrician's Mate Jim Peddie *(US Navy photo in shipmate family collection)*

Marine Cook John Arrighi *(US Marine Corps photo in shipmate family collection)*

Gunner's Mates John Snyder (*left*) and Tom Kane *(US Navy photo in shipmate family collection)*

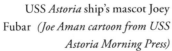

USS *Astoria* ship's mascot Joey Fubar *(Joe Aman cartoon from USS Astoria Morning Press)*

The "vengeance ship" *Astoria* as Captain George Dyer first saw her, languishing in partial completion at Cramp Shipyard in January 1944. *Astoria* was already months overdue for delivery to the US Navy. *(National Archives photo in records group 19-LCM)*

Inductees lined up for receiving at Navy Training Station Sampson in upstate New York, circa fall 1943. New "boots" reporting to Sampson drew from the nine northeast-most states. *(US Navy photo in author's collection)*

USS *Astoria* CL-90 underway on the first day of her shakedown cruise, June 20, 1944, photographed from a Navy blimp off Norfolk, Virginia. She suffered a catastrophic engine failure the same afternoon. *(National Archives photo in records group 19-LCM)*

The first photograph Herman Schnipper took with his Navy-issue press camera, *Astoria's* stripped turbine bearing at the outset of her shakedown cruise. The turbine was damaged beyond repair. *(US Navy photo taken by Herman Schnipper)*

Shakedown woes continue. Gunnery Officer Ken Meneke oversees Pharmacist's Mates tending to injured men left at their deck station during main battery live fire exercises on July 3, 1944. *(US Navy photo taken by Herman Schnipper)*

In one of the earliest Joey Fubar cartoons, two drunken sailors return from liberty in Balboa, Panama Canal Zone, with the apprentice seaman between them, September 1944. *(Joe Aman cartoon from USS Astoria Morning Press)*

USS *Astoria* at Mare Island Navy Yard on October 21, 1944. Repairs for her second turbine failure have just been completed, and the cruiser is undergoing engine trials. *(National Archives photo in records group 19-LCM)*

Astoria skipper George Dyer and exec E. W. Armentrout (*background*) going through the enlisted men's chow line for Thanksgiving dinner at Eniwetok, November 23, 1944. (*US Navy photo taken by Herman Schnipper*)

The Fast Carrier Task Force at anchorage in Ulithi, circa December 8, 1944. A *Cleveland*-class cruiser is at center foreground. (*National Archives photo 80-G-294145*)

USS *Santa Fe* rolls heavily to starboard in the typhoon December 18, 1944. Twin sister *Astoria* recorded rolls of 42 degrees, dangerously close to unrecoverable for a *Cleveland*-class cruiser. (*US Navy photo taken by Paul Madden*)

Soaked crewmen tend to a damaged Kingfisher on *Astoria*'s starboard catapult, December 19, 1944. Kingfisher floatplanes did not have folding wings and could not be lowered into the ship's hangar. *(US Navy photo taken by Herman Schnipper)*

The bow of USS *Astoria* crashes down in heavy seas that persist on December 23, 1944, as the Fast Carrier Task Force retires for anchorage at Ulithi Atoll. *(US Navy photo taken by Herman Schnipper)*

Christmas Eve entertainment on the fantail of USS *Astoria*, December 24, 1944. Nighttime lighting restrictions were typically not enforced within the confines of Ulithi anchorage. *(US Navy photo taken by Herman Schnipper)*

USS *Halsey Powell* returns Gerard Armitage to *Astoria* on January 14, the day after the destroyer rescued the overboard Marine Captain in typhoon conditions in the South China Sea. *(US Navy photo taken by Herman Schnipper)*

Marine CO Gerard Armitage is awarded an "Extinguished Service Cross" in the *Astoria* officers' wardroom, along with a poetic send-up written by Fire Controlman Fred Lind. *(US Navy photo taken by Herman Schnipper)*

Senior Aviator Charlie Tanner launches from *Astoria* on January 21, 1945, for a rescue mission of a downed USS *Lexington* pilot. His plane would never return. *(US Navy photo taken by Herman Schnipper)*

A shivering Joey Fubar is told that relief is coming. The joke is that 3rd Fleet and 5th Fleet are the same ships, just under different command. The fleet designations were meant to confuse the Japanese. *(Joe Aman cartoon from USS Astoria Morning Press)*

Inspection in white uniforms upon returning to Ulithi, February 3, 1945. *Astoria* Captain George Dyer enforced high expectations for order and discipline, even in the far-flung reaches of the Pacific. *(US Navy photo taken by Herman Schnipper)*

USS *Astoria* steams ahead of USS *Essex* as the Fast Carrier Task Force is underway for Tokyo, February 15, 1945. *Essex* F4U Corsairs and F6F Hellcats carry markings that identify them to their air group. *(National Archives photo 80-G-308591)*

An *Astoria* gunner reads a comic book at his 40mm mount during a chilly gun watch on the second day of strikes across the Tokyo Plain, February 17, 1945. *(US Navy photo taken by Herman Schnipper)*

A smoke ring rises from USS *Pasadena* as she fires on Iwo Jima. Photo taken from *Astoria*, on station astern of *Pasadena* in their fire support sector. Heavy cruiser *Boston* is in the background. *(US Navy photo taken by Herman Schnipper)*

Astoria men observe shells landing on Mount Suribachi on February 21. It would be two more days before Marines took the mountain and raised the flag for one of the most iconic images of the war. *(US Navy photo taken by Herman Schnipper)*

Brass casings from six-inch shells stacked along *Astoria*'s weather deck. The light cruiser fired her main and secondary batteries completely empty in support of the Marines on Iwo Jima. *(US Navy photo taken by Herman Schnipper)*

"Good News Joey! It's Washington's Birthday! Holiday Routine with only 12 hours G.Q To-day!"

3 days of G.Q at IWO JIMA

A haggard Joey Fubar is informed that "holiday routine" only means twelve hours of General Quarters during shore fire support of the Iwo Jima invasion, February 22, 1945. *(Joe Aman cartoon from USS Astoria Morning Press)*

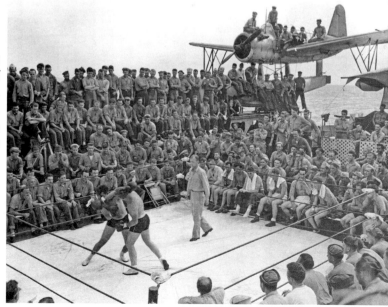

The crew watches boxing matches on the fantail of *Astoria* at Ulithi anchorage, March 10, 1945. *(US Navy photo taken by Herman Schnipper)*

USS *Randolph* after a Japanese suicide plane crashed through her flight deck at Ulithi the next night, March 11. The Fast Carrier Task Force was days away from strikes against the Japanese home island of Kyushu, and *Randolph* was put out of action for a month. *(National Archives photo 80-G-274122)*

USS *Indianapolis* (*left*) and *South Dakota* underway to support the Okinawa invasion. Taken from *Astoria* at sunset, March 18, 1945. The next morning introduced *Astoria*'s toughest days of the war. *(US Navy photo taken by Herman Schnipper)*

Astoria shoots down her first *Kamikaze* plane diving on *Essex* on March 19. The plane's bomb is splashing into the ocean ahead of the carrier. The plane followed seconds later, missing by mere feet. *(US Navy photo taken by Herman Schnipper)*

Joey Fubar lands a punch to the enemy, signifying *Astoria* bringing down three consecutive *Kamikaze* planes while protecting *Essex* off Okinawa on March 19, 1945. *(Joe Aman cartoon from USS Astoria Morning Press)*

A Japanese suicide plane overshoots *Hancock* and hits the stern of *Halsey Powell* in the afternoon of March 20. Photo taken from light carrier *San Jacinto*, directly behind *Astoria* in the formation. *(National Archives photo 80-G-328523)*

A Japanese plane makes a run on *Enterprise* while taking fire from the task group on March 20. *Astoria* is partially visible at right. Taken from light carrier *Bataan. (National Archives photo 80-G-334850)*

USS *Enterprise* astern of *Astoria* as the task group has turned to let the wind pull smoke away from the carrier's decks and superstructure. *Astoria* 40mm gunners watch in the foreground. *(US Navy photo taken by Herman Schnipper)*

Thirty minutes after *Enterprise* is hit, *Astoria* is also struck by friendly fire during a low-flying attack on March 20. A shell hit her bridge armor, sending shrapnel into Captain Dyer, Gunnery Officer Meneke, and several other men. *Astoria* managed to bring down the enemy plane. Taken from *San Jacinto*. *(National Archives photo 80-G-328671)*

Boatswain's Mate 2nd Class Stanley Dargiewicz and Buglemaster 2nd Class John Johnson at *Astoria*'s public address system calling for another alert in the evening of March 20. *(US Navy photo taken by Herman Schnipper)*

down..." "Another thing we like is the way our boys are bearing up under the strain of all these unexpected liberties. They want to go out and get into the melee..." With men policing themselves, Dyer couldn't be more pleased. Despite a few exceptions, his crew showed the signs of emerging as fighting sailormen. Certainly well trained by now, they just might be turning into the best ship *not* fighting the war.

The layover at Mare Island also allowed time to pursue the matter of Lemon. Surely the bunch who jumped ship expected *Astoria* to be well into the Pacific by now, but the bearing issue gave Dyer plenty of time to work the case while stuck stateside. Nine men, including four petty officers, with his old *Astoria* man the ringleader. Dyer had immediately sent Armentrout to investigate with the gunnery division petty officers (the ones remaining) that knew Lemon. The outcome of the investigation left Dyer speechless.

The gunnery department men came clean to Armentrout. Lemon had made his sales pitch to many men, and a few bought in. Those who shunned him and remained aboard gave a universal answer: "He's going to report in at New Orleans." *Lemon talked to everyone about it*, Dyer realized. *He might even lose his rate, but if he does, so what? He just wants out.*

Armentrout dug further, the outcome to their collective dismay. Lemon had been down this road before, along with other Savo survivors of the first *Astoria* and *Vincennes*, back when they were reassigned to the light cruiser USS *Santa Fe* in late 1942, before this *Astoria* was even launched. After a thirty-day "survivor's leave," the men had been reassigned to New Construction to go right back out. At that time a group of ten had jumped ship on the West Coast. All had been rounded up and strongly punished except Lemon. By blind luck he received a slap on the wrist, merely a warning, when he reported in at the 8th Naval District. The district, based in New Orleans, extended into his home state of Texas, and his outcome had been one of chance. He was further given a cushy assignment aboard a patrol craft in Florida, avoided a year of sea duty in action, and was even promoted twice. More pay for duty far from any war zone. Following that, word had spread like wildfire among veteran enlisted men, from the New Orleans Naval District up to New Construction—simply miss sailing for the Pacific and report back in at New Orleans if you want to ride out enlistment stateside.

Dyer wrote directly to the chief of naval personnel, calling out the New Orleans Naval District to be investigated as a possible haven for stragglers, lax in punishment. The allegation sent shock waves through the bureau, and his letter began to circulate with "snappy and forceful endorsements." Within days he had received a detailed response from the Navy Discipline Office in Washington, along with a lengthy series of attachments.

The problem of men missing sailing had been a known issue for months, first raised by an Academy classmate of Dyer's, the commanding officer of light carrier USS *Cabot*. When he suffered men missing ship out west, he had written a forceful letter of his own: "There is every reason to believe that missing ship has become a racket in the United States...it is considered necessary to over-complement carriers leaving the East Coast about 5% in order to ensure the vessels would actually sail for the combat areas with full crews." "Deadbeats," he wrote, "report in shortly after the ship sails and then hang around receiving ships for long periods where they tend to demoralize new men." Indeed, Dyer had seen his share of these and pulled them back as he could. In her wake, *Astoria* had also left a number of men either in disciplinary barracks or discharged for "constitutional psychopathy."

However, the Navy belief had become that veterans who missed ship did so because they weren't receiving an equitable exercise of annual leave compared to those in other commands. The Navy's Bureau of Personnel had dismissed the whole matter in May as "isolated" cases "which have occurred in the past and which do not accurately reflect the situation as it is today." *Hogwash*. With so many new men o' war coming on-line, the matter now approached critical mass. Dyer's letters swatted the dormant beehive.

He further pointed out a new wrinkle, not just men overstaying liberty to miss sailing. Lemon had developed a smarter game, he argued. Targeting a lenient naval district with cozy coastal assignments to offer put a sailor in position to ride out his enlistment at full pay, close to family, and safe from harm. For Dyer, the issue was more than just a practice that needed to be stopped. He requested his resolute desire to get his veteran boatswain's mate back aboard "in the interest of discipline in this ship" and to make a point with the bureau; leaders don't dismiss problems or pass them off to the other guy.

Some of Lemon's conspirators had been relatively easy to round up within days while others remained at large. Navy practice called for issuing reward declarations for such stragglers, sent to their next of kin and local chief of police. Bounty hunters also worked the cities surrounding the navy yards, and even rail lines. Two such men had just been brought back, apprehended at a train depot in Salt Lake City on their way back east. Dyer would keep these flight risks in the brig, their summary courts-martial pending, until sailing from Mare Island.

The bureau assured Dyer they would begin looking into comparative punishments for missing ship across stateside naval districts, with close scrutiny on New Orleans. They further acquiesced to return Lemon once they had him. The process would be slow and complex—transferring one man across country and then from ship to ship out to the Western Pacific. In a 1944 Navy where men were assigned in alphabetical chunks, attempting to move a single sailor halfway across the globe to a specific ship was simply not a practice, yet Dyer successfully pressed his point. Time would tell; the captain was sure his man would show up in New Orleans again.

* * *

Meanwhile, Armitage had developed his own racket, although it fell more into a category of savvy opportunism than anything nefarious. Over the past five months he had grown very close to *Astoria*'s senior aviator, Charles Sayers Tanner. The men came through similar college military programs—Armitage from Boston College, Tanner out of the University of Missouri. Buddying up with Chuck Tanner gave him a peer of rank aboard ship, and not one like the Academy Class of '42 grads who brought occasional moments of friction. The pair stood the same watch schedule. They also flew together at times, with Armitage spotting practice fire from the rear seat of Tanner's Kingfisher floatplane. Now inseparable, the two men had figured out how to work the system for their own personal car service, courtesy of the US Navy.

As far back as Philadelphia, the pair had come to realize that many naval personnel didn't understand that a cruiser carried two captains—the ship's Navy commanding officer and the CO of the Marine detachment. As a Navy captain with twenty plus years' service, Dyer far outranked his young Marine captain and rated access to official transportation. Tanner and Armitage concocted a scheme to "work that little misunderstanding to maximum advantage." Tanner would phone the Navy Yard transportation office and request a sedan for "Captain Armitage of 'Astoria.'" Once the car pulled up near the ship, Tanner would intercept the driver and inform him, "The captain likes me to drive him personally. I'll drop you back at the motor pool." One round trip later to dump the original driver, the pair had their own car.

Back in Philadelphia, Armitage once required a trip to Washington for official business. The two grew brave and tried their scheme to request an aircraft from the Naval Air Station. To their pleasant surprise, early the next morning a twin-engine Beechcraft SNB awaited. Climbing aboard, they were met by two full Navy commanders in the cockpit performing preflight check. "Who the hell are you?" one demanded.

"Good morning, Commander, I'm Captain Armitage."

"You mean to tell me I got up at four o'clock a.m. to fly a goddamned Marine?" Nevertheless, the flight left for Washington with the conniving pair flying first class. Tanner justified the trip for the men in the cockpit, as an "easy milk run" enabled deskbound pilots to accumulate hours in qualifying for monthly flight pay.

Chuck Tanner made for the perfect flying buddy. "Fly low, fly slow, fly VO," the scout/observation flyboys would quip about their branch of naval aviation. Far from a brash fighter jockey, Tanner held the cool demeanor of an Alaskan bush pilot. His consummate professionalism at the controls resonated with his Marine buddy. While there might not be anything glamorous about flying slow, ungainly seaplanes, their handling required much training and skill. A Vought Kingfisher might carry the awkward proportions of its avian namesake, but the planes proved maritime workhorses.

By their layover at Mare Island, Armitage and Tanner were running a veritable ferry service for fellow officers, shuttling them the thirty-five miles to and from San Francisco in their borrowed car. Armitage wrote of a strange and memorable incident he and Tanner witnessed one evening while in Frisco. "On a sultry evening as we approached Union Square, with a patter of bare feet, two eight-year-old urchins rounded the corner at flank speed and dashed downhill. Seconds later, more pattering feet, and a third little lad, no more than four or five years old, rounded the bend, naked to the navel, clutching his shorts with one hand, furiously waving the other, and shouting at the top of his lungs, 'Wait for baby, you dirty sons of bitches!'" The pair of officers fell out laughing at the scene. They adopted the phrase as their war cry and employed it whenever possible.

Perhaps it embodied the saga of their ship getting into the war, now given MacArthur's return to the Philippines. *Wait for baby, you dirty sons of bitches.*

* * *

Liberty ports didn't come much better than Frisco, with its grand sights and diverse experiences to take in. For the sailor, passing under the Golden Gate Bridge really brought entry into a larger world. Chinatown alone offered the exotic-sounding but very American creation chop suey. Fred Lind branched out in his liberties, visiting the surrounds of Vallejo, Oakland, and Berkeley, even Napa Valley. He wrote, "I found that wherever I went on liberty, not one civilian ever said one word to me. They would respond politely to my requests for direction to the ballpark or to the football field, but there was a definite cool air in their voice that said 'Hands off, sailor!' Guess I should have asked people other than the prettiest women."

Pappy Kane and John Snyder ran up their share of experiences in the city, sights and movies and three-dollar steaks. Free coffee and donuts awaited every man in uniform. Kane grew a mustache and they hit up the tattoo parlors for ink. *Wasn't that what sailors did?* Yet the mid-thirties Kane remembered daily that he was a married father surrounded by youngsters. He missed home, writing to his wife, "Honey, you don't know what it's like to be away so far. It doesn't seem to fit into my life, I seem to be in a strange world. Then I happen to notice I have a uniform on and then I wake up." He closed with "I'll be seeing you," a reference to the popular song recorded in 1944 by Bing Crosby that captured the country's feelings of being separated from their loved ones. He set up a cottage shop aboard ship to write poems with drawings for other older men to send home to their wives.

Herman Schnipper again broke a regulation. He mailed a postcard made from redwood to his mother announcing his presence in San Francisco. He once again signed it Sholem, this time with no other information. It couldn't be tracked back and the post office was none the wiser. With a one-word message he let his family know he wasn't following his brothers into the European Theater. He was headed for the Pacific War.

* * *

Before *Astoria* slid from her berth on October 25, Dyer gave the crew another pep talk about their duty and being aboard for sailing. A new trend had emerged: men checking into the Mare Island Navy Hospital for medical reasons while on liberty. There existed a high correlation between these medical cases and men who had previously gone absentee, AWOL, or straggler. When the ship pushed back from the dock in the early morning, she did so down eleven men. Eight were alleged hospital cases. But only three officially missed sailing. Two of them, including a rated gunner's mate, would end up in disciplinary barracks, and the third would be discharged for inaptitude. The *Astoria* Report of Changes that removed them from the ship's crew, a ritual always performed at sailing, listed a cryptic destination for the ship: "The Fray." *Astoria* at long last was headed into war.

Herman Schnipper photographed the scene from the rail, Mare Island civilian employees scrambling to arrive on time for work from their Vallejo ferry as his cruiser steamed past. Two other Navy ships brought their engines online in the background, smoke venting from their stacks. *Astoria* would have company out to Pearl Harbor, for the first time moving with ships of her class: twin sister *Montpelier* and heavy cruiser *Baltimore*. The three were set to sail in company, cover one another, and perform drills as they headed west into the Pacific. Yet curiously neither of the others had even left her berth.

Morning fog had burned off by the time *Astoria* passed under the Golden Gate Bridge, where she picked up her escort blimp guarding against submarines. Plenty of solo gunnery practice ensued as she waited for her cohort. The other two cruisers had put to sea two hours behind her, off schedule, and the Mighty Ninety's gunners seized the opportunity. *Astoria* shined in antiaircraft practice into the afternoon with her assigned plane towing sleeves.

Montpelier and *Baltimore* joined up in the late afternoon for more aerial and surface firing exercises while they still had towed targets and daylight available. The trio set out for Pearl, with Harry Hoffman, the captain of *Montpelier*, assuming tactical command of the formation. Perhaps it was a matter of Academy class pecking order, perhaps being shown up on the departure and exercise, or perhaps he simply had a thing for Dyer. But when *Montpelier*'s skipper assigned call signs for all three ships, he reserved a special one for his *Astoria* peer: *Lowlife*. For Dyer's part he carried his own opinion of the rival. While some might adhere to Hoffman's nickname of "the Horse," to Dyer and some other captains he held the moniker "Hasty" Hoffman. The late arrival of *Montpelier* and classmate Carl Fink's *Baltimore* furthered the mystery for Lowlife.

Six days to Pearl Harbor brought exercise after exercise, each ship in turn dropping out of formation to play target for the others in tracking drills and offset gunnery. The wilds of the Pacific also brought cold days and rolling seas. For the first time men ate meals on deck or at their stations because the messing compartment couldn't be set. The patchwork camouflage of *Montpelier* and *Baltimore* occasionally disappeared from view due to the height of the waves, only their masts and radar arrays visible.

Fred Lind discovered the serious nature of his optics shop role in the rough seas. Cleaning lenses on the range finders and telescopes up in Sky Forward and Aft required shinnying out upon them, and a rolling ship swung him out over open ocean, some seventy feet in the air. Strong leg muscles soon accompanied quick lens cleaning. He further learned that perching for personal business in the head required a seat in the middle of the row of toilet seats. Configured fore to aft, the squat-trough could sling its contents up on those seated at either end. "Shit's up!" men would warn. *Some things weren't found in* The Bluejackets' Manual *or any other.*

Throughout, Chuck Tanner and his aviators performed antisubmarine patrol and spotted from overhead. Herman Schnipper, his sea legs solid and his darkroom clear of paint, rode the swells and took photos of men at the rail watching the gunnery exercises, cotton or fingers in their ears. He made sure to shoot from a discreet location behind or above to avoid the swarm his camera would summon. Despite the weather, Fred Lind and Jim Thomson could take pride in their gunfire control. "Left the Pacific strewn with sleeves," wrote Thomson, referring to their antiaircraft targets. "We were gaining quite a reputation as a hot firing ship. Also a clean ship." Joey Fubar appeared in the papers with his pants blasted off from the gunfire.

Throughout, "Lowlife" Dyer fretted. His absentees worried him "all the way to Honolulu," he later recalled. He had reported his numbers to his superiors out in Pearl Harbor. "I had concocted half a dozen speeches that I was going to make…because I had really worked on the crew by making talks to them to keep the number of absentees very low." *Get them to fight the war.* Despite his efforts, eight landed in the hospital, three over the hill. And this was on the heels of Lemon's group.

In the early morning of October 31, 1944, the three cruisers sighted Oahu. Planes met them for antiaircraft gunnery drills, and in keeping with Jim Thomson's written braggadocio USS *Astoria* blazed away with accuracy, knocking down fourteen of twenty sleeves offered to them as targets. When *Astoria* rounded the turn toward Pearl Harbor, Fred Lind found himself at a loss for words to describe the beauty of Oahu, waves rolling toward Waikiki Beach. Entering the harbor itself brought an equally indescribable view, although a sobering one by comparison. Almost three full years after the Japanese attack on Pearl Harbor, evidence remained: the righted hull of USS *Oklahoma*, and behind her the sunken tomb of *Arizona*, now stripped of her superstructure.

Captain Dyer's thoughts lay elsewhere when they docked. As he feared, he and his fellow skippers had been summoned for a meeting with Rear Admiral Walden Ainsworth, the newly installed commander of cruisers and destroyers, Pacific Fleet. Absenteeism certainly would be a topic.

With all three captains in his office, Ainsworth led by saying, "Well there's one man I want to talk to, and that's Captain Dyer."

After a pause, Dyer replied, "Yes, sir?"

"How did you do it? Here's the list."

The three cruisers, each with similar complements, had put to sea together from Mare Island with striking outcomes. While *Astoria* fired at sleeves in her assigned drill outside the Golden Gate, *Montpelier* and *Baltimore* searched for missing men ashore. *Montpelier* left her berth with thirty-eight absentees. Her crew had previously lost five more to disciplinary barracks and twenty-two hospitalized, resulting in a sixty-five-man shortage for "Hasty" Hoffman's crew. *Baltimore* had taken even longer to get underway, for she initially discovered eighty-four absentees at morning muster. Her hours-long delay came from extensive searching in the area to pull men back. Only once at sea did her skipper even realize they had recovered six more men than originally thought, but she still sailed short fifty. Vindicated, Dyer shared his efforts covering discipline, morale, and inspiration. In a fiery mood, Rear Admiral Ainsworth blasted his other two skippers, "just gave them the very devil" as Dyer recalled.

The victory proved short-lived. *Astoria's* final test before leaving Pearl would be a four-day training course firing at the Navy's gunnery range on the small island of Kahoʻolawe, southwest of Lahaina Roads. The course focused on long-range gunnery with both main and secondary batteries. Other exercises would focus on surface targets towed by a tug and some more antiaircraft fire. Just as *Astoria* was set to get underway for the training course, gun boss Ken Meneke informed Dyer of a new development: 6-inch turret number three had developed an elevating screw casualty. The turret would be useless for the exercises.

Meanwhile the wire reports in the *Astoria Morning Press* brought news of a recent tremendous American naval victory, off Leyte in the Philippines where MacArthur had landed. Calling it "the greatest sea battle in history," the story asserted sixty-four Japanese warships lost— carriers, battleships, cruisers, and destroyers, truly a crushing blow against the Japanese Combined Fleet.

Now she had a main battery turret out of action that would require more days of repair. Dyer once again received permission to proceed with a casualty. Down a screw en route to Trinidad, now down three of twelve main rifles to Kahoʻolawe. Dyer winced at the thought: he missed the Philippine Sea, missed Leyte Gulf...now another certain delay at Pearl. Meanwhile J. Cary Jones and USS *Pasadena* had already crossed the International Date Line far to the west, headed to join the fleet. *Neptune's Curse for a renamed ship.*

* * *

2,000 feet over Kahoʻolawe, Hawaiian Islands
November 5, 1944

Despite the relentless drone of the Pratt & Whitney radial engine and constant circle pattern, monotony never set in for Captain Gerard

Armitage. A lifelong fascination with flying grew acute now that he had a taste for it. He even considered applying for flight training once he returned stateside, war over or not. From the pilot's seat in front of him, Lieutenant Chuck Tanner demonstrated the effectiveness of American pilot training programs, even for such a slow and vulnerable aircraft as the Kingfisher floatplane.

Learning to handle a Kingfisher, or "gooney bird," took hundreds of hours of training. Like all naval aviators, Tanner first learned to fly the infamous N3N "Yellow Peril," a biplane trainer so named for its brilliant paint scheme and knack for washing out would-be pilots. From there he advanced to VOS (aviation, observation-scout) training at Naval Air Station Pensacola, where he was introduced to seaplane trainers. By the time he left the advanced schools, he was an expert at the controls of the Kingfisher. He could fly and land by instruments, vector to a specific set of coordinates, perform bombing runs, and evade faster fighter aircraft by utilizing the plane's maneuverability over speed.

The final stage of training for a seaplane aviator assigned aboard a cruiser or battleship meant learning how to return to his ship. Four different recovery methods based on sea and ship movement required unique approaches from the aviator, who maneuvered the plane into position to hook up and be hoisted back to its fantail perch by a large recovery crane. Tanner and his fellow Kingfisher aviators learned to "sail," using a rudder at the tail of the plane's main pontoon to handle waves and a ship's wake through prevailing winds. Armitage marveled at his buddy's skill.

The Marine captain brought his skill to the equation as well. From the rear cockpit, he spotted fire as *Astoria* blasted away at target points across Kahoʻolawe. Armitage would observe the shells land relative to the target, then call back to *Astoria* for fire adjustments. Fun as it might be, the pair weren't even supposed to be in the air for the day's exercises. In the morning, training tug *Lamberton* had lost the target float intended for their long-range surface-fire practice.

Improvising afternoon exercises, *Astoria* sent Tanner and Armitage aloft for shore bombardment practice. Fine with Armitage, for the Marine captain never got tired of the catapult launches that sent the plane skyward from the ship like a slingshot. After hours of spotting, *Astoria* reported yet another casualty—the number two turret lost its elevating screw exactly as number three had. Two turrets out of commission, more work to be done back at Pearl.

As dusk approached, Dyer again improvised training. Amid preparation for landing, Tanner received the radio instruction, "Remain on station to spot night firing by flare." Darkness closed fast, and night floatplane recovery aboard a ship was a thing unheard of. Dyer directed Tanner to detach at completion of the exercises and put in overnight at Ford Island in Pearl Harbor. They could collect the ship's mail, and in the morning fly out to rejoin *Astoria* and her destroyer escort USS *Hull*. Over the next hour, *Astoria* launched star shells to illuminate the target as Tanner circled and Armitage called adjustments. Afterward, low on fuel, they peeled off for Pearl Harbor.

After an hour flying in total darkness, the Kingfisher approached a blacked-out Pearl. Tanner radioed his identification to the Ford Island tower, requesting the markers in the landing channel be illuminated. Even so late in the war, lighting up in blackout conditions remained no trivial matter, and a squabble with the tower watch officer ensued. The watch officer demanded aircraft number and ship name, while Tanner insisted on the proper protocol of only giving *Astoria*'s call sign and frequency. He emphasized that his fuel was nearly exhausted. Fifteen minutes of circling passed, precious fuel burning, before the tower gave clearance.

"You are five miles from touchdown. Landing lights will be turned on for three minutes only." Ford Island's main runway lit up in front of them.

We have pontoons, not wheels. Furious, Tanner fired back, "This is a seaplane, you idiots! Give me the channel markers!"

Without response, the runway lights snuffed out. In equal silence from the tower, the channel lights leading to the seaplane ramp illuminated. Tanner realigned as the engine sputtered. He shouted back to Armitage, "Double check your harness, we're out of fuel! This could be a hard landing!" The engine coughed and cut out as Tanner gave one last go at the throttle. The Kingfisher glided just over a crash boat on station and smacked into the water, drifting to a stop. Hooking up to their plane, the shaken boat crew towed the pair in to the seaplane ramp. Seething, Chuck Tanner stomped off to the tower, only to learn that the watch officer had stepped away on some matter of importance.

* * *

Pearl Harbor Navy Yard
November 8, 1944

With her return from the gunnery course, yard workers began immediate repair on *Astoria*'s turret elevating screws. The crew learned that President Franklin Roosevelt had won an unprecedented fourth term, beating Republican nominee Thomas Dewey in an Electoral College landslide. For the men of the Mighty Ninety, however, more important news was announced: the turret repairs required an unscheduled layover at Pearl, which meant surprise liberty in Honolulu, at Waikiki Beach, and the surrounds.

Herman Schnipper pressed his dress whites in his darkroom and headed to tour a pineapple plantation. Pappy Kane and John Snyder posed in a club with exotic *wahines* in leis, a cottage industry for some local women. Maybe just one photograph their wives might not see. Jim Thomson received the worst news—orders to start his three-month rotation scrubbing trays and utensils in the scullery, something all men rotated through. *Where is the scullery?* "Don't ask that cook!" joked Fred Lind.

Lind centered his liberties on the Royal Hawaiian Hotel, which had been turned over to the Navy for wartime use. He listened to bands play, strolled Waikiki, and even watched a live performance of a radio program he listened to back in Rochester, *Hawaii Calls*. Any free activity sufficed, as he rarely drew pay. Other guys might blow money on crap games and such, but anything he drew he sent home for his family. Instead he strolled and window shopped, always fascinated to see local school girls carrying textbooks titled *My English.*

Others weren't so well behaved, as Captain Dyer quickly learned. Men returned on shore patrol report: improper uniform, hat not squared, crossing the street to avoid saluting an officer. While his punishments were light for such first-time offenses—warnings or loss of one liberty—Dyer had Armentrout republish "Instructions on Military Courtesy." He took an even more firm tone in an address to the crew:

"It is a matter of regret to me that a few members of this fine crew have caused the *Astoria* to be publicly branded as a ship in which the ship's company cannot be trusted ashore to maintain those customs, traditions, and standards that have made the United States Navy the finest military or naval organization in the world." After detailing grievances and expectations, he closed with, "Let every manjack of you be a man o' war's man, clean, competent, and an outstanding example of an outstanding Navy."

Despite maintaining emphasis on discipline and adherence to regulation, Dyer could clearly see progress in his crew through fewer infractions meriting lesser punishment. His sailormen were griping about the right things too, such as Navy chow and pay. They grew salty, but they were also growing into a team.

* * *

On the morning of November 10, a sickening sight entered the harbor. *Astoria* men paused in their work to lay eyes on twin sister cruiser USS *Birmingham.* A casualty returning from the Leyte Gulf battles, holes and shrapnel scars peppered her stacks and superstructure. Herb Blodgett had seen his share of action at Sicily and Taranto, but certainly nothing like this. He had never seen anyone hurt or killed. As the young slugger watched the devastated ship steam slowly past, it sank in that "war could be dangerous to your health."

The next morning brought Armistice Day, a fitting day of remembrance for the crew of *Birmingham*. They had stood alongside the crippled light carrier *Princeton* to assist after she was bombed, only to have *Princeton*'s torpedo stores detonate in a savage explosion. The blast decimated *Birmingham*'s topside crew; nearly half the ship's complement lay killed or wounded. After Purple Hearts were awarded for some two hundred of the men still aboard ship, *Birmingham* got back underway for repair at Mare Island, essentially making *Astoria* her relief with the fleet. As the battered cruiser stood out, her bugler played out, "California Here I Come" over the public address.

The efficient Pearl Navy Yard completed work on *Astoria*'s turret screws within days. Replenishing munitions became the next order of business. From predawn until evening, sailors and Marines brought aboard their full combat allowances of ammunition, each division handling their stores. For Armitage's men, this meant schlepping steel cases of 20mm shells across the length of the ship to fill the ready ammo boxes at their mounts from forecastle to fantail. They then volunteered to assist the 40mm men with their larger shells, men with whom they cross-trained on the Bofors heavy antiaircraft mounts.

These tasks completed in the evening, Armitage formed his Marines for dismissal when he received a message from his boss, gunnery officer Meneke, to assist the 1st Division with their rounds for the forward-most main turret. Taking his men forward, he found the 1st Division loading on their own, with no Navy division officer in sight.

Fuming, he ordered his lieutenant and first sergeant to take over the situation. They rotated the turret 90 degrees to shorten the haul, and Marines formed up alongside 1st Division sailors to make a bucket brigade for moving the hundred-pound shells. As the work drew to a close, 1st Division officer Lieutenant Jack Karfgin walked up and realized what he was seeing. *Presumably back from dinner in the wardroom.*

"Captain Armitage, what the hell are you doing? Officers don't handle ammunition!"

Armitage's lieutenant, an Irish wit named Diveney, looked out from the turret hatch where he and two men passed shells down into the handling rooms. "Ah, good evening, Mister Karfgin. I wondered where you were. Please stand aside, sir, so they can pass me those last few shells."

Hours later the light snapped on in Karfgin's stateroom, rousing him from slumber. In the doorway stood Armitage, showered and pressed.

"Jack," he said, "Just so you'll know. We Marines are good shipmates. If you need our help, just ask. No need to go crying to the gun boss." After a pause, he added, "One other thing, Karfgin. When Marines chow down, their officers eat last. In other words, we don't send them, we lead them." The Marine left the stateroom without bothering to turn off the light.

The tale spread like wildfire throughout the ship. The Marine CO might have furthered a degree of rivalry with the Academy Class of '42, but he was confident none of them would ever leave a working party unsupervised again.

Meanwhile, Captain Dyer fought his own battle with the Operations Section of the Commander in Chief, Pacific Theater (CinCPAC). His orders upon leaving Hawaii directed him to proceed independently, unescorted for the more than four thousand miles of open ocean to join the fleet at their forward anchorage of Ulithi atoll. Dyer did not contest the relatively safe span of ocean between the Hawaiian Islands and the midway fueling depot of Eniwetok, but he felt quite differently about the 1,400-mile journey that lay further west, past enemy-held islands. *Astoria*'s captain remained a submariner through and through. He fully respected the danger of coming across a Japanese sub so deep into the Western Pacific. He knew what torpedoes could do to a light cruiser.

He requested a destroyer escort and was flat-out refused. Taking his case directly to a friend in the Operations Section, he received the same reply: "I can't give you an escort. Sorry, you'll just have to sail without one." Destroyers were vital, scarce commodities, and nothing was available. Undeterred, Dyer sent a dispatch directly to CinCPAC stating, "Having been ordered to sail without escort from Pearl to Ulithi, I request escort." The CinCPAC reply finally managed to locate a destroyer that could sail with *Astoria* as antisubmarine screen for the final leg from Eniwetok to Ulithi.

"You had to put the man on the spot," Dyer would later reflect. "Otherwise the burden is on you, the Commanding Officer, you've accepted the order."

In the afternoon of November 17, 1944, six months to the day from her commissioning, USS *Astoria* released her training escort and headed west away from the Hawaiian Islands. Her turret repairs had checked out satisfactorily in gunnery drills. She departed with four functioning engines and all weaponry in service, fully fit for combat duty. Her war diary stated, "The ship is en route to forward areas. After the many trials and tribulations of the training period, at last we are on our way." No American cruiser had taken longer to do so.

The day after *Astoria* put to sea, Dyer learned of further vindication. Returning from her shakedown cruise in the Gulf of Paria, another *Cleveland*-class cruiser, USS *Duluth*, had developed a bad vibration during a high-speed trial. Inspection demonstrated the bearings badly wiped, the same problem *Astoria* and then *Springfield* had suffered. He could also take pride in his crew, for the Mighty Ninety sailed with a full complement, well-trained with high morale.

While she would pick up Dyer's demanded destroyer escort at Eniwetok, for the first time in her career *Astoria* steamed through open ocean absolutely alone. Seven hundred miles out of Pearl, one quarter of the way to Eniwetok, the crew trained on a new exercise no one aboard had performed or even heard of: "Fire drill in the after air defense station. Plane crash into superstructure." They had no knowledge of two aircraft carriers under escort passing a hundred miles to the south. Both carriers were limping back from the Philippines, victims of exactly that type of enemy attack, what would come to be known as the *Kamikaze*.

9

The Storm

Eniwetok Atoll
November 23, 1944

T hanksgiving always occurred on a Thursday, although everything felt a day off on this side of the international date line. At least such was the case for Fred Lind, who noted the loss of Monday the twentieth in his shorthand diary. "I felt cheated...I've always liked Mondays," he wrote. Crossing the line westward meant losing a twenty-four-hour period in time, an event with special significance for sailors. The service records for *Astoria* men would now forever include the cryptic entry: "Crossed the 180th meridian headed west with permission of the Golden Dragon," the time-honored unofficial Navy recognition of the moment.

Perhaps Neptune's curse didn't apply on this side of the line, or perhaps the Golden Dragon smiled upon the Mighty Ninety, for their stopover at Eniwetok coincided with the Thanksgiving holiday. Once Japanese-held territory, the atoll had been captured by American troops and utilized for forward staging of the Pacific fleet for months. Now that the fleet anchorage had relocated even closer toward Japan, Eniwetok made for a fine fueling depot. As *Astoria* replenished her "Navy special" fuel oil, the crew could cycle through a Thanksgiving meal at anchor.

Captain Dyer and executive officer Armentrout skipped the officers' wardroom, instead taking their meal through the enlisted chow line with their men. The captain's Marine orderly kept watch over them, as did Herman Schnipper to photograph the event. Inevitably some joker would show off a mouthful of food as Schnipper went to snap a picture, jam a finger up his nose, or come up with some even more creative way to spoil a good image. He made sure to take a photo of Dyer and Armentrout receiving their meal, ostensibly to capture the solidarity they demonstrated to the crew. Privately he chuckled, for in spite of the speeches about proper uniforms in Hawaii, the skipper still wore his officer's cap in the chow line against regs.

The menu read lavish enough, certainly for a warship deep in the Pacific: roast young Vermont turkey in "old-fashioned" broth, with giblet gravy and sausage dressing, creamy mashed potatoes, and early June peas. Hot Parker House rolls and pumpkin pie rounded out the offering. Lind among others found it a delicious change, yet not all carried the same opinion.

"Typical holiday chow," wrote Marine assistant cook John Arrighi. He kept his men well fed every day. The son of Italian immigrants who opened a restaurant in Massachusetts, Arrighi made for an unlikely Marine. Joining the Corps at thirty-four, he may have been short in stature and long in the tooth by military standards, but also long in desire to serve his country. Arrighi could prepare quite the meal, and thanks to Armitage's insistence on training he could also operate a 20mm Oerlikon machine-gun mount with proficiency.

Arrighi hoped he wouldn't have to do so anytime soon. The Marine detachment stayed better informed than most aboard ship, as they always had an orderly guarding Captain Dyer, usually within earshot. The final leg of their journey to the fleet would take them directly between Japanese-held Truk and the recently established American airfields on Saipan. Japanese planes were known to launch from Truk for bombing missions over Saipan, and an American cruiser crossing through the water below might make for a tempting target. "Enemy could be anywhere out here," he logged in his diary. "Made us feel a little uneasy." The crew took to soaking their white "dixie cup" hats in indigo ink, rendering them blue to blend with the deck and the ocean when viewed from above.

Between fueling and a hurried holiday feast, *Astoria* spent a mere five hours at Eniwetok. As Jim Thomson scrubbed Thanksgiving trays and utensils in the scullery, Dyer's escort reported for duty right on schedule—USS *Kalk*, a destroyer that had recently required significant repair at Mare Island after being bombed. Her path had tracked across the Pacific just days apart from *Astoria*. The pair put to sea headed due west with a further 1,500 miles in front of them. As Eniwetok sunk below the horizon, perhaps no man was happier to set foot back on deck with wind in his face than Herb Blodgett. The diesel-turned-steam engineer had missed both the date line crossing and Thanksgiving meal in sick bay with a stomach ailment.

* * *

Ulithi Anchorage
November 26, 1944

Ulithi appeared as a speck on maps of the Pacific if at all even present. Officially part of the Caroline Islands, the atoll contained one of the world's largest lagoons. In late 1944, it also served as the hub of US Navy operations in the Western Pacific against Japan. The Navy advanced their forward anchorage from Eniwetok to Ulithi once the Marianas had been taken. Its strategic value came from central proximity to the Philippines, Formosa, and Okinawa, placing all three occupied targets within striking distance.

Entering the vast expanse of calm water three days later, *Astoria* men laid eyes on the greatest assembly of naval military might the world had ever seen: patrol craft, auxiliaries, destroyers, cruisers, battleships, and aircraft carriers. One officer described the sea of ship masts "like trees of a deciduous forest in winter." Fred Lind wrote, "I didn't know we had that many!"

Astoria passed the most venerable and battle-tested aircraft carrier in service, her lines unmistakable: USS *Enterprise*. At one point in late

1942, she had stood defiantly alone in defense of the Solomons against the Japanese Combined Fleet. Her crew had placed a sign on her deck declaring, "*Enterprise* versus Japan!" Nearby lay three CVLs (light carriers): *Cowpens*, *Monterey*, and *San Jacinto*. All three began their lives as *Cleveland*-class cruisers before their hulls were covered with flattop flight decks as a stop-gap measure to reinforce *Enterprise*. Also present were four fleet carriers of the modern *Essex*-class: *Lexington*, *Yorktown*, *Wasp*, and *Hornet*. Like *Astoria*, all four were vengeance ships, each named for a carrier sunk earlier in the war. Reaching the cruiser anchorage area, Dyer noted the presence of USS *Pasadena*, his division flagship. At long last he had caught up with her.

The most awe-inspiring aspect of the whole scene would only become apparent later. Half the carrier force wasn't even present, as their task groups remained on station striking the Philippines.

Refueling again took first priority. Aging oiler *Sepulga* came alongside to pass over the lines and hoses. As fuel oil pumped into *Astoria*, men from both ships lined the rail to shout across. Oilers always carried more than just fuel—they also had the latest "dope." Fresh scuttlebutt awaited as close as the next ship, and *Sepulga* men brought plenty.

Ulithi Anchorage, strategic as it might be, kept no secrets from the enemy. The Japanese-held island of Yap and its airfield lay a mere one hundred miles to the southwest, making for easy reconnaissance. Just days before *Astoria* arrived, Japanese manned torpedoes had managed to throw the anchorage into chaos. A picket ship standing watch rammed and sunk one intruder in the channel entrance, but another manned torpedo managed to strike the oiler *Mississinewa*, rocking her with explosions and sending her to the atoll floor. Sixty-three men perished, and the plume of thick black smoke visible across the anchorage put every ship on warning that it could have been theirs.

Curiously, however, Ulithi did not enforce light restrictions. Fred Lind noted the first night that "it looked like a large city." Marine cook John Arrighi added, "At night we had movies on the fantail. I don't imagine the Japs thought that was treating them very seriously."

The next day another carrier task group returned from support of the Leyte operation, further illustrating the vast resources of American naval power. Task Group 38.2 entered the anchorage, lines of destroyers establishing screening lanes. The "heavies" arrived in column, resplendent in their jagged black and gray camouflage schemes: *Vincennes*, a sister Savo vengeance ship. *Miami*, the first cruiser Cramp had launched before *Astoria*. USS *Hancock* and *Intrepid*, two more *Essex*-class fleet carriers, with *Cabot* and *Independence*, both cruiser-hull light carriers. *New Jersey* and *Iowa* completed the column, two of the four largest and most lethal American battleships ever built. Beyond such massing of American striking power, yet another task group remained off the Philippines.

Herman Schnipper attempted to photograph the mighty collection and was instructed that any photographs required redaction—scratching out the top-secret radar arrays from his negatives. He had to laugh. The optics on his Speed Graphic didn't allow for such detail over the distance of the expansive atoll, and at best he could manage panoramic shots. He again requested longer lenses, telephoto optic attachments. Once again his request met with smug denial that he had no need for such toys.

Many of the ships brought back wounds from action. Light carrier *Cabot* berthed next to a repair ship. *Lexington* had just completed similar work. *Intrepid* was so badly damaged that she prepared for a return stateside for repair. On the heels of the scuttlebutt of suicide manned torpedoes, Schnipper and his shipmates learned the reality of the situation straight from their captain's mouth. With lines of uncensored communication stateside left behind in Hawaii, Dyer took to the ship's public address circuit to inform his men of a new Japanese tactic unveiled at Leyte Gulf:

> This is the Captain speaking. During the last month, our enemy the Jap has developed a new method of attack on our ships, the suicide dive bomber. During this period a sizable number of our ships have been damaged by these attacks...We must meet these attacks with the same resolution with which they are delivered.

Our AA batteries must kill the pilots, and destroy their control of the plane, and then literally smash the plane to bits before it can crash into the ship. We must beat this method of suicide attack, and we must do so quickly before the mounting toll of damaged ships hampers our plans to drive the Japs out of their stolen island possessions.

This information is confidential and it *shall not* be used in your letters.

The captain's announcement explained the airplane crash drill the crew conducted on the way in. Suicide airplane crashes into ships—not individual pilot decisions, but a new organized form of enemy resistance. The Mighty Ninety had entered a theater of war that appeared to be winding down. The Marianas were taken, the Philippine Sea battles had decimated Japanese air power, MacArthur had returned to the Philippines, and Leyte Gulf had demonstrated the American resolve to crush the remaining surface threat. *Astoria's* duty of guarding American aircraft carriers had appeared it might be mundane at best.

Now this. One determined pilot could knock an American aircraft carrier out of action for months, removing the force projection capability of almost one hundred aircraft, killing and demoralizing hundreds or thousands of men. Perhaps even sinking the vessel, or pulling other warships off the line to protect a wounded flattop. All it cost in return was the pilot's life. A strict gag order regarding this information intended to keep it far from the American press.

New Jersey's return to anchorage spoke volumes, for the ship served as flagship for Admiral William F. Halsey, Commander Third Fleet. His presence telegraphed that carrier-based support of the Leyte operation was drawing to a close. In fact the last of his four carrier task groups had suffered another suicide crash into USS *Essex*, and her group was wrapping up operations to return to Ulithi. No one could call Halsey cautious or timid. His words and image in the press portrayed him as the Patton of the Pacific. The naval hero of the Solomon battles left his words emblazoned upon a large sign at Tulagi for all to see: "Admiral Halsey says 'Kill Japs, kill Japs, kill more Japs!' You will help kill the yellow bastards if you do your job well."

Yet so serious had grown this new menace that Halsey saw no value in placing his precious carriers at further risk. At Leyte one escort carrier had been lost and six others required extensive repairs. He wrote, "Further casual strikes did not appear profitable; only strikes in great force for valuable stakes or at vital times would justify exposure of the fast carriers to suicidal attacks—at least until better defensive techniques were perfected." Before MacArthur's forces could move into the next phase of their Philippine liberation, the US Navy would have to change their tactics. One thing was certain for Dyer and his men. When the Third Fleet's carriers returned to action, *Astoria* would be charged with protecting them.

* * *

Fifty miles northeast of Ulithi Anchorage
December 11, 1944

Ship's photographer Herman Schnipper timed each snap of the shutter to correspond with the massive plumes of spray thrown skyward. When each volley of 16-inch shells landed astern of the ship, it created quite the show. From thousands of yards away, the battleship *Wisconsin* fired again and again at *Astoria*, or more correctly a few hundred yards behind her as offset fire exercises were designed. While maintaining safe distance from the target ship, accuracy could be determined by how closely the massive shells splashed in her wake. Tanner circled overhead in his Kingfisher, this time with an aviation radioman in the rear cockpit to report results.

Astoria opened the morning with main battery offset fire against her battleship counterparts, who now returned the favor. First *Iowa*, then *New Jersey*, and lastly *Wisconsin*. While men gathered at the fantail to watch the show, the whole experience proved unsettling for Fire

Controlman Fred Lind up in Sky Aft. "It's no picnic being fired at with sixteen-inch guns, even with a 10-degree offset," he wrote. All ships' fire had proven deadly accurate. At the close of exercises, Captain Dyer signaled to *Wisconsin*, "Thank God for the offset." The signal reply came, "Thank God you are on our side."

The exercise came on the heels of more than a week of training with a large group, the result of MacArthur postponing his next Philippine island invasion by ten days. Halsey's entire Fast Carrier Task Force had sortied from Ulithi the morning of December 1, only to be recalled within hours. *Astoria* among several other ships were tapped to stay out and rehearse together.

Just joining up with a formation of carriers, battleships, cruisers, and destroyers had proven harrowing for Dyer. He was ordered to take station in a fast-moving formation after dark, a new experience for the skipper. One mistake could result in collision, the end of a career, or worse. He relied on his radar training, a course he had decided to take while *Astoria* sat idle in Philadelphia, and successfully maneuvered through the darkened formation into position. "Really to be able to look at it and know what it means, when you have all kinds of ships on it, you really have to have a marked skill if you're going to do that well," he wrote. Later referring to the experience as "one of the hairiest times I ever had," he "thanked the Good Lord" a half-dozen times afterward for the radar training.

"Moosetrap" exercises had followed, training exercises at a task group level. The formation approximated what *Astoria* could expect once underway for the Philippines: a nucleus of aircraft carriers protected by concentric circles of protective battleships and cruisers, with destroyers ringing the perimeter. The group launched planes and simulated enemy aerial attacks with ship-based air defense.

Now with offset fire exercises complete, *Astoria* officially joined Halsey's Task Force 38, known as the Fast Carrier Task Force—eighty-seven ships in total, broken into three task groups operating independently. Each group brought several aircraft carriers that provided offensive power.

Thirteen aircraft carriers sortied in total, collectively capable of placing close to a thousand fighters and bombers in the air. Assigned to Task Group 38.2, *Astoria* and her battleship practice partners would join up with four more cruisers to protect five aircraft carriers: *Hornet, Lexington, Hancock, Independence,* and *Cabot.* Combined with Halsey's other groups, the Fast Carrier Task Force projected the greatest concentrated display of naval power that the world had ever seen. Like all other ships in Task Force 38, *Astoria* received a coded call sign so her name could not be known to enemy ears. Far from "Lowlife," Dyer could not have been more pleased with the call sign selection for the Mighty Ninety: Rampage.

The next phase of the Philippine Liberation was code-named Operation Love III. The island of Mindoro, just south of Luzon, would be ideal for establishing airfields that could support the ultimate goal: landings on Luzon. While seaborne forces came ashore at Mindoro, aircraft from the fast carriers would play a suppression role over Japanese airfields across Luzon to prevent enemy air power from getting off the ground. Halsey and his Task Force 38 commander, Vice Admiral John "Slew" McCain, also bolstered aerial coverage capability by exchanging bombers for more fighter aircraft to intercept anything that would get airborne. For *Astoria* and the other capital ships in the carrier screen, their role would be purely protective. They would play the last line of defense for any enemy plane that made it through the blanket to the carrier groups. Having both Halsey's flagship *New Jersey* and McCain's flagship *Hancock* in her task group made *Astoria*'s defensive task all the more important.

After steaming northwest for two days, on December 13 the fast carriers rendezvoused with their Logistic Support Group for their first underway replenishment of the operation. At the rendezvous point, the ships of Task Force 38 topped off with fuel oil in final preparation for their run-in toward Luzon. Speed in refueling, as Dyer had taught, played a critical factor to get on station in time. Suicide attacks had already sprung up across MacArthur's invasion fleet, with convoys of invasion craft set to land on Mindoro in the morning.

Overnight the Fast Carrier Task Force performed a high-speed run-in toward the coast of Luzon, where waves of carrier planes launched before first light from ninety miles out. For *Astoria* men, reveille came at 2:30 a.m. Dawn alert meant watch, noontime return of the first wave meant more watch, followed by afternoon strikes and recovery, then dusk alert. Men spent the entire day on heightened watches and at general quarters. Yet not one enemy plane made it through Halsey and McCain's coverage out to them. Dyer had told the crew that attack by "torpedo planes or suicide dive bombers may be expected at any time...When they come, I expect you to give them plenty of hot lead and a watery grave." Set to photograph such action overhead, instead Herman Schnipper captured images of men seated at their gun mounts—reading comic books under empty skies.

Men stationed topside only viewed one thing of note. Following the first day of strikes, Fred Lind wrote, "During the day several planes were lost in the drink, but almost all our pilots were saved. It is a pitiful and helpless feeling to watch a plane crash. The pilot must be alert in order to get out in time. After pancaking, he has about one minute before his plane goes down nose-first...It makes you feel very helpless as you watch them settle down in the deep blue waters. Some broke into flames, and inside a human being was dying for his country." John Arrighi added, "Planes came back pretty well shot up. Many crash-landed alongside the carriers. Pilots picked up by destroyers." He added, "Disappointed because all the air alerts proved false. Bogies turned back." Men were growing accustomed to the term "bogey"—radar signals of unidentified aircraft that could be either friend or foe and ultimately had to be visually identified.

Over the next three days, the aerial suppression strategy worked magnificently. The Fast Carrier Task Force provided a critical role for MacArthur, but quite a different one from Leyte. Where their bombers had dropped three hundred tons of ordnance per day during the Leyte invasion, for Mindoro they laid down a third of that. Instead, 85 percent of their aircraft sorties provided fighter coverage. The suicide attacks tapered dramatically. Once the fast carriers took station, not a single Luzon-based aircraft attacked the Mindoro invasion fleet.

* * *

Refueling rendezvous, 500 miles east of Luzon
December 17, 1944

Following the three days of flight operations over Luzon, the Fast Carrier Task Force had retired for rendezvous with their oilers for refuel. Halsey intended to perform a quick underway replenishment and get back to support of Love III. The rendezvous point lay beyond the range of Japanese fighters, yet allowed for the quickest possible return to suppress the activity of enemy airfields and protect the invasion.

"I have never seen a sunrise so sinister," Fred Lind wrote in his diary. "The background was a cross between gold and tan, blending gradually to a dark brown on the edges. The sun's rays penetrated the golden sector of the sky, turning the brown into a violent purple. Suddenly, the whole sky burst forth into a holocaust of flame, as the sun rose above the low-lying clouds. That scene will remain in my memory forever."

From the bridge of *Astoria*, conversation also centered around the morning conditions. Captain Dyer conferred with his aerographer's mate, Marvin "Clouds" Emery, who reported a plunging barometer as both wind and sea picked up. Reports out of Pearl warned of rising storm conditions, and all indicators verified such. With the fleet positioned in "typhoon alley" during typhoon season, the concern held merit. A good chance existed that a rapidly growing Pacific storm was headed directly for them. Always designed for rapid performance, these refueling operations carried an even more heightened sense of urgency.

At 10:30 a.m. *Astoria* and Task Group 38.2 made rendezvous with their service group. Four oilers formed a line three thousand yards ahead of the disposition center, with a similar distance from oiler to oiler. Two destroyers assumed patrol stations to either side of the joint formation,

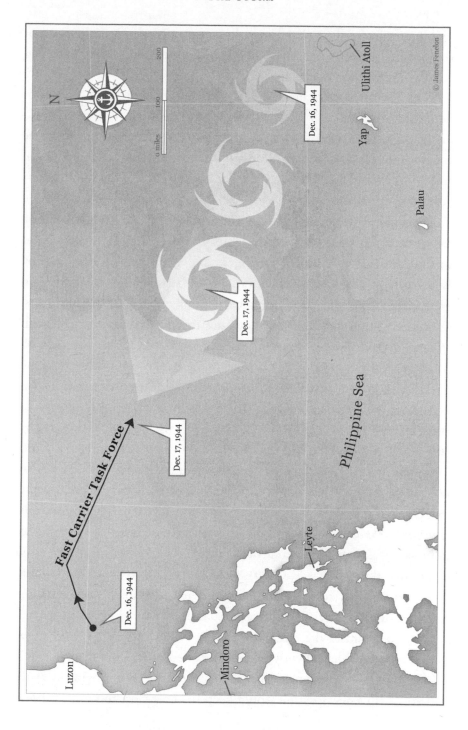

Luzon

Mindoro

Leyte

Philippine Sea

Fast Carrier Task Force

Dec. 16, 1944

Dec. 17, 1944

Dec. 17, 1944

Dec. 16, 1944

Ulithi Atoll

Yap

Palau

N

0 miles 100 200

© James Fenelon

and a patrol of eight F6F Hellcats flew protective figure-eight patterns overhead. The planes essentially guarded filling station waiting lines that stretched miles on a side.

With the barometer continuing to fall, seas swelling from the northeast, and winds up to 30 knots and gusty, Clouds Emery reported an "extra-tropical storm" forming. Reports estimated the storm to be moving north-northwest on a course that would take it hundreds of miles from the fleet. His own personal observations and measurements suggested otherwise.

On station two thousand yards astern of oiler *Atascosa* while awaiting his turn, Dyer could see the difficulties facing destroyers in line ahead of him through such conditions. Again and again, towlines and fueling hoses parted and were swept away. Other small ships attempting to transfer fuel from the surrounding battleships suffered similar problems. Within an hour of the first attempts, destroyers began to break off with no fuel received. One "tin can," as destroyers were nicknamed, USS *Maddox*, nearly collided with her oiler *Manatee*.

The Logistic Support Group also brought small escort carriers loaded with new and repaired aircraft. Their role in such operations was to transfer fresh pilots, fighters, and bombers to the fast carriers, replacing the operational and combat losses of the previous days' missions. Both "jeep" carriers canceled all air operations and personnel transfers due to consistent rolling. Their crews focused instead on lashing planes to the deck with steel cables and deflating tires to prevent losing any aircraft overboard. As the day progressed, this practice of securing aircraft was adopted by carriers throughout the fleet.

Shortly after noon, with every task group reporting similar failures to fuel and replenish, Admiral Halsey ordered all ships to cancel fueling attempts for the day "as soon as practicable." He directed a second rendezvous point to the northwest for the following morning. All units would proceed independently for another attempt at 6 a.m. Halsey made his decision based on the conclusion that the storm was moving away to the north. This new location would keep the fleet close to Luzon yet out of enemy fighter range, allowing the fast carriers to get back into action on schedule.

All ships in *Astoria*'s task group reported in with their fuel situations. Dyer was fine, along with the other heavies. All destroyers reported low on fuel, but most held enough in their tanks to make it to the next day. There were three exceptions, all approaching critical.

Beyond her near collision with her oiler, USS *Maddox* had also made a separate fueling attempt in the lee of the mammoth battleship *Wisconsin*. The pair had not even managed to get hoses across and she now ran below 15 percent fuel supply. "Very harrowing and dangerous," her skipper reported. USS *Hickox* reported similar parted lines with her assigned oiler after five attempts. The third ship, USS *Spence*, made an attempt directly from Halsey's flagship *New Jersey*. That failure played a role in the admiral's decision to wave off operations.

All three fuel-critical destroyers were ordered to remain with the oilers of the Logistic Support Group in hopes they could find a window of opportunity "to get enough fuel to make the new rendezvous" and "continue operations as necessary." As Task Group 38.2 separated from their oilers, carrier USS *Lexington* recovered several aircraft. Three originated from *Hancock* bound for Ulithi, carrying vital mail and reconnaissance photographs. They had been forced to turn back by the storm and land on their sister carrier. Fighting gale-force winds, a final two inbound planes could not land at all, and were ordered to ditch in the ocean near a destroyer for pilot recovery. All further flight operations ceased. With a base course set at 290 degrees true, 17 knots, the groups headed out to the northwest.

Captain Dyer could appreciate Admiral Halsey's predicament, caught between the proverbial rock and hard place. Stay close enough to strike, stay out of range of enemy planes, stay out of the storm's path, and yet find a spot to refuel. The calculus had to be daunting, especially without having a concrete idea of the storm's position and course relative to the fleet. Halsey's ships each suffered their own such predicaments, whether to ballast versus freeing up tanks for fueling. Ballasting and deballasting brought perils—time intensive work, along with the risk of introducing seawater into fuel oil supply that could extinguish boilers. A wrong decision either way could leave a ship dead in the water without propulsion.

Despite no concern over his own fuel situation, Dyer set the crew to work on other heavy weather precautions. He elected to partially ballast his fuel tanks. Such a move provided the ship a deeper draft in the water, which lowered her center of gravity and provided more stability in heavy seas. He ordered his forward main battery gunners to elevate their 6-inch rifles to prevent water pouring down the barrels into the turrets and ammunition handling rooms.

His Kingfisher floatplanes provided another problem. Both older and newer models of seaplane featured wings that could be folded up, allowing them to be secured in a cruiser's hanger. The Vought Kingfisher by contrast came with fixed wings. The plane had been designed prewar for battleship work, where hangars weren't present. *Astoria's* airplane hangar therefore had never been used to store airplanes, and that certainly wasn't an option now. His aviation unit made do the best they could by heavily lashing the two Kingfishers to their catapults and securing them upright with shoring timbers.

Throughout the afternoon Halsey's decision for a northwesterly course did not sit well with Dyer. The weather clearly continued to worsen as they steamed northwest. As far back as the Academy, seamanship and navigation had been Dyer's best subjects. It all felt wrong. He had Aerographer's Mate Emery break out a copy of the Bowditch *American Practical Navigator*, the Navy's seafaring bible for navigation. The pair dug into the chapters regarding storms. Bowditch had "a mouthful to say" on the subject, and it confirmed Dyer's suspicions. Strengthening seas, backing winds...nothing short of a typhoon stalked them.

Other skippers conducted similar work from their bridges. The TBS (talk between ships) radio band carried chatter of opinions and predictions based on discussions between skippers and their own aerographers. Halsey had again changed the rendezvous coordinates, yet the fleet now maintained a westward course. Consensus grew that the new refueling point lay in the path of the storm.

Heading 270 true, due west. We are violating all of Bowditch's rules. By evening watch, Captain Dyer could not stand it any longer. He radioed his division commander, J. Cary Jones, in *Pasadena* and requested Jones recommend to Halsey a course change to 180 true, due south. Bowditch made it clear that a Pacific typhoon with backing winds required a southerly course to break free in the shortest possible time. Fueling might be critical, but the force must clear the storm and survive in order to fuel at all. *One problem at a time.*

Dyer waited and waited, to no response. By midwatch *Astoria* was rolling through 20 degrees, already heavy seas for a light cruiser, and the captain elected to wait no further. He again reached out to Jones over TBS radio and referred to his original message, requesting it be passed up to Halsey. *Change course to 180 true.* This time Jones responded and passed the message along. Dyer noted that his boss did not take claim for the request, making sure it was clear it had come from Rampage, or Dyer and *Astoria*. *Surely* Pasadena *must be experiencing similar rolls.*

A response came from Halsey's chief of staff on *New Jersey*'s bridge: "Wait one."

Well, at least they're going to think about it, thought Dyer. Waiting one minute for response became two...then ultimately five minutes.

When the reply came from *New Jersey*, it was an emphatic one. "Rampage, regarding your request—*negative*."

Frustrated, Dyer held the westerly course to maintain the semblance of formation. With his ship bucking heaving waves, he knew in his heart that a turn to the south would put the sea on the ship's quarter, a much more stable method to ride such a storm.

Only hours later did the order arrive. At 5 a.m. on December 18, Admiral Halsey ordered all ships to change course to 180 degrees true— due south, Dyer's recommendation. Shortly after, he called off a potential fourth rendezvous point, and in fact any consideration of refueling at all.

Just escaping the storm became his sole priority. The order came too late; within hours the typhoon swallowed his fleet.

* * *

By midmorning, heavy sea forced most ships to drop speed to 10 or fewer knots. Winds approached "full gale force." Sickening reports rolled in over the TBS of at least seven men overboard from ships across the task group. Any search attempt by a destroyer proved impossible. Destroyers cut out boilers to conserve fuel. Ships pleaded for authorization to steam on individual courses to keep seas on their quarter, to the side and astern, and Halsey had no choice but to authorize the independent maneuvering. One destroyer approached *Lexington* in a desperate attempt to refuel in the massive carrier's lee, but no lines could be cast. *Just get south.*

From *Astoria*'s bridge, Dyer and Emery held no doubt the fleet was in the heart of the storm. The sea might be coming from the northeast, but winds over 50 knots came from the northwest. Rock-bottom barometer readings and wind backing counterclockwise, the tell-tale signs of a typhoon. Waves crested higher than the bridge. Visibility fell below five hundred yards and rain crashed against the hull in horizontal sheets, making it impossible to determine the horizon or even see other vessels in formation. *Just get south.*

As the morning progressed, each crew across the formation fought their own battle. Having tied themselves in place, *Astoria*'s radiomen relayed messages pouring in from other ships, even from other task groups. Group 38.1 reported that light carrier USS *Monterey* lay dead in the water. Severe rolling had caused her aircraft on the hangar deck to crash into one another, igniting severe fires and cutting electrical power. Shortly after, sister CVL *Cowpens* from the same group reported similar fires. The *Astoria* men transcribing such messages ended each watch exhausted merely from "always having to brace yourself or hold onto something."

Fred Lind and his watch officer Gerard Armitage adhered to their posts up in the Sky Forward directors, even though it was an exercise in futility. Armitage described the wind as a "howling banshee," screaming through *Astoria*'s rigging, radio antennae, and SK "bedspring" search radar. "Towering green walls" of water broke over the bow as the ship pitched, clearing the elevated turrets and reaching the bridge. The rolls to port and starboard brought even more concern, throwing men against bulkheads to stare "straight into the abyss ninety feet below." Lind kept his mind occupied by estimating the distance between wave crests, based on his learned judgment of such matters. By the time he came off forenoon watch and fought his way down to the messing compartment for some chow, the sky had grown "as dark as midnight on a moonless night."

Upon arrival, Lind realized there would be no hot meals, only cold Spam or peanut butter sandwiches at best. Racks of mess gear had torn away from their binding, leaving many badly damaged. He later wrote, "Bowls crashed around, and silverware and trays scooted around the deck. It was funny watching the mess cooks trying to catch it. Just when they got to where it was, the ship would lunge, throwing them off-balance, and sending the items on their way across to the other side of the galley."

Lind grabbed a sandwich along with a cup of lime juice and took a bite. Just as he did the ship rolled hard, sending him reeling into another sailor against a bulkhead and dumping juice and half-chewed sandwich all over the man. Lind choked out a laugh, but *Astoria* rolled back and sent him back downhill across the compartment, where he crashed into the opposing bulkhead. He struck a cabinet, dislodging cups, bowls, and trays. Again he started to laugh—until he stood up and the pain struck. An hour later he left sick bay with his ankle heavily taped and trying to navigate a pair of crutches. *Crutches in a typhoon?* "Good luck," the ship's doctor told him.

Meanwhile the "pill rollers" also tended to another man from a galley incident—the Marine cook, John Arrighi. Suffering a similar spill, he appeared to have a cracked rib. There was no way to know for sure, because in the morning hours their portable X-ray machine had broken loose from its lashings and also crashed into a bulkhead, ruining it. Arrighi would just have to suffice being wrapped tight and sent back to work.

Lind would spend the rest of the day strapped down in his bunk, listening to the clatter and crash of loose equipment tossed about. Men in the compartment hung coffee pots filled with water and lime juice from the overhead, so they would swing and not spill as the ship pitched and rolled. He wrote in his diary, "You can't stand up, you can't sit down, and if you lie on your bunk you get thrown against the tricing chains...It is absolutely appalling. What a beating we as a crew are taking."

As Fred Lind worked his way down lower into the ship throughout the day, Herb Blodgett worked his way up. Heavy rolls brought far less notice in the engine room, given the lack of swinging out side to side. If "black gang" men heard anything from the storm at all, it might be the pop and creak of *Astoria*'s hull under stress. Yet Blodgett knew from his telephone headset that plenty was going on. Coming off watch, he was instructed not to go out on the weather deck due to the severe conditions. "Naturally I made my way up inside the aft superstructure as high as I could go," he wrote. He encountered no one to stop him. Reaching Sky Aft, he stepped out onto a platform where he had no business, stuck his head into the blasting wind, and "just held on tight to watch the spectacle."

The experience brought back an event from his early teen years. As a paperboy in September 1938, a hurricane had raged through his home-town of West Concord, Massachusetts. Herb Blodgett had marveled to watch hundred-year-old trees crash down as he waited for a train to bring the morning papers out of Boston. Now wearing Navy dungarees instead of his Boy Scout poncho, Blodgett marveled to see a mighty ship's bow "struggle to come up from under water, shaking, quivering, creating spray that came back over the bridge, all the way back to me, soaking me to the skin." He stood mesmerized until he recalled striking the dock in San Diego. The damage to *Astoria*'s starboard bow. *Oh no*, he thought. *Wonder if she'll hold up through all this?*

Herman Schnipper also received the warning against going topside for fear of being lost overboard. While Blodgett made his way up to Sky Aft, Schnipper took his camera through the forward superstructure to the bridge. No one ever stopped him when he had the Speed Graphic handy—he could justifiably claim official Navy business. Slammed from bulkhead to bulkhead, he took care to protect the camera as he slowly navigated passageways. "A cork on the open seas," he wrote.

Reaching the bridge area deflated Schnipper. While he could see "walls of water come crashing down over the ship," attempting to capture such in a photograph would be folly. The darkness and weather rendered the concept impossible. The one thing he could do was read the ship's inclinometer, a device that displayed the degree of a ship's roll to her side. *How far before she couldn't recover? Astoria's* roll consistently hit 42 degrees, the absolute verge of capsizing.

* * *

Rolling through 40 degrees, his men could practically walk up the bulkheads. Dyer could only imagine what was happening aboard the destroyers with their much lighter displacement. By early afternoon, six flattops had seen their planes swept overboard or smashed and burned— four light carriers and two escort carriers. Even the *Iowa*-class battleships were occasionally hitting 25 degrees. Ballasted to 16,000 tons, the *Astoria* captain could only hope for the best.

Whether *Astoria* and the other *Clevelands* would hold up, the King-fishers certainly hadn't. With wind gusts reaching 115 knots, *Wisconsin* gave the first report of a floatplane wrenched from her catapult. *Miami* experienced the same minutes later, as her planes were also carried overboard. USS *Pasadena* followed shortly, both planes torn from the catapults and wrecked. At least through noon, *Astoria's* "fantail Thunder-bolts" held firmly in place with their lashing and shoring.

The paymaster's safe containing cash and pay records made for another story. When *Astoria* began to roll heavy, the massive safe ripped from its mounting bolts and began to crash about from side to side like everything else. Dyer received a report from men working to lasso the thing, yet its bulk tore through hemp rope an inch and a half thick. Putting themselves in harm's way, the lasso detail expressed legitimate concerns that the safe might actually slide out the side of the ship. At Dyer's direction, the detail eventually captured and tamed the safe with two-and-a-half-inch manila lines.

Wrangling the paymaster's safe was a short-lived victory. At 2:20 p.m., *Astoria* passed within twenty miles of the heart of the storm. Her starboard Kingfisher lifted and crashed onto the deck, crumpling its wing. The portside plane received jagged holes in the fuselage from debris that also shredded its control surfaces. Two wrecked hulks on the fantail. However, shortly thereafter they passed the center of the typhoon, and conditions showed signs of improvement beginning with a rising barometer. And *Astoria*'s roll had never passed 42 degrees.

The TBS radio continued to crackle with updates. *Astoria*'s Cramp-built sister *Miami* responded to desperate calls from a jeep carrier, *Cape Esperance*. One of the escort carriers that suffered fires from crashing aircraft, flames had reached the height of her bridge. At one point while dead in the water she lay in serious jeopardy of being lost, damaged beyond repair or worse, and *Miami* had been dispatched to assist. Now her fires had been extinguished by the same storm that had caused them, but Samaritan *Miami* called in with bow frames buckling and temporary shoring across multiple decks.

As Rear Admiral J. Cary Jones and *Pasadena* followed *Astoria* through the heart of the typhoon, they reported, "Seas mountainous, visibility zero owing to torrential rains and driving spray." More than two hundred years of maritime experience had not been given its due; ignoring Bowditch forced each ship and crew to fight their own battle.

A rising barometer and falling inclinometer brought cold comfort for Dyer. *Astoria* might be emerging from the maelstrom, but the TBS reports made it clear that many others had yet to. Some thirty miles northeast, the heart of the storm was plowing through the fleet refueling group with heartless fury.

* * *

By dawn Halsey's Third Fleet lay strewn over three thousand square miles of ocean as ships across each task group had lost formation to maneuver independently. Conditions remained rough, but the worst of the storm had passed on its march toward the Philippines. While several ships had already been directed back to Ulithi for repair, the overall state of the fleet had yet to be ascertained. A number of ships could not be hailed, and at 6 a.m. carriers launched aircraft for search and rescue. Having reached calmer waters in their 250-mile trek to the south, the groups formed up for fueling.

Throughout the early morning, stragglers and ships detached from 38.2 rejoined *Astoria's* group. First came *Miami* from her adventure assisting escort carrier *Cape Esperance*. *Miami* reported taking a series of heavy seas that "buckled her shell, main deck, and longitudinals from the stem to about frame 22," far into her fragile bow. Her entire bow was bent six inches to port. Overnight her men had heard cries and whistles from the water off the port side—men in the waves as she steamed past. A subsequent search by two destroyers had yielded nothing.

Destroyer USS *Maddox* rejoined next, one of the three fuel-criticals left with the oilers.

Even with emergency ballast, she had been unable to hold her heading as the storm passed over. *Maddox* rolled through 55 degrees, and declared, "For a while today it was touch and go as to whether we capsized or not." Her steering engine room flooded and her TBS antennae were torn away. Only by cross-connecting her engines did she manage to conserve enough fuel to finally hook up with an oiler in the 6 a.m. hour. *Maddox* also brought chilling news: "Heard that *Hull* had perished in storm, others missing."

Shortly after 8 a.m. USS *Hickox* rejoined, another of the destroyers left with the refueling group. The plucky ship had been through hell. Unsuccessful at fueling throughout the day, she ballasted and hunkered down. Water disrupted her electrical systems and she lost all steering control. She managed to remain on station by creative throttling of her engines, and almost collided with another ship when the oiler formation fell apart. Only managing 3 knots, the storm took full control of the ship, swinging her more than 90 degrees by the head. She became locked in a trough. Sideways to 115-knot wind and unable to steer, her crew focused their efforts to bring flooding under control. By nightfall *Hickox* had regained steering and made contact with two other vessels. She reported lights in the water, sending the other ships to investigate. Their response upon picking up survivors confirmed the worst: USS *Hull*, *Astoria*'s old sparring partner from the Hawaii gunnery course, had foundered and the loss of life was sure to be devastating.

Not lost on Herman Schnipper was the date per the Hebrew calendar. *Astoria* and the fleet had endured the typhoon on the eighth day of Hanukkah, the day of the great miracle of the oil. Fitting, given that *Maddox* and *Hickox* had managed to stretch their threadbare fuel oil supply to navigate the typhoon. The loss of *Hull*, on the other hand... Word spread quickly throughout the ship. Equally troubling was the question of USS *Spence*, their third detached destroyer. No ship had heard from her.

* * *

The revelation of *Hull*'s loss left Admiral Halsey with three priorities. First, account for the rest of his ships and fuel them. In addition to *Spence*, there were another destroyer and two destroyer escorts unaccounted for and unresponsive. Second, expand the search for *Hull* survivors and men overboard from other ships. Third, get the mammoth task force back on station for strikes against Luzon. The planned strikes of the nineteenth and twentieth were no longer feasible, for it would take the remainder of the day to fuel and form up. The twentieth would be a day of movement, with a return to blanket the Luzon airfields by the twenty-first.

Two ships, *Tabberer* and *Benham*, worked a search grid where *Hull* men had been recovered. Halsey would keep planes in the air all day for aerial search, and add more ships to search following the current and path of the storm. Halsey directed his known cripples, light carriers *Monterey*, *San Jacinto*, and *Cowpens*, along with *Hickox* and six other tin cans to form up and proceed to Ulithi for repair. The bulk of his striking power could head back into action, following the storm's track to cover their advance and search for survivors.

Dyer's Rampage didn't seem particularly fit to return to action. In his diary, Jim Thomson cursed the damage to *Astoria*'s guns. Water in the electrical cables prevented the 5-inch and 40mm mounts from traversing properly, rendering the ship's antiaircraft battery essentially useless. The 20mm guns at the forecastle had been destroyed. Chuck Tanner's aviators could serve no purpose either, for their Kingfisher floatplanes lay wrecked on the fantail. In fact, only one Kingfisher across the entire task group survived, aboard USS *Vincennes*. New planes would have to be flown in for all the cruisers. Even had the planes survived, they would have brought limited value. Tests of *Astoria*'s catapults proved they couldn't make a full stroke for launching aircraft given their own damage.

Halsey might have most of his offensive striking capability intact, but his heavy screen ships were in no condition to provide protection to his aircraft carriers. They required days of repair, both at sea and back at anchorage where they could be properly serviced. Nevertheless, in the evening the battered Fast Carrier Task Force again set course for Luzon and steamed northwest.

The early morning hours of the twentieth brought devastating news that confirmed the worst fears of men in *Astoria*'s group. Overnight one of the destroyer escorts engaged in the search for *Hull* survivors had recovered a raft with men from USS *Spence* who had ridden out the rest of the storm against all odds, their ship lost to the depths of the Pacific. Like *Hull*, *Spence* had rolled onto her side, taken water, and downflooded. The survivors reported the sinking happened so quickly that it was unlikely that many others trapped belowdecks made it out.

Night brought reports of lights and whistles in the water; daylight brought floating debris, empty life rafts, and floater nets. *Astoria* among many others reported sightings to no avail. No men could be found in their path. Instead, weather picked up as the fleet closed in on the now slowing storm. Halsey's plan to use the typhoon as cover didn't factor not being able to launch. With his carriers again taking water over their flight decks on the morning of the twenty-first, Admiral Halsey called off further operations and informed General MacArthur his force was retiring to Ulithi. Fast carrier support of Love III had ended.

In Captain Dyer's morning address of the twenty-second, he revealed a third grim revelation to his crew. While other missing ships had been located, a third destroyer had been sunk—USS *Monaghan*. He went on to point out the normal set of the current as twenty miles per day, with survivors recovered "slightly better than sixty miles from where the ship had sank." *Three days in the water.* Dyer closed with, "It is to be regretted that during this strike against the enemy, the *Astoria* didn't get an opportunity to actually shoot at enemy planes, but I am sure that opportunity will come sooner or later and when it does our gunners will prove their worth."

Halsey called off the search for survivors at sundown on December 22. Ninety-three men had been pulled from the water over the course of four days. All three lost ships—*Hull*, *Spence*, and now *Monaghan*—suffered terrible casualty rates. A mere twenty-four sailors were recovered from *Spence*. In the case of *Monaghan*, only six men survived. In total 790 souls perished from the three lost destroyers, plus dozens more overboard from other ships, or crushed or asphyxiated aboard the burned-out light carriers.

Returning to Ulithi, the seas remained heavy enough that *Astoria*'s bow crashed down, throwing up spray. Days after the storm, Herman Schnipper captured his coveted shot of *Astoria* braving heavy seas. The image would make a fine addition to his wall of photographs in the darkroom. Of the Love III operation and typhoon disaster, *Astoria*'s war diary declared, "The storm has dealt us a blow which the enemy would have liked very much to deliver himself."

* * *

Ulithi Anchorage, Berth 145
December 24, 1944

Scuttlebutt played its usual role. By the time of Christmas Eve festivities, men spoke of winds clocked above 150 knots and rolls past 45 degrees. The "radar equipment was smashed, searchlights were ripped off, catapults were bent..." Exaggeration of truth, all were rooted in realities. One Kingfisher proved a total loss and was cannibalized for spare parts, its smashed carcass heaved over the side afterward. The other was hoisted off for extensive repair.

Christmas Eve night brought entertainment on the ship's fantail, featuring an accordion player backed by the ship's band. A sailor dressed as Santa Claus made an appearance in the tropical heat, followed by a movie. The festivities meant to boost morale, but Herman Schnipper's photos told a different story. The crew packed onto the fantail barely watched the show. Many of them appeared lost in their own thoughts, perhaps of the typhoon they just experienced. An inaugural mission where they never even saw the enemy, yet where so many died. *It could have been them.* For almost one thousand sailors and Marines who went to sea with them, there would be no more holidays, just families soon to receive telegrams.

Fred Lind wrote, "The awful fate of those who didn't make it hung over us. How the survivors ever made it in those waters, I'll never know...No one will admit how they feel—we are tough guys, right? Yeah, right...Everyone is exhausted from the strenuous operations. The crew seems in relatively good spirits, considering the heartache everyone is feeling way down deep."

He continued, "The best Christmas present that could be had was mail from home, and we received lots of that...my thoughts left this world and returned to Rochester, New York, where I could picture everyone as we always were on Christmas day." Certainly each sailor's family weighed upon his own mind. This Christmas would be the first away from home for most men, on the other side of the globe for virtually all. Yet many bags of Christmas mail and gift packages arrived soaked and ruined from their transit across the Pacific.

Work resumed on Christmas Day, for Third Fleet would be headed out again within days. Fred Lind soon returned his crutches to the Medical Division. John Arrighi's cracked rib didn't give him much trouble. "If I never see another typhoon it's OK with me," he wrote. Jim Thomson and the fire controlmen brought the gun mounts back into operation. Chuck Tanner and fellow *Astoria* aviator John F. "Jack" Newman flew replacement Kingfishers down from Guam. Rampage, aka the Mighty Ninety, would be back in fighting trim on time: ready, reloaded, and resupplied. Across the anchorage crews and service units scrambled to conduct similar repairs and preparations.

When the official mail arrived to his attention, Captain Dyer received the best possible Christmas present. On cue, Boatswain's Mate Rousseau Lemon had reported in at New Orleans.

10

The Private Lake of Japan

Introducing one January, one nine four five,
In the hopes that in twelve months no Japs be alive,
Finds the trim Mighty Ninety of Task Force Three Eight,
Steaming Northwest at two-two to keep a hot date...
We are steaming in darkness with truck lights forbidden,
With fourteen destroyers around Circle Seven.
This completes the first log of the year forty-five,
May the Bureau remember they're still on our side.
—Excerpted from Astoria's *poetic first deck log entry,*
New Year's Day 1945

Bashi Channel, south of Formosa
January 10, 1945

F red Lind followed the flaming plane all the way down as it spiraled and splashed in the predawn darkness. Overhead, Cupid 3, the call sign for a night fighter from *Independence*, ran up his score. This marked his third kill in twenty minutes. Lind estimated the burning plane as eight miles out from the ship, and the first enemy plane he had ever seen, even if only as a shooting star–like streak near the horizon.

"A while ago I would have considered this a tragedy," he wrote, "but today I found myself smiling." The task group's round-the-clock

Combat Air Patrol (CAP) proved both efficient and persistent, doing more to ensure *Astoria's* war would be an exercise in tedium than Cramp construction or faulty bearings ever had. Fellow Fire Controlman Jim Thomson wrote, "Our CAP was on the job and two Jap boys soon went on a journey to visit honorable ancestors." He further expressed the crew's desire to get into the fight and groused that "we have yet to fire an offensive gun!"

Overnight the Fast Carrier Task Force had slipped quietly into the South China Sea through Bashi Channel, a sea lane sixty miles across, stretching from the southern tip of Formosa to a small island group north of Luzon. Enemy snoopers made it clear that the American incursion was known, yet the Fast Carrier Task Force pressed on. Their entry into the waters served a singular purpose—Admiral William Halsey chasing his white whale.

Following the surface actions of Leyte Gulf in October 1944, Admiral Halsey had champed at the bit for an opportunity to finish off the Japanese Combined Fleet. Intelligence suggested the remaining capital ships that had survived the Leyte battles were divided into two sections—one group in the Inland Sea of Japan and the other down in Cam Ranh Bay. Having missed the opportunity at Leyte, Halsey desperately wanted to engage the remaining Japanese surface threat. Heading to Cam Ranh, in French Indochina, could provide his opportunity.

In early January 1945, the logistical requirements of MacArthur's Luzon invasion, code named Mike I, made this desire a practical reality. The possibility of Japanese warships in the South China Sea posed a significant threat to the American supply lines for Luzon. Enemy airfields along the coast of French Indochina and China also lay within striking distance of these supply lines. The timing proved ideal for a Task Force 38 incursion into the Japanese-controlled waters, both to hunt for formations of surface vessels and to strike other targets of opportunity along the way.

After five days in anchorage to perform quick repairs, the Fast Carrier Task Force headed back out. Missions against Formosa airfields over previous days had netted minimal results due to heavy weather. On January 3 and 4, afternoon sorties had been scrubbed altogether. *Astoria* men had little to do except trade scuttlebutt and again read comic books or *Forever Amber* at their stations. The thick cloud cover also prevented the Japanese from sending out planes in response.

On the sixth and seventh, the fast carriers had hammered Luzon airfields from the east in preparation for Admiral Thomas C. Kinkaid's Seventh Fleet to run in at Luzon from the west. "MacArthur's Navy" was nevertheless struck by suicide attacks as they advanced northward up the Philippines. Breaks in the weather and subsequent holes in blanketing tactics permitted some Japanese planes to get airborne and attack the invasion force. Although CAPs prevented any planes from getting through to the fast carriers, several ships in the invasion force approaching Linga-yen Gulf were hit. "The Japs are getting desperate," Lind wrote. "These tactics don't succeed in sinking many vessels, but they put them out of commission by rendering them inoperative, and kill a lot of sailors."

Of damaged American planes he observed returning to their ships, he added, "Most tried to pancake into the water, and luckily, the majority of the pilots were rescued. They had about one minute to escape the cockpit before the plane went down nose-first. Some damaged planes elected to try a landing on the carrier decks. A few made it, but most crashed into the bulkheads and exploded. Others came back with only one landing gear, and broke the arresting cable. Some shot right over the side of the carrier. It was a sickening sight."

The fast carriers attempted to blanket Formosa for "S-Day," MacArthur's Luzon landings of the ninth at Lingayen Gulf. Poor weather once again restricted the carrier planes to targets of opportunity. Some missions were recalled while others found breaks in the weather and pushed on to their targets. Despite conditions, the operations achieved their goal. No Japanese planes from Formosa airfields were able to provide resistance against the invasion.

Now with American troops ashore at Lingayen Gulf and advancing on Manila, Halsey unleashed his fast carriers to detach from support of MacArthur and go hunt their big game. Joining up were *Enterprise*, freshly modified for night carrier support, and a third member of J. Cary Jones's Cruiser Division 17—USS *Wilkes-Barre*. The "Willie Bee," as her crew called her, carried the original name of *Astoria*. She had spent the December typhoon in the safe confines of Ulithi, waiting to join up when the fast carriers retired.

Following morning GQ, Captain Dyer gave his daily address, which Thomson referred to as "George's morning *tête-à-têtes*." "This morning is the first time since the early days of 1942 that units of the United States Fleet have been in the South China Sea...We hope to run into Jap shipping or units of the Jap fleet or Jap aircraft...Everyone topside saw the plane burst into flames, then break into two parts on its way down to a watery grave...I have seen no dispatches as yet in regard to our landing on Lingayen Gulf, but there is no reason to believe that it is not going well. That's all."

Astoria and her cohort had steamed into the enemy waters, first past mines and then the reconnaissance aircraft overnight. Due to the three-year gap since any American incursion, the South China Sea carried the nickname "the private lake of Japan."

Of each call to general quarters, John Arrighi wrote, "Didn't lose any time getting to our battle stations because we always figured this is it." He added what many were feeling: "About this time we decided that we never would see any Jap planes—If they didn't come out now, they weren't coming out ever."

With two days of steaming ahead, Dyer turned his attention to the Lemon matter. The 8th Naval District had not complied with Bureau of Personnel direction, whether by bureaucratic mishap or intent. Boatswain's Mate Rousseau Lemon was not on his way back to *Astoria*. He had actually been granted shore duty on request, based upon his assertion that he already had three full years of sea duty under his belt. While technically true, he had spent half of that time in stateside ports, including many months of gaming the Navy system aboard *Santa Fe* and then *Astoria*.

Following a summary court-martial, the 8th District had administered punishment of a mere loss in pay: $48 for three consecutive months, totaling $144. The man even retained his second-class petty officer rate. Now he marked time in New Orleans awaiting shore assignment. The update left Dyer livid. He sent a second round of letters to the Bureau and the 8th Naval District, requesting further investigation and again demanding the return of Lemon. "The whole handling of Lemon in the Eighth Naval District has a smelly odor in my humble opinion," he wrote the bureau.

* * *

Fifty miles southeast of Cam Ranh Bay
January 12, 1945

Mail and fuel oil hadn't been the only things that circulated after fueling. "The scuttlebutt also began to fly," wrote Jim Thomson. "Startling news... We were to bombard a port on the coast of French Indochina. The ship was aflame with excitement—our first active action. The port was the Bay of Cam Ranh in which Tojo was reported to have a good portion of his fleet."

The rumors proved accurate. Now nine hundred miles deep in the private lake of Japan, *Astoria* was ordered to detach and join a composite group to bombard Japanese warships in Cam Ranh Bay. At dawn she formed up with many of Halsey's heavies, battleships *New Jersey* and *Wisconsin*, heavy cruisers *Baltimore* and *Boston*, and the other Division 17 light cruisers, *Pasadena* and *Wilkes-Barre*. Along with a destroyer screen, the composite task group received orders to move in close and fire at targets of opportunity over the small island of Tagne at the entrance to the bay. Halsey sent the ships a message in his unmistakable style: "You know what to do. Give them hell. God bless you all. —Halsey."

"The idea was to drive out whatever was in the harbor then let fly with everything we had," wrote Thomson. "It didn't sound too good to

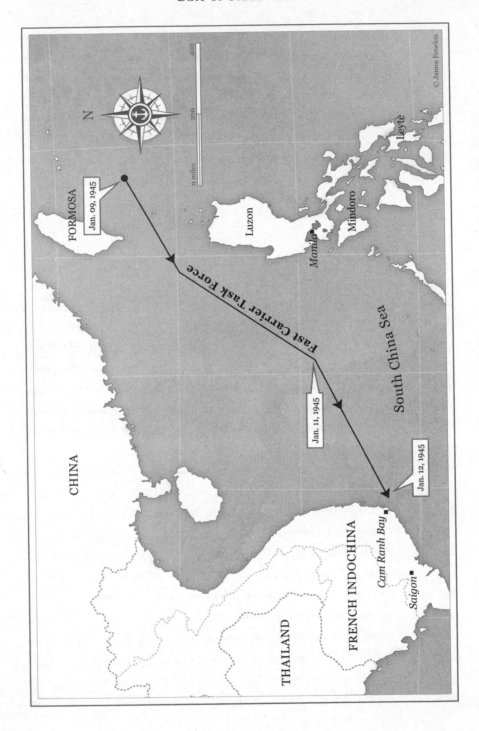

the topside stations. Four thousand yards was rather close for comfort especially against the shore installations which the Japs must have." He and the cooks on the mess deck had to "go like hell" so he could reach his general quarters station, the gunfire director for the forward 5-inch, by 7 a.m. "The crew was strangely quiet," he continued. "All it needed was the smell of liniment to make it feel like a track meet. For the first time I had to wait in line to use the head. No one complaining of constipation this morning."

Yet the next ninety minutes of anticipation proved short-lived. *Pasadena* slowed ahead in the column, then the word came across. *Enterprise* planes over the target area reported no combatant ships sighted. The Japanese Combined Fleet was not in Cam Ranh Bay, nor any other scouted surrounding area. Frustrated, Halsey ordered the surface strike unit to turn back and reconstitute his carrier task groups. "Was that a sigh of relief I heard?" wrote Thomson. Arrighi echoed both disappointment and relief in his diary.

The focus for the day turned to making the most of aerial raids against smaller Japanese surface vessels, merchant shipping, and port facilities. Scattered strikes proved enormously successful despite the absence of capital ships. Planes from *Ticonderoga* destroyed an entire convoy of enemy fueling ships and escorts, sending a line of thick black clouds skyward from oil fires. Admiral Halsey did not exaggerate in calling the day's actions "one of the heaviest blows to Japanese shipping of any day of the war," and stating that "Japanese supply routes from Singapore, Malaya, Burma, and the Dutch East Indies were severed, at least temporarily."

Twelve hours after their aborted fire mission, Task Force 38 steamed away from Indochina for a fueling rendezvous with the Logistic Support Group. Seas began to pick up, as seemed to be the trend for fueling days. For entertainment, men would listen to the radio broadcasts they could pick up from the sultry-voiced Japanese propagandist Tokyo Rose, along with the accompanying songs from home meant to make them miss loved ones. But this broadcast was meant for them specifically. With their presence now well known deep in enemy waters, Tokyo Rose took to the airwaves to call on the admiral. She asked, "We don't know how you got in, but how will you get out?"

* * *

The following morning, weather conditions continued to deteriorate as the task force steamed on a northeasterly course. Their high-speed departure from the Indochina coast had served two purposes: to prevent an enemy search, and to outrun what was looking like another approaching typhoon so they could fuel. By the time fueling operations began at 8 a.m., winds gusted to 40 knots over heavy swells. The first ships again parted lines while attempting to pass across fueling hoses. Aboard *New Jersey*, Halsey contemplated the feasibility of continuing the operation versus shutting down to locate calmer water. He needed a litmus test.

Thirty minutes into the attempts, *Astoria*'s bridge received a TBS call from Halsey's chief of staff. "Rampage, you make a try at it. If you can't do it, nobody can do it." Halsey had just called Dyer to the front of the queue and did so over the open radio for all to hear. Rear Admiral Jones must have passed along a good word, Dyer guessed. He knew Jones to keep an "S.O.B. book" with the things his ships did or did not do well. Jones closely observed fueling time and efficiency, for one. *Astoria* had developed a reputation for sound execution in refueling operations, quickest in Cruiser Division 17. Now Halsey singled out *Astoria* to make an attempt and demonstrate conclusively whether fueling was possible or not.

Dyer broke formation and proceeded toward his assigned oiler. *Rougher than all Harry*, he thought, before returning his attention to an operation his Marine captain had in progress down on the weather deck.

Slewing guns. *It never failed*, groused Armitage to himself. Foul weather, and the Marine Detachment had not been notified in advance so they could properly secure their 20mm mounts. Now, up on the forecastle, a pitching bow had broken his guns loose and they needed to be secured. The Marine captain elected to go himself, suited up in a kapok life jacket, and enlisted four volunteers to move forward with him. They would unmount the guns and pass them down to be struck below—an especially important procedure since the two previous guns had been wrecked in the recent typhoon. This could have been performed hours ago had he only known what to expect.

From the open bridge, Captain Dyer called down to "Soldier" through a megaphone, "Now you tell all your people to be careful, because that water comes over and it doesn't give you any second chance."

"Aye aye, sir."

With *Astoria* bucking waves, water cresting the bow, the Marine group clutched *Astoria*'s perimeter lifeline as they crept up the slippery deck. From crest to trough, the bow heaved some fifty feet up and down in the sea. Green foaming water soaked their legs as they reached the bow mounts, twin heavy 20mm guns swinging freely. Two men undogged a hatch and descended to receive the weapons below. Two more set to work unstepping the Oerlikon guns to hand them down as Armitage supervised.

The bow plunged as the first machine gun was handed off. The men braced themselves against splinter shields as the ship recovered, again rising some fifty feet. Just as the second gun was handed off for stowage, *Astoria* dove into a trough that submerged the entire forecastle, hurling the topside men across the deck. The gun dropped through the hatch and water poured in. Armitage's two men on the weather deck rolled against the anchor chains and cleats as seawater drove them aft, forcefully slamming them against metal, rending flesh to the bone.

When the ship righted again, one Marine writhed bleeding near the anchor capstans. Another lay unconscious at the base of turret one, knocked out by impact. As for Marine captain Gerard Armitage, he was simply gone. *Overboard.*

From Sky Aft, Fred Lind located his watch officer in the water right away, "a body turning end over end on a huge wave." As man overboard sounded, he placed his target designator on Armitage and relayed the information to the main battery director where they could track the Marine officer's movement as if he were a target.

From the bridge, Dyer watched in horror as his Marine CO passed to port. For a moment he thought Armitage was waving to his shipmates, but then he recognized something deeper at work. From the water, Captain Gerard Armitage was saluting the colors as he passed. *That's a Marine for you*, he thought. He reported his man overboard to surrounding ships.

Chuck Tanner also realized the gravity of the situation, his best friend over the rail in typhoon seas. He sprang into action, ordering aviation division men on the fantail to toss dye markers into the water to mark Armitage's position. Soon the water surrounding the officer glowed yellow-green as he faded into *Astoria's* wake. The fleet couldn't stop. *Wait for baby, you dirty sons of bitches.*

* * *

Armitage spun end over end, deep beneath the surface with no concept of up, until his life jacket thrust him to the surface. *Avoid the ship's screws,* he thought, and began to kick. Realizing he stood far clear of *Astoria* as he broke free of undercurrent, he watched her entire length pass him, strangely fascinated by his vantage point.

While perhaps too young and invincible to be terrified, Armitage did resort to his devout Catholic faith. As the massive vessels of the task group steamed past, he "recited an Act of Contrition, a prayer to my Guardian Angel, a prayer to the Blessed Mother consigning my fate into her hands." With prayer behind him, the young man next chose to sing Irish ballads in order to keep fear at bay.

"Enormous slate green walls of water bore down upon me and sped me," he wrote. "Horizontal sheets of rain hammered me like lead shot, and wind screamed and tore at me. The next moment I would shoot down into a steep sloping valley, silent now, out of the wind's howl and the rain's reach."

Armitage crested mountainous peaks and disappeared into troughs, falling farther and farther into the wake of the fleet. Yet between Lind's vectoring and Tanner's dye markers, soon the leaden gray hull of a destroyer from the edge of the formation approached. Locating the man might be one thing, but recovering him would be quite another.

A first pass by the tin can proved futile, so the destroyer skipper angled his ship broadside to the sea when he came back around. The lee created by the maneuver enabled Armitage to float closer to the ship, yet each swell pushed him back out. The destroyer eventually managed to get a line out to the soaked and exhausted Marine officer. Gripping the line with his remaining might, he pulled and swam toward the ship.

* * *

With a tin can dispatched to tend to Soldier, Dyer returned his attention to the fueling attempt. He had positioned his best helmsman in place, yet the ship swung over heavily. The oiler alongside, *Nantahala*, took her own heavy rolls, and both ships yawed in the swells. Maintaining distance at the specified forty feet kept the pair in danger of collision in such conditions, while separating farther would part the hoses. *Nantahala* had already been struck once in the operation, an earlier collision with another oiler. A section of her stern had been ripped open and she rode high in the water, her screws lifting above the surface at times and slowing her. Just matching speed proved difficult, as *Astoria* would surge ahead and strain the fueling equipment.

At 10 a.m. with lines and hoses across, the pair crested a wave simultaneously and swung in opposite directions. A fuel hose stretched to its limit and burst, splattering the decks with thick black Navy special. Promptly the signal came across from *New Jersey*: "Cease present exercise." *It couldn't be done.* Fueling would have to wait another day, as Halsey searched for a new rendezvous point. It was clear no one could fuel, and there could be no repeat of December's catastrophe.

* * *

The morning of the fourteenth brought a cartoon of Joey Fubar waving to his overboard officer crying for help in the *Astoria Morning Press*. It also brought squalls and wind, but an opportunity for successful fueling operations. Halfway back to the South China Sea exit channels, the fleet rendezvous point lay more than four hundred miles from any Japanese air base in French Indochina or China. *Astoria* again waited her turn to fuel from *Nantahala*. The oiler was now towed by *Independence* to keep her speed constant, given her damaged hull. Rampage was not scheduled to fuel until midafternoon, yet she received a morning visitor.

At 11:30 a.m. a sleek *Fletcher*-class destroyer slid up on her starboard side. The ship's small hull number "686" identified her as USS *Halsey Powell*. From the bridge, her skipper signaled to Dyer.

"*Melrose* has directed me to deliver your dried out Marine now," came the message, referring to the group commander, Admiral Gerald Bogan. "We have Armitage. What do you have?"

Captain Dyer contemplated the traditional ransom request. His ship's galley contained an ice cream maker and the typical destroyer did not. He directed the reply, "Ice cream. Usually we give 20 gallons, but due to the fact it's a Marine, 15 gallons." Agreement reached, a lead line came across.

Astoria men packed the rail to watch the show, and Schnipper held his camera at the ready. Once a highline was rigged in place, Dyer's men sent over a tub of chocolate ice cream, actually twenty-five gallons. Ransom successful, *Halsey Powell* sent Captain Armitage back across via boatswain's chair to cheers from the crew. As *Halsey Powell* moved off, Dyer signaled, "Thank you. In this exchange we feel that we have made a slight gain."

The destroyer replied, "We made out ahead in the deal, in that we enjoyed the company of your Marine and have the ice cream."

The first thing Armitage did back aboard ship was speak to gun boss Meneke about implementing his "oft-repeated recommendation to stow the bow guns and man them only in calm weather."

The ice cream would have come in handy, for it happened to be Armitage's twenty-fourth birthday, one he almost did not live to see.

That evening in the wardroom, his fellow officers gave him a rousing send-up. Instead of "Happy Birthday," they serenaded him with their own rendition of the well-known bawdy service tune, "The Mademoiselle from Armentières":

> The Captain of the Marines went over the rail, *parlez-vous.*
> It happened in a terrific gale, *parlez-vous,*
> He slipped on the deck and slid on his tail,
> You'll never teach a Marine to sail,
> Inky dinky *parlez-vous...*

The officer cadre also awarded a new service medal they had created to the blushing, uncomfortable Marine. Having him stand, they draped an oversized cross on a chain around his neck. They had named the nonexistent military award the Extinguished Service Cross.

* * *

The January 15 *Astoria Morning Press* again covered the Armitage adventure in the South China Sea, depicting the Marine captain "secured" for heavy seas with the rest of the "loose gear." He was drawn lashed to the ship itself.

Greeting Lind at their watch station in Sky Forward, Armitage shook his head. "I thought you were my friend," he chided. Lind had been revealed as the source for the *parlez-vous* song. He wrote of the incident in a letter home and composed the lyrics as a private joke for his family, only to have the mail censoring officer come across the little ditty and circulate it through the wardroom.

* * *

Given the successful destruction of Japanese shipping, Halsey was given the green light to conduct further strikes on targets of opportunity at enemy airfields and shipping in the direction of Hong Kong and the Chinese coast. Along the way he intended to continue the search for capital ships of the Japanese Combined Fleet. Weather remained terrible as the Fast Carrier Task Force steamed north, growing colder as they went. In spite of the adverse conditions, the task force launched strikes due to reported clear skies over some target areas.

From his watch station Thomson wrote, "Today our carrier aircraft struck at Canton, Hong Kong, & Formosa simultaneously. No results yet but we are standing four on & four off. George is constantly hoping for a visit from these suicide bombers but they never come!"

While reports of bogeys kept men at stations throughout the day, none managed to close on the task group before being shot down or turned away. Thomson complained, "The blasted CAP is always in there...We hear that our planes have done great damage."

Air strikes again launched in the early morning of the sixteenth. Planes returned to Hong Kong with ancillary raids conducted against Hainan Island and Canton. Weather played its role, and unexpectedly heavy antiaircraft fire from alert emplacements ashore also took a toll. Overall the results of the day's raids disappointed. One freighter and one tanker were confirmed sunk with four more ships heavily damaged. Only thirteen enemy planes were destroyed, while the fast carriers lost forty-nine, many of which fell victim to the heavy antiaircraft fire. Once again, the Japanese Combined Fleet was not in the vicinity, leaving the desired prize out of reach.

Of the day, Jim Thomson wrote, "It begins to look as though Tojo's Navy has gone home for keeps. We do everything but tell him where we are. Will be doing that soon, methinks. Tough sleeping in rough weather...Still fighting the battle of the mess hall...Only two weeks to go though."

By the seventeenth, the words of Tokyo Rose proved prescient. Getting out of the South China Sea indeed grew into a significant problem. Weather remained heavy and seas rough, making fueling difficult. Supplies began to dwindle. Fred Lind's diary spoke of running low on fresh food. "We are down to dehydrated potatoes and eggs and milk. Powdered milk isn't so bad, but I'll never get used to powdered eggs and dehydrated spuds. Rough seas put us back on sandwiches again. Original plans to go through the Sulu Sea were changed, and we headed north again." The only bright spot of the day became a literal one, where the sun peeked through for the first time in three days, enabling ships to get an accurate fix on their location by sextant. Their estimates had been off by thirty miles.

The next day offered no improvement, and by noon *Astoria* swung to 37 degrees in near-typhoon seas. Green water shipped over her forecastle, and destroyers reported their own challenges as they swung up to 60 degrees on each side. Facing a potential repeat of the previous month's disaster, Halsey again ignored Bowditch. This time a course south wouldn't suffice. The fleet steamed north instead, its sole focus to escape the private lake of Japan intact. There had been no concentrated enemy fleet. Other than the shipping raids of the twelfth, other strikes yielded minimal results at high cost. The Fast Carrier Task Force just needed out of this South China Sea trap.

* * *

East of Balintang Channel
January 21, 1945

Overnight the Fast Carrier Task Force made its departure from Japan's private lake, slipping through a channel a mere twenty-eight miles wide. Men on watch could see enemy-occupied land to both sides under the light of a half moon. The evening had brought isolated attacks over Halsey's other two task groups, one to each side. Jim Thomson logged that groups 38.1 and 38.3 "throw up a lot of stuff but all that comes down is shrapnel." The CAP did their job, and the closest enemy plane only came within seven miles of *Astoria*.

From his gun mount, John Arrighi referred to the Balintang passage as "suicide bay; ships went through one at a time in single file. For the first time I had a ticklish feeling. At that time you could hear a pin drop. The Japs never knew we were there or else they were afraid to let us know it."

Far from the weather of the previous two weeks, dawn broke to a beautiful day, "crisp and cool like a spring day at home," per Thomson. Fifty miles from Formosa, the fast carrier planes again swiped at its airfields as they retired toward the safe confines of Ulithi. Support of Mike I and the South China Sea incursion had made for a lengthy, questionably successful operation. The true butcher's bill still lay ahead.

In the early morning hours, the fast carriers took position to conduct more strikes against shipping and airfields across Formosa and the surrounding smaller islands. The Japanese airfields had been repaired and more planes shuttled in from the Home Islands while Halsey's ships hunted farther south over the past ten days. As the American planes launched throughout the morning, it became apparent that the weather would finally cooperate.

Japanese planes also took advantage of the favorable weather conditions. As *Astoria* shipmates watched flak bursts from a distance, the other task groups took the brunt of attacks. At noon the light carrier USS *Langley* was struck by two Japanese bombs, damaging her flight deck and disrupting recovery operations. Minutes later, a suicide plane dove from out of the sun on the fleet carrier *Ticonderoga* and crashed into her flight deck. The plane's 550-pound bomb penetrated and detonated between the hangar and gallery decks. Intense fires broke out on *Ticonderoga*'s hangar deck among tightly packed, fueled planes. Following smoke and smelling blood, a second plane crashed into her deck forty minutes later. Destroyer *Maddox*, battered by the December typhoon, also took a suicide crash from a Japanese fighter shortly after. She fell victim to a "Tail-end Charlie," a Japanese Zero that joined an American formation of planes returning from air strikes. These enemy planes were not only ramming into ships, they were carrying bombs and doing tremendous damage.

With a target formation to either side, *Astoria*'s group remained insulated from such attacks. "We have had very little time to sleep or to get any rest," wrote Fred Lind. "We had air alerts at 3:30 a.m. and 9 a.m.....We were at our Battle Stations all day. Fifteen enemy planes were destroyed in our immediate vicinity. They attacked the task group about 16,000 yards off our port bow. I witnessed the attack, and watched the tremendous amount of flak put up by the other group. I couldn't see the planes at that range, as they stayed above the clouds."

Near 1:30 p.m., *Astoria's* Task Group 38.2 suffered their casualty for the day, albeit from a different source. USS *Hancock* was recovering strike aircraft when a TBM Avenger landed with a live bomb that had failed to release from its ordnance bay. The bomb detonated on the carrier deck, immediately killing the Avenger's crew and many surrounding flight deck personnel. The explosion burst through to the gallery and hangar decks, causing multiple fires.

* * *

Like other seaplanes, the Kingfisher had been designed before the war for scouting and observation. The development of massed carrier task forces as the war progressed placed those duties largely in the hands of carrier-based aircraft, leaving the cruiser- and battleship-based seaplanes relegated primarily to duties of gunfire spotting and antisubmarine patrols over the fleet. Yet the floatplanes retained one key property that gave them unique capability—they could land and take off from the sea. A new mission for seaplanes had emerged as the war progressed: recovery of downed American aviators in the water.

While flames leapt skyward from *Hancock's* bomb explosion, *Astoria* received orders to get a plane in the air. A *Lexington* pilot had splashed on the far side of Formosa, and Chuck Tanner was tapped to go get him. Coordinates weren't completely certain, so Tanner would join the two other Kingfisher rescue planes from USS *Pasadena* to cover a search grid. Tanner had trained with the *Pasadena* pilots and knew both of them well, Lieutenants John Bowser and Robert Brownfield. Bowser would carry an aviation radioman in his rear cockpit, leaving two open seats when they located the *Lexington* aviator. He would also lead and navigate the team, accompanied by air cover from a pair of *Hancock* Hellcat fighters that had been up in the air when the bomb hit. The *Hancock* birds might as well stay airborne anyway, as they had the fuel and it would be hours before their carrier's flight deck could be patched to receive planes back aboard.

As Tanner set to work plotting the mission, *Astoria*'s aviation unit serviced and prepped his aircraft. At 2:04 p.m., after checking his control surfaces, he catapulted from *Astoria* and lifted off the deck. Herman Schnipper leaned out to snap a magnificent image of the plane just as it cleared the starboard catapult trained out into the wind. The photographer couldn't know, indeed no one could know, it was the final time anyone aboard ship would ever see the plane.

Tanner formed up with Bowser and Brownfield. Their F6F Hellcats also took station, the high-performance fighters forced to weave just to match the slow speed of the three Kingfishers. Their course could put them on station more quickly, due west to the far side of Formosa if they flew across the island, but that would put them directly over enemy target areas. Unwilling to take that risk, Bowser's plot circumnavigated the south tip of the island. It added fifty miles each direction, but mitigated risk and the resulting five-hundred-mile round trip fell well within their range. Tanner's biggest concern was daylight, for even an immediate rescue flirted with dusk. As had been the case back at Pearl, night recovery of floatplanes simply wasn't a practice. Besides, the old man had informed him the fleet would head off at nightfall. A man in the water meant a ticking clock; a moving fleet upped the stakes.

By late afternoon, an uneventful flight brought the composite group to their search area, approximately eleven miles off Takao in southwest Formosa. The trio of gooney birds formed a scouting line and looked for a dye marker, a raft, anything. After several minutes of fruitless search, Bowser's radioman, Donald Jones, reached out over VHF radio to a nearby submarine on station, USS *Aspro*. American subs also performed "lifeguard" duty during many strike days, taking station off the target areas. He established contact, and *Aspro* informed the team they already had the *Lexington* pilot aboard.

With their man recovered, Bowser turned the search team south to return. He also reported that he was low on fuel. Ten miles to the east, Brownfield confirmed that he too had low fuel. The news surprised Tanner as he formed up on Bowser. Kingfishers could hold enough gas to cover eight hundred miles, and this hop only required five hundred or so. *Had their planes not been fueled properly?* Rounding the tip of Formosa, the planes manually cut to a lean fuel mixture at 90 knots to conserve the *Pasadena* Kingfishers' supply.

One fighter stayed with Brownfield until the *Pasadena* pilot was forced to put down on the surface, his gas exhausted. The other Hellcat, call-sign Bingo 6, remained with Bowser and Tanner, weaving nearby. He declared that he could not maintain their slow speed and still make it back to base either. Despite his objections, Bowser and Tanner convinced Bingo 6 to head back to *Hancock* base and make a report of their situation. With darkness upon them, Bowser chose to land on the water, his fuel critical. Realizing lives were at stake, Chuck Tanner elected to stay with Bowser and his radioman Jones, landing nearby. He would pack them into his plane in the morning, get airborne, and listen for radio transmissions. He still had enough fuel for some three hundred miles of flying.

Bingo 6 throttled up and pulled away to join his fellow *Hancock* Hellcat. Bowser landed in total darkness, and Tanner followed 150 yards to starboard. After securing his engine, Tanner deployed the plane's sea anchor and broke out his life raft. His emergency kit held enough rations and water to hold him over until morning, maybe even a couple of days. Grounded for the night, the *Astoria* aviator settled in to grab some sleep and be ready before dawn. Maybe they would be able to raise the fleet by radio.

* * *

By 7:30 p.m. Captain Dyer rang up his superiors for an update. The *Hancock* birds had landed shortly after nightfall with no sign of his senior aviator. Even after *Astoria*'s aviation unit rigged their gear to attempt a night recovery, Tanner had not returned. From patched up *Hancock*, Bingo 6 gave a full debrief of the situation and Tanner's intentions. Dyer requested if a destroyer could stay on station to establish contact and locate the downed men.

Hearing no response to his request, Dyer pleaded his case to Rear Admiral Jones via visual dispatch: "If *Astoria* plane is not contacted prior or shortly after takeoff at dawn tomorrow, believe that chance of eventual rescue will be materially reduced because of lack of information as to where plane will eventually force land. Destroyer could arrive at plane's present reported position by daylight and establish communication and effect rescue. Request you recommend to Commander Task Force 38 that destroyer be sent."

The request proved impractical as the task force moved out. The best Halsey could promise was to have a submarine investigate the general area as the fast carriers moved away to the north. There was no choice but to leave the rescue planes behind. Gerard Armitage lamented the situation; just a week after his own "close encounter with Davy Jones' Locker," his best friend now faced his own test of Neptune. *We can't wait for baby.*

The next day, "George's morning *tête-à-tête*" informed the crew of strikes against Okinawa in the Nansei Shoto island group northeast of Formosa. The Nansei Shoto "form a stepping stone by which the Japs ferry their planes to Formosa and the Philippines . . . Okinawa Jima has a number of airfields and it is hoped that we will find a lot of planes on the ground there." Dyer also gave a very frank update regarding Tanner. "Unfortunately he did not know the course and speed that the ship was to follow during the night, and due to the fact we proceeded at 24 knots, I feel quite sure that he will not have enough gasoline to reach us and will have to make another water landing today. However, the sea is smooth and his chances for eventual rescue are still quite good." *Astoria* and her task group steamed in the best weather conditions they had experienced in over three weeks.

* * *

Back at Formosa, Tanner woke to heavy seas, his plane riding waves despite the deployed anchor. Looking around, he spotted Bowser's plane four hundred yards off his port quarter. Bowser had also spotted him, for the *Pasadena* pilot fired his engine and began a slow taxi toward Tanner. About fifty yards out, the engine abruptly cut out. Bowser truly had been out of fuel. With such rough swells, Tanner placed his uninflated life raft out on his wing and made preparations to abandon his plane should it become necessary. He held no hope of taking off in these conditions and wanted to be ready for anything.

Bowser's radioman Jones did the same, stepping out onto the *Pasadena* plane wing with their life raft. As he did, a wave shoved the Kingfisher's right wing below the surface and tossed the seaplane, upending it. Both men fell from the capsized aircraft. *No sea anchor*, Tanner thought. He had been stationary while they moved. He watched as the pair of aviators inflated their raft and clambered aboard.

Tanner tried to fire his plane to go get them. The engine wouldn't turn over. Attempt after attempt yielded no response. The rough water left him no possibility of stepping out onto his main float to manually spin the prop; all he could do was watch. The pair of *Pasadena* men paddled frantically to reach him, but a strong wind pushed them further and further away. As he rode the waves at anchor, Tanner sat helpless watching his fellow aviators grow distant and ultimately disappear over the horizon as their plane took water and sank. He decided to ride out the day subsisting on canteen water and pemmican from his emergency jungle pack. With luck the seas might calm; in the meantime he could weigh his remaining options.

* * *

Up in the Nansei Shoto, seven hundred miles from Tokyo, the weather could not have been better. "The most beautiful day we've had out here," wrote Fred Lind. "There is not a cloud in the sky, and the ocean is as clear and calm as Honeoye Lake in good old New York." After spotting a whale near the ship during the day, that evening he watched another Japanese plane plummet in flames from antiaircraft fire. His own crew had yet to fire a gun in anger.

Near the end of his stint with the galley, Jim Thomson found a new complaint. "Mess hall breaks out some stainless steel spoons which turn out to be a little less stainless and even less steel. They rust even quicker than the old ones." Captain Dyer agreed, as he had Herman Schnipper take photos of the worthless utensils to send back. Thomson scrambled from galley to scullery to his fire director. "Again it is watch and watch but no trouble appears," in weather he described as "beautifully cold."

The next morning, January 23, Captain Dyer announced a change in command for the Fast Carrier Task Force. Third Fleet would become Fifth Fleet; Task Force 38 would become Task Force 58. The same ships and overall force composition received new names under new leadership to convolute overall American power to Japanese ears. Halsey and Mc-Cain would rotate out as of today, to be relieved by Admiral Raymond Spruance and Vice Admiral Marc Mitscher, respectively.

The Okinawa strikes brought destroyed Japanese aircraft totals to over 1,100 planes for the operation, a devastating blow to Japanese air power. While Halsey never found his white whale of a concentrated surface fleet, the operations had been an overall success. With Manila captured, the liberation of the Philippines no longer lay in doubt. After nearly a month at sea, the fleet retired to Ulithi for rest, repair, and a little recreation.

In his parting message to his sailors and Marines, Admiral Halsey stated: "I am so proud of you that no words can express my feelings. This has been a hard operation. At times you have been driven almost beyond endurance but only because the stakes were high, the enemy was as weary as you were, and the lives of many Americans could be spared in later offensives if we did our work well now. We have driven the enemy off the sea and back to his inner defenses. Superlatively well done. —Halsey."

Jim Thomson's secret diary dealt more in daily realities than superlatives.

"Really stinks below decks," he wrote. "Checking back I find there to be a day unaccounted for which is a sad state of affairs... The extra day, who knows, they are all alike." He closed by expressing a nagging lack of closure on one issue: "No word on Tanner."

* * *

Waking again in his cockpit, Chuck Tanner found the morning of January 23 brought calm seas for a change. His rations and water were holding out, but there had been no sign of any form of rescue attempt; no destroyer, no submarine, no aircraft, nothing. Brownfield had flown out of sight the day of the abortive mission, and Bowser and his radio-man in their raft had disappeared over the horizon yesterday morning. The fleet had long moved on. Tanner bobbed on the ocean absolutely, completely alone.

Except for the enemy. Even with the sea anchor deployed, his plane slowly drifted toward Koto Sho, a small island just east of the southern tip of Formosa. Tanner could clearly see enemy ship masts from the island. Also the cliffs of Formosa. If he could see them, they could see him. Best case—he would become a Japanese prisoner. More likely he was a dead man. He couldn't wait any longer.

Tanner reviewed his maps of southern Formosa and the northern Philippines. They weren't contiguous, but he could piece together a route. If he managed his remaining fuel properly and headed south, he just might make it to Luzon, where Americans advanced in their liberation campaign. Determined to get underway, he climbed out onto the center-line float, dried his spark plug leads, then climbed back into the cockpit. The engine fired immediately and the prop spun.

Tanner jettisoned his sea anchor, destroyed his sensitive materials, and throttled up. His Kingfisher responded, skipping and bouncing over waves before taking flight. He set course due south for Luzon. Perhaps he had just enough fuel to get there, but he quickly learned he couldn't switch his prop into high pitch. Low pitch would leave him short. The

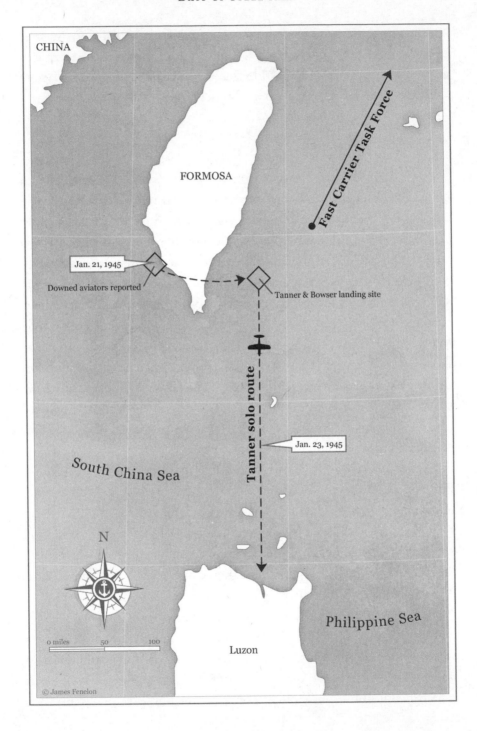

CHINA

FORMOSA

Fast Carrier Task Force

Jan. 21, 1945

Downed aviators reported

Tanner & Bowser landing site

Tanner solo route

Jan. 23, 1945

South China Sea

N

Philippine Sea

0 miles   50   100

Luzon

© James Fenelon

veteran aviator set down again, shuffled out on the float for a second time, and manually forced the prop to high pitch. He again fired the engine and launched skyward, due south.

Everything revolved around fuel conservation to stretch each possible mile. Tanner plotted his time to Luzon at two and a half hours, and his fuel supply at the same two and a half hours. He flew just above the water to conserve every possible drop of gas. *Fly low, fly slow, fly VO.* Approaching the coast of Luzon, Tanner hit heavy cloud cover and any visual landmark vanished. The maps showed mountains near the coast, one reaching four thousand feet. He climbed and leveled, his gas gauge no longer registering. Reasonably sure his Kingfisher was approaching land, Tanner calculated by watch. Six minutes. Flying blind by instruments in thick clouds, six minutes to ensure he cleared the coast but didn't reach the mountains.

Six minutes...mark. When his watch hit the six-minute mark, the aviator adjusted his parachute straps and cut the engine. Chuck Tanner climbed from his cockpit seat and took a leap of faith over the fuselage wall. As his Kingfisher sputtered to a glide overhead, he fell into thick cloud cover that swallowed him.

11

Regards from Shangri-La

I attended church services. Must be Sunday.
—*USS* Astoria *Fire Controlman Fred Lind in his*
secret diary

Ulithi Anchorage, Berth 15
January 28, 1945

Rumors circulated about Tanner's fate as *Astoria* returned to anchorage. Everyone knew they had left their rescue aviator behind and felt the loss of such a familiar face, foremost Armitage as his best friend aboard ship. Fred Lind heard that "Mr. Tanner had been rescued in a rubber raft by the Army Air Corps." Another tale said he showed up on Luzon. Yet there was simply no proof of anything, and men always liked to circulate stories. For a ship where Rousseau Lemon had led his own private mutiny and took others with him, now in combat conditions *Astoria* had presumably lost her first man.

Upon return to Ulithi, no time was lost in distributing overdue mail, which the men eagerly hauled aboard. Jim Thomson wrote of the "harbor cluttered up with hundreds of ships. A troop transport lies off our port bow...Lots of mail comes aboard, some hundred odd bags. I grab half a dozen."

Tom "Pappy" Kane received a letter from his wife, Florence, that she had written on New Year's Day, as his ship headed toward the Philippines. His son Bobby lost his first tooth. Billy was getting quite big, and Tommy Junior grew taller than his mother. The letter also covered trivial matters, such as a broken bed that would have to be replaced before he came home.

Letters from home could be simultaneously heartwarming and excruciating for the family man at sea. Florence wrote to Tom, "I guess you must be seeing plenty of action where you are. I'm trying not to worry although it's nearly a month since I heard from you...I guess the way the war is going we'll be missing you for quite some time...Glad the holidays are over as I can settle down to work again...I have too much time to think and getting no mail, it was terrible." She closed with, "Well honey, all the love in the world to you and I hope this year brings you home where you belong. As ever yours, Flo and the kids."

The evening featured movies on the fantail. "Good to see a show that night," wrote Thomson. "The first female on the screen raises hell with the boys." Beginning the next morning, groups of sailors were granted brief liberty. They packed aboard landing craft and headed across the anchorage for the Fleet Recreation Area at Mog Mog, an island on the northernmost end of the atoll. Areas designated as baseball fields, a sandy beach, swimming area, and shady grove sounded far more glamorous than their rugged reality of intense heat, relentless sun, and sharp coral. On the plus side, refreshment stands dispensed beer, soft drinks, cigarettes, and cigars.

The enlisted men's areas were always crowded—fifteen thousand men at a time packed into just over half of an island that was only sixty acres in area. Sailors on liberty at Mog Mog were only allowed ashore for three or four hours. They were given ration chits redeemable for three cans of warm beer that could be opened using nails hammered into palm trees. A complex barter system developed, with men trading cash, smokes, and future liberty for others' ration chits. Inevitably some men found ways to get drunk as a result.

Fred Lind wrote, "Three cans of beer were issued, and since I didn't drink yet, I was a very popular companion on liberty. Softball fields were available, but the extreme heat dissuaded any participants. Baseball is my thing, and I passed it up for a beach session, where I added to my sunburn. We didn't realize it, but our complexions were a very dark brown. The more we were topside and exposed to the weather, the darker we became."

Herb Blodgett braved the heat to umpire a game on the ball field. Jim Thomson wrote, "Drank my ration of beer. Went swimming for the first time. Not bad but no females." When their allotted time ended, Thomson and the others met at the landing berths designated "Hollywood and Vine" to catch their LCI transport for return to ship. "It never fails. Two guys are 'over the hill' and finally get back at nine that night," closed Thomson.

Officers' Country provided a comparative degree of luxury. Officers drank at thatched-roof clubs where they purchased as much beer as they desired, and even sipped shots of hard liquor in relative comfort. "Crowley's Tavern" read the name of the junior officers' club on Mog Mog, offering a slight taste of home for an anchorage appropriately code-named "Horror."

Dyer gave his officers a stern warning about conduct, based on a letter Admiral Halsey circulated to his captains before departing, "making each Commanding Officer personally responsible for the conduct of the officers attached to his ship while ashore at Ulithi." Without specifics as to any particular incident that brought Halsey's concern to the fleet, Dyer stated, "On the occasion of my only visit... there were a large number of young officers who were either drunk or putting on a very good act. In addition, there were several specific instances of young officers who were distinctly discourteous to their seniors.

"It is an unforgivable offense for an officer to get drunk in public and in uniform," he continued. "In accordance with Admiral Halsey's orders, it will be my duty to either accompany officers going ashore in Ulithi or to view them upon their return when I am aboard ship. In my absence the Executive Officer will meet you. I have full confidence that this meeting will be an unnecessary safeguard in the case of officers of this ship. Forewarned is forearmed."

While the crew rotated through recreational liberty, *Astoria* swarmed with activity: resupplying, overhauling machinery, and preparing for a captain's inspection. A full four weeks at sea left the ship in need of a thorough cleaning. Men scrubbed bunk bottoms and lashed mattresses to the lifelines so they could air out. With preservative paint in short supply, Badger, the first lieutenant, put men on details in a "vigorous campaign against widespread rust" throughout the ship.

Herb Blodgett and the engine room men set to work on the turbines once again. As a precautionary measure, the Bureau of Ships had ordered the bearings replaced and inspected to ensure no repeats of stripped components and damaged engines. The work took several days right up to the scheduled captain's inspection of February 3.

The F Division men discovered that the 40mm sights and directors weren't matching properly; "not according to Hoyle," Thomson noted. "Spent three rugged days getting them in shape," more maintenance running up close to the inspection.

On a somber note, the ship received a replacement plane for Tanner's lost Kingfisher. Ensign J. R. Horner would soon report aboard as an aviation junior officer, replacing Chuck Tanner in *Astoria*'s pilot complement. In the meantime *Astoria*'s remaining aviators, lieutenants Jack Newman and Don Comb, would carry the load and continue routine local flights. Tanner's loss permeated the ship.

A huge boon for morale came in the form of promotions, which abounded following examinations for advancement in rate. *Astoria* had opened the year with 375 seamen and firemen second-class aboard ship, and now fully 150 of them were promoted to first-class. Additionally, many of the existing first-class sailors earned promotion to petty officer rates, and more senior petty officers advanced to the next highest rate as well. All promotions meant higher pay grade, and men scrambled to stitch new rating patches to their uniforms prior to inspection.

A beaming Herman Schnipper moved from seaman first-class to

photographer's mate third-class. For him there was more to it than becoming a third-class petty officer; it meant he wasn't just filling a role aboard ship anymore by default. Despite never attending a photographers' school, he could declare himself a bona fide US Navy combat photographer.

The process left Herb Blodgett puzzled. The diesel-trained man who had never worked on diesels at sea had certainly learned his share about steam propulsion. All the bearing difficulties in his engine room and the different roles he assumed within the division taught him plenty. He had taken the exam for advancement to machinist's mate second-class and passed with flying colors. Yet while other engineering men who passed their exams advanced, Blodgett's name did not appear on the list. After well over a year as a third-class, he remained in his rate. No one could give him a clear explanation why. *SNAFU, perhaps?*

Jim Thomson believed he received the best promotion of all, despite not being eligible yet to advance in rate. January 31 marked his last day on the mess deck, and the next morning brought a return to standing watches in Main Plot.

* * *

Despite the heat of Ulithi atoll, Captain Dyer directed his crew to wear dress whites for captain's inspection on February 3. *Astoria's* crew packed the weather deck, standing at attention in crisp lines. Dyer, Armentrout, and divisional officers walked the ranks, inspecting their men front, back, even having them turn out their white hats for interior inspection. Review of upper decks and living spaces followed throughout the day.

The skipper held his men to the highest standard for accountability and adherence to regulation in the most important areas, but Dyer also had a good feel of what to overlook. The hot plate for coffee the fire controlmen had rigged up in Sky Forward, for example; even officers high in the superstructure went out of their way to stop by and pour a warm-up. Also overlooked were the pinup collection in the heavy machine-gun shop, along with "Mother Murphy's kitchen," a coffee and snack counter rigged up by the 40mm antiaircraft gunners.

Afterward, Dyer presented performance commendations to several sailors in front of his crew now assembled on the fantail. As he had worked and watched new ships enter anchorage over the past several days, Lind wrote, "the ship looks trim again. Big things are in the making." After Dyer presented awards he confirmed such. "The next time out we will see the whites of their eyes," Lind heard from the captain, "and if the Japanese fleet doesn't come out and fight, it will shorten the war considerably." Thomson wrote, "We are given the word that we are going right into Tojo's backyard next trip. Draws a cheer from the mob." Thomson just felt good to be back in whites for a while. The fact that the F Division fire controlmen received the highest inspection mark on the ship iced the cake.

* * *

150 miles northeast of Saipan
February 12, 1945

The work on the 40mm sights paid off. With the heavies of their new task group, 58.3, lined up in column for antiaircraft practice, Fred Lind bragged, "The *Astoria* continues to knock down more sleeves than any other ship." Jim Thomson added, "Some beautiful shooting. Five-inch lay out 125 rounds to get drone. Forties look better than ever." Each day at sea ran together: daily routine, group firing practice. Thomson didn't even realize until later it was his birthday.

Astoria's lengthy delays actually gave her a leg up on some other ships in such firing exercises, given her extensive training opportunities. For example, newly arrived carrier *Bunker Hill* had turned over a large percentage of her crew during stateside overhaul, and her green gunnery contingent received precious little practice in a virtual dash across the Pacific to return to frontline duty.

Herb Blodgett could take pride in the work of his department belowdecks. Their replacement engineering officer, Lieutenant Commander Simon, had really proved his worth over the past few months. Not only had the bearing replacements come off without incident and on schedule, but during her subsequent three-hour high-speed test run *Astoria* had maintained 31 knots. She would have no issue keeping pace with any move the task force might make.

The men in the *Astoria* Sky stations surmised a pretty good idea of what that move might be. They had become adept at determining the formation's base course across open water, even despite course changes and zigzagging. Daylight brought access to a ship's compass, but they also learned to navigate on a clear night by drawing a mental line through the constellation Orion's stars. By the evening there remained no question; Task Force 58 turned north, having skirted the east side of the Marianas. Confirmation came in the morning when the crew was issued cold-weather gear as the temperature dropped.

They had never operated in such latitudes. "We are really going to make history this time," predicted Lind. "It will be the closest thing to Japan yet... We expect to get into a climate similar to that of New York state. But where are we going? Guess it really doesn't matter, as long as we are underway. It means real trouble for the Japs again." Herb Blodgett also speculated in his diary. "Invasion of Bonins or Kuriles?" Both island chains contained Japanese strongholds. Yet soon enough scuttlebutt spread like wildfire of an even bigger mission. Task Force 58 might be headed to strike homeland Japan.

* * *

February 14 brought Valentine's Day, with Tom "Pappy" Kane creating a hand-drawn Valentine for his wife. There could be no telling when she might receive it, given the sporadic nature of mail delivery coming and going. Anything sent from the ship had to clear the censor, be bagged and transferred through the Logistic Supply Group, then make its way from ship to ship back across the Pacific. Even paying the postage for airmail required arriving at a point where it could be flown out. Kane penned a short poem on the paper, which read in part:

> Here is the best I could do for a card,
> To send to my loved one though we're far apart...
> Take it for granted that all is sincere,
> The picture I vision is having you dear,
> So for Valentine's Day what I'm trying to say,
> I love you as always, sweetheart far away.

The date also brought continued fueling for the vast fleet, five hundred miles east of the Japanese island fortress of Iwo Jima. "Largest group ever assembled," wrote Thomson. "Five units. Probably 15 carriers...Lookout Tojo." Thomson's estimate fell close to the mark. With the addition of three fleet carriers—*Bunker Hill*, *Randolph*, and *Bennington*—Task Force 58 fielded sixteen flattops spread across five task groups, four for daytime strikes and one for night operations.

With the arrival of fresh ships at Ulithi over the past two weeks, Admiral Spruance had reorganized his task groups. *Astoria* and Cruiser Division 17 shifted from Task Group 58.2 to Task Group 58.3 and its carriers *Essex* (Admiral Frederick "Ted" Sherman's flagship), *Bunker Hill* (Admiral Mitscher's flagship), and USS *Cowpens*, nicknamed "the Mighty Moo." Spruance led the entire force from their group from his flag bridge aboard *Indianapolis*, and the entire Task Group 58.3 teemed with top brass.

There was, however, an underlying cause for apprehension; almost half the air groups involved would be conducting their first combat mission due to rotation in and out of theater. Carrier deck personnel stayed busy painting new tail and wingtip markings, geometric shapes on each plane's tail and wings to identify which air group and carrier it was assigned to and to avoid confusion in the air.

Lind noted the day's minor encounters, both dangerous and harmless:

"A mine passed about 100 yards off our starboard beam. The cruiser ahead of us missed it by about 50 feet. A submarine contact turned out to be a whale."

By the morning of the fifteenth, the Fast Carrier Task Force turned to a northwest heading and increased speed. Passing east of the Marianas, giving Iwo Jima such a wide berth, the lengthy route had been carefully selected to guarantee secrecy and avoid detection for the longest possible period. The new heading could only mean one target—the Japanese Home Islands. When Captain Dyer received authorization to inform his crew of their destination in his morning address, spirits soared and cheers rose. Thomson took to his journal: "News is out that it is Tokyo!"

They would launch strikes the next morning against an unsuspecting enemy and hit him at his core. Tokyo had not endured a carrier strike since the famous Doolittle Raid three years before, when sixteen Army B-25 bombers had launched from USS *Hornet* on a one-way mission. Asked where the mission originated, at the time President Roosevelt had answered with "Shangri-La," a mythical secret base. Just as in 1942, the new strikes meant to land a profound impact on morale for both friend and foe. Yet this time there would be no doubting the "Shangri-La" source. Far from a handful of Army bombers, the next morning's Operation Jamboree would bring a fleet of American carriers to bear, sending the ferocity of hundreds of US Navy and Marine fighters and bombers over the Tokyo plain.

Jamboree fit into a larger strategic framework, meant both for diversion and suppression of Japanese defense of the real target: the tiny volcanic hulk of Iwo Jima. Situated 750 miles to the south of Tokyo, the ash island lay almost exactly halfway between American air bases in the Marianas and Japanese air bases on the home island of Honshu. Iwo Jima's prospects offered a cold, simple calculus. In Japanese hands, it provided early warning for inbound American B-29 bomber raids, and airfields for Japanese planes to intercept them en route. In American hands, Iwo Jima's airfields could be leveraged both for fighter escort of their bombers and as an emergency landing strip for wounded B-29s. On the heels of taking the Marianas to open a strategic bombing campaign against Japan, the decision to seize Iwo Jima was clear; it had been made before *Astoria* even left San Francisco.

Ostensibly meant to serve as a distraction and limit Japanese air power over Iwo, the decision to direct the carriers against Tokyo also drew fierce criticism at the top levels of the Marine Corps. Resources were at a premium for aerial and shore bombardment in the lead-up to invasion, and ships and planes sent to raid Tokyo meant fewer available for the Iwo Jima prep and landings. After much in-fighting, a resulting compromise called for the carrier force to conduct limited strikes against Japan and then retire south to send ships and planes to bear in support of the Marine landings at Iwo Jima.

At 7 p.m. The Fast Carrier Task Force initiated a high-speed run toward their launch stations, where the carriers took position at dawn the following morning, February 16. The careful precautions in their course and heavy weather en route ensured Mitscher's strike force arrived undetected. Newly added Navy and Marine F4U Corsairs carried 5-inch HVAR "Holy Moses" rockets under their wings. Avenger and Helldiver bombers completed the striking force, with Hellcats providing fighter support.

Beginning at 6 a.m. on February 16, hundreds of American planes launched into heavy overcast from positions sixty miles off the coast of Honshu. Weather immediately played a factor over the target areas—heavy clouds, wind, rain, and snow. As a result, strikes on airfields surrounding Tokyo met with varying degrees of success throughout the day. Overall the Japanese put up little opposition, and more planes were strafed on the ground than engaged in the air. Combat was largely confined to airspace over the target areas.

With no attacks over her carrier group, the mission tasking of *Astoria's* crew grew long, tedious, and cold. Her well-trained gun crews again marked time at silent mounts. Fred Lind wrote of his watches high in the ship's gun directors:

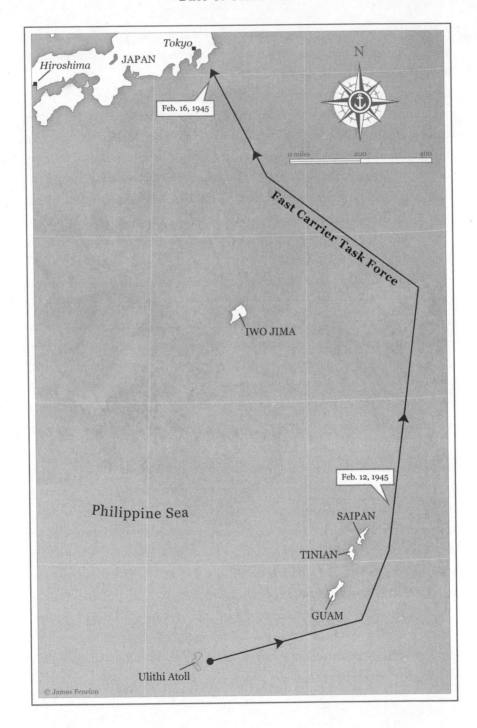

Tokyo

Hiroshima   JAPAN

N

Feb. 16, 1945

0 miles   200   400

Fast Carrier Task Force

IWO JIMA

Feb. 12, 1945

Philippine Sea

SAIPAN

TINIAN

GUAM

Ulithi Atoll

© James Fenelon

For clothing up here I am wearing my longhandles, dungaree shirt, woolen sweater, dungaree jacket, parka, Navy jacket, dungaree pants, Navy trousers, watch cap, and two pairs of gloves. That, along with my life jacket, and I make quite a bundle. Battle helmet and telephones complete my outfit. We aren't going to knock 'em dead in any fashion show! The temperature is 40 degrees, but there was ice on the target designator. The hair around my ears is coming out, and the skin is all red. This is from the constant wearing of battle telephones, with foam rubber linings on the ear pieces."

John Arrighi groused about the effectiveness of the nonstop Combat Air Patrols surrounding the fleet. "Our CAP seems to be very efficient, too efficient for us. We are anxious to see some action and pretty disgusted when nothing has happened yet—only 65 miles from Tokyo."

In the afternoon, three Japanese picket boats were spotted near the *Astoria* group. The destroyer USS *Haynsworth* sunk all three boats within viewing range. Fred Lind wrote in his diary: "I derived some sinister pleasure in watching the destroyer's guns cause severe explosions and dense smoke from their targets. After the sinkings, nine survivors were picked up. One was a 17-year-old kid who didn't know that all those ships were American until we started firing. Apparently the Japanese public isn't getting much news on what is happening. Well, we are happy to inform them."

Jim Thomson also had a vantage point from the gun director, and he wrote: "The black oily smoke billows high in the sky, flames visible at its base…Terrific explosions as the 'can' gets a direct hit on one ship…At 10 p.m. we secure from air emergency. It was a tough day." Japanese survivors from the picket boats were transferred aboard USS *Essex* and placed in the ship's brig for interrogation. As raid results poured in, Thomson wrote, "we lie 50 or 60 miles off the coast. All day is spent at air battle stations. Weather is tough with low overcast & rough seas. Very cold. The strike is very good and we get about 450 planes plus numerous shipping & several factories are hit."

The next morning brought more of the same—miserable weather, early reveille, and long hours at general quarters. The second day of strikes on the Tokyo plain were called off in midmorning due to impossible conditions over the target areas. Such weather worked both ways, equally limiting any enemy response. Rain turned to snow over *Astoria* and the task force; there would be no action for the ships defending the American carriers. Jim Thomson wrote, "Our strike is limited to the morning. 10 a.m. planes hit motor factory, goodbye motor factory. Still no opposition from Tokyo. Boys are disappointed. Couple of bogies get in to 13 miles but we don't even sound an alert."

Lind added, "If anyone ever told me that we could cruise up and down the Japanese coast and not get an attack of some sort or other, I would promptly call him the biggest fool in the world. But that is exactly what is happening... Don't they have anything? Where is the Imperial Navy? We are all flabbergasted." Unlike Thomson and Arrighi, the absence of enemy attacks on the fleet was perfectly fine with Fred Lind.

All further strikes over Honshu canceled, the Fast Carrier Task Force retired south for their next support mission—the invasion of Iwo Jima. February 18 brought refueling and a very welcome cache of mail from the replenishment group. The *Astoria Morning Press* reported results from the Tokyo raids: forty tons of bombs on the Nakajima engine plant, a sunken light carrier, 258 Japanese planes shot down, and another 149 destroyed on the ground. American aircraft and crew losses were minimal, counted at 29 planes.

Despite mixed results over two days mostly due to weather, news of the carrier raids on Tokyo were quickly dispatched back to the US. The opening thrust of a bombing campaign against homeland Japan made for front-page headlines back home on February 19. The day brought an even more momentous event closer to the fleet: after steaming overnight at 25 knots, the carriers launched planes to support the 3rd, 4th, and 5th Marine Divisions assaulting the Iwo Jima stronghold.

Under clear skies and calm weather the morning of the nineteenth, planes launched and returned from raids. Men spent tense hours at their stations waiting for a Japanese response, but other than a few harassing aircraft on the perimeter of the fleet, no attacks materialized until evening. At dusk, the *Astoria* men topside could see gunfire over the horizon—picket ships. Several raids by bogeys—unidentified aircraft closing the task force—interrupted evening chow and caused Rear Admiral Sherman to order all ships in Group 58.3 to make a smoke screen to provide cover.

Jim Thomson observed, "Tojo's flying sons are all around us and catches us with our planes on deck. Things look bad for a while... This is an eerie feeling to dash through the darkness of the night amid an avenue lined on either side with smoky black trees. As usual there is firing all around us but we don't open up." By the twentieth his diary entries were jumbled due to the scramble of watches, general quarters, and air alerts. It was easy to lose a day in such a blur of tension and monotony.

By the evening of the twentieth, there was a stark break in routine. *Astoria* was given a new mission based on the Navy-Marine compromise over force allocation in the operations: detach from her carrier group and head at high speed to Iwo for shore bombardment. The invasion was meeting intense resistance, and her guns were desperately needed to relieve other ships on station as they replenished ammunition.

The ship again buzzed with nervous energy and scuttlebutt at the expense of sleep. Lind recalled air emergency at 10:30 p.m. "It developed that the bogey was an Army pilot who radioed that nothing would please him more than staying away from our formation." He had abstained from sending any pay home on the outbound logistics ship. "February 20th was payday, but I am not drawing any out here. It is risky sending it home from this place."

While her role in the monumental Tokyo raids had largely involved marking time against a nonexistent enemy threat, the next morning would certainly bring something very different. *Astoria* was headed for the hottest spot on earth, and she might finally get into the war.

12

Detachment

Those poor bastards.
—*USS* Astoria *yeoman Deno Dolci, on the*
Marines ashore at Iwo Jima

Iwo Jima Northwest Call Fire Sector
February 21, 1945

I n the hour before sunrise, a soft glow danced along the horizon punctuated by flashes of brilliance. Closer and the light began to take
shape: green luminescence crisscrossed by streaks of red tracer. Closer still
and the rhythmic pounding of man-made thunder stretched across the
water. Even from this distance, men on watch could see they were steaming toward pitched battle.

With no sunrise in the heavy overcast, darkness lifted gradually. A wall
of sound greeted the new arrivals to a scene perhaps suited to Dante's
Inferno. Dawn had broken over the third day of the Iwo Jima invasion.
Fred Lind referred to the sight as "the firing of star shells that lit up the
island like a night baseball game...Noisy darn place!" By 6:15 a.m. the
crew had manned battle stations.

The island stretched out before them, no more than five miles across.
It had but one noteworthy geographic feature: a swollen expanse of rock
at far right that gave the island a peculiar unbalanced look. For Marine

skipper Gerard Armitage, the target held something personal. Those were Marines fighting their way inland, his brothers, likely including men he served with at Guadalcanal. "Dark, menacing, spitting fire," came his description of the island stronghold. "A brooding Mount Suribachi on the right, and to the left, steep slopes rose up from the beach the full length of the island to form a level plateau. There, the two airfields, Motoyama Number One and Motoyama Number Two, had been installed by the Japanese."

Diametrically opposed to the landing beaches on the southeast side of Iwo, *Astoria* and her cohort approached from the northwest. Their target areas would fall beyond the lines of American advance, on the airfields, buried emplacements, and troop concentrations identified by aerial spotter aircraft. Each salvo would be meant to protect the men advancing.

As they approached their fire station, plumes of smoke churned skyward. Dozens of mottled gray shapes littered the surrounding waters—the American invasion fleet of Task Force 54. For men accustomed to the expanse of an entire fleet solely in tranquil anchorage, this was something new.

The encirclement of ships came in all sizes. Small transport craft, LSTs, destroyers, and cruisers formed a mosaic of modern weaponry against the rugged backdrop. Rounding out the lineup were mammoth battlewagons of another era—US battleships designed prior to the First World War. Too slow for the Fast Carrier Task Force, these behemoths, named *Arkansas*, *New York*, *Nevada*, and *Texas*, still had their strengths, on deadly display as they hammered away at the island with their massive 14-inch guns.

Texas cut the silhouette of a ship out of time, purpose-built for a clash of big naval dreadnoughts in World War I that never came to be. Built prior to the Great War, indeed a contemporary of the likes of RMS *Titanic*, her outline in 1945 bore almost no resemblance to her as-built configuration. Now gunfire directors, antiaircraft mounts, and radar arrays sat atop locations determined by availability, not design. A single floatplane catapult rested atop a main battery turret amidships.

Converted by need over decades to such utilitarian form, *Texas* and her contemporaries might not be able to keep pace with *Astoria* and the fast carriers, but their huge naval guns could be brought to bear in shore bombardment support of assaulting troops. *Texas* had spent the past eight months in exactly this capacity, lobbing massive shells from her 14-inch rifles into German emplacements at Omaha Beach, Cherbourg, and southern France. Now on the opposite side of the globe, she had spent the past few days firing the ship empty into Iwo Jima. She slid past *Astoria* to retire for fresh ammunition and rest. Alongside came the venerable old cruiser *Pensacola*, also coming off station for resupply. Two days into the invasion, the baton had been passed to fresh ships from the Fast Carrier Task Force.

Astoria had been ordered to assume *Pensacola*'s call fire station some six thousand yards northwest of the volcanic island. She had not come alone, as the remainder of Rear Admiral Jones's Cruiser Division 17 moved in with her—*Wilkes-Barre* and *Pasadena*. Also arriving were heavy cruisers *San Francisco* and *Boston*, plus a full division of destroyers. Each ship detached from the Fast Carrier Task Force would relieve a similar ship on station so they might retire and replenish, perhaps even rest.

The invasion code name brought irony—Operation Detachment. Perhaps selected at random, it reflected the role of these ships detached from their strike force, but more importantly the nature of the invasion: detaching a piece of sovereign Japanese soil from the empire. The Japanese had long anticipated the strategic value of this island and dug in deep through a network of bunkers, tunnels, and caves.

Astoria men immediately recognized a huge difference in communication protocols. Accustomed to radio silence, there was little to hide here in a full-on assault. The airwaves crackled with radio traffic. The imposition of radio silence was lifted for the expediency required in pitched battle. Individual ships were referred to by their call signs— Rampage for *Astoria*, Skullcap for *Wilkes-Barre*, and Pagoda for *Pasadena*. Each ship maneuvered into their station as relief for their predecessors moving off the line.

USS *Pensacola* passed between *Astoria* and Iwo Jima as she retired, her ammunition magazines empty and her men exhausted. She had spent four days in close fire support; two for preparatory bombardment and two more once the Marines began to come ashore. *Pensacola* also held the dubious distinction as the only heavy ship that had been struck by Japanese artillery. She had maneuvered too close to shore and received a salvo of enemy fire in return. In addition to rest and resupply, *Pensacola* had repairs to make and shipmates to bury at sea.

As the two ships passed, Captain Dyer signaled to his counterpart aboard the damaged older cruiser, "I relieve you of this tight spot." As if to punctuate the moment, a Japanese battery from Mount Suribachi fired a welcoming round that splashed off *Astoria's* bow. The trick would be to hold station slightly out of range of the heaviest Japanese shells coming from Suribachi, code-named Hot Rocks, and within range of *Astoria's* 6-inch and 5-inch guns to fire for maximum effect and accuracy. Her most lethal capability would be to outgun her opponent by range.

Armitage watched enemy batteries bracket two destroyers closer in to shore, splashes from shells landing to either side of the tin cans. His ship felt close enough, given the range of their guns. He wrote, "So close-in were we that we could see the thousands of holes dug by the Japanese to defend Iwo—and the relentless defensive fires spitting on the Marines inching up the slopes far below, shin-deep in black volcanic sand."

From Jim Thomson's fire control vantage point, he could see "hell all over…Overhead naval dive bombers & fighters continually strafed with bombs, rockets & machine guns. A constant pall of smoke hung over the island."

Astoria took position behind *Pasadena*, turning broadside to northwest Iwo. The two cruisers would serve as a fire team together, while *Wilkes-Barre* steered to the northernmost portion of the island. *Wilkes-Barre* would use her own planes for target spotting, but *Astoria* and *Pasadena* were assigned spotting planes from the escort carrier USS *Wake Island*.

The sister ships' assigned FM-2 Wildcats arrived on station to direct their fire. Much like the dreadnoughts below and even the cruisers' own floatplanes, the aging Wildcats had been given new life through shifted responsibilities. Outclassed by more modern fighters such as the Hellcat and Corsair, the FM-2s of USS *Wake Island* could orbit the island with trained pilots to direct each salvo, correcting for range and bearing.

One radio frequency brought the overhead spotter communication: "A couple of salvos on 216Q," the radio barked, referring to grid references for Iwo Jima's northwest sector. *Astoria*'s guns were dialed in. Yet a delay in ensuring the position of the American front lines caused the plane-to-ship spotting to recalibrate, lest they fire into their own advancing forces.

By 11:10 a.m. the issue was clarified. 216H proved a better target. Slightly adjusted, the first broadside salvos from *Astoria* and *Pasadena* erupted, six main guns each, shaking the ships. A cheer went up across the ship.

"Salvo one."

"Up 500, no change," came the call from the Wildcat, adjusting their fire.

"Roger. Salvo two." The aft guns fired.

The two cruisers adjusted and again opened up, their main batteries sending clouds of orange and black smoke skyward as their shells sped downrange.

"Splash," came the report to the overhead Wildcat. The twin sisters had hit their mark. A parked-vehicle area had just been obliterated.

Hour after hour the big guns fired. Inside the aft 5-inch mounts, 4th Division gunners Tom Kane and John Snyder earned their pay alongside *Astoria*'s other gunners with a massive coordinated effort to move heavy shells and powder charges from the ammunition magazines deep in the bowels of the ship, up through handling rooms, and into position in the big gun breeches. With each deafening salvo, spent casings clanged to the cruiser weather deck through turret ejection ports. Other men dragged the precious brass into huge stacks for future transfer and reuse. Each hour a *Wake Island* Wildcat would move away for a replacement spotter, consummate professionals performing dangerous work.

"I am flying over 216Q, find it difficult to pick one particular target. There are many in this area."

"Roger. We will fire first salvo and you can lead us where you think best. Over."

"Roger."

"Salvo one."

The guns erupted.

"Splash." Another hit.

Gerard Armitage spent the day directing the secondary 5-inch battery fire. In the evening he wrote that the cruisers in their division "pounded the island with every gun that would bear. Suribachi, wreathed in smoke and flame, hurled back shot for shot, some at the fleet, but primarily down on our comrades ashore. My Marines wept in frustration at their gun stations, unable to enter the fight because of the range, and helpless to support their fellow Leathernecks and pals.... The First Sergeant was sent to each gun crew with the message, 'Armitage is directing the five-inch batteries for all of us.'"

Dyer spent the day on the bridge, attending to three separate radio circuits at once. Unprepared, he quickly trained himself to listen to the three channels simultaneously. No matter who was talking, one circuit could be more important than another. Overall movement, fire control, orders from within his support sector, they all overlapped and came in at once with messages stepping on one another.

Men across the ship watched the battle through high-powered optics with "ringside seats," as Schnipper saw them. It was excruciating to see an American attack meet with resistance they could make out from their seaborne position, and watch their comrades in arms fall to the enemy. Schnipper again lamented his lack of high-powered lenses, as he photographed through his Graflex Speed Graphic. Instead he could capture *Astoria* men moving spent shell casings and sailors at their battle stations with their fingers in their ears.

By late afternoon *Astoria* could report a major gun battery destroyed by their fire, several emplacements neutralized, and a parked plane at the main airfield destroyed. *Astoria* men joked that they had gotten their first plane, never mind that it was on the ground. In the process two of their spotting Wildcats had been hit and damaged, sending them back to their carrier base.

Fred Lind captured radio reports of "a Marine pilot hovering over the invaded island to direct the naval bombardment…It was intriguing, and several times during his transmissions he would say, 'Oh oh,' as an annoying enemy antiaircraft gun would open up at him. There I was, listening to a first-hand account of an invasion opposed by 23,000 enemy troops."

Through his binoculars from his Sky Aft position, Lind watched movements of both friendly and enemy troops. Marines slogged forward knee-deep in ashen sand, and American tanks spun their treads in attempts to advance. "Hot Rocks" may have received the heaviest shelling across the island, but the northwest naval support group also received their share of return shots. Lind wrote, "Several times during the day enemy shells burst about 100 yards off our bow. Jap shells can be distinguished from friendly fire—their shells burst with a black explosion. It is not a comfortable feeling being fired at, but I can't imagine what it must be like facing our firing! The direct short-range firing of the 14-inch guns of the battleships are actually tearing off the top of Mount Suribachi."

When darkness fell, main battery crews rotated out for chow and rest. The 6-inch mains had fired continuously for nine hours, five hundred shells, with short breaks for friendly aircraft to bomb and strafe over the besieged island. With spotter planes retired for the night, fire control shifted to a Marine party ashore called Charlie 273—they would be tasked with requesting on-demand harassing fire and, more importantly, star shells for illumination. By consistently sending 5-inch star shells up over the northern and western sectors of the island, *Astoria* would provide some semblance of overnight daylight for the Marines hunkered down. The Japanese defenders were certain to form counterattacks in the darkness.

Lieutenant Junior Grade Don Comb returned from dinner to his

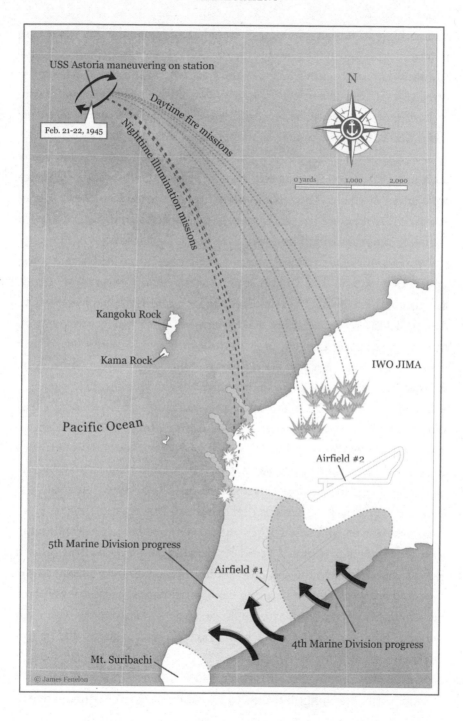

USS Astoria maneuvering on station

Feb. 21-22, 1945

Daytime fire missions

Nighttime illumination missions

N

0 yards   1,000   2,000

Kangoku Rock

Kama Rock

Pacific Ocean

IWO JIMA

Airfield #2

5th Marine Division progress

Airfield #1

4th Marine Division progress

Mt. Suribachi

© James Fenelon

station high in the aft superstructure. He had spent the day observing the battle through high-powered optics, able to see both Japanese and Americans entrenched across from one another, "all lying in that volcanic dust." His battle station would only be called upon if the bridge were to be hit; if it were, his men could run the ship from an aft auxiliary location. He had little to do but watch and think.

When Comb volunteered for the Navy from Minneapolis, he did so with two years of civil engineering study from the University of Minnesota under his belt. This education allowed him to qualify for naval aviation. On the day he left home for the Navy, his mother plucked a four-leaf clover for him. He placed it in his billfold for luck.

By the time he was training in Corpus Christi, Texas, he was given the option of what type of flying he wanted to do. Scout-observation was his last choice, but that was where he was assigned. He received his wings in August 1943, and at least he was flying, even if slow and low. Besides, he came to like the airplane. "It could fly for six hours and that's a long time to be sitting on a parachute." Before shipping out with *Astoria*, he married his sweetheart Peggy. Perhaps there was luck in the clover.

Five-inch gunfire resumed. Bursts overhead from their star shells illuminated the ship, the water, and the shore. *Tanner gone. Peggy on the other side of the planet. Men dying just thousands of yards away.* Comb considered his dinner in the wardroom, on "a table set with linen tablecloths" as the ship shook with gunfire around him. He "had made the right choice of service." Perhaps there was luck in the clover.

Astoria slowed to 3 knots, then ultimately came to a standstill, lying to with all engines stopped. From his perch above Comb's platform in Sky Aft, Fred Lind also watched the illumination rounds blast into the night from below him—one round every six minutes. The bursts of gunfire brought temporary blinding light and vicious concussion with each round. "The fives don't supply very good slumber music," added Jim Thomson.

Further south toward Hot Rocks, Marine flamethrowers also lit the night, sending long, burning streaks into caves and emplacements.

Lind further noted enemy mortar fire was "extremely heavy despite all our bombardment. Fighting conditions on the island are the toughest imaginable. The enemy is not visible, but secluded beneath rock."

We can't even see flashes enough to identify their battery emplacements, Captain Dyer thought. *Six minutes between star shells.* From the bridge, the skipper hoped his allotment would hold out, let alone do some good through the long night ahead. What stuck with him the most were the cries he could overhear on the shore-fire control circuit as the hours passed—"screams, and I mean real screams, of desperate men."

"Oh God! Keep those shells coming! Keep those shells coming!" came terrified voices over the radio.

In addition to his ship's standard allotment of star shells—six per hour—*Astoria* had a small emergency reserve to be used at the captain's discretion. Dyer later reflected,

> We shot all night. From dark 'til dawn . . . Their cries were for these star shells, keeping things illuminated, because the Japs were really giving them fits.
>
> The real test of your judgment was in knowing that the call at four o'clock in the morning might be more urgent than the call you had yielded to at ten o'clock the previous night. You had to judge when and how to allocate those small rations of emergency shells that you had. It was a real toughie, and could be made by nobody else except the commanding officer. You had to use every bit of your judgment and knowledge to do it.
>
> You never could respond to all the calls that you got. You would hear the Marines on the lower echelon pleading with their Gunfire Control Officer by voice radio for this and that. You tempered your judgment in regard to what you should or shouldn't do . . . It made a very real impression on me.

Such was the old man's burden. For the rest of the crew, the night brought sporadic rain, soaking cold in foul weather gear, and restless if any sleep. More than anything, it brought relentless gunfire booming across the water. Occasionally would come the call to cease fire immediately— further south on the island, someone's fire mission was fouled up, and American shells were raining down on US Marines. Across the ship men might be miserable, but they knew they had it far better than those poor bastards ashore.

* * *

In the hour before dawn, *Astoria* was ordered closer in to address a Japanese counterattack in progress, as enemy troops were spotted bringing small boats ashore behind the American main line of advance. Jim Peddie and fellow electrician's mates manned the ship's 36-inch GE lamps and activated them. Powerful twin beams cut the darkness and trained on the landing craft. Peddie had never felt so exposed, up in the searchlight platform where the beam drew a perfect line back to him. After thirty tense minutes, he breathed relief to hear the order to cut the light. The threat had been neutralized, and besides, daylight was breaking.

Main battery fire resumed at 8 a.m. with the 6-inch gunners back at their GQ stations after a little rest. An admiring Armitage wrote, "As we fought, a cold, clear dawn illuminated the awesome sight. At our first salvo, the great fighting ship *Astoria* came alive. Before General Quarters sounded, the crew rolled from their bunks and raced for battle stations. Main battery turrets trained out."

The targets for the morning continued to be identified by shore fire control, and many machine-gun nests called for close-support, "only 200 yards in front of our advancing tanks and troops," Fred Lind observed. "The tanks are creeping forward, and the Marines are crouched behind the tanks." By noon the secondary battery was called in for bombardment, as *Astoria*'s main guns ran perilously low on ammunition.

Lind continued, "During the afternoon, I witnessed the most amazing scene I shall ever hope to see. It was just like a front seat at a circus, but just a little different. Our Marines were advancing to the left behind a column of tanks in our firing quadrant. Our support fire was cut down to 100 yards ahead of the tanks. Then the shore-fire control party called for a salvo with a spot of 'Up 50, right 200 yards,' which would place the shell right between the tanks and the Marine troops. We fired, and the Marine captain who made the spot yelled back over the radio, 'Yeah, dead on! You knocked out an enemy pill box that had been passed up, and it was opening up with machine-gun fire at our infantry.' What guts it took to call that spot!"

Throughout the day Lind and the men in the Sky positions experienced something even more devastating to their ears and their insides: 14-inch battleship salvoes screaming directly overhead. He described "ballistics crack, an extremely sharp crack that almost tears you apart. I have never experienced anything like it, and I hope I never have to experience it again. This continued all the time the battleships were firing, and along with the effect of our own ship's concussion, everyone topside felt that every bone in their body was constantly shaken."

Helpless to do much except keep his men fed, John Arrighi wrote that "the Marines have a real tough battle on their hands. The island was a mess of smoke most of the day from the ships' shells and rockets from the planes...I was on deck most of the day and could see the tanks advancing on Japs' position and also one of the Jap tanks was hit by our fire." His 20mm mount sat silent, as *Astoria* remained far out of range of the Marine detachment's antiaircraft guns.

For the 6- and 5-inch guns, their second day of bombardment brought effective results. Jim Thomson proudly referred to their guns as the " 'no change' battery. All day we blasted during bad weather and did beautiful shooting...Early afternoon about fifty Helldivers made a momentous run. They dove vertically to drop their eggs. The scene that followed was unforgettable. The concussion waves rose in huge dome-shaped eddies & the entire northern end of the island seemed to rise entirely out of the sea, quivered and shook like jelly. What could live in such an inferno was matter for conjecture yet the Jap counterattacked."

Fred Lind echoed his sentiments from their shared platform. "The barrage of air bursts put up by the Nips over our tanks and infantry was devastating. But then came our air attack by the carrier planes carrying big bombs. The horrendous explosions of these bombs seemed to shake the whole island, concussion waves could be seen shooting up—and from our distance from shore (6000 yards), we could feel the blast."

With her ammunition rapidly depleting, *Astoria* prepared to move off the line at 4:20 p.m. when a major Japanese counterattack developed. Over the radio, Captain Armitage was alerted by the crackle, "Here they come! They're moving along the slope below the ridge line—from left to right. Tanks and infantry. Request fire support. We will adjust." Across the ship men could see the enemy advance forming, a "massive attack," this time in the open.

Within six minutes, *Astoria* had turned and moved into closer range. Her main battery roared in response, using rapid fire of high-capacity shells armed with VT proximity fuses—low-trajectory, almost point-blank range for such guns. Detonating between twenty and fifty feet off the deck, the barrage rained an Armageddon of shrapnel on the advancing troops and tanks. The Marine spotter radioed back of very accurate fire that had "completely obliterated the entire attack." Reports soon arrived that the Marines had managed an advance of a critical one thousand yards with the enemy repelled. Fleet and Landing Force radio brought praise to Dyer and his crew: "Well done." Only later did Armitage learn that Dyer had actually *smiled*.

At 5:32 p.m., the Mighty Ninety moved off the line, relieved by destroyer USS *Stembel*. The move was one of necessity; with her fire mission extended by hours due to the counterattacks, *Astoria* had nothing left to fire. She and her sister cruisers had been shot empty over the past thirty hours. Although the ships of Cruiser Division 17 left the battle unscathed, VCS-17, their aviation group, suffered a combat loss: one of *Wilkes-Barre*'s OS2N-1 Kingfishers performed a forced landing due to engine failure for a total loss. As *Astoria* moved away from Iwo Jima, she left seventy-seven tons of explosive ordnance buried in the volcanic stronghold.

* * *

Dawn of February 23 brought Cruiser Division 17 in company with Admiral Spruance's flagship *Indianapolis* on course to rejoin the Fast Carrier Task Force. Far northeast of the Iwo struggle, *Astoria*'s task group prepared to reconstitute, then turn for a second round of strikes on Tokyo after a fast run-in toward Honshu. After two nonstop days of pitched combat, Captain Dyer felt and looked as haggard as Joey Fubar in the inevitable postaction cartoons. Steaming behind *Pasadena* with *Wilkes-Barre* and *Indianapolis* in column, rejoining their task group seemed to Dyer like pretty routine movement and a good chance for him to take a personal moment.

The captain's life was a lonely one during combat operations. Dyer sailed tied to the bridge and his tiny sea cabin just behind it throughout. There he slept, there he took his meals in solitude as the other officers enjoyed the camaraderie of their wardroom, and there he even conducted his private bathroom matters. *You're on a bridge on a twenty-four-hours basis*, he reasoned. *You're on your feet much of the time, you're under strain… You've got to keep your system working.* Dyer turned over the bridge to his executive officer Army Armentrout.

After sitting in his private head for a few minutes in what he called his "morning's morning," Dyer began to shave. He was mere strokes into his shaving cream when his signal officer, Lieutenant Junior Grade Carl Houghton, burst in. "You'd better get out on the bridge." Knowing the thirty-year-old-man and former chief could recognize a bad situation brewing, the captain dropped his razor and ran.

By the time Dyer covered the short distance to the pilot house, the ship's collision alarm was blaring. The disheveled skipper, half-shaven in his skivvies, stood horrified to see the fleet's flagship *Indianapolis* at right angles across his bow, plodding from starboard to port as *Astoria* bore down on her at 20 knots. He could hear men forward shouting, "Get out of the way! Get out of the way!" and saw them waving frantically, futilely.

Dyer seized the conn back from his exec, his career flashing in full before his eyes for the third time in less than a year of *Astoria* command. Looking left—battleship *South Dakota* closing from the port bow, her own alarm wailing, the hole between getting smaller—he took to the radio. Ignoring any semblance of voice code protocol, he called to his friend Captain Charles "Swede" Momsen in *South Dakota* by name: "Swede, back down with everything you've got! I'm coming through!" He gambled that the battleship skipper was also on his bridge. Dyer then ordered all engines backed down full as he steered left, breaking the T-angle with *Indianapolis* and aiming to split the closing gap between the ships. Precious seconds passed.

From the aft main deck Herb Blodgett looked on in horror. "My God! That ship is right across our bow!" *They are at ninety degrees, right in front of us. We're gonna cut her right in half.* He felt the screws shift into reverse beneath his feet. The entire ship rumbled and shook; the stern jumped up and down. He had never felt such vibration. *We're at emergency astern.* The turn into reverse didn't seem to slow the ship much. *Astoria* plowed ahead at good speed even as she steered from *Indianapolis* toward *South Dakota*. Blodgett moved to the port rail and observed *South Dakota* respond in kind, backing down hard in her own emergency turn to port.

Somehow the battleship came parallel to his ship, slowing to drop astern and clear the imbroglio. Blodgett then returned his attention forward in time to see *Indy* clear *Astoria*'s bow by a matter of feet. The heavy cruiser also passed astern to port, so close he could have tossed a baseball onto her fantail. *God we just missed her.*

Men around Blodgett joked once out of harm's immediate way, but he shook his head. He had watched the approach from the morning chow line after securing from GQ. *What a grandstanding maneuver the whole thing had been, a big sweeping arc around the task group. It wasn't the normal way you'd come back and get your ship into position.* The veteran salt called it "one of the dumbest maneuvers" he had ever witnessed. "Got themselves in the position where they almost got cut in half."

Why had *Indy* been so slow, seemingly unable to respond herself? Blodgett's black gang concocted a theory that perhaps she snuffed her active fires in error while securing surplus boilers following GQ; perhaps she left herself dead in the water. Such events were known to happen if one brought boilers offline improperly. And the *Indianapolis* had "just sort of inched, inched out there..."

From the bridge Captain Dyer held the command perspective to understand the bigger picture. The Fast Carrier Task Force was behind schedule, overdue to meet their fueling group, with the tightest of time-lines to get the flattops back on station for further strikes on Tokyo. Hence the run-up to 25 knots, near flank speed, to rendezvous with the oilers now that the formation was sorted out. With Spruance's column of cruisers retiring from their Iwo assignment to meet the fleet, given their easterly course relative to their task group plowing ahead at full speed, the sweep around to release ships to the task group was likely necessary to conserve time. Yet nearly disastrous. Now the destroyers astern were in their own reactive maneuvers, as the rear half of the formation fell apart.

Fred Lind's stomach had been badly upset even before the near-collision. He wrote in his diary that the extended Iwo bombardment "literally shook my guts out," adding of the incident, "We came as near to being eliminated from this war as I care to." Just like Blodgett and Dyer he could see those four big stars flying from *Indianapolis*, proclaiming whose flagship they had just tangled with. If there was any amusement to be found among the fire controlmen, it was that Ensign "Wonderman" had been officer of the deck at the time of the incident.

Dyer's personal fury landed on his Executive Officer Army Armentrout. Regardless of how the situation developed, Dyer felt his exec had not reacted well enough. *He was doing it right five minutes before.* The captain was career-minded to a fault, and the experience shook him up. He made sure the *Astoria* deck logs contained a highly unusual entry:

"Executive Officer at the conn" at 6:59 a.m., February 23, 1945, and he waited to hear from Spruance. Dyer went further in recollection: "This is where my naval career pretty near ended...I owe my professional life to Swede Momsen. You never forget a thing like that."

The Fast Carrier Task Force made its rendezvous with the Logistic Support Group, only fifty-five minutes behind schedule despite the complex logistics of recovering the cruiser divisions from Iwo Jima fire missions. By early evening they were back on schedule, underway for another round of strikes on Tokyo. "Giving the Japs something to think about to take their mind off Iwo Jima," John Arrighi added.

It would be some time before the crew would learn that in their wake, their efforts were paying off. As *Astoria* refueled following her near-collision with the fleet flagship, six 5th Division Marines raised a flag atop Hot Rocks. In that moment, as Schnipper slept in his darkroom from exhaustion in between developing his images of their fire support mission, another photographer, this one on the ground, snapped the most iconic photograph of the Pacific war. Joseph Rosenthal's photograph of six Marines raising the flag on Iwo Jima ended up on the cover of many American Sunday newspapers that week and would win him the Pulitzer Prize.

Other news rolled in that was far less encouraging. USS *Saratoga*, a night carrier detached to the amphibious group assaulting Iwo, had been bombed and struck by suicide aircraft across the island from *Astoria* on the twenty-first. Casualties numbered in the hundreds, and another American aircraft carrier had been knocked off the line. Even worse, nearby escort carrier USS *Bismarck Sea* was also struck by suicide aircraft, exploded, and sunk.

Gerard Armitage reflected on their turn at Iwo Jima. Although Suribachi had fallen, many more men would surely lose their lives before the island was secured. He had known comrades transferred to the landing force and very likely would never learn their fate. Would such sacrifice save the lives of bomber crews headed over to bomb Japan? He doubted it.

Captain Dyer penned a letter later that day to the Bureau of Personnel requesting to detach his executive officer for another assignment. He later reflected: "I don't know a single top flight military leader that hasn't had to make those decisions. They're never easy to make...You have to answer to your own conscience. You have to be true to yourself. That's what makes it difficult. Are you setting an impossible standard? Are you asking too much of an individual? Or are you doing something that is for the good of the service?"

Ultimately there was no official mention of the incident. Not in Captain Charles McVay's *Indianapolis* deck logs, not in Captain Charles Momsen's *South Dakota* deck logs, not in Rear Admiral Frederick "Ted" Sherman's task group records. Nor did Admiral Spruance ever say a word of the incident to Dyer. Perhaps culpability abounded, or perhaps it was just one of those things that happens when orders and circumstances collide. Thankfully the ships didn't. They had managed to avoid the incident, and all had business with Tokyo.

* * *

The two weeks following largely brought the monotony of routine. *Astoria* and her cohort screened the fast carriers, but shortened and canceled strikes followed consistent miserable weather as they worked their way back south toward Ulithi. There was far more grousing than any action for the crew.

"We had a 55-knot wind harassing us. No attacks by the enemy. We headed south after recovering our planes, and intended to attack Nagoya, but had to abandon the attack because visibility was very bad."

"Although our CAP was shooting down planes every day, we never saw one...Even though we were called out at all hours to man the AA batteries, the only effect it had on us was a great loss of sleep."

"Took on mail. I got six letters. It's a wonder they still write. We don't get much time to answer letters. In fact, we don't even have time to get undressed. I can't remember when I changed clothes. We don't have time to shower or shave, and if we get undressed, we can't make it to our battle stations in time. We look grubby, we are grubby, and we will probably stay grubby. Topside, we are probably not too obnoxious, but below decks, no one seems to hang around us very long."

Herman Schnipper received letters from as far back as October, when the ship first got underway. He wrote to his sister Sylvia and gave her a pep talk about her high school grades, and closed with, "You would be surprised to know the places I have been to...I remember studying about these places in school, and at that time were very distant...It is impossible for me to tell you where I have been, but you have read quite a lot in the newspapers where I have been and am doing out here."

* * *

Ulithi atoll, Berth 475
March 5, 1945

Returning to Ulithi Anchorage for resupply and rest, Armitage shuffled paperwork at his desk when the stateroom fire curtain was whisked back. There stood the familiar, grinning face of one senior aviator Chuck Tanner, safe and sound following his Philippine adventure.

After a stunned silence, Armitage managed, "Don't you ever knock, Tanner?"

"You didn't wait for baby, you dirty sons of bitches!"

"That was the plan, Chucky—how did you find us?"

"I have a friend in submarines."

"Submarines? Where the hell is our airplane?"

"Our airplane?"

"Marines pay taxes too—it was on loan to you from the citizens."

"Last time I saw it, it was in a thousand pieces in northern Luzon."

Tanner's navigation had indeed proven accurate, and he broke through the clouds and parachuted down over enemy-held territory on Luzon, even as he watched his abandoned plane crash into a mountain. Ever resourceful, he managed to evade capture and link up with Filipino guerrillas. Now after two months he was back aboard ship by way of a submarine, reunited with his crew and a relieved best friend.

"What about the *Pasadena* boys?"

"They didn't make it," Tanner replied with a more somber tone. "Where's the wallet and checkbook I left with you?"

"We sent mail over the side yesterday—your dough is now on its way to the Franciscans."

"You Catholic bastard!"

"You Protestant bastard!" Armitage opened his desk safe to fish out the aviator's wallet and checkbook, pitching them his way with a grin.

* * *

Dyer decided the crew had earned a "smoker," an afternoon of boxing and wrestling matches. *Astoria*'s fantail was converted into a match ring and her best and strongest took on fighters from sister cruiser *Biloxi*. Men packed around the catapults and floatplanes on the fantail to the accompaniment of the ship's band. After the matches, Dyer spoke to the crew, commending them on their exemplary performance to date. As a finale, the detached executive officer, Armentrout, gave a farewell. Despite the near-collision, he was immensely popular with the crew, a rare feat for an exec. He received a standing ovation as a send-off.

Through official mail Dyer learned that his charges about Rousseau Lemon and the New Orleans Naval District had gone all the way to Secretary of the Navy James Forrestal and Admiral King. His letters carried the endorsement of Chester Nimitz. The chief of naval personnel came down hard on the commandant of the 8th Naval District. He issued revised instructions for handling courts-martial for deserters across all naval districts. The safe haven in New Orleans came under especially intense scrutiny.

Lemon himself had been located in Gulfport, Mississippi, detailed as a "security guard, general detail Master at Arms" in the ultimate of ironies.

He was yanked from Gulfport and ordered back to *Astoria* via a sequence of ships across the Pacific. Everyone wanted to prove a point.

With one heroic officer back aboard, one officer detached, and Dyer's biggest troublemaker headed back to him, the captain ordered movies on the fantail. The task force would soon be underway for the next operation, and morale needed to be at peak. Ships across the anchorage were lit that night with similar film screenings when an aircraft engine drone rose to a scream. An enormous explosion detonated on the stern of the carrier *Randolph*, anchored near *Astoria*. Men scrambled to quarters and darkened the ship, the film already a distant memory. A suicide attacker had managed to reach the presumably safe confines of Ulithi atoll and crashed into the carrier lit up by the movie showing on her deck. For *Astoria* men it was a sobering experience; they had never witnessed such a crash. Even home anchorage seemed no longer safe from suicide attacks.

PART THREE

DAYS OF STEEL RAIN

13

Rampage

In the vast stretches of the Pacific, war is a long
time coming—and concentrated in terrible swift-
ness when it does come.
*—Joe Custer, UPI correspondent wounded aboard
heavy cruiser* Astoria *at Savo Island*

Mugai Channel, Ulithi atoll
March 14, 1945

Nine days at anchorage. One recreation period per man at Mog
Mog. Countless hours of repair, upkeep, reprovisioning, and
bringing aboard thousands of rounds of ammunition and pyrotechnics to
replace those blasted into Iwo Jima. The "rest" period brought little of
such before *Astoria* and the Fast Carrier Task Force passed back through
Mugai Channel into open water, bound for their next operation.

Randolph was forced to stay behind for repairs when the Fast Carrier
Task Force again put to sea, a debilitating aircraft carrier casualty before
the operation was even underway. More than one hundred men lay
killed or wounded, and her aft flight deck was severely damaged. Also
gone was any consideration of movies or anything else that breached
nighttime "darken ship" protocols. The fleet had paid a hefty price for
complacency and confidence. "Jap bastards," wrote John Arrighi. With

Ulithi no longer lit up like "Main Street on Christmas Eve," movies were a thing of the past.

The plane that hit the *Randolph* originated all the way from Kyushu, but left Fred Lind to muse, "Yap is only 70 or 80 miles away from Ulithi, is Jap-controlled, and has an airfield. Wonder why we haven't taken it over? I guess that's one of the hop-scotches we are taking around this area." It was no secret that the enemy knew exactly where the American fleet dropped anchor.

These suicide attacks were now being referred to as *Kamikaze*, literally translating to "divine wind." The term referenced a thirteenth-century typhoon that ruined a Mongol invasion fleet and protected the Japanese Home Islands. After years of losses, Japan had reached a point of a fully defensive and desperate strategy to protect the homeland from full invasion. And even after five months of suicide tactics, the American public remained unaware; any mention of them in letters or press was expressly forbidden.

Kamikaze attacks had claimed two fast carriers since *Astoria* reported for duty: *Ticonderoga* off Formosa and *Saratoga* off Iwo Jima. *Astoria* had been assigned to neither flattop, as both were in other task groups. *Astoria* had in fact never even faced the challenge of an enemy plane hurtling toward the ships she protected. But a message sent from CinCPAC following both attacks resonated, especially after the shocking hit on *Randolph* at anchor: "Open fire early, accurately, and in volume."

Iwo Jima was now almost fully secure and under American control, its captured and repaired runways being put to use by American forces. B-29s were launching from Saipan and Tinian to rain fire over Japanese population centers using incendiary bombs, with Iwo both enabling fighter escorts to protect the bombers and providing a safe haven for their emergency landing when needed. The US had constricted its grasp to the point that no geographic area of Japan was out of reach, and civilian areas had become targets in an aggressive effort to force capitulation.

Astoria and the fast carriers again headed north toward the Home Islands, intent on striking the southern Kyushu airfields where many

Kamikazes were known to be based. The mission served as prep work for Operation Iceberg, the long-awaited invasion of Okinawa in a final step to bring the war home to Japan after long marches through the Pacific. As Curtis LeMay's Army Air Forces focused on strategic (and civilian) bombing targets, Navy air power would focus on tactical (and military) ones. The Army and Marines would combine to take Okinawa and its land-based runways. Japan would either surrender or face outright invasion.

The Fast Carrier Task Force numbered more than one hundred ships, with seventeen (now sixteen without *Randolph*) carriers scheduled to send planes over the enemy airfields. They were to locate and destroy as many potential suicide planes as possible, reducing what Japan could send up against the invasion fleet during what was expected to be a lengthy endeavor to invade and subdue Okinawa.

Astoria and Cruiser Division 17 steamed out for the first time as a complete unit. In early March the fourth twin sister, USS *Springfield*, had reported for duty, following her own delays with a wiped turbine bearing identical to those of *Astoria*. The cruisers and all ships of the task force had been directed to repaint from geometric multitone camouflage to dark blues and grays. The clear emerging threat would come from the air, not the sea, and blending closely with ocean water from above provided better cover. Surrounded by dark gray carriers, battleships, and cruisers, one ship left Ulithi still wearing her dazzle camouflage: *Astoria*. Whether due to paint shortage or lack of time, she stood out against her cohort and likely would to the enemy.

Others came aboard ship during the Ulithi layover. A Radioplane TDD drone unit set up shop aboard *Astoria*, filling her unused hangar with their radio-controlled target aircraft. The team was responsible for flying the drones over live-firing columns of ships during target practice. The TDD drones could turn quickly, dive, and simulate Japanese maneuvers. *Astoria* inherited the team because she kept knocking the drones down. It had been decided she should sponsor the drones, as she had an available storage hangar and didn't need the practice.

Also reporting aboard was a cameraman named Walter Duggan from a Navy combat photography unit. The unit was split into several ships across Task Group 58.3 to record action off Kyushu and Okinawa in the coming weeks. Armed with a Bell & Howell 16mm turret movie camera stocked with color film, his presence rankled ship's photog Herman Schnipper for several reasons. Schnipper felt perfectly capable of using such equipment effectively. His darkroom would no longer be a personal place of solitude. And he still couldn't even convince the chief store-keeper to order better lenses for his trusty Speed Graphic. He reluctantly welcomed Duggan into his personal space.

The first day back at sea brought practice, practice, and more practice. *Astoria* launched her new drones from her catapults as other ships fired. Tracking exercises and night battle exercises followed, with calls to GQ and air emergency stations throughout. Jim Thomson lamented, "Still playing stinking games with GQ at all hours. No sleep last night. Oh why did I leave home?" He thought often of his little brother Bobby, now playing semi-pro baseball while awaiting discharge from the Army Air Forces stateside. Meanwhile Jim, older brother and mentor, remained stuck on a fire control platform across the globe and again headed into action.

* * *

Spruance's five task groups proceeded northward en masse, once again as the largest assemblage of men o' war in human history. The scale dwarfed that of any predecessor power—ninety miles across, groups of ships in concentric circles expanding twelve miles from their center points. Task Force 58 lay spread across more than one thousand square miles of ocean, carrying some one hundred thousand sailors and Marines unified by common purpose—bringing the war to Japan's doorstep.

Just as with the February Tokyo raids, surprise was again critical. Yet continuing to conceal a force of such magnitude grew more challenging with each operation. Whether spotted advancing or not, defense of the precious offensive power of aircraft carriers came down to three layers. Ideally enemy planes would be caught on the ground or engaged by American aircraft over the target areas. Those that made it out to sea would be addressed by Combat Air Patrols flying large patterns around the carrier groups. Any remaining combatants that got through the first two layers would have to be handled by the destroyers, cruisers, and battleships in formation with the flattops from a purely defensive posture. The idea was to reduce hundreds to dozens, then dozens to hopefully singles or none. The strategy had proven quite effective in the Philippines and during the Tokyo raids. Neither *Astoria* nor any cruiser in her division had been tested by a single enemy plane that survived such a gauntlet of protection.

March 17 brought St. Patrick's Day, it brought the final run-in toward Kyushu, and it brought Fred Lind's mother's birthday. "Sorry, Mom, but we had a rotten birthday party," he wrote. Another day at air emergency stations with bogeys in the area, but no visible targets. A message from USS *Hornet* circulated providing a warning: "Their persistence and maneuvers left little doubt that they were enemy planes and that the approach of the Task Force has been detected."

Dawn of March 18 broke with red skies, an ominous portent for centuries of seafarer superstition. Flares dropping around the perimeter of the task force betrayed an enemy presence searching for them, feeling them out. Even in calm seas with mild wind from the north, men quickly realized their presence was no surprise. Night fighters both scattered and shot down some enemy planes, but determining friend or foe by fire control or radar proved difficult. Visual identification would have to suffice as the sun rose. Partly cloudy skies might mean a great day for raids over target areas, but such clear visibility also worked both ways.

At 6:04 a.m., from across the task group USS *Bunker Hill*'s aft air defense officer reported a "bandit," a confirmed enemy aircraft, spotted through binoculars—a twin-engine "Frances" Japanese fast bomber. Ships immediately opened up, including Fred Lind's 5-inch guns. "He ran into a cloud, and we lost him. A little while later we fired on a plane

I never saw. Part of the reason was that the elevation of the five-inch guns right beside us was such that the concussion was knocking us cockeyed. Ducking below the splinter shield didn't help much." The planes had merely been snoopers, taking advantage of high cloud cover where they could. The invading Frances was subsequently brought down by Combat Air Patrol outside the formation, but assuredly the advancing force's presence had been reported.

Across the task force men began to learn hard lessons through sporadic moments of chaos. Firing at target sleeves and drones in column was one thing, but firing over and toward your fellow ships in formation— something completely different. It fought human tendency not to shoot, and to remain mindful of the range of your guns lest the smoke and bursts interfere with another gunnery team who had the range correct. Such teamwork required trust. USS *Alaska* brought down an American F6F Hellcat by error, but the pilot escaped via water landing—another hard lesson learned.

American pilots over their target areas were surprised to discover so few Japanese planes on the ground. Just as the Fast Carrier Task Force sent waves of planes inland, the Japanese had sent their own planes out toward the carrier groups. The opposing forces met in aerial combat, with the more numerous and experienced American pilots scoring most of the victories and pushing on to their target locations. Puzzled flyers also noted a lack of antiaircraft fire over Kyushu airfields. *Why weren't they firing back?*

Task Force 58 took a number of hits through the day, all in Task Group 58.4. While *Astoria* men could only see flak bursts and smoke from over the horizon, *Enterprise* endured a dud bomb while *Intrepid* and *Yorktown* both suffered damage and casualties. In *Astoria's* Task Group 58.3, almost all attacks developed miles away over USS *Bunker Hill*. *Astoria* men could do nothing but watch over *Essex* due to fouling of range and bearing— they were cautious not to fire into their own ships.

Bunker Hill recorded: "The cloud cover was ideal for enemy purposes— either dive bombing or suicide crashing. The result was an almost constant nerve-racking alert by lookouts and gunners. Every sighting, every radar contact required check and double check. Even so, the second attacker was able to sneak in undetected until in his dive... The Japanese habit of sending in small uncoordinated groups of attackers presented a difficult problem with weather as it was and scores of friendly planes in the vicinity." A Japanese Zero would approach in the clouds and from the sun, falling in behind returning "fighters on the friendly approach bearing." Approach was shallow glide with flaps down, and "could have been dismissed as friendly if it were not that personnel were alerted." The plane never indicated any intention of a suicide dive, but given its approach it could have "stood more than an even chance of making a successful suicide crash."

By day's end the Fast Carrier Task Force may have been dealt a bloody nose in the *Intrepid* and *Yorktown* task group miles away from *Astoria*, but it had paled in comparison to the devastation unleashed against the Japanese in the air and over airfields across Kyushu. Tomorrow would bring a new day and a second day of strikes.

* * *

Herman Schnipper was determined to get his shot. Maybe to prove something to himself, or to his command, maybe to prove something against the likes of Walter Duggan from Fleet Photog. On the morning of March 19, he loaded his Graflex Anniversary Speed Graphic, now a virtual extension of his hand, and he positioned himself up on Jim Peddie's searchlight platform, his favorite vantage point. Planes would be launching soon, and if yesterday was any indicator, that meant a response from enemy aircraft. As much as *Astoria* gun crews wanted their crack at Japanese attacks, so did he.

Astoria steamed off the port quarter of USS *Essex*, the lead ship of her class, damaged by an early *Kamikaze* in the Philippines and now one of several flattops launching Navy and Marine Corsairs in addition to her Hellcats, Avengers, and Helldivers. The proximity of screen ships to the integral carriers might change during any operation, but *Essex* would be stationed closest to *Astoria* and therefore her primary responsibility was to protect the carrier for Operation Iceberg. Schnipper made sure he kept the carrier in clear view. He gripped his camera and waited.

In the early hours flares burst overhead, illuminated their ships, and Captain Dyer knew what the day might bring. *They are onto our tactics of staying on station for two consecutive days of strikes before moving.* Regardless, hundreds of planes across the fleet launched shortly after to strike inland again. As dawn broke, men at their stations nervously rotated out for chow, noting the continued low, broken clouds—perfect *Kamikaze* conditions.

It took less than two hours after American planes left their carriers for a Japanese response. With strikes inbound for the newly nicknamed "*Kamikaze* Alley" southern air bases of Kyushu, a lookout next to Fred Lind spotted a plane approaching from dead astern—a "Judy," a Japanese Navy dive-bomber. The pilot had made it off the ground, evaded the CAP, breached the perimeter of the formation, and now had his sights set on *Essex*, the nearest aircraft carrier. *Astoria*'s responsibility. *Here we go.*

Lind wrote, "The plane shot out of a cloud and was in a vertical dive straight at the carrier *Essex*. After sighting the plane, the lookout dropped his binoculars onto his shoulder strap, and the binoculars hung on his chest. We relayed the target to the director, they matched up with our target designator, got the guns on target, and commenced firing." Jim Thomson added, "Noise terrific as we opened up with everything. Down he came though the sky was living with bursting flak…down and still down and we couldn't stop him."

As *Astoria*'s gunners tracked the target, so did Schnipper. Amidst cacophonous fire, tracer rounds, and smoke, the young photographer kept his camera on the Judy as it fell. Hits struck the plane and its wing surfaces shattered, sending it into a spiral. The pilot released his bomb as he lost control, hurtling down. Only a split second remained for Schnipper's shot. *Click.*

The bomb splashed just ahead of *Essex* as she steered in an emergency turn to dodge the attack, detonating as the suicide plane slammed into the sea off her starboard bow, a close shave. With a sharp clap, a geyser of water hundreds of feet high shot skyward, its spray thundering down across the carrier's forward flight deck. *Essex* steamed through unscathed. *Splash one bandit.* Men cheered from their gun mounts. Rampage had her first plane. For the first time the ship's 40mm and Marine 20mm guns had contributed, able to open up due to the close range. Schnipper cycled his camera and prepared for more, hoping he too got the shot. He wondered about Duggan nearby with his movie camera. *At least I can develop my stills aboard ship.*

Antiaircraft shrapnel had rained down across the ship, plinking off Navy gray M1 helmets and clattering to the deck like steel gravel. From Sky Control, Fred Lind's lookout approached him. "Look at this!" Shrapnel from exploding antiaircraft shells had struck the casing of the man's binoculars, ruining them. Both men realized that the binocs hanging from his chest had stopped the shrapnel from meeting flesh and bone. *Lucky.* As charge of the ship's optical shop, Lind ran down to issue a new pair. And for the men topside, something troubling, something visible to the naked eye couldn't be ignored—a huge, mottled white plume of smoke expanding steadily higher from over the horizon. *Essex* might be safe, but something big just happened in another task group. The day was far from over.

Lind had returned to his station when a second plane broke through at 8:15 a.m. Another Judy? A Zeke? Hard to tell at a distance and in bright sun behind the approach, but definitely Japanese. *Clearly another suicider,* thought Jim Thomson. Again the plane targeted *Essex,* and again the *Astoria* fire team locked on and opened up. Other ships joined in, but *Astoria* had the solution. The fire controlmen trained their guns from Sky Aft, and the 5-inch battery of Tom Kane and John Snyder responded. Proximity fuses did their job and the plane took a direct hit, breaking apart and spiraling. A second splash barely missed *Essex,* this time just off the port bow within a hundred feet.

"Hit the drink. Bomb misses," wrote Thomson. Schnipper was sure he had the shot, snapping his Graflex from the searchlight platform just as the destroyed aircraft crashed. From the fantail, John Arrighi checked in with his fellow Marines at their 20mm mounts. Shrapnel had again pelted *Astoria*'s weather deck, falling from exploding American shells overhead. This time three men had been hit. A bursting 20mm round from another ship struck the men at their mount. All wounds proved superficial, but Arrighi would write, "It proves we are not playing marbles." The individual attacks, meant to crash into American ships, were bringing an unexpected element: making those same ships fire into each other.

The smoke on the horizon continued to belch skyward. Within fifteen minutes the radiomen of *Astoria* had their answer. "Dixie hit by a suicider and is burning fiercely…Estimate eighty men in water. Recommend destroyer…" USS *Franklin*, a sister *Essex*-class carrier in nearby Task Group 58.2, had been bombed. Exploding ordnance and burning aviation gasoline mixed into the black and white smoke plume. *Essex* might be safe, but overall the task force now faced a serious cripple, a carrier that might actually sink, on top of the previous day's ship casualties.

In the late morning the task group received a respite. Radar picked up inbound aircraft, and the only planes overhead proved to be friendlies returning from their Kyushu strikes. The pilots reported that over the target areas, antiaircraft batteries sprang to life where they had waited in silence the day before. The tactic was meant to lull American flyers into false security, reaping a greater harvest against American attackers who flew lower to the ground and strafed their targets longer. Much heavier antiaircraft fire meant more downed comrades than the day previous.

Despite the battered strikes returning, Fred Lind took advantage of the lull over the task group to telephone Commander Meneke, the gunnery officer. They spoke of the shrapnel problem and he asked to keep the ruined binoculars as a souvenir. With them set for scrap anyway, Meneke agreed.

Reports continued to arrive into the early afternoon. USS *Wasp*, from Task Group 58.1, had taken a bomb hit within a minute of *Franklin*'s attack. The bomb had ruptured many of her fire mains, completely destroyed her galley and laundry, and caused extensive damage to her hydraulics. Unknown casualties. Even given such carnage, *Franklin*'s situation sounded far more serious. Extensive burning of her flight deck, ordnance cooking off and exploding, the ship in a list with mass casualties. While *Astoria*'s task group fended off suicide attackers, the other groups were being bombed. *Astoria* men could do nothing but stand vigilant at their stations, trade what little information they had, and watch the horizon for anything inbound.

A second round of *Kamikazes* soon broke through. With flight launches and recoveries in progress across the clustered carriers and tightened protectors, two new bogeys were picked up shortly after 1 p.m. Other ships began to open fire at the inbounds as far out as eight miles. Armitage's men checked their fire as the planes approached from astern, realizing quickly that the now-confirmed bandits were being closely pursued by Combat Air Patrol. The lookouts and fire controlmen, so thoroughly drilled on aircraft identification friend versus foe with many months of delay, locked down firing so as to not hit a friendly.

The lead plane, a Japanese Zero, flamed and plunged into the ocean, brought down by the CAP fighter in tight pursuit even as ships fired on both. A second enemy plane pressed on as its American opposer broke clear of the flak, crossing through clouds ahead of the formation. *Astoria* lookouts confirmed the newcomer as a Tojo, a single-engine Japanese army fighter. Approaching *Astoria* from the bow, the attacking plane lined up for *Essex*. *Another suicider.* At four miles out, the Mighty Ninety again erupted in defense. *Essex* joined, followed by other ships.

The Tojo pitched into a dive on *Essex*, crossing *Astoria*'s beam from port to starboard. Lind kept his aim on target, the guns beneath him raging, orange-black powder smoke rising. He could see the plane spewing smoke from the tail as hits landed. With forties pounding away to their thumping rhythm, the heavier 5-inch battery unleashed. The larger shells detonated and scored hits, blowing the plane apart directly over *Astoria*.

Herman Schnipper managed to click the shutter then dove to the deck.

Flaming wreckage rained down across the after half of the cruiser, a wing landing on the port quarter. At the aft 40mm and 20mm mounts, men crumpled in cover, before rising afterward to cheer once again. The destroyed plane had fallen short of its target, and the third near-miss of the day for *Essex* brought a near-miss for *Astoria* with it. *Three for Rampage. Essex* safe on station. Another *Astoria* man wounded by friendly fire.

Lind wrote, "One of the guys struck by shrapnel aboard ship was only about 15 feet from me. He climbed down over the side, and I told him we were still on battle station. He said he was headed for sickbay. He turned around, and I saw five holes in the back of his foul weather jacket."

Lind had seen the pilot tossed from the destruction. *No chute. If he wasn't dead from the terrific explosion, he was when he hit the water.*

Minutes later, *Astoria* was ordered to detach from *Essex* and her task group even as more planes were breaking through. The *Franklin* situation had grown dire given her massive fires; she lay dead in the water as men scrambled to get her underway. Task force commander Marc Mitscher elected to shift his entire force configuration to protect the wounded carrier. Captain Dyer received the order to join a screening group hastily organized to put themselves in harm's way between *Franklin* and Kyushu. *Franklin* likely could not survive another hit.

With sister cruiser *Wilkes-Barre* ordered to take station near *Essex*, the Mighty Ninety peeled away from the formation and rang up flank speed to 30 knots. In her wake a new attack developed over *Essex* as she moved off. *Astoria* could not make a difference; she had her orders. Her new assignment lay across a twenty-mile expanse of open ocean.

Both Schnipper and Duggan kept their cameras trained as angry puffs of smoke again magically appeared in the sky astern, the drumming of gunfire barely audible over the crash of water passing around their ship speeding away. Herman Schnipper tried a photo as it appeared that *Wilkes-Barre* flamed the plane short of *Essex*. Schnipper knew the shot would be distant; if only he had that damned lens. Duggan had multiple options for magnification while he didn't. But he was confident that despite all the flak and debris, he had captured all three planes dropped by Rampage.

14

Friendlies

> I was a chap who had been wounded; I knew you
> could get wounded. Most people think the other
> guy gets wounded, but I never get wounded. I
> knew you could be.
> —*Retired Vice Admiral George C. Dyer*

50 miles east of Kyushu, day 6 at sea
March 19, 1945, 4 p.m.

As *Astoria* left her task group at flank speed to assist the *Franklin* group, men across the ship regrouped and collected their thoughts. Despite the day's victories in protecting *Essex*, Jim Thomson was shocked by what he saw from some men under fire for the first time, including some of his officers. He wrote, "Many of the young enlisted men completely lost their heads and stared fascinated at the diving planes." A first loader on a 40mm mount had reached for the next clip of ammunition, only to find his second loader watching an enemy plane approach. He slapped the man's helmet, jolting him back. "Dammit, this is for real!" Training had been one thing, but now men were learning to perform in a real life or death situation. Thomson was also furious with his telephone "talker," a man wearing a wired communications headset, who "completely forgot to give the word commence firing on our first run."

Focused on the plane's approach, crucial moments passed before Thomson realized his mount below was not firing. Several times the talker had failed to call ranges. Thomson would write, "All in all it was a very confusing scene and picking up the target is most difficult as the bursts were scattered all over the sky."

Fred Lind's own telephone headset might keep his ears raw and hair rubbed out, but he saw having his ears covered as a small price to pay to reduce concussion from the 5-inch guns. When the dual-purpose fives were elevated near 90 degrees skyward, he could reach out and touch the barrels from his position in Sky Aft. He wrote that at one point the concussion "took one sailor and threw him over a four-foot-high splinter shield...The constant blasting tears the guts out of you."

While transiting the two task groups, *Astoria* raced past a distant destroyer on picket station at the halfway point. Watching American flights return from strikes, he witnessed an attack on the lone picket. An enemy plane sent a bomb down at the destroyer, which just missed. Instead of circling back, the bandit proceeded toward *Astoria*'s former group. *Another inbound.*

From within the task group formations, it was difficult to appreciate the scope of work the aerial patrols were doing to prevent attacks. This far removed, the crew had a different viewpoint. "There was our Combat Air Patrol," wrote Lind. "One Corsair made one pass at him, and the Jap plane went down. The feeling was just like scoring a touchdown, which I guess was exactly what we had done. Hooray for our team!"

Astoria was chasing down a task group on the move. While a small group of defenders encircled *Franklin* as she lay dead in the water, *Astoria*'s new screen assignment in Task Group 58.2 headed west toward Kyushu to form a front guard. Placing themselves in between the airfields and *Franklin*, their role would be to repel any and all attackers while emergency repairs were performed and *Franklin* could get back underway.

Even though not in view to *Astoria* men, reports came in from *Franklin*. Casualties were devastating, men still being accounted for. By midafternoon the stricken flattop had been taken in tow by heavy cruiser *Pittsburgh* to get her as far off the line as possible. But *Pittsburgh* towed a listing, smoldering target, struggling to hold a course at 5 knots. The movement of an entire task force in retirement for refuel was now dictated by the movement of *Franklin* and her small salvage group. Attacks were certain to come. The enemy knew she was wounded and smelled blood. *Astoria*'s Task Group 58.2 assignment would stand between *Franklin* and the enemy.

At 4:20 p.m. the Mighty Ninety arrived on station and reported for duty in the covering force. Two battle cruisers, *Alaska* and *Guam*, subsequently detached to bolster the rescue group surrounding *Franklin*. Her surviving crew would work through the night to perform enough temporary repair to get her internal power back, engines running, and screws turning. With darkness falling, *Astoria* settled into her protective screen. Her new flattops to watch over would be *Hancock* and *Enterprise*, the latter the only remaining fleet carrier in action from the beginning of the war. *Enterprise* had been configured to perform night duty. Men ate at their stations and tried to sleep near the same—either at their mounts or finding a spot to lay down on the deck. All they could do was rotate through watch and wait for signs of any new attacks that made it past the night patrols.

Such a cold calculus of attrition, sending hundreds of planes out to meet the Americans. It only took one to get through, one man to successfully penetrate the defensive layers and crash into his target to cripple or sink a carrier. His life was a trivial forfeit in return.

Captain George Dyer pondered such a concept from his sea cabin following the Mighty Ninety's most active day so far. For the ship's war diary, he wrote candidly with respect for the enemy he fought. "The Jap pilots showed great skill, courage, and determination in pressing home their bombing or *Kamikaze* attacks, and they were defeated and the task group kept from all damage only by the skill and timing of emergency maneuvers, the highly organized and effective system of interchange by ships of enemy bogey information . . . by the excellent work of the combat information centers, and the top notch gunnery of the antiaircraft batteries." *Respect your enemy.*

He further addressed the emerging friendly fire problem. "20mm and 40mm firing was at times very dangerous to this and other ships." Several *Astoria* sailors and Marines had been wounded to various degrees. Dyer reflected back to the experimental flak suits they had been asked to test. Trinidad in July had been the worst possible environment for testing, scorching heat leaving them a mess of perspiration and odor. Plus it had been an early training environment, not combat. Now men were lining up for Purple Hearts due to shrapnel wounds. He vowed to revisit this with his officers in the morning. *Wear your suits.*

Despite Jim Thomson's criticism of some of the men around him when under real aerial attacks for the first time, Dyer wrote a far more complimentary evaluation of his crew as a whole, for he was familiar with the chaotic nature of combat. They had ensured *Essex* was not hit by another suicide plane, as she had been once off the Philippines before their watch. "Personnel performance in their first attack by dive bombers and *Kamikaze* was all that could be desired. The efficiency of the Gunnery organization, Lookouts, and Combat Information Center was outstandingly and consistently high."

Dyer's final concern centered around the switch in task groups due to the *Franklin* hits. Task Group 58.3 under Sherman had developed a strong system of communication and fire by sector and range so as not to fire into one another, and yet friendly fire came. Now in another task group without such protocols, what might tomorrow bring?

* * *

Three planes, three photographs. Three fleeting moments of opportunity that could never be reclaimed. The images that emerged in a pan of developer fluid under red lighting, tucked away deep in the bowels of a man o' war, would tell the story—or they wouldn't.

As Herman Schnipper had conducted his craft over many months, a body of art took shape. There emerged no singular iconic photograph of war; images such as Joe Rosenthal's now famous Iwo Jima flag raising required fortune of location and timing in concert with skill. For *Astoria*'s ship's photographer, the whole of his work grew to be greater than the sum of its parts. Together the images formed an extraordinary composition of fighting men at sea—the determination, the humor, the trials and tribulations. They captured monotony, tension, and fatigue, of which there now appeared no end. Maybe his work once sent in would make *Our Navy* magazine.

The gun boss and the skipper reviewed the new photographs with satisfaction. In dramatic detail, there were the day's events frozen for eternity: The first attacker tumbling into the ocean at the precise moment its bomb fell wide, cutting the surface mere feet ahead of *Essex.* The second plane, equally broken, crashing in a thunderous spray just off the carrier's port beam as *Astoria* men craned their necks for a view. The third, shot straight overhead, a burning fuselage plummeting past *Astoria*'s mainmast. All complete with Schnipper's signature talent, perfect framing of the shot.

Captain Dyer ordered enlargements to accompany the ship's antiaircraft reports. If pictures spoke a thousand words, then these photographs held the power to persuade admirals awarding credit for downed planes. Almost as an afterthought, Schnipper ran one additional enlargement of the first attack, the Zero spiraling down. Where black paint had been stripped from the darkroom bulkhead months earlier on the other side of the world, another photograph of *Astoria*'s war was now taped in place.

* * *

170 miles east of Kyushu, day 7 at sea
March 20, 1945

Hard-working yeomen had the ship's daily schedule printed and posted long before reveille at 4:50 a.m. the next morning, March 20. In notes to the crew, gunnery officer Ken Meneke wrote, "Long hours, hard work, irregular meals! That's gunnery, but yesterday's 'Jap splashing' was the payoff. To the lookouts who 'spotted 'em,' and to the director and gun crews who 'scratched 'em,' well done to you all." Captain Dyer added, "Yesterday the *Astoria* played a real part in protecting the *Essex* from three suicide dive bomber attacks... To all the antiaircraft and lookout personnel, well done." Ship's cartoonist Joe Aman added his own brand of commentary, with an empowered Joey Fubar landing a huge punch against a Japanese caricature. "Today I'm a man!" On Joey's newly muscled arm was written, "3 planes."

Reveille largely woke men at stations, not in their racks. For the men actually in bunks, it meant placing flameproof bunk covers over mattresses strung from tricing chains. For all hands, it meant stowing all "burnable material, including papers, in lockers and desk drawers." Everything to prevent serious fire, especially after *Franklin*. Men were given twenty minutes before dawn alert.

Overnight the task groups had headed south, away from Japan, retreating to get *Franklin* underway to the relative safety of Ulithi atoll for more significant repair and return stateside. The Japanese had tracked each fast carrier group and struck hard over two days. *Franklin*, reduced to a floating inferno after bombs laced her decks amid fueled and armed planes, lay so badly crippled that offensive operations for the entire Fast Carrier Task Force were halted so the massive armada could get her off the line and into safe waters.

Shortly following dawn alert, *Franklin*'s remaining men had her engines turned up and closed on regaining steering control. The groups would start moving faster shortly, but the wounded carrier continued to limit 105 ships to an average of 6 knots in moving away from enemy territory. Dawn alert and the full morning brought no enemy planes. Combat Air Patrol brought down a few snoopers, but conditions proved ideal for topping off destroyers and sharing fuel oil as the force retired.

Despite relative quiet, Captain Dyer set the tone for the coming day over *Astoria*'s P.A. for his morning address. "We are now a part of

Task Group 58.2...the task group that had a carrier hit yesterday. We are now less than eighty miles from the Jap homeland, the island of Shikoku, and we are closer to Japan than we were when we launched the first strikes...We are to act as a buffer to protect the crippled carrier. It is anticipated that the Japanese will make every effort to destroy the crippled carrier and therefore it is expected that we will also receive some attention."

Dyer informed his men they would again remain at air emergency stations throughout the day, ready to spring into action on a moment's notice. "Everyone must be on the alert and work at this job today. When those planes come in, they come in fast, and they come in with only one purpose in mind, and that is to wreck and sink ships."

He issued a warning: "This task group does not have in effect the excellent system of exchange of information that was in effect in the task group that we just left...every ship is more or less on its own. For that reason, our lookouts and antiaircraft personnel must be particularly on the alert to detect and identify enemy planes, since you cannot expect to receive the tipoff from other ships.

"The difference," he concluded, "in getting a battery on the target five seconds earlier is the difference between knocking the plane out of the sky or having it hit the carrier or the *Astoria*. Let's turn to and do a good job, as good a job as we did yesterday—which was tops in every respect."

The carrier nearest *Astoria*, USS *Enterprise*, was nothing short of a legend. She had been a mainstay in the war since the December 1941 attack on Pearl Harbor. Her twin sister *Yorktown* had been sunk following the Midway battle. For a long month in late 1942 she stood sentinel as the only American carrier operating in the Pacific, and by now she had operated in more major engagements than any vessel in the United States Navy. If the new *Essex*-class carriers floated as symbols of American wartime production efficiency, *Enterprise* cut the distinctive silhouette of a ship out of time. Perhaps better suited to the clean lines and gleaming peacetime paint of her 1938 commissioning, seven years later she remained unmistakable from any angle. Even in her dark gray livery, even loaded down with added antennae, radars, and antiaircraft guns, at her core the "Big E" maintained the lines of a graceful ship from another era.

USS *Hancock* also steamed nearby, along with the two light carriers *San Jacinto* and *Bataan*. These four flattops would send planes airborne throughout the day for protective cover, and also were tasked to intercept anything headed farther out toward the *Franklin* group. Joining *Astoria* for screening protection were cruisers *Flint* and *Baltimore*, battleships *North Carolina* and *Washington*, with a destroyer squadron clustered to the western side of the formation. Together they assembled a gauntlet of defensive guns and offensive air power that any Japanese attacker would have to thwart to get to the wounded ship.

Throughout the morning, reports came in of unidentified planes on approach. Most "bogeys" turned out to be "friendlies," although one enemy snooper was shot down by Combat Air Patrol. With the task group at a more relaxed posture, destroyers lined up alongside carriers for refueling. Although the group did not require fuel overall, fuel oil transfer redistributed on-hand supply from ships with the biggest storage tanks to those with the greatest need, a process designed to be quick and keep the group moving away from Japan. By 2 p.m. a report came in that *Franklin* steamed under her own power, towline cast off, and she was making 15 knots. The screening group also increased speed, and men held hope that *Franklin* might actually get clear without further incident.

With temperatures in the low seventies, the sun shined through scattered clouds. In other circumstances the weather would be regarded as ideal, but this day it merely meant ideal for attacking enemy planes. Men shucked their foul weather jackets in the sunshine. Meanwhile Captain Dyer stressed to his officers to keep the hated flak suits nearby in case of air emergency stations, to set an example and order the same of their men. The warmer weather raised the unpopularity of the order, but Dyer did not want a repeat of yesterday's woundings or worse.

From his watch station on the Sky platform, Gerard Armitage amused

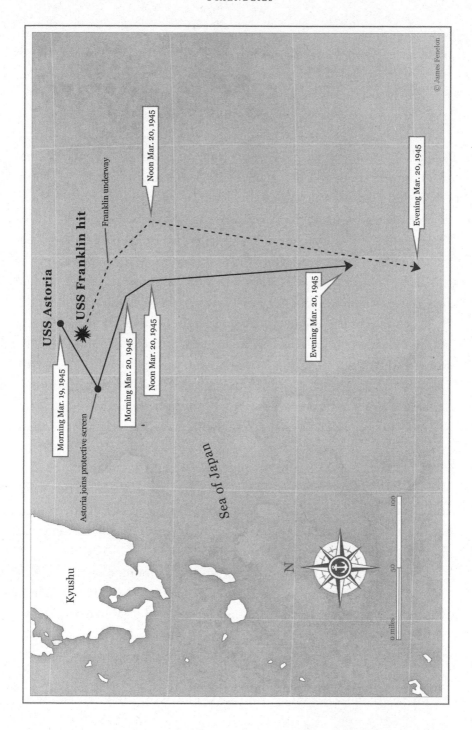

Kyushu

Sea of Japan

USS Astoria

USS Franklin hit

Franklin underway

Noon Mar. 20, 1945

Evening Mar. 20, 1945

Morning Mar. 19, 1945

Astoria joins protective screen

Morning Mar. 20, 1945

Noon Mar. 20, 1945

Evening Mar. 20, 1945

N

0 miles   50   100

© James Fenelon

himself observing the destroyer *Halsey Powell* transfer two pilots via highline to *Hancock* as she lay alongside. The same tin can that had fished him out of the South China Sea and ransomed him back to *Astoria*. Fuel transfer, mail transfer, now recovered aviators, all taking place off their port side. Surely the plucky destroyer managed another demand of ice cream in exchange for the *Hancock* aviators. As the second man was being sent across the highline at 2:46 p.m., a report came in—a bogey closing from thirteen miles. The ship rang up air emergency stations.

Aboard *Hancock* and *Halsey Powell*, men also scrambled. With the aviator suspended via highline between the two ships, crews worked the lines to complete his safe return to the carrier as their shipmates prepared to cast off and separate. Together the two ships made for a ripe target.

Astoria lookouts identified the inbound as a Judy, a dive-bomber, headed for *Hancock*. Confirming they had the range, Armitage and Lind's fire control team trained the 5-inch battery to port over the carrier. From the gun mounts, Tom Kane and John Snyder's team loaded proximity-fused rounds. Lined up, *Astoria* opened fire on the bandit. Plumes of orange-black smoke blasted from the barrels below the Sky platforms, sending the proximity rounds hurtling toward the intruder. Immediately behind *Astoria* in the formation, light carrier *Bataan*'s gunners also sprung to life.

Halsey Powell's men completed the transfer and *Hancock* sailors pulled the aviator to the deck even as both ships also opened fire. Hits peppered the rapidly descending Judy, and the plane was torn apart in its final seconds. The left wing shattered and the fuselage split. Still it plummeted, far past the point where its course could be altered.

Armitage watched in horror as the ruined airframe cleared *Hancock* and showered wreckage onto the fantail of *Halsey Powell*. Its bomb detonated close aboard in an eruption of water and flame that towered over both carrier and destroyer. For the men of *Astoria* the thunderous detonation arrived a split-second later—a sickening soundtrack out of sync with the image.

The return of silence brought smoke in a skyward curl as the two ships

Downed aviators safe in dry clothes with their rescuers: (*left to right*) *Hancock*'s Pete Somerville recovered by Jack Newman, and *Cabot*'s David Kelleher recovered by Donald Comb on March 29, 1945. *(US Navy photo taken by Herman Schnipper)*

Light carrier *Cabot* in an emergency turn a split second before being struck by a *Kamikaze* plane on April 6, 1945. The plane overshot but damaged the ship's main search radar array. *(US Navy photo taken by Herman Schnipper)*

The immediate aftermath of a suicide crash on the flight deck of *Hancock*, taken from *Essex* on April 7, 1945. The carrier suffered 133 casualties but amazingly her crew had *Hancock* operational within an hour. *(US Navy photo in author's collection)*

A Japanese *Judy* is blown apart by *Astoria* and *Essex* in the afternoon of April 7. It was the final attack of the day. *(National Archives photo 80-G-321933 taken by Paul Madden)*

The onslaught continues on April 11. One day after returning to Task Group 58.3, *Enterprise* was attacked repeatedly throughout the afternoon. This near-miss was photographed from *Astoria*. *(US Navy photo taken by Herman Schnipper)*

A close call for *Pasadena* comes on April 11. Antiaircraft fire sheared an enemy plane's wing off as it dove on the cruiser, causing the plane to spin out of control and crash just yards away. *(National Archives photo 80-G-316902 taken by Paul Madden)*

Wilkes-Barre weathers a near miss within the same minute as *Pasadena*. *(National Archives photo 80-G-315756 taken from* South Dakota*)*

One minute later a plane targets *Astoria*. Even as the plane is brought down short of its target (*splash at right*) *Bunker Hill* continues firing. The flash visible from the carrier fired a 5-inch round into *Astoria*'s aft funnel just as Herman Schnipper clicked his camera shutter. The detonation sent shrapnel into Schnipper and Chaplain Lusk as the men hit the deck of their searchlight platform position. *(US Navy photo taken by Herman Schnipper)*

After summoning a Navy corpsman, Herman Schnipper took this photo of the combat medic tending to a badly wounded Chaplain Lusk, checking his pulse in *Astoria*'s searchlight platform. *(US Navy photo taken by Herman Schnipper)*

As Lusk and Schnipper were tended to, a Judy made a low pass at wounded *Enterprise*. *Astoria* (*pictured*) opened fire as the plane cleared the carrier, the two ships together shooting it down. *(National Archives photo 80-G-324306 taken from Enterprise)*

May 3 brings some much-needed good news to the task group, as *Astoria*'s Charlie Tanner rescues *Bunker Hill* Marine pilot Walter "Barney" Goeggel after his Corsair makes a forced water landing. *(US Navy photo taken by Herman Schnipper)*

An *Astoria* twin-40mm gun crew at quarters on May 7. The sailor at far right illustrates the isolation of Black Americans in the segregated World War II United States military. *(US Navy photo taken by Herman Schnipper)*

On May 11, 1945, *Bunker Hill* is struck by two *Kamikazes* within sixty seconds. The view from *Astoria* shows the carrier burning across the formation. Flak peppers the distant sky as *Wilkes-Barre* brings down a third attacking plane. USS *Enterprise* is in left foreground, back from repairs for a third time. *(US Navy photo taken by Herman Schnipper)*

Exhausted yet tied to their battle stations, members of an antiaircraft gun crew catch some sleep under one of *Astoria*'s main battery turrets in the afternoon of May 11. *(US Navy photo taken by Herman Schnipper)*

Hospital ship *Bountiful*, painted bright white to indicate she is non-combatant, takes aboard casualties from *Bunker Hill* to port and *The Sullivans* to starboard on May 12, the day before Mother's Day. *(National Archives photo 80-G-350765)*

Attacks resume early the next morning. *Enterprise* is hit for a third and final time, sending her forward deck elevator 400 feet into the air. The blow knocked the "Big E" out of the war for the final time. *(National Archives photo 80-G-323565)*

Astoria (*in background*) brings down a second *Zeke* short of *Essex* on May 14. She also shot down another diving enemy plane four minutes later. Over seventy-nine days, no *Kamikaze* plane ever got to *Essex*. *(National Archives photo 80-G-324121 taken by Paul Madden)*

Minutes after the attacks end, *Astoria*'s aviation unit prepares to launch both Kingfishers for an unprecedented rescue mission into the Inland Sea of Japan to recover a *Randolph* bomber crew. *(US Navy photo taken by Herman Schnipper)*

Later the same day: The recovered aviators with their rescuers: (*left to right*) Charlie Tanner with *Randolph* pilot John Morris and Don Comb with airdale Cletus Phegley. On this day, Tanner and Morris learned they shared a common dear friend in *Astoria* Marine CO Gerard Armitage. *(US Navy photo taken by Herman Schnipper)*

Joey Fubar takes credit for the "Mighty Ninety's" gunnery prowess in late May 1945. *(Joe Aman cartoon from USS Astoria Morning Press)*

Friday evening Jewish prayer service aboard *Astoria* on May 25. Chaplain Al Lusk, recovered from surgery, continues to conduct religious services for Catholic, Protestant, and Jewish faiths aboard ship. *(US Navy photo taken by Herman Schnipper)*

At last retiring to anchorage, *Astoria* men paint a scoreboard on her bridge armor. *Astoria* received solo credit for thirteen Japanese planes at Okinawa, top honors across the Fast Carrier Task Force. *(US Navy photo taken by Herman Schnipper)*

Herman Schnipper receives a backlog of mail on June 6, 1945, including weeks' worth of his hometown newspaper *The Bayonne Times* and various dried and canned foods sent by his mother. *(US Navy photo taken by Louis Rodrique)*

Danger arrived in many forms. USS *Randolph* is hit by a plane for a second time at anchor, on this occasion by an Army Air Corps P-38 Lightning that was horsing around over the fleet on June 7. *(US Navy photo taken by Herman Schnipper)*

In his final day aboard ship, June 9, 1945, Captain George Dyer presents Chaplain Al Lusk with a Purple Heart for his wound sustained at Okinawa. *(US Navy photo taken by Herman Schnipper)*

Before leaving ship, Captain George Dyer takes a photo over the "Mighty Ninety" scoreboard with Air Defense Officer H.G. Leahy (*center*) and Gunnery Officer Kenneth Meneke (*left*). *(US Navy photo taken by Herman Schnipper)*

Astoria sailors on liberty shop and trade with Filipino locals on Samar, June 15. *(US Navy photo taken by Herman Schnipper)*

Astoria S-Division sailors pose with a Japanese flag during liberty on Samar on June 25. At front center is George W. Ostrander, a thirty-six-year-old ship's cook who died of a heart attack six days later. *(US Navy photo taken by Herman Schnipper)*

Chaplain Al Lusk gives a eulogy at the funeral service for George W. Ostrander just hours after *Astoria* returns to sea on July 1, 1945. *(US Navy photo taken by Herman Schnipper)*

Astoria firing upon a target sleeve in column behind *Essex* on July 2. *(National Archives photo 80-G-373831 taken by Paul Madden)*

A public relations photo depicting men from the Rochester, New York, area taken on July 14, 1945. N Division officer Lawrence Doty (*right*) instructs men on use of a sextant. Fire Controlman Fred Lind is third from left. *(US Navy photo taken by Rudy Guttosch)*

Air Group 83 Avengers from *Essex* drop bombs through solid overcast in a radar-guided raid on Aomori on July 15, 1945. Weather hampered Fast Carrier Task Force operations through July into August. *(US Navy photo taken by Paul Madden)*

A PR photo captures Joe Aman, Joey Fubar cartoonist on July 20, 1945. *(US Navy photo taken by Rudy Guttosch)*

Astoria and Task Group 38.3 conduct the first nighttime underway replenishment in US Navy history, July 20–21, 1945. Herman Schnipper managed a few photographs before being ordered to cease. *(US Navy photo taken by Herman Schnipper)*

The Boys from Bayonne. Herman Schnipper (*lower left*) with six other men from his hometown of Bayonne, New Jersey, for a local writeup in late July 1945. *(US Navy photo taken by Rudy Guttosch)*

Astoria's second commanding officer, Captain William V. Hamilton taken on August 3, 1945. *(US Navy photo taken by Rudy Guttosch)*

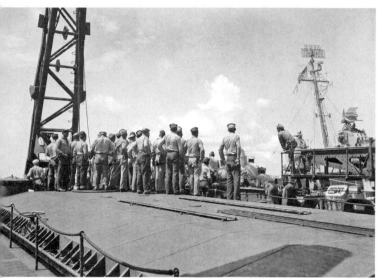

Astoria men cease work in the morning of August 15, 1945, when they learn of Japan's surrender. Destroyer *Chauncey* was alongside for mail transfer when the announcement came. *(US Navy photo taken by Herman Schnipper)*

Astoria shipmates pose for a PR photo to celebrate the announcement of the end of hostilities with Japan. After these photos, the men went right back to work in their daily duties. *(National Archives photo 80-G-337360 taken by Rudy Guttosch)*

Sunbathing men from multiple ships pack *Astoria*'s main deck during the voyage home on August 30, 1945. *(US Navy photo taken by Herman Schnipper)*

The first ships to leave the Fast Carrier Task Force for the US following the armistice signing. Left to right are *Astoria*, *San Jacinto*, and a *Fletcher*-class destroyer on September 3, 1945. *(National Archives photo 80-G-265834)*

Passengers from other ships sleep in *Astoria*'s hangar bay/basketball court on September 5 as the ship steams off the Aleutian Islands headed for the west coast of the United States. *(US Navy photo taken by Herman Schnipper)*

Recording artist Ella Mae Morse backed by a Navy band sings for the *Astoria* crew and passengers, welcoming her arrival at Terminal Island Navy Yard on September 15 after eleven months in theater. *(US Navy photo taken by Herman Schnipper)*

An *Astoria* sailor song request in chalk on the ship's superstructure below the bridge scoreboard as the crew packs the starboard side to listen to Ella Mae Morse sing. *(US Navy photo taken by Herman Schnipper)*

Joey Fubar speaks for the crew in saying goodbye to the first round of *Astoria* shipmates headed for civilian life or other assignments on September 15, 1945. *(Joe Aman cartoon from USS Astoria Morning Press)*

Herman Schnipper and *Astoria* shipmates on a "homes of the stars" tour in March 1946. Schnipper and a friend pose on Mary Pickford's diving board in Hollywood. (*Photo taken by Herman Schnipper*)

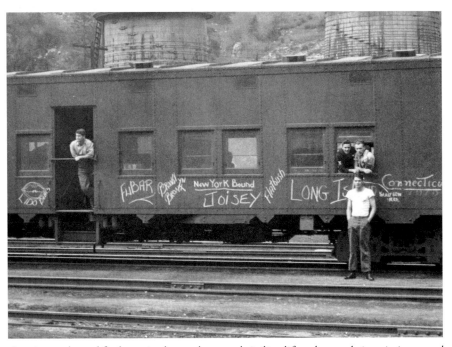

Astoria men bound for home in the northeast and civilian life, taken as their train is stopped to switch engines on April 18, 1946. (*Photo taken by Herman Schnipper*)

became anthills of activity. The aviator may have been safe back aboard *Hancock*, but shrapnel and wreckage took his place across *Halsey Powell*'s stern. Men on the fantail lay butchered from the impact. The destroyer veered first to starboard, then back to port, her rudder jammed from the damage, all steering control lost. She careened across the bow of *Hancock* in a near collision.

A second destroyer, USS *The Sullivans*, was dispatched to stand by *Halsey Powell* and render aid. The plane's bomb had punched a hole through her stern and she sat lower in the water as she was brought back under control. Armitage felt sickened at the sight of it. That could have been him on the highline, and those were the men who had brought him home to *Astoria*. Tensions remained high for the group following a report of a bomb near miss on *Franklin* to the south, also from a Judy. Might it have been the same plane? An hour passed before *Astoria* secured from air emergency battle stations. With men exposed on deck, *Halsey Powell* had taken some forty casualties. *Astoria* had fired thirty-five rounds. Jim Thomson's forties and John Arrighi's twenties could never even fire; they would have jeopardized hitting the two ships under attack at that range and altitude.

The lull lasted a mere fifteen minutes before radar picked up more inbounds. Just after 4 p.m., men raced back to their air emergency stations and the task group began to execute emergency turns. Less than a minute passed before another Judy was sighted from the northwest at high altitude, diving hard at *Enterprise*. Again *Astoria* and the task group opened fire. Flak bursts painted the sky black as the plane dove, lower and lower. The antiaircraft fire followed the dive-bomber down as the pilot released his bomb and leveled out low to the water. The bomb missed *Enterprise* astern, but descending antiaircraft fire struck the venerable carrier in her forward gun tubs. *Astoria* had checked her fire in the final descent. Another ship in the group did not.

As the Judy cleared the task group at very low level, smoke and flame began to pour from *Enterprise*. A victim of gunfire from her own ships, her damage control crews scrambled. Ammunition cooked off in the gun tubs. The wind drove thick black smoke into her pilothouse. All *Astoria* men could do was watch from their stations and stand vigilant for more. The Judy had escaped.

A standing protocol for a wounded carrier dictated that the ship maneuver as necessary, and the task group would conform to her movements. Herman Schnipper and Walter Duggan trained their cameras first with *Enterprise* astern, then to starboard as the task group performed with the carrier. Her starboard turn brought the wind around so the thick smoke blew away from her island structure. Across the forward flight deck, new bursts of flame erupted as fueled planes caught fire. The friendly fire incident not only killed men on the carrier, but it changed the calculus. Task Group 58.2 no longer just stood between *Franklin* and Japan, it now had its own wounded aircraft carrier to protect as well.

Within minutes another plane passed through the task group. *Astoria* again opened fire until the plane passed between ships. They did not need another friendly fire incident in the group. Fire controlman Jim Thomson observed, "The Jap dove and dove, and not one could we hit. Again his bombs were missing but they flew close to the water after pulling out and streaked clear through the formation. The carrier we were escorting, the *Enterprise*, was hit by our own shell fire and went up in flames. Ammunition exploded all over the place."

Men realized these planes were not *Kamikaze*; far from it. Their pilots maneuvered well, completing their runs mere feet above the ocean surface as they weaved through the task group. Antsy gunners dropping their fire too far was proving the biggest danger.

Despite the concussion of the nearby 5-inch guns, Captain Dyer kept command from *Astoria*'s open bridge. His Marine orderly, Corporal Hugh Gibbs, realized the skipper had neglected his own flak suit despite his orders. He grabbed the suit and approached the captain, informing him he needed to don the protective layer.

Dyer shouted, "Lad, don't bother me now!"

Gibbs replied, "Captain, your wife told me to look after you. Now please put your arms back." Dyer acquiesced because he knew the corporal was right—not just for his wife, but for the example. Nearby, gun boss Ken Meneke was wearing his suit per Dyer's orders.

Minutes later another plane came in, high to starboard. With fires still erupting on *Enterprise*, the plane lined up in an apparent attempt to finish her off. The task group exercised an emergency turn to port to unmask their guns. From a 45-degree dive the plane dropped a bomb on *Enterprise* that also missed. The plane pulled out low, and ships across the task group opened fire.

An explosion rocked *Astoria*'s open bridge mere feet from the captain, knocking Dyer, Meneke, and other men to the deck. *Astoria*'s aft battery continued to thunder as the plane cleared the group. Dyer and Meneke clambered to their feet while Armitage and Lind's 5-inch guns pounded away astern. The men up in Sky Aft shortly reported dropping the plane, observing it crash four miles outside the formation. *Astoria* had been the only ship firing as it smoked and fell.

As the skipper and gun boss composed themselves, they found the nose cap of an exploded 5-inch shell—American. A gaping hole in the open bridge splinter shield let light through just eleven feet from where they had been standing. A friendly fire round had exploded against the control tower. Dyer counted thirteen shrapnel holes in his flak suit. Meneke's suit bore a large tear right over his heart; he had been struck heavily in the chest. The experimental suits had saved their lives. They would be bruised tomorrow, but they had survived. Several other men on the open bridge displayed superficial wounds. Sky Forward reported three more men wounded from the shrapnel. All would be eligible for Purple Hearts. Dyer joked with his men, "I was running the fastest, and they were the ones that got caught." He summoned Herman Schnipper to photograph the hole in the bridge armor for evaluation.

Standing at his aft 20mm mount, John Arrighi was approached by the Marine top sergeant, Israel Friedman. The top, a veteran of Guadalcanal like CO Armitage, sported a huge grin. He showed off a bloody leg. "I got hit—look." Another shrapnel wound. He reported another man in the 40mm tubs who had been wounded by friendly steel as well. Arrighi would write in his secret diary of the enemy planes "five feet from the water—we couldn't fire for fear of hitting our own ships and he went through the whole formation that way—our CAP shot him down later."

Within minutes the ship was firing on another lone attacker that passed through the formation. The task group commander informed overall task force commander Marc Mitscher, "We are under heavy air attack." Just after 5 p.m., as *Enterprise* brought her fires under control, two more enemy planes breached the perimeter. *Astoria* and other ships unleashed on the first, shooting its tail off and dropping it in the middle of the formation. An F6F Hellcat just launched from USS *Bataan* engaged the second plane as some ships continued to fire.

Fred Lind called it "the most spectacular attack of all. Two Judys dove on our formation, with one of our F6F fighter planes right after them. One of the enemy planes was hit about 5,000 feet up, and went into a helpless spin. The other guy kept coming, dropped his bomb, which was a near-miss, and then was shot down. Some of the ships did not recognize our F6F, and opened fire on him."

The Hellcat burst into flames at twilight and burned brightly as it descended across the entire group. Duggan had his camera rolling, and Schnipper took a still. The American fighter cleared the formation and splashed near a perimeter destroyer. Lind concluded, "I was proud to see that the *Astoria* didn't fire on him. Later, we received word that our pilot was picked up in good condition. Bet he won't forget that one right away!" The ship's war diary confirmed, "*Astoria* did not fire on the Hellcat."

It would be much later before the early reports proved erroneous. The pilot, Commander Walker Ethridge, did actually perish in the flaming crash. He had been USS *Bataan*'s air group commander, brought down by friendly fire.

* * *

The night brought snoopers, enemy planes tasked with monitoring the task group's position, but no serious attacks. Task Group 58.2 sent up fire to chase them off, which Lind compared to "a butterfly with about nine hoses spraying on it. The butterfly broke into a flaming ball and crashed. We had bogies in the area all night." He continued, "That night I enjoyed the best sleep I've had in months."

Jim Thomson wrote, "We were a hot shooting ship. The new unit was not as well coordinated as our own and there was much confusion and much shooting into our own ships...The *Asty* was riddled with shrapnel. A shell plowed thru the shield six feet from my head unnoticed in the roar of the fives. Salvos were landing all around us. Decidedly uncomfortable." He joined Dyer in praising the enemy, "They were mostly beautiful fliers hugging the water while passing through our ships. Many of them feigned crashes letting out smoke, only to straighten out in time. Many of them crashed in flames as the forties hit them as they left the formation. They caught fire very easily & their wing fittings seemed very weak. Generally when we hit them the outer wing panel would come off...The sky was covered with five and forties and it was beautiful to watch the white and red tracer as they arced thru the skies."

The morning of March 21 brought calm seas and overcast. *Franklin's* group continued their trek south, and by early afternoon only the longest-range enemy planes could reach the fleet. At 12:33 p.m., a twin-engine Frances bomber was spotted on *Astoria's* starboard beam. Radar had tracked the plane in from fifty miles out. *Astoria* had the range and bearing, and the ship opened up. Walter Duggan captured the film footage as the Mighty Ninety pounded the plane from the time it passed overhead. Herman Schnipper also photographed the attack, again losing any semblance of fear as he channeled his focus through his camera viewfinder. Hit after hit landed as the bomber dropped a bomb in futility, before its right engine caught fire and it crashed near the perimeter of the formation. The ships of Task Force 58.2 passed burning wreckage, finally clear of the danger zone.

Franklin and *Enterprise* steamed safe from further harm.

Securing yet again from general quarters, men left their positions exhausted and grubby. They had been through hell for three days. All meals at battle stations.

Men caught up with their diaries. One *Astoria* sailor wrote, "It rained steel for three days," a sentiment echoed by his shipmates. Lind added, "After seeing fighter planes all the time, a twin-engine bomber seemed like a monster... It looked the size of a bus." He concluded, "I am getting testy from lack of sleep, but aside from fatigue, I am all right. At least I can still control myself enough to keep from mouthing off to officers. Glad I'm still a civilian at heart."

Jim Thomson had to reevaluate the performance of his shipmates relative to what they had experienced from other ships in their temporary task group reassignment. "Altogether we had a dozen odd men hit by shrapnel which was good all things considered... Many of the ships seem to open up just for the sake of firing. The noise is terrific and you are unable to make yourself heard to a man standing alongside you... We got credit for half a dozen planes, but it seems silly and impossible to say that one ship did the damage there is so much stuff going up."

Chuck Tanner found his planes riddled with shrapnel holes, reflecting much work ahead for his aviation division. Gerard Armitage negotiated with Tanner a loan of one of the .30-caliber machine guns from the gooney birds. He further enlisted the Construction and Repair Division to weld mounts on either side of his post at Sky Aft. If they were going to make these kinds of attacks, he wanted to be able to shoot back.

When the crew reported through the messing compartment for breakfast in the morning, they would receive an extra message from the captain. Gunnery officer Ken Meneke's flak suit had been stuffed and placed at the head of the chow line, shrapnel damage visible through shredded layers directly over the chest area. The sobering message was clear: wear your suit and live.

15

For the Boys

We would go to such extremes to rescue one guy,
but it really boosted morale.

—Astoria *aviator Don Comb*

Philippine Sea, 600 miles south of Kyushu, day 9 at sea
March 22, 1945

Across the task force the bombings and suicide attacks had been shockingly effective. With just two days of strikes completed and the invasion of Okinawa looming, Admirals Spruance and Mitscher had lost a quarter of their aerial strike capability. Three fleet carriers had been knocked off the line and required retirement for repair—*Wasp, Franklin*, and *Enterprise*. A fourth, *Randolph*, sat back at Ulithi Anchorage, also under repair from the suicide attack before the operation even got underway. Sending three more carriers off the line also meant pulling away vital support ships for escort.

The Japanese tactics further wrought havoc through the secondary phenomenon of causing Americans to fire into their own ships; *Astoria* and *Enterprise* were not alone in being struck by American shells. The turn of events brought such profound impact as to cause a massive reorganization of the Fast Carrier Task Force. Five task groups had approached Japan three days ago; now Admiral Mitscher consolidated his remaining ships into three groups.

As the task groups restructured, *Astoria* men briefly got a view of the crippled carrier they had been protecting. *Astoria* steamed in company with sister cruiser *Santa Fe* off the starboard beam of *Franklin*, and Walter Duggan captured a sight on film that defied imagination: *Franklin's* foremast, oddly canted under the weight of its main search radar. Five-inch mounts and island superstructure blackened and peeled from raging fires. The entire football-field length of her aft flight deck charred and gutted. As they steamed in formation, the crack of rifle reports carried over the water. The men knew what this indicated. From the portside elevator, out of view, American boys who had died from their wounds were being committed to the deep, slid over the side from under American flags as their shipmates stood at attention.

John Arrighi and other men wrote of "790 survivors," and word spread quickly. This would prove inaccurate, as other survivors had been plucked from the water by destroyers or spilled aboard *Santa Fe*, which had stood alongside after the attack. Nevertheless, nearly half *Franklin's* complement of 2,700 men lay killed, wounded, or missing. The ruined ship made for a sobering backdrop to men in desperate need of rest.

Eight men were killed and thirty-seven wounded aboard *Enterprise* in the friendly fire incident of the twentieth. The carrier had held a commitment service for the dead in the afternoon of the twenty-first, once out of range of enemy planes.

Halsey Powell also buried her dead at sea on that day, then joined up with the escort ships formed around *Enterprise*, *Wasp*, and *Franklin*— *Santa Fe* and a destroyer squadron. All would be headed back to Ulithi for repair and assessment, maybe back to Pearl for further work. There could be no question that *Franklin* would head back to the States and out of the war. Having earned her radio call sign Rampage, *Astoria* was ordered to return upon refueling to her station near *Essex* in Rear Admiral Ted Sherman's Task Group 58.3.

Essex had emerged without damage or casualty. *Wilkes-Barre* had indeed taken care of the fourth plane attempting to crash her as *Astoria* moved away on the nineteenth. Arrighi wrote, "The *Essex* wasn't very well pleased that we were leaving her and requested the task group commander to send another cruiser. They give us credit for saving the *Essex* from a couple of dive bombers, presumably suicide bombers. They really appreciated our being around." *Astoria*'s total credit for the harrowing three days grew to five confirmed planes with several assists.

The morning brought rough seas along with the Logistic Support Group for resupply. John Arrighi wrote, "We fueled and took on ammunition while underway—quite a job because the sea wasn't too calm, made steering hard. The lines parted before we completed the job. We did manage to get some five-inch ammunition aboard." Replenishing ammunition while underway remained a new process, first experimented with at Iwo Jima. The ammunition ship *Mauna Loa* had never transferred resupply of such to a cruiser or other heavy ship, and the swells kept raising her propellers out of the water. *Astoria* would surge, then have to back down, then increase speed. *Astoria* had to move away after a partial ammunition load transfer. That was fine with Fred Lind, who could not wait to get rid of the ammo ship, all of which were alarmingly named for volcanoes and packed bow to stern with explosive contents.

By contrast, the oiler *Millicoma* proved quite experienced, a "steady steamer," and *Astoria* took aboard more than three hundred thousand gallons of fuel oil in seventy-six minutes. The crew also brought aboard food and supplies during refueling, sent over wrapped in cargo nets. "Somehow or other," Lind wrote, "when loading food supplies, the better-tasting stuff would sometimes be rerouted to under one of our bunks such as orange crates, etc. No onions ever got misrouted. Fresh food at sea was a luxury."

When the groups separated, *Astoria* took her position off *Essex* shortly before twilight. With a quarter of their carriers out of action, the three newly consolidated task groups steamed toward Okinawa. *Astoria*'s Task Group 58.3 now covered five aircraft carriers—*Essex, Bunker Hill, Hancock*, and light carriers *Cabot* and *Bataan*. With *Kamikaze* bases reduced at Kyushu, the carrier forces would shift their focus to Okinawa, providing air support for landing forces until the Army Air Forces could occupy airfields ashore. Only nine days remained before the landings began, and the task force had targets to soften.

Despite the heavy blow absorbed, the Fast Carrier Task Force received high praise. The two days' raids had yielded a devastating blow to Japanese airpower. Between planes shot down and destroyed on the ground, 528 aircraft never made it to the fast carriers. Apart from the three carriers out of action, all other planes that broke through had been brought down. The cost in return was some 300 American planes off the line aboard carriers out of action, scores more shot down over the Home Islands, and many hundreds of sailors and Marines killed. Cold calculus aside, the US Navy was gradually winning a war of attrition.

* * *

The next day, March 23, brought the fast carriers northwest to conduct raids over airfields on Okinawa and the surrounding Nansei Shoto from 150 miles out. Japanese antiaircraft batteries again remained silent on the first day of strikes as American air groups bombed and strafed targets on the ground. Fred Lind wrote, "We went right back at it, launching attacks against Okinawa. We sure were persistent—no let up. Many bogeys were in the area, but they couldn't find us because of heavy overcast. I prefer clear weather, when visibility is good—maybe the Japs did too, but the clear weather was nice and peaceful."

Jim Thomson observed, "Beautiful sight to see our planes thunder overhead. So far no alerts. Before the day was over we were up and down half a dozen times. Hard to figure Tojo. He was overhead all day but didn't come down." Despite calls to air emergency with bogey alerts, no attacks materialized. Both afternoon and evening chow were interrupted by calls to air emergency stations, both to no avail.

The most noteworthy event of the day from *Astoria* was observing a *Bunker Hill* Helldiver bomber fail to achieve takeoff speed. Realizing the plane would not get airborne, the pilot threw his SB2C ("Son of a Bitch, Second Class") onto its right wing before hitting the water. The maneuver likely saved the lives of both crewmen, as the plane rolled onto its back and cleared the carrier to starboard. Both men made it out of the cockpit and emerged unhurt other than vomiting mouthfuls of seawater and dye marker. A destroyer serving as plane guard picked them up via whaleboat.

For the newest member of Cruiser Division 17, USS *Springfield*, the afternoon brought being straddled by dropping bombs through mist and overcast. Despite initial concerns, the incident proved far from an enemy attack. The bombs had been jettisoned by a plane from another task group before landing with no visibility as to what lay below.

* * *

Philippine Sea, 70 miles southeast of Okinawa, day 11 at sea
March 24, 1945

The morning hours brought the second day slated for air strikes over Okinawa. Fresh off the midwatch in his engine room, Herb Blodgett stood at the rail in predawn darkness, puzzled to see ship running lights appear across the task group, a first in combat conditions. The formation was in the process of a significant turn to starboard, each ship holding relative position as they assumed a new course, reversing to almost due south after steaming north. *Running lights sixty miles off Okinawa? Before morning strikes?* Blodgett noted USS *Indianapolis*, Spruance's flagship, peeling off to detach. *Now where is she going?*

From the pilothouse, Captain Dyer focused on the "difficult and risky movement" the formation was performing in the dark. Other ships joined *Indianapolis* in detaching—battleships *Washington* and *South Dakota*. The running lights proved necessary to avoid collision as the heavies detached during the course change. Spruance had ordered them to form up with the five other fast battleships across the other task groups. Together they would serve as seaborne heavy artillery for shore prep while Mitscher brought the air power of his remaining carriers to bear over the airfields.

Midmaneuver, the lights abruptly went out on all instruments across *Astoria*. Gyros stopped. Steering refused to answer, and all communication went down. The ship had lost electrical power. With the engines still churning to produce 25 knots and no way to communicate, *Astoria* steered off course in the formation. Electricians scrambled to cut over to other generators, and there was precious little Dyer or anyone on the bridge could do. Fortunately only a couple of harrowing minutes passed before the electrical gang brought alternate generators online and the ship resumed station. *At least we didn't almost collide with* Indianapolis *again.*

Arriving for general quarters a half hour after, Fred Lind took his station oblivious to the scare. All he noted after sunup was that the battleships were gone. "They just quietly snuck out...I sure would hate to have been on the receiving end of this mission!"

Dawn broke to scattered clouds and strikes headed inland to Japanese airfields across Okinawa. If an American offensive strategy had developed, so had a Japanese defensive one. Antiaircraft batteries over the target sites sprang to life and shot down scores of American planes from the carriers.

Astoria's rescue planes held first watch for the task group on the day. At 9:15 a.m. their two Kingfishers were called to launch for a downed *Bunker Hill* Corsair aviator off Okinawa. Don Comb led the mission. Twenty minutes out from the location, with four *Bunker Hill* fighters in escort, Comb received a message from other pilots on station that the downed aviator was fading very quickly in the water.

Comb landed as quickly as he could, splashing his Kingfisher's floats into the ocean near a pool of dye marker and an uninflated life raft. With the plane's prop running, he steered by rudder and approached the man bobbing in his flight gear and life jacket. He realized waves were breaking over the aviator's face; the man was gone. Comb hadn't realized the strength of the wind and sea before setting down. The waves were too rough to even attempt to deflate the dead man's life jacket for a proper Navy burial at sea.

Left with no choice but to fight heavy white-capped waves to launch airborne, he throttled up. Cresting a swell, the plane dipped and coasted into the following trough. One moment Comb could see nothing but sky, the next nothing but ocean. *I should never have landed in the first place*, he thought. *Yet here I am.* After riding several such waves, he timed the top of a swell and gave the Kingfisher full throttle. The plucky floatplane sprung free and lifted airborne. Relief spilled over him, for he had feared he would "auger right in." Following his return trip to *Astoria*, Comb learned his futile rescue attempt had left another carrier's air group without a commander.

All four cruisers of *Astoria*'s division, by now coined the "WASP Division" after the first letter of each ship name (*Wilkes-Barre*, *Astoria*, *Springfield*, and *Pasadena*), were ordered to dispatch their Kingfisher floatplanes to retrieve downed airmen. By late afternoon, the other three ships had conducted successful rescue missions.

At 3:35 p.m., having cycled through all the available rescue planes in the task group, a new request came through for *Astoria*. Another *Bunker Hill* crew was down, a Helldiver pilot and his radioman. The task group commander called on *Astoria*, sending the cruiser's aviation division scrambling. As Chuck Tanner's men serviced his planes, they determined one was out of commission due to an unbalanced propeller from heavy seas experienced earlier in the day. Despite the pending twilight, Tanner volunteered to pilot the remaining plane. His request to fly out a single rescue plane deviated from standard procedure, and the prospect of returning after dusk added unprecedented complication. Cruisers in theater didn't typically recover Kingfishers in the dark. Nevertheless, Tanner informed Captain Dyer that he could perform the mission, and Dyer acquiesced.

Tanner spun up the number two plane and launched solo from *Astoria*'s catapult. The downed airmen's situation grew dire as his own had been approaching dusk off the Philippines, and he was not about to leave them out there without a rescue effort. Tanner was confident he could get them back before sundown.

Once airborne, overhead he met up with fighter cover from *Bunker Hill* also determined to rescue one of their own. The formation headed for the southern tip of Okinawa based on Tanner's map work. Crossing the island would be far too dangerous due to antiaircraft fire; they were forced to take the long route around the southern tip.

Tanner had no trouble finding the crew in the water as a *Bunker Hill* plane circled overhead. He spotted two men floating in a raft, fighting considerable chop. Initially he was skeptical he could safely set down in the "12 to 15 foot swell." *We can't leave these men out here.* With light fading, Chuck Tanner informed his flight cover he "was going to try it."

Three bounces into his landing, he lost sight of the raft and overshot his target by fifty feet, but he made it down. With seas too rough to try to turn back toward the raft, Tanner idled and steered by rudder on the central float while dropping the plane's flaps as a makeshift sail. Between the Kingfisher backing up and the men paddling closer with their small metal oars, they closed the distance. Tanner threw a line over from the wing and lowered his rope ladder. Tanner later reported that, as he worked to help the exhausted men, "I could only leave the cockpit for a few seconds because the plane would commence to turn out of the wind. Had I allowed it to turn as much as 45 degrees from the wind, it would have capsized immediately," something the aviator knew all too well from his experience seeing it happen to the *Pasadena* plane back in January. While Tanner worked to prevent this for his plane, the Helldiver pair's raft flipped over in similar fashion.

In fading light and with his plane pitching wildly, Tanner managed to hoist both exhausted crewmen aboard. Next came the problem of squeezing three men in a two-seat aircraft. The *Bunker Hill* radioman, J. D. Mahoney, looked the smallest, so Tanner elected to stuff him in the seaplane's baggage compartment. "This was as close as I could get him to the [plane's] center of gravity," Tanner wrote. "In the event we capsized, he would have had a better chance to get out face down than face up." He then strapped the Helldiver pilot, Lieutenant C. J. Davis, into the rear cockpit. The flight back would be cramped, but a rescue was a rescue.

Tanner's report continued, "I waited for a swell with a small amount of chop and started my takeoff. It was rough, to say the least. I used maximum available power and my takeoff run wasn't too long, but the plane took a terrific beating."

In his own statement, *Bunker Hill* pilot Davis sure felt that the takeoff run was long. "Must have been a mile run over swells," he opined. Radioman Mahoney noted, "The plane seemed to stop momentarily on contact with each swell and I expected the pontoon to break loose, but the exceptional skill of the pilot triumphed over the elements." *Floatplanes made for a very different kind of flying than carrier launches.*

Davis and Mahoney were just relieved to be off the water and back in an American plane. From their raft, they had seen three other Kingfishers fly past them earlier in the afternoon. Not knowing they were returning from rescue missions of their own, he had assumed the heavy seas weren't suitable for a landing attempt. Davis "settled down to the belief it would be the following day before rescue would be made." Yet after three and a half hours in the water, he had spotted a lone Kingfisher with fighter escort headed directly for his raft. He watched as Tanner "circled and made a hazardous landing in rough seas." Now airborne at twilight, his lone rescuer steered the burdened aircraft back toward their task group.

In preparation to retrieve their plane, *Astoria* performed a sweeping turn and cut a hard rudder, causing the ship to slip sideways. Referred to as Charlie Method recovery, this maneuver created a temporary slick in rough seas, ensuring their plane had the calmest possible surface upon which to land. Just as darkness fell, Tanner set down near *Astoria* in the slick and taxied up. He drove his plane onto the deployed net sled trailing astern, the hook on his central float caught, and the stern gang retrieved him via ship's crane. The overloaded Kingfisher was hoisted back aboard in the pitch of night.

With two soaked *Bunker Hill* aviators safe aboard ship, Captain Dyer put Tanner in for a Distinguished Flying Cross, an award rightfully earned for his selfless courage. Admiral Sherman further praised the successful rescue. *Astoria* had just completed her first rescue at sea, and a night effort at that.

* * *

The next day brought refueling and rearming. It also brought Palm Sunday. Fred Lind wrote of the "Padre," "I attended church services. Our chaplain has Catholic Mass, and follows that with Protestant services. Maybe he's a Rabbi as well." Chaplain Al Lusk, a "jack of all faiths," indeed conducted weekly Friday night prayer services for his Jewish shipmates, including Herman Schnipper.

Palm Sunday might not have carried meaning for Schnipper, but on that day he wrote to his mother. Due to strict censorship he couldn't mention that his photos now included enemy planes hurtling down at ships. "The mail situation is not very good because of the way we get around," he continued. "I have not received any letters for over three weeks. I am still in the best of health and am getting along alright. Your son, Sholem."

John Arrighi wrote of the only noteworthy event out of the routine for the day: a man who lost balance and went overboard while handling lines during resupply. "Destroyer picked him up quickly. We made the usual offer of ice cream for his return—destroyer answered 'we make our own ice cream, we'll keep the man.' He was put in bed for a rest—probably get him back tomorrow."

* * *

Minami Daitō Jima was a hunk of nothing. A scant four miles across on its longest side, the island had roughly the area of Iwo Jima. It would not retain the notoriety of Iwo, which lay at the midpoint between the Marianas and Honshu, nor did it require invasion. But it did have an airfield, one the Americans did not require but did need to prevent Japan from using. On a chart, if one placed a compass at its center and drew an arc through approximately two hundred miles away, the resulting circle passed through Okinawa and the upper Nansei Shoto to the northwest, and the track of Task Force 58 to and from Kyushu to the east. Such a speck of land in the north Philippine Sea might be tiny, but it was worthy of a wide berth...and frequent bombardment to keep the airfield out of action. Such was the mission the WASP Division found themselves tasked with on the night of March 27.

John Arrighi wrote, "After daylight we got the word we're going to a small island to bombard it—The bombardment was for tonight, seven or eight cruisers and the rest destroyers, seventeen in all. Midnight—General Quarters. Minami Daito Jima is the island. We have the ammunition dump and 3 air strips to knock out."

The cruisers lined up with *Astoria* again behind *Pasadena*. Arrighi continued, "When we moved in we could see other ships shelling and a faint outline on the horizon which was our objective. The island is comparatively flat, highest point about 240 feet above sea level. Could see our shells exploding." As an antiaircraft gunner, he had no responsibilities while the battery gunners like Snyder and Kane took their turn. He concluded, "Soon got tired of the whole thing and found a place to sleep—funny how you can sleep with guns firing all around you. Someone woke me up about 3 a.m. and said we have been secured."

Jim Thomson added, "The aim was to raise hell with a large airstrip and installations including an ammunition dump. We started large fires but no dump. We go back to fuel and get a couple of raids on the way back by Tojo's planes." Fred Lind wrote, "Other than the bombardment, nothing exceptional happened...It sure lit up the place at night!" The main battery gunfire in the dark was bright enough that Herman Schnipper could even take photographs.

The bombardment lasted mere minutes—a target of opportunity due to location. Lind's team picked up bogeys on the radar, but they turned out to be American B-29s en route to bomb mainland Japan. Arrighi closed with, "We rejoined task group 58.3 early in the morning. Glad to see the rest of the ships again—we only had left them last night. Always better to have planes flying around us (our own of course)."

*　*　*

Philippine Sea, 120 miles southeast of Kyushu, day 16 at sea
March 29, 1945

The fast carriers were sent back up to Kyushu to chase reports of Japanese ships underway. The reports proved false, and planes were diverted to secondary targets—"wharves, warehouses, factories, barracks, and a seaplane base." In the early morning missions, disaster struck for Ted Sherman's Task Group 58.3. In heavy overcast *Bunker Hill* Helldiver bombers in close formation suffered a five-plane collision, sending the *Wilkes-Barre* floatplanes out to retrieve any survivors. They were only able to locate and rescue two of the ten aviators involved. Shortly afterward two *Hancock* Helldivers also collided in the thick soup, one chopping the other's tail off with its propeller. The mortally wounded plane fell into a spin deep over Kagoshima Bay at the tip of Kyushu, a hotbed of activity for Japanese air bases in *Kamikaze* Alley.

The pilot of the plunging aircraft, Lieutenant Junior Grade Ronald L. "Pete" Somerville, tried to radio his rear seater to get out. Receiving no response as the plane hurtled below eight hundred feet, Somerville popped his straps and bailed out, pitching a life raft over the side with him.

Hitting the water shortly after his plane pancaked the surface, Somerville nearly drowned. His feet had become tangled in the shroud lines while deploying the chute and he broke the surface headfirst. The wet parachute promptly dragged him under as he struggled to free himself. Starved for air, he pulled his sheath knife and frantically cut at his captive ties to the chute. He repeatedly bobbed up for air, lungs burning, using "that air to pray," and sawed first the harness and then the shroud lines. Somerville eventually broke free.

He inflated his life jacket and spotted the nearby raft he had thrown from the plane. The exhausted aviator swam over and struggled his way aboard. He had seen no other chute as his canopy deployed and his plane plunged into the water. His back-seater, Louis Jakubec, must have gone down with it. Alone in Kagoshima Bay, catching his breath, he could do nothing further but wait and watch as four Hellcats from *Hancock* circled overhead. The Hellcats made it clear they were there to protect Somerville until help could arrive. Two flew low over him with the other two higher up for top cover.

Any reassurance Somerville felt quickly faded as he spotted eight Japanese Zeros flying along the east side of the bay. One spotted him and peeled off, heading directly toward the raft. Somerville thought, *I got out of the last spot, but maybe this is the real one.* The Hellcats also spotted the Zeros, added power, and charged in to attack—four against eight over a lone man on the water.

* * *

Aboard *Astoria*, Captain Dyer received the order to launch for rescue, which would again send *Astoria*'s aviators out from their stand-by status. This time Jack Newman and Don Comb received the call. The pair catapulted at 9:47 a.m. and formed up with their fighter rescue cover to head into the bay and retrieve the man. The *Astoria* planes brought quite an escort toward pitched battle—twenty-four fighter planes from *Hancock*, *Cabot*, and *Bataan*.

Approaching the recovery site seventy miles up into Kagoshima Bay, Comb observed splashes in the water—planes being shot down. The four *Hancock* fighters covering their downed comrade had been set upon by enemy Zeros. Comb realized he and Newman were flying into an active dogfight. Despite their Kingfishers having no combat capability, they pressed on into the bay and spotted a dye marker.

The battle over Somerville raged. He had seen "a real fight" from the water. "They milled all over the sky. It seemed unreal to me, sitting in that little raft. That Jap that had dropped down to look me over went out early." At one point Somerville saw a Hellcat chasing a Zero, with another Zero on the Hellcat's tail, with another American fighter on him, another Zero on the second F6F, and yet another Hellcat on the third Zero, all in line. The American pilots proved superior, and within minutes five of the eight Japanese planes had been shot down.

Somerville observed one Japanese pilot bail out nearby, splash, and inflate his own raft. He figured, "This would beat it all, a naval engagement, rubber raft to raft, with a Jap in Kagoshima Bay." The event never materialized, for the enemy pilot disappeared from view.

Two more enemy planes joined the fracas. The *Hancock*, *Cabot*, and *Bataan* rescuers powered up to jump in and relieve Somerville's protectors as *Astoria*'s pilots put down and went to work. Newman took the lead and dropped his plane, splashing its floats into the water and taxiing up to the aviator in a life raft. He could see that the man was struggling and exhausted. Newman climbed from the cockpit onto the main float and reached out for the man in the raft, managing to grab his hand. With much effort he pulled a soaked Pete Somerville up and helped him into the rear seat of the plane.

Somerville looked at Newman and said, "Mister, what's your name? 'Cause I'm gonna remember it for a very long time."

"I'm Jack Newman, from Battle Creek, Michigan." Always the first offering, Newman handed him a cigarette.

With fighters still engaging overhead, Newman throttled up the Kingfisher and took off from the water to get out of the fray as quickly as the slow floatplane could manage. *Leave the Japanese planes to the agile Hellcats and Corsairs.*

A veteran of USS *Enterprise* and *Intrepid* before his air group operated from *Hancock*, Lieutenant Junior Grade Pete Somerville had ditched once before, and quite recently at that. On March 18, the first day of strikes in Operation Iceberg, his entire flight ran out of fuel returning from their Kyushu mission. Multiple planes splashed short of *Hancock*, leaving Somerville and others to be rescued by destroyers. With two destroyed aircraft over two weeks, Somerville climbed aboard Newman's

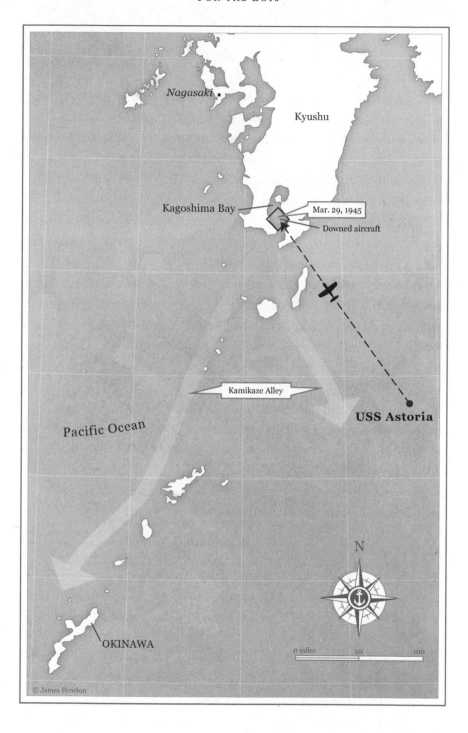

Nagasaki ∎

Kyushu

Kagoshima Bay

Mar. 29, 1945

Downed aircraft

Kamikaze Alley

USS Astoria

Pacific Ocean

N

OKINAWA

© James Fenelon

0 miles   50   100

gooney bird a charmed man, plucked from what he called the "Japanese birdbath." A harsh footnote was the loss of his radioman Jakubec.

In the other *Astoria* plane, Comb circled the splash areas at the entrance to Kagoshima Bay. Flying at five hundred feet, he looked through the canopy to see a twin-engine bomber flying wing to him. *We don't have twin-engine bombers out here.* He recognized the outline of an enemy Frances. Comb could see into the cockpit very clearly, the pilot with goggles up on his leather helmet. In short order two Corsairs of Comb's fighter escort pounced, sending the bomber down with flames trailing from both engines. Other planes of the group scoured the bay for any additional survivor, but found no dye marker, no sign of Jakubec. Jack Newman brought their sole survivor out.

Retiring from the bay, one division of escort Corsairs received permission from the flight leader to make strafing passes over an observed seaplane base nearby, a target of opportunity to destroy some more Japanese planes. During their second pass, one Corsair took hits in the belly tank and burst into flames. As he headed south out of the bay, the pilot dropped the tank but his plane continued to burn. He descended and bailed out of the cockpit, leaving the Corsair to splash unmanned.

Comb observed the Corsair pilot bail out, "so low that his chute had barely opened when he hit the water." He landed his Kingfisher and taxied up to find the man struggling under his silk canopy, in serious danger of drowning. Comb maneuvered in close, leapt from the cockpit, and worked to reel in the parachute shroud lines until the flailing Corsair aviator was able to reach an outboard float. Traumatized, the man clung to the floatplane's strut and called out, "Take me home!"

Comb replied, "You've got to get in the rear cockpit!" The pair worked together to get the soaked man up and into the back seat before taking back to the air. Once aloft, Comb learned he had recovered Ensign David Kelleher from USS *Cabot.* He also learned that Kelleher had ingested a lot of seawater, for the man began to vomit. Comb would recall, "He threw up again and again. It all landed in the bilge, and on a Kingfisher, the draft is all from back to front. The smell was a little rough."

A running battle with Japanese Zeros worked its way south toward the fast carriers as the slow, burdened floatplanes headed back to *Astoria*. Once within close range of the task group, a voice came over the radio directing Comb and Newman to veer off. The final Japanese pursuers were destroyed by gunfire from ships in the group, and both floatplanes were successfully brought back aboard along with the recovered men in the early afternoon. Corpsmen threw blankets over both retrieved pilots and walked them to sick bay for evaluation, where they were deemed in good condition. A shot of Old Grand-Dad bourbon worked wonders.

Fred Lind wrote, "These were anything but pleasure flights... The pilots and the rescued pilots always get an enthusiastic welcome aboard... Kingfishers are not known for their speed and elusiveness. Setting a big target down in enemy bays is no picnic. These guys have guts, and countless downed pilots owe their lives to cruiser gooney bird pilots. To complicate matters, some of the rescuees are shot up. Others are dead. It is one of the toughest jobs aboard ship, and the entire crew is extremely proud of our pilots."

The "Battle of Kagoshima Bay" marked the first time a surface rescue was ever performed in inland Japanese waters. Of Somerville, *Hancock* sent to *Astoria*, "The whole ship cannot give your pilots a hand that is big enough. A more than excellent job done in a more than excellent manner." For Kelleher, *Cabot* added, "Greatly appreciate your rescue of our pilot." Proud of his aviators, Captain Dyer put both of them in for Distinguished Flying Crosses.

That night John Arrighi wrote, "We got the dope today on our next objective, Okinawa Jima. We had heard rumors about it but this is straight dope. L-Day (invasion landing) is set for April 1, Our battle wagons are over there now shelling the beach day and night." With *Kamikaze* bases reduced, the Fast Carrier Task Force's next mission would be direct support of the invasion of Okinawa on Easter Sunday.

Reports of Japanese fleet units were the sole reason the task group had been ordered away from Okinawa. The goliath Japanese battleship *Yamato* still lay out there somewhere, along with remaining portions of the fleet.

16

Casualties of War

Giving up your pie at meal time is tantamount to
giving your girlfriend's address to a shipmate.
Thank you, Main Battery. Now how about your
girlfriend's address?

-*USS* Astoria *Fire Controlman Fred Lind*
in April 1945

Philippine Sea, 50 miles east of Okinawa, Area Eagle, day 19 at sea
April 1, 1945

B ack in February, Task Group 58.3's Rear Admiral Ted Sherman
wrote in his private diary, "Ho hum, the war is getting pretty mundane as far as we carriers are concerned." March had proven this notion
wrong with four carriers off the line. The Okinawa invasion, Operation
Iceberg, brought the likelihood of more carnage. Following D-Day in
Normandy, a name popularized in the Western press, the term had become so associated with the invasion of Europe that it had been retired
and replaced. "L-Day," for Landing Day at Okinawa, came off on Easter
Sunday, April 1, with American landings largely unopposed.

Astoria went to general quarters at dawn alert as planes launched across
the group. While the carrier aircraft struck Okinawa targets and four
Army and Marine divisions went ashore, the men of the Mighty Ninety

found themselves with very little to do. No counterattacks emerged as reports rolled in; the ship never even took air emergency stations for any inbounds. In his Gregg shorthand diary Fred Lind wrote,

> It was a combination of Easter Sunday for us and April Fool's Day for the Japs. We even had time for church and communion. The Easter meal was very good... Reports came in this morning that the landings were successful, and two airfields had been taken. The Jap strategy seems to have changed, falling back to establish strong positions inland, and not opposing landings. It at least was allowing us to get organized ashore before all hell broke loose. I'm sure Okinawa will be no cake walk...
>
> Our job was to provide an umbrella for the landing forces and the transport ships. They were very vulnerable when anchored for disembarking troops and equipment. The faster they got unloaded and out of port, the safer they were. Air attacks of any kind slowed things down, so if we could do the job of intercepting raids and caught them before they arrived at the harbor, we could facilitate matters for the landing forces.

The next day brought resupply for the Fast Carrier Task Force. Despite photos from Herman Schnipper and film shot by Walter Duggan, images simply couldn't capture the ferocity of resupply—the urgent efficiency, one ship casting off and moving away with the next in line moving in. Every minute counted when a task group was at its most vulnerable. Deck hands who manned the guns at quarters instead put their full weight into keeping lines taut, hauling pallets of supplies and barrels of fuel across. Mini-storms emerged between two ships forty feet apart traveling at more than 20 knots, manmade breakers and rolling of the ships bringing masts and antennae perilously close to one another. On April 2, such operations proved to be even significantly harder by strong wind and heaving seas. Yet no enemy planes appeared.

The ship also received bags of mail. For Herb Blodgett, delivered mail and dispatches brought a double-whammy of bad news. While he had aced his exam for advancement in rate, he had not received any notification, unlike others around him. Now he had the answer. The Bureau of Personnel had made a decision not to let motor machinist mates (diesel engines) change rates to machinist mates (steam). Blodgett found himself stuck with practical experience in a role where the Navy would not let him qualify for a higher rank and more pay.

Engineering officer Simon made the decision to transfer Blodgett from the engine room to A (Auxiliary) Division. After more than two years in a role aboard first *Boise* and then *Astoria*, he would finally be a diesel man, which he was initially trained for yet had forgotten everything about. He would essentially have to start from scratch.

Further, Blodgett received a letter from Betty ending their engagement. Her family was moving away from West Concord, and as devout Catholics they didn't want her marrying a Protestant boy anyway. Betty was out of his life, leaving him devastated.

The icing on the cake became his new assignment to the aft diesel auxiliary engine on watch. Accustomed to wearing a telephone headset and feeding updates from topside to the other men, working a throttle in his engine room and surrounded by fellow engineering sailors, this change in role would place him waiting to operate an auxiliary diesel engine only needed in time of emergency. As the only man in the compartment, ready if needed, Herb Blodgett would stand watch utterly alone.

* * *

Returning for further air strikes over Okinawa on April 3, Captain Dyer cautioned his crew about complacency toward the enemy in his morning address: "During the last few days we have had very little attention from the Japanese. I want to express a word of warning, however. The amphibious forces around Okinawa have had considerable attention from the Jap aircraft. *Kamikaze* pilots have been thicker than bees around a sugar bowl…As we move closer to Okinawa to provide close air support, it is essential that our lookouts and our combat team give their very best attention to locating any Japanese planes that may show up…We must not relax our vigilance because we haven't had any action during the last week."

Acutely aware that men were fighting ashore as *Astoria* steamed without event, men still recorded such monotony. Fred Lind wrote,

> Regular routine, with reveille at 4 a.m., launching of flights, and all-day sessions at our Battle Stations, followed by Condition Watches at night. We sure were getting fresh air! It was funny how very few crew members we became involved with.
>
> The only people we saw were those on our Battle Stations or Watch Stations. When we ever did get to our sleeping quarters, everyone was sacked out. We didn't even see the reveille Petty Officer, because the horn was three feet above my head on the bulkhead, and it blasted us out of the sack for Air Emergencies, General Quarters, or for any reason that pops into the Captain's mind. That boatswain's whistle pierced your eardrums, and the bugler walloped you out of your sack. The anti-aircraft personnel slept with their clothes on, and cleared out of the compartment immediately. The Main Battery grumbled about the damn Japs, but learned how to fall right back to sleep. Usually their terminology was not that polite.

* * *

Philippine Sea, 160 miles southeast of Okinawa, day 24 at sea
April 6, 1945

Astoria Captain George Dyer's predicted counterattacks began with dawn raid launches; the enemy knew quite well by then where the fast carriers were operating. Combat Air Patrol did their effective work in destroying inbound planes until overwhelmed by targets in the noon hour. At air emergency, *Astoria* opened fire at 12:26 p.m. Duggan and Schnipper were up in their searchlight platform to capture a plane that barely missed USS *Cabot* as the light carrier made an emergency turn. *Cabot's* maneuver worked, and she barely evaded a hit as the plane overshot.

Also watching for once was Herb Blodgett. With his new role, his air emergency station changed. He might stand watch, which really amounted to sitting and reading books in a lonely compartment, but under attack he was now assigned to damage control topside, where he could after long months actually see what was happening.

Within minutes another enemy plane dove on *Cabot*, which again went into emergency maneuvering. Blodgett watched as *Astoria's* 5-inch battery fired in thunderous claps, thick flak bursts surrounding the aircraft as it made its suicide plunge. The suicide plane overshot its mark, again narrowly missing the flight deck of *Cabot*. The plane's left wingtip clipped the ship's SK "bedspring" radar and tore away sections of its cables, knocking the sensitive array out of commission.

As *Cabot* completed her emergency turn and swung clear of the attack, two friendly 5-inch rounds from a flat trajectory slammed into the stern of the ship beyond her—USS *Pasadena*. Both rounds detonated against the cruiser's aviation crane, which had been raised for her responsibilities in the day's search and rescue rotation. The boom of the crane blew apart, sending metal fragments spiraling as far forward as the ship's forecastle. The crane's pulley assembly crashed to the deck along with severed electric and hydraulic cables. Shrapnel ripped into sailors and Marines manning the 20mm mounts surrounding the crane.

The scene horrified Blodgett as he learned what a topside view looked like. Far worse, the rounds came from his vantage point—*Astoria. My God, we fired one burst too long. One too many. We might have killed some people.*

Armitage could see quite plainly what had happened—yet another friendly fire incident. Not only had men clearly been hit, but a fellow VCS-17 rescue team had been knocked out due to the loss of their recovery crane. He immediately moved and relieved the Sky Aft officer for what he felt was "panicking under fire and causing damage and casualties to an adjacent ship as a consequence." The man had failed to cut off fire in time to avoid hitting another ship. It proved to be the final attack of the day, allowing *Astoria*'s leadership to regroup.

As the day closed, Dyer, Armitage, and gun boss Ken Meneke discussed the friendly fire issue. The 5-inch guns had emerged as a big problem across the fleet. While quite accurate as dual-purpose weapons for both surface and antiaircraft fire, Japanese *Kamikaze* tactics changed the calculus. Enclosed inside the gun mount, the gunners themselves certainly couldn't see their target, and the guns were directed by fire controlmen like Fred Lind and Jim Thomson training their sights on a diving enemy plane as they followed its path. Knowing when to cut off required a split-second decision subject to human sensory limitations. The result of this combination of factors kept putting ordnance downrange into fellow US Navy ships.

After USS *Enterprise* was knocked off the line, *Astoria* took friendly hits herself and then she tragically fired into *Pasadena*, the *Astoria* officers had seen enough. Captain Dyer recalled how he had addressed a gunnery problem aboard USS *Biscayne* back in Salerno. The group agreed to station an officer behind each 5-inch fire controlman to watch the background and squeeze the man's shoulder to cease fire once their field of fire was fouled by friendlies. There could be no more of this.

Astoria men were not the only sailors and Marines to keep secret diaries; *Pasadena* men did as well. Wrote Marine Darwin Lewis,

> We were hit in the fantail with two five-inch shells. Since the fantail is my battle station I was surrounded

with shrapnel. Another landed within two feet of me. So I dived for what little cover I could get. I was hit in the arm and three places in the leg but not bad. Two of my buddies back there were seriously hurt. One lost a leg, don't know if he will live, another lost four fingers on right hand, hit in head and neck also in hip. Don't know if he will live.

All but one out of around ten of us were hit but not bad. The first thing I did when the first shell hit was to pray and I think the Lord was with me. I hope I never have to experience a sight like that again. The boy with the leg shot off was still conscious and crawling around but nobody could help him because shrapnel was still falling. The tail caught fire and he was in the center. We didn't know to run or remain on stations because of gas and ammo stores there. But we remained.

Seaman 1st Class Frank "Ski" Lapinski had borne the brunt of the impact. Falling steel tore one leg from his body and crushed his lower abdomen. Marine Private Louis Lepere lost the four fingers of his right hand and suffered head trauma. In total six men were hit by shrapnel, including Darwin Lewis.

Later Lewis added to his diary, "Ski came from Connecticut. Just got married. Died at 11:09 p.m." The cause of death was listed as "compound comminuted fracture at left upper leg and partial avulsion." He bled out and would be buried at sea the following morning.

* * *

April 7 brought a new day, a new gunnery methodology, and almost assuredly new attacks. The *Kamikaze* activity of February and March had been almost sporadic by comparison; now it grew systematic and every man knew it.

From his position in fire control, Fred Lind wrote of *Kamikaze* patterns that had clearly emerged. "Most suicide attacks were vertical dives starting at 10,000 feet, generally with the plane suddenly appearing in view when penetrating through a covering cloud directly overhead. Others came in at water level, threaded through ships in the formation, arriving at a carrier, and taking a tight loop, diving into the deck of the carrier. These were obviously more skilled pilots, and the attacks were difficult to shoot down because of fouled range."

He also noted, "Ranks and ratings disappeared in battle conditions, where everyone was in the same boat. The focus was not on internal affairs, but the issue became the enemy, and each and every man was totally absorbed in his job to protect the fleet and our ship."

Of the previous day, John Arrighi found a bright side. He wrote, "We got credit for two assists today. The planes of the *Essex* alone reported splashing 52 Jap planes in our vicinity... They were sent out to intercept the planes going to Okinawa Jima. I suppose the planes that came after us were sent from the main body... Our task group today accounted for 245 Jap planes."

The morning of April 7 brought all eyes to a Japanese naval force sortieing for Okinawa, assembled in formation around superbattleship *Yamato*. Her class included the heaviest battleships in the world with enormous 18-inch main guns. While Admiral Halsey had long eyed her as a supreme prize, now Admiral Mitscher's task force held the opportunity to sink her in his stead. Search planes had reported contact southwest of Kyushu. With the window of opportunity to wreck the remaining Japanese fleet, Mitscher launched everything he had available—fully loaded Helldiver dive-bombers and Avenger torpedo bombers—covered by Hellcat and Corsair fighter cover. Combat Air Patrol would remain airborne around his task groups, but coverage would be thin. Most planes would be devoted to the mission, so *Astoria* and her surrounding escort ships would have to primarily cover the carriers.

Just after noon, with the fleet's air cover more than two hundred miles northwest, inbound bogeys were reported like clockwork. John Arrighi wrote, "Seems the Japs always come out after us at chow time. A Jap Zero comes in high on starboard beam and dives on carrier *Hancock*. He comes in so fast that there wasn't much flak sent up."

Stepping away from his new station, Herb Blodgett was en route to the engineer's head forward when the plane came in. With new orders in place to prevent firing into friendly ships, *Astoria*'s guns remained silent. The plane dropped low and firing carried a high risk of hitting another ship. "Nobody could shoot!" Blodgett later recalled. "I saw him come in right around broadside and fly right into the hangar deck of the *Hancock*." Protecting American ships from friendly fire clearly traded off with vulnerability to enemy attack. While *Astoria*'s guns did not hit *Hancock*, nor did any other American ship's in the task group, the Zero did.

The plane exploded on the flight deck near the carrier's forward elevator, bringing a thunderclap over the water. Men aboard ships from all sides watched, helpless. John Arrighi wrote, "The carrier seemed to burst into solid flame. Heavy black smoke rolled out and covered the ship completely." For *Astoria* men, despite their experiences covering *Essex*, protecting *Franklin*, seeing *Enterprise* hit, and watching in horror as their own rounds hit *Pasadena*, this was the first time they had ever seen an actual successful *Kamikaze* strike.

Smoke belched from *Hancock*, engulfing the ship as her damage control crews scrambled to fight fires. A black column soon filled the sky. From 1,700 yards away, again covering *Essex*, there was simply nothing *Astoria* men could do but watch. From his 20mm mount John Arrighi would write, "Looked like she was lost but repair party worked very well and had the fire completely out in a half hour. She left the formation for a while and went into separate maneuvers during the fire fight in order to use the wind to her advantage." The firefighting school men had attended across stateside naval bases paid off: *Hancock*'s damage control crews managed her fires despite the initial look of things. Still, the carrier would have to be evaluated for operational capability and it likely meant yet another aircraft carrier knocked off the line for extensive repair.

Herman Schnipper photographed the blaze from their distance, again lamenting his lack of higher-quality optics. Walter Duggan stood along-side, filming in color for the Navy as *Hancock* blazed. The smoke formed an overhead screen that other carriers took advantage of, moving under-neath for concealment from any other inbound planes. *Pasadena* steered into the wake of *Hancock*. Although a cruiser wasn't suited for plucking men who had been thrown or jumped overboard, and there were many, her deckside crew tossed life jackets and dye markers in the hopes that a following destroyer could retrieve the men.

Aboard *Astoria*, exhausted men remained at stations as the task group performed emergency turns to conceal their heading, "seldom staying on one course for more than five minutes." The CAP, thin as it might be, performed its job "intercepting the enemy aircraft and destroy-ing them" during the concentrated attack. Yet at 2:20 p.m., another Zeke managed to break through, and the suicide pilot set on *Essex* once again.

During the two-hour respite between inbound bogeys, Fred Lind had elected to remain at his air emergency station, fully expecting more action despite not being on watch. He guessed correctly, for he sat in Sky Aft reading a magazine when a plane was spotted—another Zero. *Astoria's* 5-inch battery erupted, guns elevated near his position.

Lind wrote, "I had no battle helmet or battle telephones on, and the concussion blew me from one side of Sky Aft to the other. The five-inch twin mounts fire every three seconds, so I made numerous trips back and forth across Sky Aft." The forties also opened up as the plane crossed *Astoria's* stern in a shallow dive, this time aimed at *Essex*.

The *Astoria* war diary reflected the outcome: "The *Astoria* scored a five-inch hit on the Zeke, which after dropping its bomb abeam of the *Essex*, crashed flaming into the sea off the *Essex'* starboard bow. *Astoria* claims destruction of this plane." Once again, both bomb and plane missed the carrier *Astoria* protected. Lind came to his feet reeling: "The wind had been blowing, and I had a firm grip on the magazine. When firing stopped, I looked down at the magazine, and the top half was gone, destroyed by the concussion."

Down on the ship's fantail at his 20mm gun mount, John Arrighi received a much more up-close view of the aftermath, seeing his first dead Japanese who had attempted to bail out. "We passed the body of the pilot by not more than 30 feet. His parachute was open. He looked very young and little, almost like a boy—he was dead. About 200 yards out from him was another man in the water alive and waving. Never found out for sure who he was but we think he was one of the men from the *Hancock* who had gone overboard when the ship got hit."

Near 3 p.m. the task group carriers commenced aircraft recovery from their raid to huge celebration regarding the outcome. The proverbial white whale, IJN *Yamato*, had been sunk by bombs and torpedo hits. "Japan's largest!" wrote Arrighi. "Two cruisers and a destroyer—leaving three destroyers burning and three undamaged." Turning to a somber note he added, "Haven't heard of our losses yet in planes nor the number of men lost on the *Hancock*...Many men from the *Hancock* jumped over the side during the fire, and destroyers were sent out to pick them up." He later added, "*Hancock* losses were 28 killed, 52 injured, 15 missing. Had an idea they were very lucky—it surely looked bad over there."

Fred Lind's tone in his Gregg diary painted a similar bittersweet reflection on the day's turn of events: "Here we are with surface fleets that could wipe out anything the Japanese Navy could put up against us, and the Japs are destroyed without ever getting a salvo fired at our ships! Such is the power of carrier forces. The table is turned, and now they are on the funky end of the stick. We can place planes within comfortable range and bomb them out of the water. Their carriers have been sunk, their pilots and planes have been decimated, and the ball is in our court."

Lind closed with thoughts regarding the *Hancock* crew. "These were men blown overboard, or those who jumped to escape flaming gasoline on the flight deck. It was a sickening sight to watch it burn. I couldn't sleep when I finally hit the sack."

Resistance had also picked up ashore as the invasion force made progress deeper into Okinawa, and by the evening of April 7 it grew apparent that the services of the fast carriers would be required for an extended period of time. Despite two more wounded carriers moving out of action for repair, Admiral Mitscher decided to place his remaining task groups into a rotation—two on the line at any time as the third retired for rest, resupply, and repair. While this ensured a constant presence in air cover for the invasion, albeit heavily weakened, Task Group 58.3 wasn't going to receive relief anytime soon. They were slated last in the rotation.

* * *

Refueling rendezvous off Okinawa, day 27 at sea
April 9, 1945

Beyond the typical spectacle of refueling and resupply, scuttlebutt buzzed. The men of the Mighty Ninety packed the weather deck and manned lines to bring a familiar face back aboard—Rousseau Lemon. Following a lengthy transit across the Pacific from ship to ship, the original *Astoria* boatswain's mate was hauled aboard via highline after his six months of trying to work the Navy system. Captain Dyer's efforts to bring him back aboard had been successful.

Lemon met glowering faces. Where once neophyte boots had seen him as a leader, now a battle-hardened, galvanized crew received him back aboard. He had not lost his rate, and the man had barely even been punished through loss of pay for his second act of desertion.

Captain Dyer directed the men to bring him to the bridge upon arrival. The skipper studied his returned crewman and said, "Well you're back." Dyer viewed the sailor as a "line petty officer deserting in time of war," and "legally beyond any punishment that I might be able to assign him." The captain told him, "Whatever treatment your shipmates give you, that's what you're gonna get as far as this ship is concerned." Dyer then spoke over the ship's loudspeaker and informed the entire crew of Lemon's return. He informed them that there could be no other official punishment for the man. "I have assigned him where none of you will be under his command," Dyer stated, "because I think he's unfit for command."

Rousseau Lemon, still qualified in antiaircraft gunnery, was assigned to the 5th Division, starboard side 40mm cannons. The captain then assigned Lemon to oversee the boatswain's gear storage space. His newly returned petty officer might serve on a quad-40 mount at air emergency stations, but he would have no charge over a single crew member, a de facto demotion for a petty officer like Lemon.

Captain Dyer had essentially turned Rousseau Lemon out to his shipmates for whatever they saw fit. The crew immediately responded by not even speaking to him. The men he returned to were not the same ones he had left; boys he had once regaled with tales of combat in the South Pacific were now salty combat veterans of the Philippines, typhoons, Iwo Jima, and so on. They had spent the past three weeks repelling Japanese suicide attacks and just saw one of their carriers badly hit two days prior. To the men of the Mighty Ninety, Lemon was now a man who had cut and run when the rest of them went to war together. Boatswain's Mate 2nd Class Rousseau Lemon found himself with no friends aboard a taut, tightknit ship that was effectively protecting her charges and dropping enemy planes. Not everything about the Navy could be found in *The Bluejackets' Manual*.

The accompanying mail brought further action on the part of the Bureau of Personnel. The chief of naval personnel had sent a memo to all continental naval districts, illustrating the wide range of punishments administered to men who missed sailing with *Astoria*, from prison sentences down to probation. The memo scathed: "The above shows that the spirit and letter of the Bureau's directives are not being fully carried out... The only complaints received from the fleet have been the laxity of the shore establishments in enforcing it. That these complaints have been justified is well supported in the case of the USS *Astoria* CL-90. Such laxity endangers the state of discipline and morale in the fleet."

If Lemon had been gaming the system, so had the 8th Naval District in New Orleans. So overwhelmed were they with court-martial cases, they were reducing sentences just to clear the docket. Their brigs were overflowing and they merely wanted men out of their queue, not realizing the vicious cycle their lenience created. The bureau directed additional officers to New Orleans to expand their court and manage their caseload properly.

Rousseau Lemon had lucked into discovery of this sequence of perverse incentives and capitalized. Now he managed an equipment locker off Okinawa in combat conditions, a pariah to 1,300 men.

* * *

Strike Day over Okinawa, day 29 at sea
April 11, 1945

Fully four weeks into Operation Iceberg, the tedium of routine weighed on men as heavily as any other stressor. Every morning brought general quarters at dawn alert. Then back and forth, up and down ladders, returning to stations to don helmets and flak suits as bogeys were picked up on radar. As food supplies dwindled and hours at emergency stations increased, men were reduced to eating K rations, simple combat packs of food, at air emergency. *So much for the "ice cream service branch,"* thought Fred Lind.

Heavy clouds and limited visibility meant assured attacks, and men stood antsy at their posts. At 1:45 p.m., USS *Alaska* reported from another task group what appeared to be a "major attack" developing. Two groups of planes, one estimated at four to six planes, the other at about ten, closing from sixty miles to the north. Shortly before, Combat Air Patrol over Kikaijima had reported many planes in that area. Once again men scrambled to their air emergency stations. Then a third group was picked up, heading in from the northeast. *This could be big, stand by to repel pending air attack.*

The first Zeke to penetrate the formation screamed in at 2:05 p.m. USS *South Dakota* opened up across the formation, and the plane dropped in flames astern of *Enterprise*—a near miss. A second *Kamikaze* Zeke fell burning astern of *Bunker Hill* moments later. While the carrier steamed in *Astoria*'s sector of the formation, she checked her fire due to the updated coordination system. Her bearing was fouled and the risk of firing into a friendly ship too great. On radar picket station at the perimeter of the formation, the destroyer *Kidd* reported being hit low on her hull to starboard by a suicide dive-bomber and severely damaged.

Throughout the afternoon, there was never a time that bogeys weren't within fifty miles of them. Enemy planes in the mass attack penetrated the surrounding air cover, and once inside the American formation many guns would be out of action due to both range and the concern over friendly fire. All indicators suggested *Astoria*'s Task Group 58.3 was again set to bear the brunt.

At 2:14 p.m. it was *Essex*'s turn yet again. Another Zeke, diving on *Astoria*'s charge. The Mighty Ninety blasted away, this time accompanied by sister WASP Division cruiser *Pasadena*. With the sky a mottled black and gray from flak bursts, the Zeke spiraled out of control and crashed within fifty yards of *Pasadena*'s quarter, sending up tremendous ocean spray over the maneuvering ship. Despite more intruders, the fire management by sector appeared to be working.

From the searchlight platform he had adopted, Herman Schnipper smiled to himself, as much about the successful defense as the photographs he was capturing. While he might be exposed on deck, he held a unique role in no assigned air emergency station—just get the best angle. Weighted down with his flak suit and helmet, he cycled his camera once again...and his jaw dropped when he turned to see the chaplain standing behind him.

Wearing no protective gear, the padre had climbed up to the platform to watch. A shutterbug by nature, Al Lusk wanted to see combat for once and discuss Schnipper's equipment with him. Schnipper stood aghast, knowing how many more bogeys were inbound. Yet he was an enlisted man, far from able to tell an officer what to do.

At 2:59 p.m. *Astoria* again opened fire on an inbound Zeke. Her range and bearing clear of friendlies, she joined other ships across the task group pounding away at the bandit with forties and 5-inch. The plane crashed close aboard *Enterprise*, missing its target but throwing debris onto the forward flight deck in a heavy explosion. F6F Hellcats ready on the Big E's catapults began to burn. Schnipper saw men scramble across the bow section of the ship and launch the burning planes pilotless into the ocean to stop the fires. Throughout, Lusk, the ship's "jack of all faiths," crouched behind Schnipper akin to a baseball umpire behind a catcher.

Aft of Schnipper and Lusk, Fred Lind and Gerard Armitage had access to reports from the task force commander, intercepted and translated from the Japanese air coordinator frequency. Lind wrote, "We intercepted a message indicating that the Japs were on their way to attack with suicide planes…we intercepted raids coming in about fifty miles from our formation.…Despite many clouds and limited visibility, our anti-aircraft fire was marvelous. Eleven planes attacked, diving straight at the carriers. Not one of them got through to even drop a bomb! It was the most devastating fire I have ever seen! Many friendly shells burst directly over our head."

From his perch on the open bridge, Captain Dyer would later recall, "two planes that got very close to the ship, headed right for us very obviously *Kamikaze*-bent. We destroyed one of them when it was about 1,000 yards from the ship where it exploded and disappeared. The other one came boring in, burning all over, but still coming on. It got in about 300 yards from the ship. It got inside the range where your five-inch shell explodes. Everything in the ship, of course, was shooting at it…It splattered the ship with all kinds of machine gun bullets until the very last minute. They were shooting at us, they had good aim, they couldn't have much else."

Schnipper tracked the plane with his camera as it crossed over the bow starboard to port and he snapped an image. The photographer shifted his position across the platform and Chaplain Lusk stayed right there with him, umpire and catcher. The plane aimed for *Bunker Hill*. *Astoria's* starboard battery checked their fire as her portside guns took over. Just as the Zero lined up for a run on the carrier, *Astoria's* 6th Division gunners found their mark. Flashes of light and pops of smoke danced across the wings and fuselage where 40mm shells tore into the plane.

The Japanese pilot realized he would not make it to *Bunker Hill* under such murderous fire and pinwheeled the stricken plane back toward *Astoria*, trading a carrier for a cruiser. John Arrighi and *Astoria*'s fellow Marines opened up with their 20mm machine guns. *Bunker Hill* also opened fire as the Zero closed the distance on his new target. In a moment that many men would later recall as feeling personal, *where the plane appeared headed at them individually*, Schnipper stood his ground and framed his next photograph.

Astoria's guns struck the plane a fatal blow and it heeled over, falling toward the sea. *Bunker Hill* fired another burst as it fell. "Get down!" the chaplain yelled. He leapt onto Schnipper just as the photographer tripped the camera shutter. The two men landed in a heap on the platform. A low 5-inch shell from *Bunker Hill* struck *Astoria*'s aft stack and exploded, showering the pair with shrapnel in a thunderclap. A plume of water splashed down where the Zero struck the surface. Smoke drifted skyward from gun barrels on both American ships. All fell silent.

Collecting himself, Schnipper struggled out from under a groaning Chaplain Lusk. The padre was hit, and bad. The photographer scrambled to his feet, leaned over the platform railing, and called down for a corpsman. Within an eternity of seconds one of *Astoria*'s pharmacist's mates worked his way up a ladder to the searchlight platform, his medical pack slung over his shoulder. Still in full flak gear, the corpsman tended to Lusk as he lay on the metal decking. With no flak suit, Lusk had been vulnerable and exposed. Schnipper took a photograph of the pair, a study in contrast of protective armor: the corpsman in helmet, goggles, flash hood, and flak gear, holding thick gloves as he checked the pulse of the chaplain clothed only in officer's shirt and coat. Only then did Schnipper realize he himself had also been hit by slivers of steel in his face.

The chaplain had a pulse, but shock was setting in. He had shrapnel lodged in his back near his spine and urgently needed surgery. Schnipper and the corpsman gingerly lifted Lusk and wrapped him in the medic's hooded jacket to control shivering in the stiff wind. They worked with men on the boat deck below to rig a boatswain's chair from rope. From a deck below, Walter Duggan, the fleet photographer, rolled his Bell & Howell and captured color footage of the team lowering Lusk from the searchlight platform. Lusk managed to work his hands and feet down the rungs of the ladder, his weight supported by the men above and below, his olive hood and jacket whipping in the wind.

As Schnipper and Duggan filmed the chaplain's drama in the late afternoon, the lookouts and fire controlmen tracked another bandit. At 4:16 p.m., the Zero passed low between *Astoria* and *Enterprise*. The Mighty Ninety gunners checked their fire so as not to shoot into *Enterprise*, their gun mounts swiveling, trained on the plane. Thomson, Lind, and the gunners received their first up-close view of their enemy, a Japanese pilot. He had neither requisite eyeglasses nor prominent front teeth so common in countless racist propaganda drawings. Instead behind the canopy, goggles, and scarf lay young eyes trained back toward *Astoria*'s men and her guns leading him, the eyes of a terrified boy who knew his fate. Yet the hard reality of a human enemy mattered little to the outcome. As the Zero passed clear of *Enterprise*, *Astoria*'s starboard side battery erupted and tore the plane apart. The pilot bailed out to a partially opened chute as he pancaked into the ocean and ruined metal rained into the sea.

In short order, the ship's senior medical officer, Lieutenant Commander J. H. Keller, approached Captain Dyer on the bridge. Chaplain Lusk had a large piece of shrapnel lodged in his kidney. It had missed his spine by an inch.

At first Dyer thought to transfer him off the ship to a hospital vessel. But Dr. Keller informed the skipper, "The chaplain is just pleading to stay with the ship. He doesn't want to go to a hospital ship and then be transferred home. He wants to stay with the ship. As far as the operation is concerned, I assure you I am perfectly competent to do this operation just as well as it can be done anywhere. I recommend the patient stay with the ship."

While livid with his chaplain for his unapproved shutterbug adventure up in the searchlight platform, Dyer's urgent issue remained the padre's medical condition. He acceded, replying, "You do the operation and we'll keep him." Keller returned to sick bay to prep for the operation. Dyer made a special visit from the bridge to wish the chaplain well and also chew him out heavily for his ill-advised adventure.

* * *

In addition to the standard antiaircraft arrangement for a late-war *Cleveland*-class cruiser, *Astoria* carried an additional weapon: Marine Captain Gerard Armitage's "air-cooled thirty-caliber machine gun borrowed from the aviators." He wrote,

> It works very well and we get to use it a few times on attacking planes within range.
>
> When at General Quarters, because of the *Kamikaze* divers, all air handlers and other power units are shut off; all lighting and fires extinguished. Below decks for damage control are hospitalmen, stewards (stretcher bearers), fire control men and engineers—the sense is one of a darkened tomb. The sounds of battle above echo through the ship.
>
> One salty hospital corpsman was heard to say, "I don't pay much attention when the five-inch mounts go off; I listen real good when the 40s and 20s start to shoot; but I tell you this…when that Marine opens up with that machine gun, it's time to kiss your tail goodbye."

With darkness approaching and Chaplain Lusk being tended to in sick bay, attacks came in unrelenting. With *Essex* listening in on the Japanese frequency, the next round would arrive around 7 p.m. K rations were again distributed to weary men at all stations. In line with expectations, flares began to fall at twilight. All returning American planes back aboard the carriers, the ships of the task group engaged in emergency maneuvers to disrupt their paths.

With darkness the snoopers drew closer. From his regular duty station in Sky Forward, Gerard Armitage recorded one example of the professionalism in fire coordination that had developed aboard *Astoria* through the telephone headsets and talker system:

"Sky Forward from Plot."

"Go ahead Plot."

"We have a bogey at Angels Eight, bearing two-five-zero; range 35. Closing. Over."

"Thank you, Plot. Watch him please. Out."

Thirty minutes later: "Sky Forward from Plot. Bogey still with us. He's all the way up on our port beam. Same Angels, range 20. He's just come about on a heading of one-two-zero. Over."

"Plot from Sky Forward. He's a snooper—probably a flying boat. He's looking for you, chum. If he stays on present course, how close will he come? Over."

From Plot: "Wait one!"

"Sky Forward from Plot. Maintaining present course, bogey will cross our port quarter at approximately twelve miles…he has come down…present Angels Four. Shall I inform bridge? Over."

"Plot—hear me…If he continues on this course, what does snooper see? Over."

Armitage continued. "Sky Forward from Plot. He could spot the fleet's tail end. Over."

"Plot. This snooper knows we're here—he's after a better fix on us. Start tracking him on Fire Control Radar. We may get lucky and pick him up. Negative on informing bridge. Let them sleep."

Within a few minutes, Armitage received the word: "Sky Forward, this is Plot…he turned away. Heading south…out of range. Over."

"Plot, be patient. He may zig again. Sky Two (aft) shift to neutral."

Within minutes, a reply regarding radar tracking came. "Sky Forward from Plot. Bogey has come about. We have him at Angels Three, range 15 and closing. Course zero-eight-eight."

Sky Forward: "Roger Plot. Start solution when snooper is in range."

"Sky Two from Sky Forward. Shift to auto-match pointers. Mounts Four, Five, and Six."

"Sky Forward. We have a perfect solution out at the end of the string."

"Roger Sky Forward."

"Bridge from Sky Forward. Request permission to engage a snooper bearing 190 relative at max range."

By then the bridge watch had woken up Captain Dyer from his cabin. He spoke directly to Armitage in familiar terms. "Good evening, Soldier, commence firing when ready. Over."

Armitage replied, "Good evening, Captain. Snooper is at max ordinate and range. We may wake the Fleet watch for nothing."

"Thank you, Soldier, we understand."

"Sky Two from Forward. Three salvos, commence firing!"

Armitage wrote, "Eternity stalled as 18 five-inch VT rounds expressed into the night. Endless seconds crawled past as the watch crew waited and counted in Sky Plot, in the bowels of the ship, in the stifling confines of mounts four, five, and six, in the armored shell of Sky Two, in the clear cool air of Sky Forward where the Air Defense watch trained their binoculars aft, on the port wing of the bridge," where Captain Dyer observed patiently through binoculars, deep into hours with no rest.

Gerard Armitage observed, "A sudden flash of orange light illumined the sky far to our rear, hard by the stern. The flame arched from the sky, plummeting into the sea, darkness restored."

"Bridge from Sky Forward. Splash one snooper."

"Bridge aye. Thank you, Soldier," came Captain Dyer's reply.

"Sky Plot, Sky Two, mounts four, five, and six from Sky Forward. Scratch your Bogey—he flamed. Well done, we're proud to stand watch with you. Out."

Captain Dyer gave a final response. "Sky Forward from Bridge. For my watch log—did you observe any other vessel firing? Over."

Armitage was proud to give the response. "Bridge—Sky Forward. Negative. This bird was ours. Out." The Mighty Ninety had racked up another plane.

That night Armitage watched the radar in fascination as a solid line of B-29 bombers headed in toward Japanese cities. As well informed as a crewmember could be, Fred Lind wrote of his chaplain, "Stay off searchlight platforms!" John Arrighi chimed in, "The Old Man said 'now he'll have something to pray about.' He isn't supposed to be on the topside anyhow.... Our score today was three down—unknown assists."

He continued, "15 planes made dives at our group—one destroyer was hit killing 20, injuring 40...We had K rations...Most all Japs made it a point of diving at carriers—only taking another when flak becomes so heavy that it is impossible to get through. Today many of them dived on destroyers and cruisers when their first attempt was beaten off. One of them made an unsuccessful try at us and came within 300 yards before we hit him. He then made a steep bank, out of control, nosedived into the water 100 yards out. Everyone breathed again."

* * *

Strike Day over Okinawa, day 31 at sea
April 13, 1945

Three days of strikes had brought precious little sleep, for the harassing attacks continued. So many Japanese planes made it past the protective Combat Air Patrol and into the formation that the ships could barely notate them all in their action reports. Through the course of the week all four cruisers of the WASP Division had evaded near misses as planes dove on them, and any man asked would swear it was coming straight for him. USS *Enterprise*, freshly returned to the group after repairs, had been targeted repeatedly and received yet another blow, again igniting fires on her forward flight deck. No sooner was she back in action than she was in need of further repair and retired for Ulithi.

Perhaps the only positive note regarded Chaplain Lusk; the padre came through his surgery successfully and lay in sick bay recovering. For the rest of the *Astoria* crew, rest could hardly be a consideration. Air emergency station calls by boatswain's whistle and bugle came almost hourly.

Yet men managed to continue writing in their diaries. Fred Lind wrote,

> Friday—Dawn broke on the calmest sea I ever seen in my life—almost smooth as glass—very beautiful and calm day—Sunrise was like a picture... Lucky Friday the 13th... we were plenty tired by this time and didn't give a lot of thought of anything except when we could get some rest.
>
> *Astoria* claimed two planes, one possible, and many assists. The Combat Air Patrol had a field day, but no reports were in yet. With massed targets, they didn't have to chase them all over the place. One of the planes the *Astoria* got was 16,000 yards away when it burst into flames. We had taken it under fire when it was in range, and we were the only ship firing on it. I saw it burst into flames, but we won't get credit for it. No matter, there's one less enemy plane to worry about.
>
> An F6F chased a Zeke right through our formation, with the fleet firing at both of them. That didn't stop the F6F, though, and he stuck with him and finally shot him down... Destroyer *Kidd* was hit by a suicide plane that went right through her. It was a sad sight, but she is still afloat and making 25 knots.

Fellow Fire Controlman Andy Lavin added of his experience with the 5-inch battery, "When we'd finish, I had to have my fingers pulled straight. I'd grab hold of that thing and I'd squeeze down, and the guys in the turret would roll the five-inch shells in there, and as soon as they closed them up, boom. They went off, because I kept the firing pins connected at all times. So all they had to do was shove them in there, and close them up, and instantly they were on the way."

From the bridge, Captain Dyer and gun boss Ken Meneke had to make a quick decision for one plane that had passed through the group with distance opening quickly. As the plane approached the limit of *Astoria's* 5-inch battery, task group commander Ted Sherman radioed, "Rampage, you better save those shells for the next time." Dyer replied, "We have a solution," and the ship maintained firing. Sherman tersely replied, "Rampage, cease fire." In that moment the rounds found their mark and the burning plane spiraled into the ocean. Dyer replied to Sherman, "Flame one Jap." The rear admiral responded, "Congratulations. I'm sorry."

General quarters carried into the evening, and chow was again reduced to K rations. Fred Lind never minded that however, because K rations meant a chocolate bar. "We don't get good stuff like that except in K Rations," he wrote. "At 1900 they came in again, but the Combat Air Patrol had them pinpointed, and knocked them all down. One raid, consisting of three Bettys, was splashed just before sunset. Other raids were shot down before they got to us."

By the late evening, with men already at a demoralized low after three days of attacks, sickening news arrived. President Franklin Delano Roosevelt, the only president many of the crew could ever even remember, had died. John Arrighi spoke for his crew in writing, "It was a shock to all. No one said much about it. Best that way."

17

Tetsu no Ame

Eventually it all works itself into an emotional
tapestry of one dull, dead pattern—yesterday is
tomorrow...and when will we ever stop and God,
I'm so tired.

— *War correspondent Ernie Pyle*

Resupply operations, 330 miles southeast of Okinawa, day 32 at sea
April 14, 1945

With the announcement of the president's death, Fred Lind wrote,
"No news was shocking by this time. Good news or bad news, it
was accepted as fact. None of the guys on our station seemed to know
who the Vice President was. All flags were immediately flown at half-
mast."

Pure fatigue had brought morale to a nadir. From his sick bay bed,
Chaplain Lusk continued to lead services and work to boost spirits.
Between the loss of FDR and his own injuries, he said to the men, "The
Lord plays no favorites." One bright spot came through a form letter
authorized by the Navy that men could sign and send home to their
families, informing them of past operations they had participated in.

Men had developed tips and tricks for their letters home. They learned
to put their name at the bottom of each page, lest a Navy censor mix

up an envelope or lose a portion. Some even numbered each envelope, so their sweetheart would know the sequence even if a date was snipped away by censoring scissors, or if the letters arrived out of order as they commonly did. A "passed by naval censor" stamp with the censoring officer's initials at the center always accompanied the postal cancel on the envelope.

Herman Schnipper circulated pictures in an informational document about a newly discovered guided suicide rocket bomb called an Ohka, found at Okinawa air bases. Fred Lind wrote, "Jeez, I couldn't wait to see one of these. It was hopeful that they would never penetrate our Combat Air Patrol perimeter. One good thing was that the pilot had only one way to go—down. I'll bet the pilot assigned to this was really thrilled, having such a huge bomb all his own to 'fly'! I couldn't understand the Japanese philosophy. First, *Kamikazes*, and then this crazy thing."

Schnipper also continued to develop his photos from the darkroom and discovered something startling: he had captured the exact moment *Bunker Hill* fired the round that hit him and Chaplain Lusk, muzzle flash visible in the frame. The padre tackled him just as he snapped the shutter.

By the end of the week, six of seventeen available American fast carriers were out of action, more than one-third of Admiral Mitscher's striking power. Despite repaired ships returning for duty, the asymmetric nature of *Kamikaze* attacks was proving effective. The Japanese were knocking carriers off the line quicker than replacements could be brought back. The ever-lengthening support of Okinawa frustrated Admiral Spruance and Mitscher, as being tied to the island invasion robbed the fast carriers of their primary advantage of movement. They were quite simply tethered to the area and easy to find. Morale across the Fast Carrier Task Force continued to dip and was at its worst with Sherman's men. The "hard luck" group drew another short straw: Spruance decided to rotate the groups back to anchorage for rest and resupply, and Sherman would be last in the rotation. A dog-tired Joey Fubar reflected the attitudes of the men in his comics.

By this time the ship's newspapers printed aboard the admiral's flagship *Pasadena* and that of *Astoria* had diverged completely. The *Pasadena* paper remained wholesome, fully censored down to the date of printing, and ready to be mailed home to family. *Astoria*'s paper was for shipmates only—bawdy, irreverent, filled with updates of the immediate combat situation.

The ship's newspaper shared relevant humor. "Sailor, walking into recruiting office: 'Gimme that ol' sales talk again. I'm getting kinda discouraged.'" Sleep deprivation became a pervasive subject. The M Division reporter wrote, "Draughn is the only man in the division who can get out of his sack, stand a watch, and return to it without waking up. Heroes are not made."

A long-running joke landed in the lap of gunnery officer Meneke, as an anonymous wardroom humorist wrote, "The only explanation of the Gun Boss' absence from meals lately is the report that he now has *Forever Amber*." When one fortunate officer days later learned of surprise orders to rotate home, he emphatically stated, "I'm going back to the States to *live* *Forever Amber*."

* * *

The onslaught continued. On April 15, Fred Lind wrote,

> At 7 p.m. I witnessed the largest flak barrage I will ever
> see. A twin-engine Francis [*sic*] approached the Group
> from the rear, and was sighted by the Astoria at 12,000
> yards. We were the first ship to open fire, and the entire
> Task Group threw everything they had into the air. The
> tracers were like sparklers, shooting across the sky and
> pinpointing on the target. These tracers emanated from
> every ship in the vicinity, and formed a dome, focused
> on one hapless Jap. It wasn't long before there was a
> trail of smoke from a crashing Jap plane arching through

the sky. We fired 196 rounds of 5" shells at this one target. The intensity of Anti-Aircraft fire can be better-appreciated knowing that 5" twin barrels fire every three seconds. When you were right next to them, "appreciated" may have been a misnomer. It was like having multiple cannons in your living room. Thank God for battle telephones and battle helmets!

The next day John Arrighi wrote of being "kept awake all night by air alerts—Fired at intervals at planes dropping flares—after daybreak until about 8:30 a.m. all was quiet then we got the word of a large formation closing on us...Before nightfall and after several more emergencies we got word that a bogey was known to be over us at 35,000 ft. and starting a dive. Almost immediately the five-inch opened up and we spotted the plane diving at a steep angle. It was hit in the middle of his dive...he didn't burst however but kept coming very straight. He hit the water aft of a carrier on our port quarter...We had a busy day."

On April 19, Lind wrote, "We received word that Ernie Pyle was killed on Ie Shima, a tiny island off Okinawa...Our planes continued air strikes. These sessions involved a steady routine of early reveille, and battle stations interminably." The reporter had been a beloved press outlet for the men, a voice for the American fighting man through his on-the-ground reporting from before most of the crew were even inducted into service.

* * *

In the April 21 ship's newspaper, the anonymous 5th Division reporter wrote tongue-in-cheek, "We were surprised to see Lemon, BM2c report aboard a few days ago and see him in very good health. Since he reported aboard he has been working very hard for the division." Around this time Rousseau Lemon voluntarily requested Captain's Mast. George Dyer recalled, "He said 'Captain, I've been punished enough. By this time I'm very, very sorry for what I did,' and so forth and so on. He had a good song and dance." Dyer replied, "'I'm not going to do a blooming thing about it. When the crew relents on you, they'll relent on you.'"

Men found outlets for family despite their sequestration. Herman Schnipper wrote to his mother, "Dear mom, this is going to be another short V-mail just to let you know that I am alright and in the best of health. Since everything is practically the same out here, which is as far as the censor will allow me to write, I have nothing very much to tell you. So until a later date when I can write you a letter, I'll close. Your son, Sholem."

As April drew to a close, the American public was learning the word *Kamikaze.* West Coast ports were packed with American ships under repair, and the carrier *Franklin* was sent up east to Brooklyn Navy Yard for the extensive work she needed. Her gutted and charred decks could not be hidden from sight entering New York City, nor could thousands upon thousands of sailors and Marines be expected to keep quiet about what was going on in the brutal fighting of the Pacific. Reignited anger fueled public sentiment.

* * *

On May 1, *Hancock* pilot Pete Somerville, who had recently been rescued in Kagoshima Bay by *Astoria* aviators, was featured on the NBC radio program *Everything for the Boys.* Sent via shortwave radio, the interview had been selected by his command and the Armed Forces Radio Service. His rescue was just the sort of thing the weekly NBC radio program looked for, blending firsthand stories from the front lines with celebrity variety acts. Bombshell blonde movie star Betty Grable served as the guest host with Dick Haymes, promoting their new movie *Diamond Horseshoe* premiering in the US the next day. In detail Somerville depicted the dogfight overhead and his recovery by *Astoria*'s rescue pilot Jack Newman, from Battle Creek, Michigan, without naming ships. Not mentioned in the radio show was the death of his gunner, nor the reason he was in a position to give the radio interview to Grable at all: his carrier *Hancock* was back at Pearl Harbor for repairs following her *Kamikaze* hit. Nor was any *Astoria* sailor in a position to hear it.

The next day on May 2, the crew received word of Adolf Hitler's death. Speculating on the outcome of the war on two fronts, John Arrighi simply wrote, "We wonder." Others made no mention in their diaries at all. Despite an event of such enormous significance to their country back home and in Europe, *Astoria* men were fighting a completely different war. Out in the Pacific, there were far more relevant matters to attend to. Fred Lind penned, "Air attacks were unceasing. During three previous days, 135 Jap planes were destroyed by our planes. One Jap suicide plane dove into the US Hospital Ship *Comfort* near Okinawa, and killed thirty, including six nurses. This made a statement regarding the quality of our enemy. 'All's fair in love and war?'"

Rescue of downed aviators could be routine given the circumstances. On May 3, Marine First Lieutenant Walter Goeggel took fire over Takuno Island airfield, south of Kyushu. The *Bunker Hill* pilot managed to close within fifty-five miles of the task group before losing oil pressure and setting down on the water. At 6 p.m. with darkness closing, *Astoria* launched Chuck Tanner for a second evening solo operation. Four fighters escorted him, but none were needed. Another *Bunker Hill* plane on station vectored Tanner directly to Goeggel, and in calm seas Tanner lifted another grateful man into his rear cockpit. The recovery aboard *Astoria*, "a night Charlie" as Tanner called it, had also become routine.

Goeggel ("Barney" to his squadron buddies, after the popular cartoon character Barney Google) was returned to *Bunker Hill* the next day to fight again, after Herman Schnipper photographed him with Tanner. *Astoria* recorded her fifth life saved in Japanese waters. The entire operation had taken less than two hours from the time Goeggel hit the water.

On May 4, Lind wrote, "Being this close to Japan, all their remaining planes were available for attacks against us. Repetition was monotonous, but describing it is easier than enduring it." The Okinawa support at sea had hit day 52, and the constant requirement for the Fast Carrier Task

Force's air power demonstrated the slow progress ashore. With no end to operations in sight, the men of *Astoria* and the fast carriers would stay on station.

* * *

The May 5 edition of the *Astoria* ship's newspaper shifted in tone, less emphasis on humor and more on pep talks and team effort. One reporter penned a lengthy entry offering oblique advice aimed perhaps at Rousseau Lemon: "We have made mistakes in our past which we deeply regret. By these mistakes we have oft times made impressions on others which shame us greatly." He wrote of redemption, of the opportunity to "improve ourselves and to change the impressions we have made on others." He further appealed to the crew as a whole: "A moderate amount of initiative and effort on our part will make ours not only a better man o' war, but a far better place in which to live." The pharmacist's mate closed with a flourish: "Let the world know we were here."

Another entry reiterated sections of Rocks and Shoals that focused on swearing, fighting, shirking, and "any other scandalous conduct tending to the destruction of good morals." The authorless entry, likely written by the new executive officer, concluded, "Where the policy is so clear it seems unnecessary that so many of us participate in such violent misuses of the English language. It is a fact that we ought to start disciplining our tongues now before we slip someday and get the 'book' thrown at us, or slip at home and reveal that we have definitely let down on our habits while in the Navy."

While foul language continued unabated, home was too foreign a concept to consider for most men. Their daily reality was open water and sleep deprivation; there was no end in sight for their war cruise. When one radarman had the audacity to wash his dress blues, his division mates wondered "if he has lost his mind, or does he really think that we are ever going back to the States?" A storekeeper was reported as "rapidly becoming the most eligible bachelor in the division. Every mail call brings announcement of the loss of one of his prospective wives via the marriage and engagement route." Three signalmen waited for word from wives that were expecting. But even mail could take a toll on morale; a starboard-side gunner learned of the death of his mother at the same time a port-side counterpart was informed of the death of his wife. Sympathies for both were expressed in the Mother's Day edition of the ship's paper.

A day later the crew was informed their orders had changed; they were now to remain on the line for at least two more weeks, as yet another task group retired to anchorage in their place. No explanation was offered. A promised smoker, replete with boxing matches and entertainment on the fantail planned for the ship's commissioning anniversary, would be postponed. The *Astoria* birthday cakes would have to wait. Instead they received a congratulation message from Admiral Sherman and *Essex*, equally weary of their lengthy ordeal.

* * *

When Germany capitulated to Allied forces in Europe on May 8, it hardly mattered to the men of the Western Pacific. *Might as well be on the other side of the world*, grew the ironic sentiment. It had no bearing on the men of the Fast Carrier Task Force, except maybe guys headed home from Europe to take up after their girls and land jobs. The lights might be back on in London, but *Astoria* and her cohort still darkened ship every day at dusk. May 8 merely meant *Astoria*'s fifty-sixth consecutive day at sea.

Ashore at Okinawa the battle slogged on, reduced to World War I–esque trench warfare in rain and mud. Tethered to the operation, Ted Sherman's task group ran short of supplies. *Astoria* had exhausted her fresh food holdings two weeks before, frozen goods a week after that. At each "resupply" rendezvous, the oilers and ammunition ships simply had nothing else to offer. By the fueling of May 10, *Astoria* was down to K rations.

That night, the WASP Division was detached for a second island bombardment of Minami Daitō Jima, still a staging base for Japanese air-craft within range of Okinawa. The Japanese were proving able to repair the runways and facilities on the island as quickly as US Navy cruisers and destroyers could send it back into shambles.

Opening fire at 11:16 p.m., *Astoria* pounded targets via aerial spotter, firing 180 rounds of 6-inch and 360 rounds of 5-inch shells. In line with her, *Pasadena*, *Wilkes-Barre*, and *Springfield* did the same. Afterward, open fires could be seen raging over the bluffs into the heart of the small island. A report from the task unit commander stated, "The boys in the planes say it was damn good shooting...that's the stuff."

* * *

Philippine Sea, 80 miles east of Okinawa, day 59 at sea
May 11, 1945

The WASP Division cruisers returned to their carriers at 5 a.m., just as further strikes were launched against Okinawa targets. Later in the morning, Japanese planes followed a returning flight of Marine Corsairs landing on *Bunker Hill*. Within sixty seconds, two bomb-laden *Kamikazes* crashed through *Bunker Hill*'s decks, reducing her to a pyre reminiscent of *Franklin* two months before. Time slowed and smoke began to pour forth like blood from a wound before men could even begin to comprehend what just happened.

Just off watch and as the self-declared least important man in engineering, Herb Blodgett had gone topside for A Division mail call. He recalled, "I watched them hit...I saw what looked like five hundred men, bodies were blown all over the place. They were hitting out all over the water, and she of course immediately burst into flames. And we never fired a shot...Never a shot."

Wilkes-Barre was able to open fire and flame a third plane intent on finishing off the flattop, then she moved in close to fight fires and rescue men trapped in the inferno. Herb Blodgett along with many other sickened men stood at their stations across the task group. They could do nothing but watch helplessly as burning American boys spilled over the stern of the carrier; they had their own carriers to protect. Across the task group, exhausted *Astoria* men tried to put the sight out of mind and grab a little fitful sleep at their battle stations while guarding *Essex* from a similar fate.

In his diary John Arrighi wrote, "It was hell. A fellow from my home town is on that carrier—had a few words with him one day not too long ago when we were fueling. Wonder how he is."

Fred Lind wrote, "Major things happened when a carrier was hit by a *Kamikaze*. Fires broke out, gasoline and oil caught fire and flaming gasoline flowed across the decks. When this happened, the Captain turned to port or to starboard, to dump the gasoline over the side. When any personnel were in the path of the oncoming flaming gasoline, there was only one direction to go, and that was overboard. Jumping overboard was no bed of roses, either, because not only did you have sixty or one hundred feet or more to drop, but now you were dropping into gasoline burning on the surface of the water…Only a few destroyers were assigned to pick up survivors. Fortunately, they were very efficient in performing this assignment. Today, 168 guys could attest to that." He added, "This day made sixty days at sea."

That same morning *Enterprise* returned for a third stint in support of Okinawa following her second round of repairs. The Big E effectively replaced *Bunker Hill* as the group made rendezvous with a hospital ship to transfer the wounded. Over the two days that followed, hundreds of American dead were committed to the deep through burials at sea. Sunday, May 13, marked Mother's Day back home, and for hundreds of *Bunker Hill* mothers, Western Union telegrams informing of the deaths of their sons would follow closely on the heels of the cards those sons had sent for the occasion.

The next morning *Enterprise* was hit yet again. A *Kamikaze* plane diving on the ship crashed into her foredeck, causing an explosion that launched her forward elevator four hundred feet into the air in a giant mushroom cloud. The elevator came down to land on the ship in a thunderous clap, and the war's most legendary and veteran aircraft carrier was finally put out of action for good. *Astoria*'s range had been fouled by the disposition of other ships in the task group, and she was unable to fire a shot. Men shook their heads about *Enterprise*; the crew of baseball fanatics had taken to calling her "the catcher's mitt" and were proven correct again.

Shortly after, however, *Astoria* again proved her mettle in protecting *Essex*, bringing down a series of attackers that culminated with the final diving plane blown in half. Herman Schnipper captured images of men at their guns as the flaming portions of the suicide plane plummeted into the ocean short of its target. Fred Lind wrote, "One plane (George) gave me my worst scare so far. He was diving at us and we hit him when he was 2,000 yards out. He broke into flames, but kept coming straight at us. Our firing was terrific, and we shot his tail off. He was blazing directly overhead, and we never knew whether he would fall on us or not. Then we hit him again, and blew him completely off course. He landed about 400 yards off our port beam. During the day, we claimed one shot down, and three assists."

John Arrighi wrote of the day, "We stayed on our guns until 11 a.m. without any chow. At seven a Jap plane got in and hit the carrier *Enterprise*. It was a suicide plane—the plane was hit before hitting the carrier but not bad enough that it couldn't do its job."

* * *

At 8:28 a.m., *Astoria* received orders for another risky rescue mission: a *Randolph* Helldiver crew was reported down deep in the Inland Sea of Japan. *Astoria* held the rescue duty for the day. The message directly from Admiral Sherman read, "*Astoria* stand by for rescue of two survivors in raft, distance twenty-five miles bearing 115 from point Tollgate. *Randolph* will provide four VF [fighter] escort." Additional *Essex* planes would accompany them en route to their own target areas, comprising eight fighters in all.

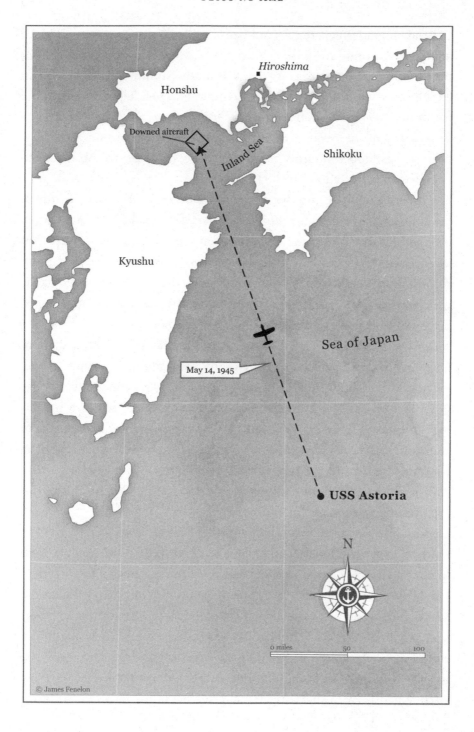

Honshu

Hiroshima

Downed aircraft

Inland Sea

Shikoku

Kyushu

Sea of Japan

May 14, 1945

USS Astoria

N

0 miles   50   100

© James Fenelon

Ready pilots Chuck Tanner and Don Comb were to form up with their fighter escort and head into the waters between Honshu and Shikoku, then keep going further in. As the aviation division prepped his aircraft, Comb was left with plenty of time to think. He "just kept running to the bathroom." *Oh my God*, he thought. *I'm flying into the Inland Sea...into the heart of Japan.* Such a surface recovery operation had no precedent. Even once strapped into his plane and on the catapult, Comb remained "visibly concerned about the flight."

Tanner catapulted into the sky at 9:31 a.m. from the opposite side of the ship, and Comb readied himself. He focused on the familiar—firmly placing his head against the headrest, prop at low pitch—and waited for the catapult officer to launch him. *Just breathe.* A sharp crack rang out, throwing his weight into his seat. and acceleration over sixty feet into the wind in mere seconds followed. Every time he launched, Comb hoped he wouldn't dip and hit the water—and once again he didn't.

Airborne and climbing, he could see Tanner's plane ahead of him. Only once they formed up did Comb "start to calm down a little." He would have a 205-mile journey into the heart of enemy territory to settle himself, and he had a buddy with him. "Tanner helped a lot," he would write. "He was very reassuring." Back at base, the carriers would continue recovering, arming, and launching planes for further strikes on Kyushu. *Astoria* and the other ships in the screen would protect them, and hopefully Comb and Tanner would have their base on station for their return. *Just breathe.*

With the Kingfishers traveling at some 90 knots, their fighter escort "had to make continual S-turns to stay over them." The gooney birds might be superbly functional for surface recovery efforts, but with their low power-to-weight ratio they took their time to get there. Clear skies eventually gave way to haze as the formation reached Kyushu some ninety minutes later. Visibility dropped to five miles. While such conditions would make the rescue planes more difficult to spot and fire toward, it might also impede their ability to locate the downed men. The Helldiver aircrew had been in the water for almost five hours in a raft, paddling hard against current to stay away from enemy shores, adrift and surely a distance from their original reported crash location.

Tanner, Comb, and their escort passed between Kyushu and Shikoku into the Inland Sea, deeper into Japan than any surface rescue had ever been attempted. Flying under one thousand feet, Comb made note of antiaircraft batteries below, but the emplacements did not open fire. Tanner made contact with fighters on station circling the helpless men in their raft, and the fighter cover was able to vector the rescue group accordingly. The *Randolph* planes ahead had been standing watch over some of their own, and twice had strafed and turned away Japanese destroyers attempting to intercept.

Fifty miles into the Inland Sea, Tanner and Comb spotted yellow dye marker in the water and dropped to make their landings. As the fighters who had been standing watch over their brethren moved off to return to their carrier, the fresh rescue escort assumed top cover.

Tanner landed first, and almost immediately shore batteries erupted, shells splashing closer and closer as the enemy sought their range. Tanner taxied up and idled his engine. He climbed out on the wing with a coil of rope, which he tossed to the men in the raft as he glided past. Both men grabbed it, and Tanner reeled the raft in. Using the plane's rope ladder, he assisted the *Randolph* pilot into the rear cockpit of his floatplane with little difficulty. He then moved away so Comb could maneuver to retrieve the radioman. He elected to stay on the surface in case something went awry. The shell splashes closed.

Comb landed fast, and overshot the raft. He taxied a circuit around for a second pass. As he did so, he witnessed their fighter cover shoot down two Japanese planes over the rescue scene. A second pass and he missed again—the plane was simply throttling too fast for an easy lineup with the raft and the radioman. Comb circled again, and this time watched his fighter cover strafe a Japanese destroyer closing from a distance. *So much effort for one man, but he's one of ours.* He elected to cut his engine and coast up to the raft. Leaping out of the cockpit, this time he managed to help the weakened aviator into the back seat of the plane.

To restart his plane from the surface, Comb needed to fire a starter gun into an engine cylinder to crank the engine over. He kept a box of starter shells in the cockpit for this purpose. He loaded a shell, lined it up, and fired into the engine. *Click.* Nothing happened. Discarding the shotgun-esque cartridge, he grabbed a second one from the box, loaded, and fired. *Click.* The second did not work either.

With shore fire moving closer, he grabbed a third round. *Bam!* The engine cranked and sputtered to life. After strapping in, Comb joined Tanner as both pilots throttled up at 12:15 p.m. and left the water behind. They had been on the surface of the Inland Sea for thirty minutes while effecting rescue under fire. Ascending and departing the Inland Sea at five hundred feet, their formation took further fire from antiaircraft batteries, "light but accurate." Although flak burst around them, neither plane was hit.

After two hundred miles in return flight and once safely aboard the Mighty Ninety, the rescued aviators were given the usual shot of Old Grand-Dad bourbon by *Astoria's* junior medical officer, George W. "Doc" Slagle. The *Randolph* crew certainly needed their nerves settled. Ensign John Morris, the Helldiver pilot, and Cletus Phegley, his radioman, had been hit during a bombing run, losing their engine. Morris had managed to perform a survivable water landing, and both men exited the plane with their life raft as they had practiced many times. While working to inflate the raft, Morris was abruptly yanked underwater as the sinking plane caught a strap on his life jacket. Oxygen starved and sinking, he fought his way free, arriving at the surface exhausted. Phegley helped him into the raft and they waited for hours, watching planes battle overhead and fight off surface threats.

Morris described his thoughts: "I wondered why me? There was a sudden realization that I would never see my parents again, never get married, and never have a family…We decided to stay right where we were and keep the water dye marker visible as long as we could." The pair expressed the hope they regained when hours later they spotted "two tiny specks on the horizon with a division of F6Fs circling them."

Morris also received a special visitor to sick bay: *Astoria's* Marine CO Armitage hailed from the same hometown of Haverhill, Massachusetts. The men had grown up together and now met up on the other side of the world, both having endured near-death experiences.

The Inland Sea rescue would be hailed by a United Press story as "one of the most daring actions of the war." Admiral Mitscher would declare that the Navy could recover its aviators "right out of the Emperor's fish pond on the Imperial Palace grounds." Both *Astoria* pilots would receive oak leaf clusters for Distinguished Flying Crosses earned in their earlier rescue operations. Admiral Jones sent a teletype to Dyer that read, "Extend my hearty congratulations to your Kingfisher pilots upon another job performed in typical *Astoria* fashion and CruDiv 17 manner. Well done to all hands in *Astoria*."

It was only once safely back aboard that Don Comb realized the third starter shell had been the very last one in the box. Perhaps the four-leaf clover brought luck.

* * *

Deep into May, Rousseau Lemon again requested to see the skipper at Captain's Mast. He expressed remorse for his actions, asked for the men to stop treating him as an outcast, and even requested transfer. Captain Dyer repeated to him that no transfer would be granted, and that he was quite pleased with the stance the crew had taken. When the man had earned his keep, the crew would accept him as one of their own. For the duration of the Okinawa operation, no sailor worked harder within his division. Lemon pulled consistent 4.0 ratings for proficiency and conduct. The Mighty Ninety crew gradually warmed to him; the most telling proof of his eventual acceptance was his name being included in the jokes that poked fun at one another in the ship's newspaper.

Fred Lind wrote, "Our operations were becoming redundant. It was more of the same daily. We were not in a routine—we were in a numbing field of action, and felt like robots. A few nights ago we were getting ready to secure from Condition Watch at 0400, and I started to head out of the Anti-Aircraft director. When I got to the trap door, one of our crew was sitting on the hatch, half-asleep. I tapped him on the shoulder, and told him that we were securing from watch. I naturally expected him to willingly get up and head down the ladder, but he just sat there. So I picked him up and moved him off the hatch. He snarled, "You go down that hatch, and I'll kick your head off." I said, "Start kickin', cause I'm going down." Guess he fell asleep again, because I didn't get kicked. It just shows the condition we were all in—everybody was worn down and nerves were on edge."

For the rest of May the Fast Carrier Task Force remained at two-thirds strength: two carriers had returned to service, but eight were off the line for repair. No further *Kamikaze* attacks developed for the rest of the month, and after the other task groups had completed their two weeks of rest and recovery, Ted Sherman's battered group was at last able to retire for anchorage. Their official time continuously underway was logged at seventy-nine days, a record for the US Navy. However, only a handful of ships in the group when it arrived at a new anchorage in the liberated Philippines had been present for the full duration, such was the turnover. The four cruisers of the WASP Division all carried the honor, as did three destroyers, battleship USS *Washington,* and two aircraft carriers, *Essex* and *Bataan.*

Ultimately the verdict from the Navy came that such an uninterrupted operation was simply too long for the well-being of the men involved; *Essex* was suffering dozens of cases of combat fatigue and "situational psychoneurosis." Some of the crew were left unable to function, shaking, even incapable of responding when being addressed. Admiral Sherman's task group had been hit far harder than the other groups, fought off heavy swarming attacks, and suffered more than half the aircraft carrier losses endured at Okinawa. The men of the group had borne witness to more than a thousand sailors and Marines killed and wounded in action. Admiral Mitscher's reports stated that with exact figures not available, "the Task Force lost over 1,500 men killed or missing in action and a larger number of wounded." "Aircraft of Task Force 58 shot down

1,488 enemy aircraft, ships' gunfire shot down 141, and 11 more were destroyed by suicide crashes on ships of the Force, making 1,640 airborne enemy aircraft destroyed." Astonishingly, despite many wounded in action, *Astoria* did not lose a man.

Back in March when *Astoria* left anchorage for Okinawa operations, she had yet to fire on an enemy plane. Now bandaged men hung over her damaged bridge armor to paint rows of Japanese flags into a scoreboard. Also back in March her pilots had yet to successfully retrieve a single downed airman. Now her floatplanes had cartoon life rafts with hash marks for lives saved painted on their cowlings. During the seventy-nine-day operation, the Mighty Ninety took top honors, firing upon and receiving credit for more enemy planes than any of the other 122 ships that served in the Fast Carrier Task Force at Okinawa: forty-one total planes taken under fire, twenty-seven brought down, thirteen solo credits. Her rescue pilots also finished on top, retrieving the most downed aircrew of floatplane-equipped vessels. "First in Battle, First in Rescue" became the motto for George Dyer's *Astoria*. The skipper could not have been prouder of his misfits.

Her division sister *Wilkes-Barre* scored second in both categories, and the other two ships of the WASP Division, *Springfield* and *Pasadena*, also performed at the top. The story of the WASP Division as skilled *Kamikaze* killers was picked up by *Stars and Stripes*. Their pockmarked, riddled superstructures served further testament to their efforts under fire as they steamed into San Pedro Bay in the Philippines, their new anchorage.

Fred Lind reflected on their experience against the *Kamikaze*: "The expertise in Damage Control saved our stricken carriers...No one can ever repay our Navy and Marine Air Forces for their selfless involvement in daily raids over enemy territory. Their skill and determination meshed with the fleet's capabilities, giving Japan more than they could handle. America's morale spiraled, knowing that the Japs were on the receiving end, and the most significant contributor to that spiral was the pilot, who made continuous raids daily."

Astoria had kept *Essex* and her air group on the line for the full seventy-nine days.

18

Relief

Boys, beware of receiving a telegram that you are
now a proud father of a 9 lb. child. As you know
you haven't been home in 10 months.
— *1st Division reporter, Mighty Ninety newspaper, July 1945*

As naval support of Okinawa operations concluded, a letter arrived from USS *Randolph* addressed to Captain George Dyer. In
neat longhand penmanship it read: "Dear Captain Dyer, I'm taking the
liberty of writing you in order to express my appreciation and gratitude for your efforts on my behalf. I refer to my rescue, daringly
executed by pilots under your command, from the Inland Sea off the
north coast of Kyushu on May 14. It is difficult to find words to ad-
equately express the gratitude felt by my aircrewman, Phegley, and
myself but hope you will accept from us both our heartfelt thanks.
Sincerely, John Morris, Ensign USNR." Dyer shared the letter with
Chuck Tanner and the aviation unit, then tucked it away in his personal effects for safekeeping.

Days of liberty ashore followed at Leyte, fought for by other ships
back in October. It was the first soil under the *Astoria* crew's feet in three
months. John Arrighi wrote, "Liberty was at San Antonio Beach—They
give two cans of beer, no soft drinks. It's hell on me...Kids go around

trading things for food—what they want most is oranges." All he wanted was a Coca-Cola.

Men came back aboard with the possessions they gained through trade with the local Filipinos; especially popular were Japanese flags. More than a few mattress covers went missing in return. Jim Peddie snuck one out with a mattress cover wrapped around him under his uniform. When he returned aboard, he brought back a machete in a bamboo sheath.

Fights broke out with men from other crews—"You bastards, you got credit for our plane!"—and numerous *Astoria* men received extra beer chits courtesy of appreciative *Essex* sailors for keeping the *Kamikazes* off their backs.

A significant portion of the crew grew sick with fever, the likely culprit being swimming in the stagnant San Pedro Bay water. A moratorium was subsequently placed on the activity. Of the incident, Fred Lind wrote,

> Liberty nearly did me in.... We were walking along the beach, and I said, "Roy, grab me." I fell flat on my back, and there was no way that I could get myself upright. My head started to spin, and everything went black. When they finally got me back to the ship, the doctor laughed, and said, "You don't get seasick, do you?" I told him no, and he said, "well, you got land sick." Apparently my body had become accustomed to the vibration and movement of the ship, and the earth was so solid and so still that my system couldn't accept it.... This port duty wasn't all it was cracked up to be.

John Arrighi added, "The water or something is getting the fellows sick—even our compartment is now sick bay. I was sick for 3 days."

Marine Captain Armitage learned that a man named Joe Broscia, a roommate from Corona Naval Hospital, was killed aboard USS *Franklin*. The fellow Marine captain was one of the 772 killed in the attack.

Herman Schnipper landed a large haul of food and Bayonne newspapers sent from his mother. When the latest *LIFE* magazine arrived, men had to laugh. An article featured photos of Ulithi with no explanation as to why, and certainly no American ships in any photograph. *Propaganda for the Japanese perhaps?* One *Astoria* sailor would write that Ulithi was "a small atoll in the Caroline Islands that is ignored on most of the world maps. Contrary to popular belief that it was a tropical paradise, as inspired by *LIFE*'s glowing article, to us it was merely an anchorage and a rough one at that. We made liberty there, and on occasion to Mog Mog, one of the small islands that formed the atoll. There we could swim among the razor sharp coral and drink our three cans of beer. With no women and very little song it became just a spot of beer cans and coral where we could rest our feet from the steel decks of the ship."

Fred Lind wrote, "On June 1, I was sworn in as Petty Officer (Fire Controlman Third Class), as a result of the examinations we took some time ago. Three of us in our Division were made Petty Officers. This won't affect our assignments much except in port, where we will probably draw Shore Patrol duty, etc. We will get a few dollars more in our pay. I think it meant that we were worth about eleven cents an hour now. Things were really looking up. I couldn't wait to have Mom hear about this?? How did they ever sell us on putting up with all that crap for that kind of money?"

On June 7, men on deck were jolted by a terrific nearby blast—a complete shock while once again at anchor. As *Astoria* went to general quarters and smoke again poured skyward from nearby, Herman Schnipper ran for his camera to take photos of whatever was happening. Arriving back on deck, he realized the carrier *Randolph* had been crashed into again across from *Astoria*, this time by a reckless Army Air Force P-38 Lightning pilot showing off for the ships at anchor. "Must have been *Randolph*," mused Fred Lind. More sailors were killed, and *Randolph* earned the unenviable reputation as the only ship ever hit in anchorage and twice at that: once by the Japanese and now once by the Army Air Forces.

The remaining fast carrier task groups steamed into San Pedro Bay, now led once again by Admiral Halsey. This brought Navy support of

Okinawa operations to an official end, but did so in tragically Halsey fashion, for the ships had endured yet another typhoon under the admiral. Where the typhoon back in December had been most cruel to the destroyers and escort carriers, this one exacted its toll on cruisers and fleet carriers. Heavy cruiser *Pittsburgh* lost one hundred feet of her bow, several other cruisers were badly damaged, and the carriers *Hornet* and *Bennington* had their forward flight decks crushed against their hulls from smashing headlong into heavy seas. By the end of the month the Fast Carrier Task Force would be going back out again under Halsey, but would do so less ships once again knocked out due to a combination of enemy and weather. *Astoria* men shared a sentiment: *He did it again.*

On June 9 the crew prepared for their long overdue smoker and ship's birthday celebration. Before the festivities, there was a more somber matter to attend to—*Astoria*'s first change of command ceremony. The crew assembled in dress whites on the fantail for the second time in their war cruise, this time to show respect and say goodbye to Captain George Dyer. He read commendations and handed out awards, including a Purple Heart to the chaplain he had so heavily dressed down for putting himself in mortal danger. The skipper then had tears in his eyes as he read his orders and addressed his crew. Men who had stood at mast, served in the brig, lost liberties and pay, been busted in rate, and received additional work detail surrounded Dyer. Even Rousseau Lemon, fully back in good graces with his shipmates, attended.

The time had come for Dyer to say goodbye to Rampage and the crew he had cultivated. The men's underground diaries made note of the captain's tears streaming down his cheeks as he read his orders. Pharmacist's Mate William Dixon, one of the lead contributors to the ship's newspaper, read a statement from the men of the Mighty Ninety to their beloved first captain:

> Let it be known to all men that George Carroll Dyer,
> a Captain of the United States Navy, while serving as
> Commanding Officer of his valiant and fighting ship,

the USS *Astoria*, has by his courage and untiring efforts inspired and led this ship and crew through strenuous days of training and into battle against the enemy. These efforts have greatly aided the establishment of the fine reputation this ship now holds in the fleet. The Mighty Ninety has successfully met and stopped all enemy resistance on every front she has yet fought.

Know you all that as Captain George Carroll Dyer leaves this ship on this 9th day of June, in the year of our Lord 1945, his merits of leadership, determination, and courage shall live on in those of us who remain behind. It is with regret that we see him depart. Godspeed and good luck in his new assignment. May we be fortunate enough to serve with him again.

The officers and men of the USS Astoria

Dyer posed for photographs with gunnery officer Ken Meneke over the ship's scoreboard, followed by photos with his heads of departments. He then left a ship and crew he dearly loved and climbed into a whaleboat, destined for a job in Washington and his long-desired promotion to flag rank as a rear admiral.

Dyer's relief skipper was a stocky Texan named William Hamilton, a former destroyer man. Perhaps he knew the key to success for relieving a disciple of Kelly Turner was to "ease up on the thumbscrews a bit," for he ran things in a slightly looser manner. Dyer never would have been seen having a drink with his officers, as Hamilton did on liberty. He surely would have had the crew pose for division photographs in dress whites, not work dungarees as Hamilton permitted while Herman Schnipper photographed. For some young replacement officers, Hamilton's style immediately demonstrated a vast improvement over Dyer's. Yet the replacements had not been through the year-long saga of *Astoria*, nor had they been there long enough to appreciate what the first skipper accomplished with his green crew. Hamilton had inherited an efficient, competent man o' war, and it was certain they were going out there yet again, for there was no indication Japan would yield.

Back in the United States, a Navy Department film with footage recorded by Walter Duggan played in theaters to inform the public of what America was up against. Titled "The Fleet That Came to Stay," the film compiled the footage shot aboard *Astoria* and several other ships in Ted Sherman's task group at Okinawa. It graphically depicted the *Kamikaze* attacks they had endured for months, eliminating any stateside question whether the Japanese were "fanatical" and "suicidal," stopping at nothing to oppose the Americans drawing closer to Tokyo. A horrified American public had never seen anything like it.

Additional fleet photographers were assigned aboard *Astoria*, roaming the ship to take public relations photos of groups of men for their hometown newspapers. Public support and continued funding of the war effort were deemed critical; all hands knew that the invasion of the Japanese Home Islands loomed in the near future. Scuttlebutt crossed the fleet that the absence of suicide attacks was proof that the Japanese were hoarding planes in preparation for a bloody showdown when they invaded. Reports emerged of training efforts across the Home Islands instructing even women and children to fight to the last with sharpened bamboo poles once the Americans came ashore. Casualties in the planned Home Island invasions were expected to be catastrophic.

19

Ghosts of Nansei Shoto

As we left San Francisco some months ago we all
wondered how long it would be before we again
set eyes on the beautiful Golden Gate Bridge.
We're still wondering.
—*A Sailor Writes Home, censor-approved USS*
Astoria *form letter*

En route for Japan
July 2, 1945

Hours after getting back underway, *Astoria* lost her first man. A
Navy cook, an overweight sailor who would have never qualified
for service in the absence of a draft, was found dead in his bunk of a heart
attack. George Washington Ostrander's nickname in his division was
"five by five," referring not just to his height and girth but how squared
away he was as a cook and sailor.

Marine and fellow cook John Arrighi wrote in his diary, "Left Leyte
at 6 a.m. One of my buddies died about 9 a.m. of a heart attack. From
New York State, he had a wife and three kids. Can't come any better than
him...Everyone was asked to be at the fantail. Our Marines were there,
mostly everyone was there."

A popular man among the crew, Ostrander was buried at sea as men packed the fantail in driving rain and a fully recovered Chaplain Lusk conducted the service. The ship's crew collected a hefty sum from undrawn pay to send back to his widow. The man had survived Okinawa only to die after a rest period—just days after he had posed ashore for Schnipper photographs with a Japanese flag. "Had he died a few hours earlier he would have been buried on land," noted Herman Schnipper.

Arrighi added, "We have seven days training ahead of us—Air Emergency, General Quarters, air attack from our planes, firing at drones—we'll do about everything. Something big coming up sure as hell." During the week of such grueling exercises, the men would learn their new mission.

A popular tale that circulated among the task force spoke of the "Nansei Shoto Ghost," an enormous radar signal indicating a large number of incoming planes that would suddenly vanish, because they were nonexistent. The "ghost" eventually proved to be a product of weather and early radar, a complete anomaly, but it foreshadowed the task force mission post-Okinawa. For the first time in *Astoria*'s tenure, the ships were not tied to a specific invasion. Instead Halsey was free to move as he pleased. Throughout July into August the fast carriers would range freely up and down the Japanese coast, striking quickly and moving, to soften landing areas for the planned invasion of Japan.

He sent waves of American planes to destroy port facilities, combat ships, merchant vessels, even rail lines. Hunting such targets of opportunity fit the admiral's freewheeling style, much as the strict requirements of the Tokyo raids, Iwo Jima, and Okinawa had suited the meticulous nature of Spruance. As Halsey hunted naval targets and coastal infrastructure, Curtis LeMay's Army Air Forces would continue to methodically fire-bomb cities and their populations with the intent of forcing capitulation.

As the task force trained, a new issue broke out. Fred Lind wrote, "Strange things were happening at sea. We were cruising off the coast of the Philippines, and were due to head north to continue our attacks on Tokyo. For some strange reason, we were heading in circles, and I couldn't figure out what was going on. Watching maneuvers, I noticed that one plane had nose-dived into the ocean when taking off, and another plane suddenly dropped out of formation, went into a sudden descent, and crashed into the water. One of my buddies was standing by my bunk talking to me, and fell flat on his face in the middle of a sentence."

An epidemic had hit the fleet—catarrhal "cat" fever. The pharmacist mate "pill rollers" scrambled across ships to distribute sulfa pills, a precursor to antibiotics, and inform everyone they had to get shots. For Lind the effort proved too late. He wrote, "After the midnight watch, I secured at 4 a.m., went to the head, and as I was leaving the head, I grabbed the doorknob. Everything started to spin, and I fell on my back in a pool of sweat. I was so slippery that it took six guys to carry me to sickbay."

Lind couldn't recall the three days that followed, even as the group formed columns to fire at drones and perform exercises. *Astoria* operated the target drones and conducted firing drills with what healthy men they had. Several compartments were converted into overflow sick bays. When Lind finally broke fever and awoke, he found himself in Marine quarters. He climbed out of his sack and approached a pharmacist's mate. "He looked at me funny, and asked if I was all right now. Apparently, I had done some strange things when I was out of it. After about a week, things cleared up in my head, and I was okay again...Wonder what I did? Whatever it was, it sure was impressive!"

* * *

425 miles southeast of Tokyo
July 9, 1945

Gunner's Mate Tom Kane caught wind of their objective. He could already tell, as the temperature continued to drop. Clearly they were headed for the Home Islands. The scuttlebutt spoke of a "very dangerous operation, expect 25% casualties." He pushed any fear from the forefront. Like so many sailors and despite the typhoons, Kane was proud to sail with Admiral Halsey, "leading the way aboard the *Missouri*." John Arrighi just enjoyed the change in weather: "Getting cooler every day— that's what we've been hoping for—destroyer blowing up mines... We'll soon see what the Japs have."

Flight operations for strikes over the Tokyo plain began early the next morning, bringing the full strength of 1,000 planes. Fred Lind wrote, "Reveille was at 2:10 a.m. on the 10th, and we were at General Quarters from 3 a.m. until 7 p.m. Our position was 100 miles from Tokyo. One Dinah was shot down off our port beam by the Combat Air Patrol. I watched from my binoculars, and it fell from about 25,000 feet, and was a tremendous sight. We had K Rations on station."

Arrighi added, "Our last strike was just going in when five hundred B-29 Superfortresses were leaving Tokyo—I wonder if the Japs liked it." Kane noted, "Carrier pilots report no resistance over target. Admiral Halsey broadcasts challenge to the Japs, 'We are out here, come and get us.' Saw a Francis [*sic*] flaming into the sea after being shot down by a Corsair at 1:30 p.m.... Daylight, full daylight, at 3 a.m."

A second day of strikes brought nothing over the task group. All action was focused over the Tokyo Plain target areas. On the twelfth they moved off for refueling, and Lind noted sleeping under blankets for the first time in a while. Results of the previous day's raid came in: "110 planes destroyed, and at least 200 more damaged. Ground installations were hit. Again we headed north. The weather was bad." Amid rough seas and with poor visibility, Admiral Halsey sent the task force a "well done" for the strikes on Tokyo.

Beginning with July 13, weather dictated any offensive action against homeland Japan. Strikes launched at 3:30 a.m. were called off after just a few aircraft due to overcast, dense fog and rain. For John Arrighi this was a blessing: "Sack time the rest of the day." Tom Kane noted, "Japs broadcast confusion as to the strikes the fleet is making, not knowing where they'll strike next." *Ghosts of Nansei Shoto*.

Weather cleared the morning of the fourteenth and strikes resumed. Lind wrote, "Our planes were hitting Hokkaido for the first time.

Railroads, shipping, and harbors were the juiciest targets. One Betty was shot down by the Combat Air Patrol near the Group. We had K Rations again. We were 40 miles from Japan this morning; I could see land without my binoculars."

In the late afternoon the WASP Division of cruisers detached to conduct an antishipping sweep along the Honshu coast. Any target of opportunity was up for grabs. With a division of destroyers forming a screen ahead and another in column behind, the four cruisers moved down the Honshu coast, resulting in nothing. An "anti-sleep sweep," the men called it. Fred Lind wrote, "We were at General Quarters from 6 p.m. until 3 a.m., but couldn't find any ships. So we rejoined the fleet, and they were at General Quarters—so now we had duty until 5 p.m. or 7 p.m. We came within 15,000 yards of Japan, and I could see land. No sleep in several days."

John Arrighi wrote, "I had the battle telephones on. We had to up and down the coast for 30 miles until 2 in the morning. About 11:30 p.m. Sky Forward told us we were 20 miles from shore, later it was 16 miles, then 12 miles—getting too damn close. Then we were told we were 8 mi. from Japan's coast. We are the first ships since the war that ever came that close to Japan; up to two we ran up and down but not a damn thing happened. I just couldn't believe it."

* * *

While operating up and down the Japanese Home Islands, *Astoria* received word that she was to head stateside for refit after so long at sea. Fred Lind wrote, "Names were being submitted for first and second leave parties. I asked for a transfer, hoping to catch a new construction. From all appearances, the leaves would be 22 days from the west coast. That wasn't much, but anything beat staying out there. Everyone was mighty excited, and the war seemed to have taken a back seat."

With fewer enemy planes, no *Kamikaze* attacks, the biggest enemy became the tedium and monotony of daily watches. With so many

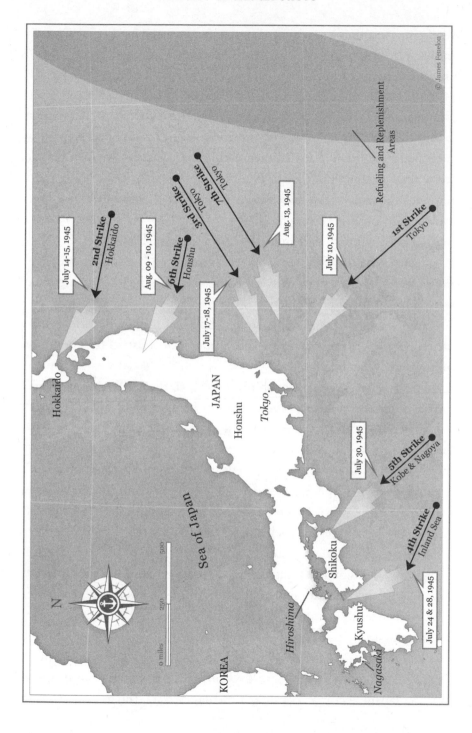

© James Fenelon

Refueling and Replenishment Areas

2nd Strike
Hokkaido
July 14-15, 1945

6th Strike
Honshu
Aug. 09 - 10, 1945

3rd Strike
Tokyo

7th Strike
Tokyo

Aug. 13, 1945

1st Strike
Tokyo
July 10, 1945

July 17-18, 1945

5th Strike
Kobe & Nagoya
July 30, 1945

4th Strike
Inland Sea
July 24 & 28, 1945

Hokkaido

JAPAN

Honshu

Tokyo.

Shikoku

Hiroshima

Kyushu

Nagasaki

Sea of Japan

KOREA

N

0 miles   250   500

servicemen coming home from Europe, being stuck in the Pacific grew intolerable. On August 2, Herman Schnipper finally had enough when an officer asked for personal pictures. He said the wrong thing to the officer in reply and immediately found himself at Captain's Mast. He was stripped of his rate in a manner that no one else aboard ship had been except two black mess stewards. The S (Service) Division had boasted of their "all-allied lineup," listing men with Italian, Polish, Russian, Dutch, Irish, English, Filipino, Czech, French, and Chinese heritage. They did not include their black mess stewards, and now Schnipper had been evaluated in the same manner.

Fred Lind wrote, "They must have been serious about our going back to the States, because on August 3, we started cannibalizing the ship. All excess stores, spare parts, etc., were being transferred to other ships; but we still had Anti-Aircraft practice."

The next day John Arrighi wrote, "Still waiting....All strikes were cancelled. Fleet abruptly turned and headed northeast to far north end of Honshu. What was up?"

In the August 5 issue of the ship's newspaper, the 1st Division updates included remarks about Rousseau Lemon. "Lemon, BM2c, who has years of experience as a salesman, seems to lose most of the arguments he has with Sanders. Boys, if you want some entertainment, get those two started telling sea stories." Grady Sanders was a well-liked and respected boatswain's mate, a veteran of the Sicily and Anzio landings aboard USS *Brooklyn* before reporting aboard *Astoria*. His friendship indicated that indeed Lemon had been accepted back among the men as one of their own.

By August 7 morale was looking up for the men of *Astoria*. The lull in fighting brought the cruiser alongside *Wilkes-Barre*, with orders to cannibalize parts and equipment and send them across to her twin sister ship. Men happily manned the lines and worked the block and tackle, for this was a sure sign *Astoria* was soon headed home for a long overdue refit and overhaul. Yet that afternoon, all work was stopped as Captain Hamilton announced of a "new kind of bomb" that had been dropped over the Japanese city of Hiroshima the day before. The devastation was tremendous, and orders were to stay north and wait for any Japanese response.

At noon on August 9, 1945, the routine daily task of logging the ship's position was performed aboard USS *Astoria*, just as it had been for hundreds of days previous. A sextant reading confirmed *Astoria*'s position as 37-54-48 North, 144-38-00 East. Within one minute of this log entry, 786 miles to the west-southwest, the sky collapsed over Nagasaki, Japan. *Astoria* men didn't receive word until the following day that a second "atom bomb" had been dropped. Men rushed to the rail and looked out to see any sign, even though they were some seven hundred miles east of the former city. Seeing nothing, they had no idea of the complete devastation. Through the following days, diary entries again repeated daily: "Nothing yet... waiting... why won't Japan just give up?" *We want to go home.*

Tom Kane wrote, "A million rumors flying around the ship... Snyder & myself assigned to the riot squad with sawed off shotgun with bayonets. I can hear Flo saying, 'You damn fool.'"

The morning of August 15 had brought planned heavy strikes. Whole air groups were airborne, carriers turned into the wind and launching more planes, when the word came. *Astoria* had a destroyer alongside transferring guard mail when Captain Hamilton came over the PA: Japan had formally agreed to unconditional surrender. Work ceased; men stopped in their tracks and stood listening to the full announcement, processing.

The announcement was relayed across all ships and to the airborne squadrons, for the formation turned and began landing planes immediately. The fleet PR photographers aboard *Astoria* snapped photographs of men celebrating, cheering, and tossing their hats in the air. Signalmen ran a large battle ensign up the ship's foremast. But all was for the papers back home; Schnipper took pictures of the reality. Show over, men immediately returned to work hauling mail and scrubbing decks. Hostilities might have ceased, but they were still on station many thousands of miles from home.

Further news tempered spirits. USS *Indianapolis*, Spruance's former flagship and steaming partner of *Astoria* throughout 1945, the ship she narrowly avoided collision with thanks to Captain Dyer's fast action, was reported sunk by a Japanese submarine. Most of her crew was gone with her.

Two days after the surrender, it was confirmed that *Astoria* was indeed headed home. Fred Lind wrote, "Aerial pictures were taken of the fleet. Guess we made the newsreels back home. All the ships congregated, and formed ranks…I had never seen more than one Task Group in formation, and the sight was unbelievable. This really punctuated the awesome sea power of the United States of America, and we were proud to be a very small portion of that power. Unseen were the thousands of heroic pilots and long-suffering seamen. Missing from the picture were the heroes who died in combat, and their doomed ships. The haunting question will never vanish: 'Why them, and not me?'"

Supplies and mail continued to arrive from home after months in supply lines. He concluded, "On that day I received a Christmas package from home. It contained chocolate chip cookies, that by this time had been pulverized. Hershey syrup in a can survived, though. The package had been following us for nine months—shows how much we had been on the move."

The following days brought tension and uncertainty; instead of confirming a return to the States, all signs pointed to possible occupation duty. The Marine detachment conducted small arms refresher practice with gunner's mates, firing various weapons out over the side. Sailors were issued lists of phonetic Japanese phrases such as "Hands up!" and "Come here to me." Jim Peddie was handed a shotgun. "I didn't know how the hell to use one. A .45 was bigger than me." The scuttlebutt mixed anger, frustration, and excitement depending on who was talking. Herman Schnipper for one wanted to go ashore and load up on Japanese camera equipment.

This uncertainty continued for almost two weeks, even as the fleet performed massed maneuvers for aerial PR photos—Operation Snapshot—

and practice runs of a thousand aircraft overhead in formation to make an impression in Tokyo Bay. Only when other ships began coming alongside to transfer "high-points" men, meaning those with lengthy service who merited priority for discharge, did the crew of *Astoria* realize they were indeed heading home for overhaul. The news was perhaps more welcome than the surrender announcement.

Ship after ship packed men aboard the plucky cruiser. Passengers dropped their seabags and mattress covers anywhere they could find space—on deck, even in the ship's hangar (which had never been used to house planes anyway, instead modified into a basketball court). The weather deck became a sea of sunbathers. For the great-circle route from Japan past the Aleutians to California, no one would complain about the crowded spaces—they were headed for Uncle Sugar Able, the good old US of A.

As Halsey led his occupation force into Tokyo Bay, *Astoria* formed up with a handful of ships headed the opposite direction. The ship's band gleefully played "California, Here I Come." Light carrier *San Jacinto* had strung a lengthy "Homeward Bound" banner in her wake, suspended behind her by weather balloons. And steaming alongside *Astoria* was her charge for the very long seventy-nine days off Okinawa—USS *Essex*, also headed for refit but otherwise unscathed. The pair would be the first ships to return from the combat zone following the surrender, victorious.

20

Uncle Sugar

I want to offer my sympathy to those men receiving "Dear John" letters... Mine is marrying a
soldier. Who is yours marrying?
—*5th Division reporter, Mighty Ninety newspaper, August 1945*

Cartoonist Joe Aman spent the journey home re-creating his favorite
Joey Fubar cartoons, compiling a "Cavalcade of Humor" printed
compilation that men could take with them as a souvenir. Joey Fubar
ultimately won his creator a Navy commendation for boosting morale.
The lead scribe behind the *Astoria* press self-proclaimed his promotion to
"Civilian First Class" as he prepared to leave ship on points, and he offered a list of helpful reminders to his shipmates such as how to behave
around women and family, and how to return one's vocabulary to words
with more than four letters.

Essex detached to head into Bremerton, Washington. Men packed her
flight deck, waving, as her ship's whistle blared farewell to the Mighty
Ninety, the guardian that kept her safe those long months.

Astoria continued south down the coast to Los Angeles and approached
her pier assignment at Terminal Island Navy Yard. Captain Hamilton
ordered the Kingfisher floatplanes ahead to retrieve mail, a move that
backfired when they returned packed full of Dear John letters, informing

sailors that their girls had moved on. Morale plummeted when it should have been at a peak, but the men of *Astoria* were late coming home with the war in Europe long over.

Herb Blodgett was one of several men selected to go ashore in a boat ahead of the ship to secure the lines when she docked. He recalled,

> Since I was in A Division and theoretically had some knowledge of diesels, I was occasionally assigned to do something in the whaleboat...As we approached Long Beach, the typical early morning haze and fog was so thick that you couldn't see beyond the bow of the ship. So they sent us in the little whaleboat ahead of the ship, not to guide the ship, but just to be in there to handle lines if it was necessary. Well, on the way in, we came by this big shape that loomed out of the fog and it was the USS *Boise*! And I had tears down my eyes, oh, my old ship! So there was one chance to wave goodbye to her.

He was further surprised to learn that a complement of sailors awaited to handle the mooring lines for them.

The full reception ran the length of the pier. WACs, WAVEs, and press all lined up. Front and center he spotted a truck-mounted bandstand with a Navy band fronted by famous recording artist Ella Mae Morse. Hailing from Mansfield, her Texas twang and hit song "Cow Cow Boogie" brought a taste of home for the few Texans aboard. *Astoria* men and their passengers packed the starboard rail, whooping at the women and writing song requests in chalk on the ship's superstructure—"Don't Fence Me In." Morse declared over her microphone that she would kiss the first sailor off the ship, and men jockeyed for position at the brow. Herman Schnipper photographed the actual winner receiving his prize from the recording artist.

Crowds packed the pier, and the homecoming reception was featured in all the regional newspapers, replete with photographs of *Astoria*'s scoreboard of island bombardments and Japanese plane credits. The accompanying articles spoke of her protection of *Essex* against *Kamikaze* attack, referred to as "terrier duty" for the big carrier. *Astoria* was the first ship to return to Los Angeles after the surrender.

Refit work began immediately on the ship, as construction crews replaced sailors on liberty. Two-week leaves were granted for all men who did not have enough points to be discharged, and the leaves were split into two sections. Fred Lind wrote, "While a bunch of my buddies left for home, I enjoyed liberty in the good old USA. Twenty-two days leave doesn't translate into too much time at home on the East Coast, because it meant five days via train each way."

Jim Peddie and 117 other men drawn for the second leave had time to plan. They knew the train ride cross-country both ways for a largely Northeast crew would consume much of their leave. Some men managed commercial air travel, but the flights were difficult to book, crowded, and expensive. One sailor had a buddy who was a former pilot with the Flying Tigers and had been home for a while. He and a group of investors had purchased surplus Budd Conestoga airplanes and started their own air cargo service locally, National Freight Service.

Peddie and the others had plenty of money from undrawn pay, so they chartered five cargo planes to fly them up east and back, two each to Boston and New York, and a fifth to Buffalo. $175 each earned them a rented mattress and box lunches for the journey, $100 cheaper than a commercial booking. Flying "cargo class," they rode on the deck and maximized their time with their families and sweethearts as a result. The story made the *New York Times* with the article headline, "Blow In for a Blow-out."

Fred Lind penned, "Reunion with the family is indescribable. We had tough times at sea, but we could see what was happening. At home, Mom and Pop could only read the news and pray. Parents suffered unbearably, but family gatherings seemed to overcome all the problems."

By November, *Astoria*'s crew had a 50 percent turnover. Gone were most of the veteran petty officers like Blodgett and Arrighi; now the

Sampson men were rated and senior. The Mighty Ninety, fully repainted and refit with updated antiaircraft guns, took part in a fleet review to wish farewell to Admiral Halsey, now back from Tokyo. Each ship gave the retiring fleet admiral a seventeen-gun salute in turn as his barge passed by, his five-star blue-and-white flag whipping in the wind.

In December *Astoria* returned to sea, heading to Pearl Harbor to pack full again with men returning home as part of Operation Magic Carpet, which turned warships temporarily into transports. Some passengers were former POWs, many not used to sea travel, and the trip back to Terminal Island became a nightmare of stench and vomit. Still, passengers kissed the ground upon arrival in California. They would be home in time for Christmas, and Mighty Ninety sailors were acutely aware that meant these men would add to the masses lining up ahead of them for girls and jobs.

Late in 1945, newly promoted Rear Admiral Dyer ran into Halsey's five stars at Main Navy for the first time in many months. Gripping his hand, looking him in the eye, Halsey said, "Wouldn't you just be the son of a bitch with the right course." *180 degrees true.* Halsey walked on, having admitted that Dyer had followed the centuries-old Bowditch *Practical Navigator* and advised the correct course out of harm's way during the December 1944 typhoon maelstrom. Halsey had wanted too badly to stay on station. Listening to *Astoria*'s skipper earlier could have saved more than eight hundred men.

The trial of Captain Charles McVay, skipper of the doomed *Indianapolis*, had also begun for failings in the loss of his ship.

Dyer reflected on his former ship's sinking, which stood in stark contrast with his handling of *Astoria* given similar orders earlier in the war. Dyer had "put the man on the spot" and repeatedly requested escort when ordered to sail alone through similar waters. Had McVay requested escort, he opined, "She would have had escorts instead of being sunk by a Japanese submarine."

Through March 1946, while still assigned aboard, Herman Schnipper and his buddies did their best to terrorize Hollywood, posing under the real Hollywood and Vine sign (as opposed to the one at Ulithi), taking tours of the homes of the stars, and photographing themselves walking out of Bing Crosby's nightclub like they owned the place. Yet tragedy struck for Schnipper when he learned that his father had suddenly passed away. He arranged for a flight home in time to sit shiva, the Jewish rite of mourning with his family, only to be denied permission by an officer. "You bury your people too quickly," he was told. In an example of what sailors called "Navy chickenshit," Schnipper was released from duty within a week, on the same day that shiva ended. Another instance of anti-Semitism for the young photographer.

Under her third commanding officer, Captain Frank Walker, *Astoria* spent the rest of 1946 on a victory cruise up the West Coast. Declared "Victor in War, Guardian in Peace," her wartime scoreboard was painted over. She became a celebrity ship, hosting dignitaries and ferrying the Portland Rose Festival's queen and court down the Columbia and Willamette Rivers to the festival. She made another stop on the Columbia River returning to sea—the first time a ship named *Astoria* had ever visited Astoria, Oregon. Her victory cruise further took her to her predecessor's old haunts of Bremerton, Vancouver, and Dutch Harbor, Alaska. Instead of her success in the Pacific, word of mouth persisted of Neptune's curse, and sailors with their ears blown out while trapped at their station during main battery fire, an event that had dated back to *Astoria*'s shakedown cruise regarding gun mounts that no longer even existed, as they were replaced after. New Boots wondered what kind of duty they had drawn.

Also fading from memory was the Navy experiment of the Cramp Shipbuilding Company. All remaining contracts were canceled by war's end, all work stopped in 1946. Efforts by Cramp to attract civilian work were largely unsuccessful, and the last Cramp cruiser hulls were scrapped on the shipways. In shuttering the yard, which would eventually return to a desolation of rust and weeds, management issued stockholders a $1 dividend per share from their remaining funds. It was the only return investors in the company would ever see.

Astoria remained in commission through February 1949, one of the last *Clevelands* to be retired. She served occupation duty in China and spent sixteen months operating in the Marianas through late February 1948, also operating out of Terminal Island for midshipmen cruises. At one point her crew sighted and destroyed an old Japanese mine. While this would have been routine duty three years earlier, in 1948 it became a novelty that made the *New York Times*.

After decommissioning, *Astoria* spent more than twenty years sitting idle at an inactive reserve facility in San Diego, her hull popping as metal expanded and contracted with each dawn and nightfall. Not one Mighty Ninety veteran was present as she was towed out on a cool morning in 1971, passing under the Coronado Bridge to meet her fate with the breakers up the coast in Richmond. Sold by the Navy in 1970, she was to be scrapped. Ever defiant, the ex–light cruiser's hull number 90 remained visible in its war-era small stencil, her guns still in place.

In 1972, surviving shipmates from the two cruisers named *Astoria* held their first reunions. The decisions to meet were independent, but men from both ships realized with events thirty years behind them, no one was getting any younger.

The reunions reflected the regional nature of their crews. For *Astoria* CA-34, the lost predecessor, her sailors and Marines met in Gearhart, Oregon, just south of Astoria at the mouth of the Columbia River. She had been aptly named, always a West Coast ship with a predominantly West Coast crew. Her loss at Savo Island ensured a somber remembrance as part of the reunion.

For *Astoria* CL-90, her avenging namesake, men and wives met in Boston. The Mighty Ninety began her life as a Northeast ship with a Northeast crew, and Rochester's own Joe Aman drew up Joey Fubar flyers to spark old memories. Retired admirals George Dyer and William Hamilton both attended.

After many separate reunions, the two crews decided to have a joint reunion in 1995. It would be the only one. As one shipmate related regarding the memories, "It just got too painful." Men retreated into the Silence.

Epilogue

Guardians in the Setting Sun

Nobody would really realize, and you can't explain
it unless you was there.

—*Albert W. Farris,*
USS Astoria *sailor 1944–1946*

Reflecting in later years, Gerard Armitage wrote, "It would be contemptible to set down a record of *Astoria*'s war cruise unless proper tribute was paid to those valiant young Bluejackets who stood fully exposed in that open platform. High in the ship, through attack after attack—as the flak literally rained down upon the ship—and when it was virtually impossible to tell whose ship the *Kamikazes* were diving upon until the last minute. Through it all, these youngsters in their late teens or early twenties, calmly went about their spotting or transmitted their messages or otherwise performed their duties with the highest order of decorum, dedication, and courage. To be privileged to serve with them was a most memorable experience."

While most men took pride in their contribution, they did so quietly. How could one tell a wife or children about watching burning men blown off a ship? Planes exploding under black skies? How could they relate to the endless days of sheer fatigue, seeing another man lose his nerve and crack or cry for help while flailing in his own blood? Wives came to know on their own, for they didn't have to be told. They experienced it firsthand in the restless sleep of their husband, the cries at night, and the dreams that were memories. They learned how to bring their husbands back, to soothe and calm, fighting their own battle that lasted many more years than the Pacific war.

For their part, the combat veterans were given no counseling or assessment for what was then called "battle fatigue," now acknowledged as post-traumatic stress disorder. The limits of such things in the 1945 military were letters from a separation center chaplain to a wife. For example, *Astoria* shipmate William Theaker's wife received a letter from his chaplain that stated, "We must remember that life in the military service, of necessity, is much different from life at home. I am sure you will do all you can to assist him to readjust himself as a vital part of his family, his church, and his community... My sincere prayer is that his return home will measure up to his hope and expectations."

For the vast majority of men, the Silence carried forward for years, often a lifetime. Most simply wanted to put the war behind them, and many struggled. Some men found security in alcohol and squelched demons by drinking. Others turned to religion for guidance, or ongoing education. A number of doctors, politicians, and degreed professionals emerged from the *Astoria* cadre. Yet the pain of experience, both firsthand and the impact on their families, remained.

HERB BLODGETT

With his focus returned to baseball, Herb Blodgett earned a one-hour tryout with the Boston Red Sox. "I was the smallest guy on the field," he told me. "I was only about 5'8", and could not hit with power. But I could play the outfield, I could throw, they appreciated that, but they wanted sluggers and I didn't fit the bill...the debate was about if you were able to hit that left field wall." Herb met his future wife, Ruth, the love of his life, and they celebrated sixty-eight anniversaries before he passed. Blodgett remained a baseball and softball player until retirement when he was eighty. He left a legacy of four children, and as of this writing four grandchildren and six great-grandchildren. Blodgett remained passionate about his US Navy service and contributed heavily to this project. He cried privately when he learned from the author that men had suffered casualties aboard *Astoria*.

FRED LIND

Of his brother Paul, Fred Lind wrote many years later, "Loss of my best buddy, two years older than me, has been devastating throughout my life. I didn't know much about grief until then, and I felt like I had swallowed a bucket of cement that had set up in my throat. I think a lot of it is still there."

Lind's secret diary written in Gregg shorthand provided much rich color to this narrative, and he served his country with honor and distinction following the loss of his brother. He returned to work in capacities he loved: Eastman Kodak, recreational camps, and bowling alleys. His life was further enriched by multiple grandchildren and great-grandchildren. His family still has the damaged binoculars from the Japanese attack.

JIM THOMSON

By 1951, the close-knit fire controlmen of *Astoria* had set up a large network, locating one another through mail and by phone, the first ship division to do so. They agreed to begin meeting in New York City. They could see the Giants play—Jim Thomson's little brother Bobby was gaining notoriety as the "Staten Island Scot," a slugger for the big-league team. Jim Thomson had joined the New York Fire Department and was doing well in his own right, but that October Bobby stole the show by hitting the "Shot Heard 'Round the World" against Ralph Branca of the Brooklyn Dodgers, destined to become the most famous home run in major-league history. Ever humble, Bobby took the ferry home after the win and the first person he visited was his mentor Jim. Jim Thomson made a career with FDNY and passed away in the late 1970s. Younger brother Bobby and Jim's son both contributed to this project. Bobby Thomson's signature on letters was a spot-on match to his baseball card autographs.

JOHN ARRIGHI

When John Arrighi returned to civilian life in Massachusetts, he picked up where he left off in food service. After working in a number of establishments, he opened his own restaurant in the same building where he had worked for his parents before the war. An avid sports fan, he played basketball and baseball into his sixties, and sponsored a championship softball team through his restaurant. He fathered five children along the way.

ROUSSEAU LEMON

Rosseau Lemon applied with the US Army Reserve after his naval service ended. He then spent years as a painter foreman in civil service at Kelly Air Force Base in San Antonio, maintaining ties to the military long after his wartime service and discharge. A fully redeemed man, he died of congestive heart failure in San Antonio in 1977. He is buried in Fort Sam Houston National Cemetery.

TOM KANE

Tom Kane returned home to his beloved wife. After work in a lumber yard, he made a career as an exterminator. Even when his son joined the Navy, he never talked about his own experiences. John Snyder came to visit him once in the 1950s, but they only shared the one reunion experience. Perhaps the only thing they had in common after all was the war, and the Silence took over.

JIM PEDDIE

Returning home a veteran of Sicily, Salerno, and *Astoria*'s Pacific war cruise, Jim Peddie put his Navy electrical training and experience to use. After marrying his wife, Grace, in late 1945, he began a career as a journeyman electrician, working the big presses for local newspapers. He later received a call from an old Sunday school teacher asking if he had a job, which took him to similar work for the *Christian Science Monitor*. He retired after thirty-eight years of post-Navy electrical work, having two daughters. He was also an organizer for the *Astoria* reunions beginning in 1973. As of this writing, Peddie is the lone surviving shipmate from the narrative. At 98, he resides in Massachusetts with his beloved dog Sammy.

DON COMB

After leaving military aviation, Don Comb returned to complete his degree in civil engineering. He worked with his father constructing airfields across the Midwest for many years, then finished his career with 3M. He and his wife, Peggy, left a legacy of five children with many grandchildren and greats. He kept the same four-leaf clover in his billfold throughout.

HERMAN SCHNIPPER

In 1975, Herman Schnipper took one last photograph of mighty *Essex*. One of America's most decorated World War II veteran ships sat rusting away in the Bayonne shipyard near his home. He captured her defiant stern nameplate through a barbed wire fence. Unscathed survivor of Okinawa, she was now losing the one battle her crew could never save her from, not *Astoria*, not anyone. She was being cut apart for scrap. She had done her duty and her time was over.

The Navy handed Schnipper's photographs over to the National Archives, which promptly destroyed almost all of them, along with that of fellow combat photographers, "to make room." Of close to 1,300 images, the archives preserved a mere twenty-seven in their holdings. However, Schnipper preserved the history—he had left *Astoria* with a print of every image he took packed into the bottom of his seabag. In almost every case he retained the only surviving copy.

Herman Schnipper attended the reunions and broke out his collection for men to view. Laughter would turn to somber silence as his shipmates moved through images that took *Astoria* deeper into her war. If no words could be exchanged with family members, in the company of shipmates no words were necessary.

Schnipper spent his years with a passion for his time in the Navy. As a reservist after the war, he served as ship's photographer aboard USS *Wisconsin* during an Atlantic cruise in 1947. Yet he served as a seaman first-class, not a photographer's mate. He never received another opportunity to advance in rate, and the circumstances remain subject to scrutiny.

He made a career as a printer and lithographer, and raised two daughters. In later years he appealed to the Navy Board of Corrections to have his rate restored—not for back pay or benefits, but for what he did during the Pacific war and the questionable justice he received in losing his rate as a photographer's mate. His appeals carried to the time of his passing, and all were denied, despite the involvement of this author and a retired Navy captain.

GERARD ARMITAGE

Gerard Armitage remained in the Marines and remained close to George Dyer, Chuck Tanner, and others. In February 1948 he wrote to his former CO, "I should like nothing better than to go out there with the Admiral...Our good friend Tanner is still busy at the same old stand. He is now in helicopter work at Lakehurst NAS. From the Mighty Ninety he went to Pensacola, then to Norfolk and aboard a carrier for a trip to the North Pole. Later he joined the South Pole Carrier Experimental Cruise and narrowly escaped when he dunked a helicopter in the water in sub-zero weather. He and his very sweet wife (hometown childhood sweetheart) are expecting their firstborn this month." He closed offering Dyer a paid subscription to *Time* magazine.

Armitage commanded a battalion of Marines in the Battle for Bunker Hill in Korea, August 1952. He later spent twenty years as a construction executive including overseas work and passed in 2009 with a large family of children, grandchildren, and greats. Colonel Armitage was buried in Arlington National Cemetery with full Marine honors.

GEORGE CARROLL DYER

As for Vice Admiral George Carroll Dyer, USN (ret.), Gerard Armitage wrote, "Our first skipper was a true professional in every sense—talented leader, superb ship-handler, tactician and fighter. He loved his ship. Unlike many of his seafaring peers, he understood precisely what she was intended for—to close her guns within range of the enemy and to carry the fight, to yield nothing. 'Astoria' was happiest when her guns were engaged. On more than one occasion in the wardroom, this Marine Captain defended this purpose when 'purists' murmured at the perceived recklessness of 'Astoria' for volunteering us into harm's way time and again. This Marine was proud to sail under Captain Dyer's command. So indeed was the entire Detachment."

Dyer served as commander of Task Force 95, the United Nations Blockading and Escorting Force, in 1951 during the Korean War. He later wrote textbooks for the US Naval Academy and biographies of other admirals. Following a series of strokes, he had no choice but to retire. Yet he never lost touch with his *Astoria* shipmates when they would write to him. He passed away in 1989, his three daughters carrying a legacy that extends to great-great-grandchildren.

Across the water inlet at the US Naval Academy, a wooden bridge leads to a small cemetery on a hill. Densely populated with grave markers, the cemetery has few living visitors at any time, save the occasional midshipman cutting through to a class at Beach Hall.

Many of the graves are elaborate affairs—statuesque, ornately carved, and adorned with quotes. The names on the markers read like a fleet review, or perhaps the index of a US Navy history book: Ernest King, Arleigh Burke, and so on. By contrast, in Section G lies Marker 12, a simple VA-style granite marker: final resting place for a vice admiral beside his beloved wife, Adaline. George Dyer, the man who took *Astoria* and a gallant, admiring crew through the maelstrom of the Pacific War in 1945.

Acknowledgments

A heartfelt thank you and gratitude to my Hachette editor Lauren Marino and her consistent yeoman's work. Sincerest thanks to Mollie Weisenfeld, Fred Francis, Bill Warhop, Michael Giarratano, Quinn Fariel, and the entire Hachette team.

To my agent Jim Hornfischer, I can only humbly hope to approach the bar you have set as an author yourself. It's an honor and privilege to even share a ballpark, and thank you for taking a shot on a rookie with an idea that was tough to sell.

Thank you to my illustrator James Fenelon for performing his craft in impeccable fashion. Sorry it took us so many redraws to get *Astoria* correct; the *Cleveland*-class isn't a simple one.

To my fellow *Astoria* devotees, all with family ties to the ship: John Moccia, Carl Theaker, Corey Bullard, Ron Schmitt, Gary DiMaio, and Dominic DeScisciolo, USN Captain (ret.), thank you for the connections we have made, your contributions over the years, and your belief in this project. Similar thanks to family members from other ships who assisted, notably Joe Madden and Peter Somerville.

To Billie and Jim Rash, Bill and Danielle Baron, and Glenna Whitley, your generosity in aiding my research means the world. Thank you.

Sincere appreciation also goes out to the staffs at the following repositories: the National Archives in College Park and Fort Worth, the Library of Congress, the National Personnel Records Center, the Naval History and Heritage Command, the United States Naval Institute, and the J. Welles Henderson Research Center at Independence Seaport Museum.

The work you and others in similar roles perform daily enables historians to do what they do.

To the families of the principal characters in this narrative, I am humbled beyond words at your grace and faith. Thank you for believing. For George Dyer, Fred Lind, Herb Blodgett, Gerard Armitage, Al Lusk, Herman Schnipper, Tom Kane, John Snyder, John Arrighi, Jim Thomson, Jim Peddie, Rousseau Lemon, Chuck Tanner, Don Comb, Jack Newman, and all their shipmates, I sincerely hope I have done these brave and noble Americans justice.

Lastly, no words can express gratitude enough to my family for their support across such a journey. Much like the journey of the shipmates of USS *Astoria*, it could never have been taken alone.

Notes

Unless otherwise stated in citation, direct quotes and statements from the veterans in this ensemble oral history come from the interviews, diaries, and memoirs listed in the attached bibliography. All are vetted against the deck logs, war diaries, and action reports for USS *Astoria* CL-90. In any instance where veteran memory in later years conflicted with official period documents, the latter has been given precedence.

Where multiple sources are blended into a paragraph or short section, the citation below starts with "constructed from." Longer sections crafted from overlapping citations are bracketed with opening and closing portions of text.

All track charts on maps and specified ship locations are derived from longitude/latitude coordinates logged in the USS *Astoria* war diary. The track chart for USS *Franklin* CV-13 is similarly derived from her war diary coordinates.

American nicknames for Japanese aircraft found in the narrative:

Betty: Mitsubishi G4M medium navy bomber.
Dinah: Mitsubishi Ki-46 army reconnaissance aircraft.
Frances: Yokosuka P1Y navy attack bomber.
George: Kawanishi N1K navy interceptor fighter.
Judy: Yokosuka D4Y navy reconnaissance aircraft.
Tojo: Nakajima Ki-44 army interceptor fighter.
Zeke/Zero: Mitsubishi A6M navy long-range fighter.

Notes

PART ONE: THE VENGEANCE SHIP

Part One photo insert: USS *Astoria* CL-90 launching at Cramp shipyard, March 6, 1943.
—US Navy photo NH 75591 (NHHC)

1. THE OLD MAN AND THE SEA

3 Captain Dyer's narrative is a blending of his oral histories to Mason Jr. and Burnett Jr.
5 USS *Astoria* CA-34 account is from Mooney, DANFS.

2. NEW CONSTRUCTION

10 "Oh, take me back to New Construction": Document of "Songs we sing" circulated aboard Cruiser Division 17 ships in 1945. (Author's collection)
11 USS *Oklahoma City* CL-91 launching account is by an unnamed author: "Your Rovin' Reporter Gets a Worm's Eye View of a Launching of the Cruiser *Oklahoma City*," *Cramp News*, March 11, 1944, 4. (Author's collection)
12 "They will man a sister ship": Introductory remarks for launching of USS *Oklahoma City* by H. Birchard Taylor, February 20, 1944, 2. (ISM)
12 Philadelphia readers followed the much larger story: Author unnamed, "15,000 Idle at Shipyard After Vote," *Philadelphia Inquirer*, January 7, 1944, 1.
12 such legacy and prestige as Cramp: Author unnamed, *Cramp...An Epic of Action*, 1943 internal Cramp Shipbuilding Company publication. (Author's collection)
13 Cramp Shipbuilding was in real trouble: Author review of Cramp Shipbuilding Company financial statements and letters to shareholders, 1941–1944. (ISM)
14 They stuffed chewing gum in keyholes: Author unnamed, "Hundreds of Autos Damaged by Vandals Near Cramps Shipyard," *Philadelphia Inquirer*, September 27, 1942, B3.
14 "Is an Agreement a Mere Scrap of Paper?": Author unnamed, headline article, *Cramp News*, January 2, 1943, 1. (ISM)

15 Locals took sides in letters to the editor: "The Voice of the People," *Philadelphia Inquirer,* February 3, 1944, 10.

15 "The only thing the four-day strike": Author unnamed, "They Merely Helped Our Enemies," *Philadelphia Inquirer*, January 11, 1944, 10.

15 "Don't slow up the ship!": Cramp Shipbuilding Company internal motivational materials. (ISM)

15 "things are going ahead slowly but surely": George C. Dyer letter to Captain J. G. Crawford of USS *Miami* CL-89, April 20, 1944, Dyer papers, LOC.

16 "There will be other cruisers": Author unnamed, "USS *Wilkes-Barre*," *Wilkes-Barre Times-Leader*, October 21, 1942, 14.

16 "named for the old *Astoria,* which dealt death to the Japs": United Newsreel Roll 41, circa March 1943, Records Group 208. (NARA)

16 "With a desire to pay back these so and sos": Dyer oral history to Mason Jr.

16 One man proved quite easy to locate: Unnamed author, "Admiral Bruce, USN Congratulates Hero Phipps of USS *Astoria*," *Cramp News*, August 21, 1943, 2.

17 Best of intentions aside: Dyer oral history to Mason Jr.

3. MAN O' WAR'S MEN

18 "the inertia of the place": E. W. Armentrout letter to George C. Dyer, April 12, 1944, LOC.

19 Armentrout had a floating city to populate: Armentrout's challenges in assembling his crew cover a number of letters to Dyer across April–May 1944, retained in Dyer's papers, LOC.

19 The Navy was exploding in size: King, 14–15.

19 sent him seamen alphabetically: While all 1944 US Navy muster rolls were alphabetical, Armentrout's seaman second-class and seaman first-class drafts held very high concentrations of these letters.

20 crippled Armentrout's efforts…Responses from Dyer made it clear: Armentrout's continued challenges in assembling his crew cover a number of letters back and forth with Dyer across April–May 1944, retained in Dyer's papers, LOC.

20 The forty-year-old's wife: Erasmus W. Armentrout census and marriage records assembled by the author from www.ancestry.com.

21 His shortages left him far more concerned: Section constructed from letters back and forth with Dyer across April–May 1944, retained in Dyer's papers, LOC.

23 Fred Lind never desired military service: Lind, 3–7. Backstory constructed from memoir and author interviews.

25 a Christian cross bore the name of Paul Lind: "Solomons Island Battle," *LIFE,* October 26, 1942, 41.

25 the Marine tankers were burned: Gilbert, 46.

26 "You'll be sorry!": Talcott, 4.

28 the vast majority of Sampson seamen second-class: Muster rolls for *Astoria* and other WASP Division cruisers.

29 Blodgett also loved to play baseball: Backstory constructed from diary and author interviews.

31 Jim Peddie, also detached from *Boise*: Author interviews.

33 On April 17, a fuming Rousseau Lemon: Constructed from Lemon service record, NPRC, and *Astoria* CA-34 accounts from DANFS, Custer.

39 The Navy and Cramp agreed on a delivery date: Dyer papers, LOC.

39 Little things still required attention: Dyer and Armentrout letters, LOC.

4. COMMISSIONING

41 Cloudless sun brought near-record temperatures: Armitage account constructed from Armitage, 4–60.

50 News reports spoke of fresh Allied attacks: USS *Astoria Morning Press*.

50 *Biloxi* was far from the only cruiser built: War Diaries for each ship listed.

51 Three hundred honored guests filed into the Philadelphia Navy Yard: USS *Astoria* deck logs.

51 Dyer kept his address short and to the point: Dyer papers, LOC.

51 The first day in commission: USS *Astoria* deck logs.

52 Of the men standing in crisp ranks: USS *Astoria* initial muster roll of May 17, 1944.

52 Herb Blodgett celebrated the evening: Blodgett diary.

5. ROCKS AND SHOALS

53 Stationed at Pearl Harbor: Dyer oral history to Mason Jr.

55 moved into roles that began alphabetically: Shipmate interviews blended with USS *Astoria* muster rolls.

55 Fighting and disrespecting the authority: USS *Astoria* deck logs.

55 These problems were nothing new: *Articles for the Government of the United States Navy.*

56 Dyer had ordered his division officers: Dyer oral history to Mason Jr.

56 Dyer and Armentrout set to work: Section constructed from USS *Astoria* deck logs.

57 found Herman Schnipper's face: Section constructed from USS *Astoria* deck logs, Schnipper photographs with captions, and author interviews with Schnipper.

58 one of seventeen men aboard: USS *Astoria* initial muster roll of May 17, 1944.

60 The Cramp-built cruiser executed a sweeping maneuver: Section constructed from USS *Astoria* deck logs.

61 "Too excited to sleep": Armitage, 61.

6. BREAKDOWN CRUISE

62 "They told us we were not supposed to keep a diary": Author interview with Blodgett.

62 He gripped the lifeline: Section constructed from author interviews with Schnipper.
63 exercises off Brandywine Shoal: Section constructed from USS *Astoria* deck logs, Schnipper photographs with captions, and author interviews with Schnipper.
65 Herb Blodgett came off watch at noon: Section constructed from USS *Astoria* deck logs, Blodgett diary, and author interviews with Blodgett.
66 Captain Dyer's frustration began: Dyer oral history to Burnett Jr.
67 Herman Schnipper tried to convince himself: Section constructed from USS *Astoria* deck logs, Schnipper photographs with captions, and author interviews with Schnipper.
70 The primary purpose of a shakedown cruise: Section constructed from USS *Astoria* deck logs, Blodgett diary, and author interviews with Blodgett.
71 a few men returned to be placed on venereal watch: USS *Astoria* deck logs.
72 Kane and Snyder grew up hundreds of miles apart: Section constructed from Kane and Snyder family interviews, shared diary, and www.ancestry.com.
73 refit battleship USS *Wyoming*: USS *Wyoming* BB-32 war diary.
74 Early on a fellow 4th Division man was approached: Author interview with Obuchon.
75 at one point the waiting line: Section constructed from USS *Astoria* deck logs.
76 "darken ship" at sunset: Ibid.
76 a later *Cleveland*-class, *Astoria* was built with an open bridge: Friedman, 268.
76 tore the open bridge plot table from its mounts: Dyer oral history to Mason Jr.
76 Training deficiencies emerged: Section constructed from USS *Astoria* deck logs, Schnipper photographs, and author interviews.
77 A related matter became protective flak suits: Dyer oral history to Mason Jr.
78 *Astoria* departed the Trinidad area: Section constructed from USS *Astoria* deck logs and author interviews.
78 Yet Lemon never forgot: Constructed from Lemon service record, NPRC, and author interviews.

7. GOLDEN GATE IN '48

80 Ninety-pound seabag over his shoulder: Section constructed from Lind memoir and author interviews.
81 Herb Blodgett held similar plans: Section constructed from Blodgett diary and author interviews.
83 Rear Admiral J. Cary Jones's flagship USS *Pasadena*: USS *Pasadena* CL-65 war diary.
83 *LIFE* magazine even saw fit: *LIFE*, May 22, 1945, 35.
83 declared "fit and ready for all action": Section constructed from USS *Astoria* deck logs.
84 Newly promoted first-class petty officers: Section constructed from USS *Astoria* reports of changes.
84 he instructed his executive officer: Section constructed from Dyer oral history to Mason Jr.

84 a sharp rise in absenteeism: Section constructed from USS *Astoria* deck logs and author interviews.

86 One spark of inspiration: Custer.

87 *Astoria* needed a nickname: Dyer oral history to Mason Jr.

87 a few volunteer "beat reporters": Section constructed from USS *Astoria Morning Press*, *Mighty Ninety* newspapers, and author interviews.

88 The captain even began a personal file: Dyer papers, LOC.

89 Back from their surprise two-week leave: Section constructed from Lind memoir and author interviews.

91 the name of James Hay Thomson: Section constructed from Thomson diary, Lind memoir, author interviews with family, and www.ancestry.com.

92 Fellows created plenty of ways: Author interviews with Schnipper.

93 four more men had gone over the hill: Section constructed from USS *Astoria* deck logs, Dyer oral history to Mason Jr., Schnipper photographs, and author interviews with Schnipper.

94 the Mighty Ninety cleared the hurdle: Section constructed from USS *Astoria* deck logs.

95 Fred Lind delighted to learn: Section constructed from Lind, 9–15, and author interview with Lind.

97 passed through the Panama Canal: Section constructed from Blodgett diary and author interviews with Blodgett.

97 Passing one house early on: Lind, 10.

98 he and a few buddies: Author interviews with Peddie.

98 shore patrol received summary courts-martial: Section constructed from USS *Astoria* deck logs.

99 Despite the early morning fog: Ibid.

99 *We're coming in all wrong*: Author interviews with Blodgett.

101 the State Pier harbor pilot: Section constructed from USS *Astoria* deck logs and Dyer oral history to Burnett Jr.

102 Gerard Armitage had no more taken position: Armitage, 63–64.

103 Fred Lind took in a movie: Lind, 10.

103 Herman Schnipper decided to break a regulation: Schnipper letter and author interviews with Schnipper.

104 Others with good-conduct records: Constructed from Lemon service record, NPRC, and USS *Astoria* deck logs.

104 *Astoria* limped from San Diego: Constructed from USS *Astoria* deck logs.

PART TWO: HERE BE DRAGONS

Part Two photo insert: A *Kamikaze* plane dives on USS *Essex* CV-9 off the Philippines, November 25, 1944.

—US Navy photo taken by C. S. Colwell (author's collection)

8. INTO THE FRAY

109 A few men sought solitude: Photographs of USS *Astoria* taken on October 21, 1944, at Mare Island, NARA 19-LCM.

110 beloved wife Adaline across country: Dyer papers, LOC.

110 The engine discussion alone: Section constructed from Dyer oral histories to Burnett Jr. and Mason Jr., and Schnipper photographs.

111 the same issue had just been reported: USS *Springfield* CL-66 war diary.

111 became the word for the culprit: Section constructed from Dyer oral histories to Burnett Jr. and Mason Jr.

112 USS *Pasadena* had leapfrogged: USS *Pasadena* CL-65 war diary.

112 the recently published *Forever Amber*: Section constructed from *Mighty Ninety* newspaper.

113 time to pursue the matter of Lemon: Section constructed from Dyer oral histories to Burnett Jr. and Mason Jr.

113 Lemon had been down this road before: Section constructed from USS *Santa Fe* CL-60 reports of changes, Lemon service record, NPRC, and Dyer oral histories to Burnett Jr. and Mason Jr.

114 The problem of men missing sailing: Captain Malcom F. Schoeffel letter of January 16, 1944, to Commander Air Force, Pacific Fleet, from 8th Naval District papers, NARAFW.

114 He further pointed out a new wrinkle: Dyer oral histories to Burnett Jr. and Mason Jr.

115 Armitage had developed his own racket: Armitage, 65–66.

116 "Fly low, fly slow, fly VO": VO in Navy terms stands for heavier-than-air observation flight.

117 Lind branched out in his liberties: Lind, 10.

118 Pappy Kane and John Snyder ran up their share: Kane and Snyder shared diary and inserts.

118 Dyer gave the crew another pep talk: Section constructed from Dyer oral history to Mason Jr. and USS *Astoria* deck logs and reports of changes.

119 Schnipper photographed the scene: Section constructed from Schnipper photographs, USS *Astoria* deck logs, USS *Baltimore* CA-68 and USS *Montpelier* CL-57 war diaries, and Dyer oral history to Mason Jr.

120 Fred Lind discovered the serious nature: Lind, 13.

120 Throughout, "Lowlife" Dyer fretted: Dyer oral history to Mason Jr.

121 morning of October 31, 1944: USS *Astoria* deck logs.

121 Captain Dyer's thoughts lay elsewhere: Constructed from Dyer oral histories to Burnett Jr. and Mason Jr., and reports of changes for USS *Baltimore* CA-68 and USS *Montpelier* CL-57.

122 6-inch turret number three: Constructed from USS *Astoria* deck logs.

122 Meanwhile J. Cary Jones: USS *Pasadena* CL-65 war diary.

122 Despite the relentless drone: Constructed from Armitage, 66–67, and *Eyes of the Fleet* (US Navy publication, 1944).

123 he advanced to VOS: VOS means observation/scout flying.

125 With her return from the gunnery course: USS *Astoria* deck logs and author interviews.

126 Others weren't so well behaved: Constructed from Dyer oral histories to Burnett Jr. and Mason Jr., USS *Astoria* deck logs, and Dyer papers, LOC.

126 a sickening sight entered the harbor: Blodgett diary, author interviews with Blodgett, and USS *Birmingham* CL-62 war diary.

127 completed work on *Astoria's* turret screws: Constructed from USS *Astoria* deck logs and Armitage, 68–69.

128 Captain Dyer fought his own battle: Constructed from Dyer oral history to Mason Jr. and USS *Astoria* deck logs.

129 USS *Duluth*, had developed a bad vibration: USS *Duluth* CL-87 war diaries.

129 "Plane crash into superstructure": USS *Astoria* deck logs.

9. THE STORM

130 coincided with the Thanksgiving holiday: Constructed from Lind, 12, Schnipper photographs, USS *Astoria* 1944 Thanksgiving menu, and USS *Astoria* deck logs.

131 "Typical holiday chow": Constructed from Arrighi diary and author interviews with family.

131 blue to blend with the deck: Schnipper photographs.

132 Dyer's escort reported for duty: Constructed from USS *Astoria* deck logs, USS *Kalk* DD-611 DANFS entry, and Blodgett diary.

132 "I didn't know we had that many!": Lind, 12.

133 " *Enterprise* versus Japan": USS *Enterprise* CV-6: The Most Decorated Ship of the Second World War, www.cv6.org.

133 Nearby lay three CVLs: Constructed from USS *Astoria* deck logs.

133 managed to strike the oiler *Mississinewa*: USS *Mississinewa* AO-59 DANFS entry.

134 another carrier task group returned: Constructed from USS *Astoria* deck logs, Paul Madden photographs taken from USS *Essex* CV-9, and Schnipper photographs.

134 Many of the ships brought back wounds: Constructed from USS *Cabot* CVL-28, USS *Essex* CV-9, USS *Intrepid* CV-11, USS *Lexington* CV-16, and USS *New Jersey* BB-62 war diaries.

134 Dyer took to the ship's public address: Dyer papers, LOC.

136 "Further casual strikes did not appear profitable": Morison, *Leyte*, 360.

136 Schnipper timed each snap of the shutter: Constructed from Schnipper photographs, USS *Astoria* deck logs, Lind, 12, and Dyer papers, LOC.

138 call sign selection for the Mighty Ninety: Rampage: Dyer oral histories to Burnett Jr. and Mason Jr.

138 The next phase of the Philippine Liberation: Morison, *Liberation of the Philippines*, 52–57.

138 After steaming northwest for two days: Constructed from USS *Astoria* deck logs, Schnipper photographs, and Dyer papers, LOC.

139 **"During the day several planes were lost":** Lind, 17, 19.

139 **"Planes came back pretty well shot up":** Arrighi diary.

140 **"I have never seen a sunrise so sinister":** Lind, 16.

140 **Captain Dyer conferred:** Dyer oral histories to Burnett Jr. and Mason Jr.

140 *Astoria* **and Task Group 38.2:** Typhoon section constructed from USS *Astoria* deck logs, author interviews, Dyer oral history to Burnett Jr., Schnipper photographs, and Morison, *Liberation of the Philippines*, 59–87.

147 **Armitage described the wind:** Armitage, 72.

147 **Lind kept his mind occupied:** Constructed from Lind, 18–19.

148 **Blodgett worked his way up:** Blodgett diary, and author interviews with Blodgett.

148 **Schnipper also received the warning:** Constructed from author interviews with Schnipper and Schnipper account in *The Jerseyman* online magazine, December 2003.

149 **Rolling through 40 degrees:** Constructed from Dyer oral histories to Burnett Jr. and Mason Jr., USS *Astoria* deck logs, and war diaries of listed ships.

151 **By dawn Halsey's Third Fleet lay strewn:** Constructed from Morison, *Liberation of the Philippines*, 59–87, USS *Astoria* deck logs, war diaries of listed surviving ships, and author interviews with Schnipper.

152 **The revelation of** *Hull's* **loss:** Constructed from Morison, *Liberation of the Philippines*, 59–87, USS *Astoria* deck logs, war diaries of listed surviving ships, and Thomson diary.

154 **In Captain Dyer's morning address:** Dyer papers, LOC.

154 **Halsey called off the search:** Constructed from Morison, *Liberation of the Philippines*, 82–84.

154 **the seas remained heavy:** Schnipper photographs and USS *Astoria* war diary.

155 **Scuttlebutt played its usual role:** Author interviews, Schnipper photographs, and USS *Astoria* deck logs.

155 **"The awful fate of those":** Constructed from Lind, 19, Arrighi and Thomson diaries, Schnipper photographs, USS *Astoria* deck logs, and Dyer papers, LOC.

10. THE PRIVATE LAKE OF JAPAN

157 **Fred Lind followed the flaming plane:** Constructed from Lind, 21, Thomson diary, and USS *Astoria* deck logs.

158 **the Fast Carrier Task Force had slipped quietly:** Constructed from Morison, *Liberation of the Philippines*, 87–92.

159 *Astoria* **men had little to do:** Schnipper photographs.

159 **"MacArthur's Navy" was nevertheless struck:** Constructed from Morison, *Liberation of the Philippines*, 101–119, and Lind, 20.

159 **Halsey unleashed his fast carriers:** Constructed from Morison, *Liberation of the Philippines*, 164–166, USS *Wilkes-Barre* CL-103 war diary, USS *Astoria* deck logs, Thomson diary, and Dyer papers, LOC.

160 **Of each call to general quarters:** Arrighi diary.

160 **Dyer turned his attention to the Lemon matter:** Constructed from Dyer papers, LOC, and Lemon service record, NPRC.

161 "The scuttlebutt also began to fly": Constructed from Morison, *Liberation of the Philippines*, 164–166, USS *Astoria* deck logs, Thomson and Arrighi diaries, and Lind, 21.

164 "but how will you get out?" Constructed from Lind, 22, and author interviews. Many men interviewed repeated this.

164 weather conditions continued to deteriorate: Constructed from Morison, *Liberation of the Philippines*, 169–170, USS *Astoria* deck logs, Dyer oral histories to Burnett Jr. and Mason Jr., Armitage, 73–74, and author interviews.

165 "a body turning end over end": Lind, 21.

166 "recited an Act of Contrition": Armitage, 74.

167 Dyer returned his attention: Constructed from Dyer oral history to Mason Jr., Schnipper photographs, author interviews with Schnipper, and USS *Astoria* deck logs.

168 her skipper signaled to Dyer: Constructed from USS *Astoria* deck logs, Dyer papers, LOC, Schnipper photographs, and USS *Astoria Morning Press*.

168 "The first thing Armitage did": Armitage, 75.

168 The ice cream would have come in handy: Constructed from author interviews, Schnipper photographs, and Lind, 21–22.

169 Halsey was given the green light: Constructed from Morison, *Liberation of the Philippines*, 170–174, USS *Astoria* deck logs, and Thomson diary.

170 Fred Lind's diary spoke: Lind, 22.

171 Overnight the Fast Carrier Task Force made its departure: Constructed from Morison, *Liberation of the Philippines*, 179–183, USS *Astoria* deck logs, and Thomson and Arrighi diaries.

173 "We have had very little time to sleep": Lind, 22.

173 Task Group 38.2 suffered their casualty: USS *Hancock* CV-19 war diary.

173 Like other seaplanes: *Eyes of the Fleet* (US Navy publication, 1944).

173 While flames leapt skyward: Constructed from USS *Astoria* deck logs, USS *Pasadena* CL-65 and USS *Aspro* SS-309 war diaries, Schnipper photograph, and 1945 History of the USS *Astoria* Aviation Unit including Tanner account.

176 "close encounter with Davy Jones' Locker": Armitage, 75.

176 "George's morning *tête-à-tête*": Thomson diary.

176 "Unfortunately he did not know": Constructed from Dyer papers, LOC, and USS *Astoria* deck logs.

177 Tanner woke to heavy seas: 1945 History of the USS *Astoria* Aviation Unit including Tanner account.

177 Up in the Nansei Shoto: Constructed from USS *Astoria* deck logs, Lind, 23, Thomson diary, and Dyer papers, LOC.

178 "I am so proud of you": Morison, *Liberation of the Philippines*, 183.

179 "Really stinks below decks": Thomson diary.

179 Waking again in his cockpit: 1945 History of the USS *Astoria* Aviation Unit including Tanner account.

11. REGARDS FROM SHANGRI-LA

182 "Mr. Tanner had been rescued": Lind, 23.

182 "harbor cluttered up": Thomson diary.

183 His son Bobby lost his first tooth: Kane letter inserted in his diary.

183 "Good to see a show that night": Thomson diary.

183 groups of sailors were granted brief liberty: Mog Mog depiction constructed from Wheeler, 88–92, USS *Astoria* deck logs, author interviews, Lind, 12, and Blodgett and Thomson diaries.

184 "It is an unforgivable offense": Dyer papers, LOC.

185 While the crew rotated through recreational liberty: USS *Astoria* deck logs.

185 Herb Blodgett and the engine room men: Blodgett diary.

185 "not according to Hoyle": Thomson diary.

185 On a somber note: USS *Astoria* deck logs.

185 A huge boon for morale: USS *Astoria* reports of changes.

186 The process left Herb Blodgett puzzled: Author interviews with Blodgett.

186 received the best promotion of all: Thomson diary.

186 Despite the heat of Ulithi atoll: Constructed from USS *Astoria* deck logs, Schnipper photographs, Thomson diary, and Lind, 23.

187 work on the 40mm sights paid off: Constructed from USS *Astoria* deck logs, Thomson and Blodgett diaries, and Lind, 9, 23.

188 Kane creating a hand-drawn Valentine: Kane diary insert.

189 "Largest group ever assembled": Constructed from Reynolds, 332, USS *Astoria* deck logs, Thomson diary, and Lind, 24.

190 By the morning of the fifteenth: Constructed from Morison, *Victory in the Pacific*, 4–25, USS *Astoria* deck logs, and Thomson diary.

191 Fred Lind wrote of his watches: Lind, 24.

193 John Arrighi groused: Arrighi diary.

193 three Japanese picket boats: Constructed from USS *Astoria* deck logs, USS *Essex* CV-9 war diary, Lind, 25, and Thomson diary.

194 morning brought more of the same: Constructed from USS *Astoria* deck logs, Lind, 28, and Thomson diary.

194 All further strikes over Honshu canceled: Constructed from USS *Astoria* deck logs, USS *Astoria Morning Press*, and author interviews.

195 "Tojo's flying sons are all around us": Thomson diary.

195 By the evening of the twentieth: Constructed from USS *Astoria* deck logs, Lind, 29, and author interviews.

12. DETACHMENT

196 In the hour before sunrise: Constructed from USS *Astoria* deck logs, author interviews, Lind, 30, Armitage, 77–78, Schnipper photographs, and Morison, *Victory in the Pacific*, 33–50.

197 *Texas* **cut the silhouette of a ship out of time:** Constructed from USS *Astoria* deck logs, Schnipper photographs, and USS *Texas* BB-35 DANFS entry.

198 The invasion code name brought irony: Morison, *Victory in the Pacific*, 7.

198 *Astoria* **men immediately recognized a huge difference:** Constructed from USS *Astoria* deck logs, author interviews, Schnipper photographs, war diaries of ships listed, and Dyer oral history to Mason Jr.

199 "I relieve you of this tight spot": Dyer oral history to Mason Jr.

199 "So close-in were we": Armitage, 78.

199 "hell all over": Thomson diary.

199 *Astoria* **took position behind** *Pasadena***:** Constructed from USS *Astoria* deck logs, USS *Pasadena* CL-65 action reports including radio logs, and author interviews. USS *Wake Island* FM-2 Wildcats spotted for both ships in column.

201 Gerard Armitage spent the day: Armitage, 78.

201 Dyer spent the day on the bridge: Dyer oral history to Mason Jr.

201 "ringside seats": Constructed from Schnipper photographs with captions and author interviews with Schnipper.

201 *Astoria* **could report a major gun battery destroyed:** Constructed from USS *Astoria* deck logs, USS *Pasadena* CL-65 action reports including radio logs, and author interviews.

202 Fred Lind captured radio reports: Lind, 29–30.

202 With spotter planes retired for the night: Constructed from USS *Astoria* deck logs and USS *Pasadena* CL-65 action reports including radio logs.

202 Lieutenant Junior Grade Don Comb returned: Zdon.

204 *Astoria* **slowed to 3 knots:** Constructed from USS *Astoria* deck logs, author interviews, Lind, 30–31, and Thomson diary.

205 *We can't even see flashes***:** Constructed from Dyer oral histories to Burnett Jr. and Mason Jr.

205 "We shot all night": Dyer oral history to Mason Jr.

206 In the hour before dawn: Constructed from USS *Astoria* deck logs and author interviews with Peddie.

206 Main battery fire resumed at 8 a.m.: Constructed from USS *Astoria* deck logs, Armitage, 79, Lind, 31–32, and Arrighi and Thomson diaries.

208 With her ammunition rapidly depleting: Constructed from USS *Astoria* deck logs, Armitage, 79, and USS *Wilkes-Barre* CL-103 war diary.

209 Dawn of February 23: Constructed from USS *Astoria* deck logs, war diaries of ships mentioned, and Dyer oral history to Mason Jr.

210 Herb Blodgett looked on in horror: Author interviews with Blodgett.

211 Captain Dyer held the command perspective: Constructed from USS *Astoria* deck logs, Dyer oral history to Mason Jr., Lind, 32, Arrighi diary, and author interviews with Schnipper.

212 Other news rolled in: Constructed from Morison, *Victory in the Pacific*, 52–55.

212 Gerard Armitage reflected on their turn: Armitage, 80.

213 Captain Dyer penned a letter: Constructed from Dyer oral history to Mason Jr. and listed deck logs.

213 **The two weeks following:** Constructed from USS *Astoria* deck logs, diaries of Thomson, Arrighi, and Blodgett, and Schnipper letter.

214 **Armitage shuffled paperwork at his desk:** Constructed from Armitage, 76–77, and 1945 History of the USS *Astoria* Aviation Unit including Tanner account.

215 **an afternoon of boxing and wrestling matches:** Constructed from USS *Astoria* deck logs, Schnipper photographs, and author interviews.

215 **Dyer learned that his charges:** February 28, 1945, CinCPAC endorsement on Dyer letter of January 11, 1945, Dyer papers, LOC.

215 **Lemon himself had been located:** Lemon service record, NPRC, and Dyer papers, LOC.

216 **Ships across the anchorage were lit that night:** USS *Astoria* deck logs and author interviews.

PART THREE: DAYS OF STEEL RAIN

Part Three photo insert: USS *Pasadena* CL-65 in an emergency turn under heavy flak after a *Kamikaze* near miss on April 11, 1945.
—US Navy photo 80-G-316903 (NARA)

13. RAMPAGE

219 ***Randolph* was forced to stay behind:** USS *Randolph* war diary, USS *Randolph* CV-15 DANFS entry, author interviews, Arrighi diary, and Lind, 34.

220 **"Open fire early, accurately, and in volume":** Dyer papers, LOC.

220 **Iwo Jima was now almost fully secure:** Morison, *Victory in the Pacific*, 67–68.

220 ***Astoria* and the fast carriers again headed north:** Constructed from Morison, *Victory in the Pacific*, 86–88.

221 **numbered more than one hundred ships:** Operation Iceberg Action Reports for Commander Task Group 58.1, 58.2, 58.3, and 58.4, organization sections. Task Group 58.5 sailed embedded in Task Group 58.2 at operation outset. Author placed these assignments in charts and tracked ships attaching and detaching through the following reorganizations.

221 **steamed out for the first time as a complete unit:** Constructed from USS *Astoria* deck logs and USS *Springfield* CL-66 war diary.

221 **directed to repaint from geometric multitone camouflage:** Navy Department Bureau of Ships direction dated February 26, 1945. Many photographs in NARA Records Group 80-G show *Astoria* as an exception during Operation Iceberg. The reason the ship had not yet complied is unknown to the author.

221 **Others came aboard ship:** Constructed from USS *Astoria* reports of changes, Schnipper photographs, and author interviews with Schnipper.

222 **The first day back at sea:** Constructed from USS *Astoria* deck logs and Thomson diary.

222 **Spruance's five task groups proceeded:** Constructed from USS *Astoria* deck logs and task group action reports.

223 Neither *Astoria* nor any cruiser in her division: Cruiser Division 17 war diaries.

223 March 17 brought St. Patrick's Day: Constructed from USS *Astoria* deck logs, Lind, 34, and Blodgett diary.

223 At 6:04 a.m., from across the task group: Constructed from USS *Astoria* deck logs, USS *Bunker Hill* CV-17 war diary, and Lind, 34.

224 USS *Alaska* brought down: USS *Alaska* CB-1 action report for Operation Iceberg.

224 American pilots over their target areas were surprised: Constructed from Morison, *Victory in the Pacific*, 94–96, USS *Astoria* deck logs, USS *Bunker Hill* CV-17 war diary, and author interviews.

224 "The cloud cover was ideal for enemy purposes": USS *Bunker Hill* CV-17 action report for Operation Iceberg.

225 Herman Schnipper was determined to get his shot: Author interviews with Schnipper.

225 *Astoria* steamed off the port quarter of USS *Essex*: Constructed from Morison, *Victory in the Pacific*, 94–96, USS *Astoria* deck logs, and author interviews with Schnipper.

226–228 "The plane shot out of a cloud"...making those same ships fire into each other: Section constructed from USS *Astoria* deck logs and action report from Operation Iceberg, Lind, 35, Thomson and Arrighi diaries, Schnipper photographs, and author interviews with Schnipper and Lind.

228 The smoke on the horizon: Constructed from Morison, *Victory in the Pacific*, 94–96, USS *Astoria* deck logs, USS *Franklin* CV-13 action report from Operation Iceberg, Duggan film, and author interviews.

229 A second round of *Kamikazes*: Constructed from USS *Astoria* deck logs and action report from Operation Iceberg, USS *Essex* CV-9 war diary, Duggan film, Lind, 35, and author interviews.

230 Minutes later, *Astoria* was ordered to detach: Constructed from USS *Astoria* deck logs and action report from Operation Iceberg, USS *Franklin* CV-13 war diary and action report from Operation Iceberg, USS *Wilkes-Barre* CL-103 war diary, Duggan film, Schnipper photographs, and author interviews with Schnipper.

14. FRIENDLIES

231 As *Astoria* left her task group at flank speed: Constructed from USS *Astoria* deck logs and action report from Operation Iceberg, USS *Franklin* CV-13 war diary and action report from Operation Iceberg, Thomson diary, author interviews, Lind, 24, 36.

232 Even though not in view to *Astoria* men: Constructed from USS *Astoria* deck logs and action report from Operation Iceberg, USS *Franklin* CV-13 war diary and action report from Operation Iceberg, USS *Alaska* CB-1, USS *Guam* CB-2, and USS *Pittsburgh* CA-72 war diaries.

233 Captain George Dyer pondered such a concept: Constructed from USS *Astoria* war diary and action report from Operation Iceberg.

234 Dyer reflected back to the experimental flak suits: Dyer oral history with Mason Jr.

234 Dyer wrote a far more complimentary evaluation: Constructed from USS *Astoria* war diary and action report from Operation Iceberg.

234 Three planes, three photographs: Constructed from Schnipper photographs and author interviews with Schnipper.

235 Hard-working yeomen had the ship's daily schedule: USS *Astoria* daily schedule of March 20, 1945.

236 Overnight the task groups had headed south: Constructed from Morison, *Victory in the Pacific*, 97–99, USS *Astoria* deck logs, and USS *Franklin* CV-13 war diary.

236 Captain Dyer set the tone for the coming day: Dyer papers, LOC.

237 USS *Enterprise*, was nothing short of a legend: USS *Enterprise* CV-6 DANFS entry.

238 USS *Hancock* also steamed nearby: Constructed from USS *Astoria* deck logs and action report for Operation Iceberg, and USS *Bataan* CVL-29, USS *San Jacinto* CVL-30, and USS *Hancock* CV-19 war diaries.

238 Men shucked their foul weather jackets: Constructed from Schnipper photographs, author interviews with Schnipper, and Dyer oral history to Mason Jr.

240–241 destroyer *Halsey Powell* transfer two pilots…jeopardized hitting the two ships: Constructed from USS *Astoria* deck logs and action report for Operation Iceberg, USS *Halsey Powell* DD-686 war diary, Duggan film, author interviews, and Lind, 36–37.

241–242 The lull lasted a mere fifteen minutes… "Ammunition exploded all over the place": Constructed from USS *Astoria* deck logs and action report for Operation Iceberg, USS *Enterprise* CV-6 war diary, Schnipper photographs, Duggan film, Thomson diary, and author interviews with Schnipper.

242–243 Captain Dyer kept command…summoned Herman Schnipper to photograph: Constructed from USS *Astoria* deck logs, Dyer oral histories to Burnett Jr. and Mason Jr., Armitage, 85, Lind, 37, Schnipper photographs, and author interviews with Schnipper.

243 John Arrighi was approached: Arrighi diary.

244 Within minutes the ship was firing…brought down by friendly fire: Constructed from USS *Astoria* deck logs and action report for Operation Iceberg, USS *Bataan* CVL-29 and USS *Enterprise* CV-6 war diaries, Duggan film, Schnipper photograph, and Lind, 37.

245 The night brought snoopers: Constructed from USS *Astoria* deck logs, Lind, 37, and Thomson diary.

245 The morning of March 21: Constructed from USS *Astoria* deck logs and action report for Operation Iceberg, USS *Franklin* CV-13 war diary, Duggan film, and Schnipper photographs.

246 "It rained steel for three days": Written on a map of the Pacific utilized by *Astoria* sailor Mario DiMaio as a diary.

246 "After seeing fighter planes all the time": Lind, 37–38.

246 Jim Thomson had to reevaluate: Thomson diary.

246 Gerard Armitage negotiated with Tanner: Armitage, 82.

246 reported through the messing compartment: Dyer oral history to Mason Jr.

15. FOR THE BOYS

247 "We would go to such extremes": Zdon.
247 shockingly effective: Composite created by author based on aircraft carriers retired for repair versus those remaining on the line, all verified by war diaries.
247 Mitscher consolidated his remaining ships: Morison, *Victory in the Pacific*, 100.
248 *Astoria* men briefly got a view: Constructed from USS *Franklin* CV-13 war diary, Duggan film, and author interviews with Schnipper.
248 "790 survivors": Arrighi diary and USS *Franklin* CV-13 DANFS entry.
248 Eight men were killed and thirty-seven wounded: USS *Enterprise* CV-6 action report from Operation Iceberg.
248 *Halsey Powell* also buried her dead at sea: USS *Halsey Powell* DD-686 war diary.
248 *Astoria* was ordered to return: USS *Astoria* deck logs.
248 *Wilkes-Barre* had indeed taken care of the fourth plane: USS *Wilkes-Barre* CL-103 war diary.
248–249 "The *Essex* wasn't very well pleased": Arrighi diary.
249 swells kept raising her propellers: Constructed from USS *Astoria* deck logs and Lind, 26.
250 the Fast Carrier Task Force received high praise: Morison, *Victory in the Pacific*, 100–101.
250 March 23, brought the fast carriers northwest: Constructed from USS *Astoria* deck logs, USS *Bunker Hill* CV-17 and USS *Springfield* CL-66 war diaries, Thomson diary, and Lind, 38.
251 Blodgett stood at the rail: Constructed from USS *Indianapolis* CA-35 war diary, Blodgett diary, and author interviews with Blodgett.
251 "difficult and risky movement": Constructed from USS *Astoria* deck logs, Dyer oral history to Burnett Jr., Morison, *Victory in the Pacific*, 101, and Lind, 38.
252 *Astoria's* rescue planes held first watch: Constructed from USS *Astoria* deck logs and 1945 History of the USS *Astoria* Aviation Unit including Comb account.
253 All four cruisers of *Astoria's* division: Cruiser Division 17 war diaries.
253–256 having cycled through all the available rescue planes… *Astoria* had just completed her first rescue at sea: Constructed from USS *Astoria* deck logs, USS *Bunker Hill* CV-17 war diary, and 1945 History of the USS *Astoria* Aviation Unit including Tanner, Davis, and Mahoney accounts.
256 The next day brought refueling and rearming: Constructed from USS *Astoria* deck logs, Lind, 38, Arrighi diary, Schnipper letter, Schnipper photographs, and author interviews with Schnipper.
256 hunk of nothing: Constructed from USS *Astoria* deck logs, author interviews, and author manipulation of Google Earth.
257 "After daylight we got the word": Constructed from USS *Astoria* deck logs and Arrighi and Thomson diaries.
258–259 The fast carriers were sent back up to Kyushu… four against eight over a lone man: Constructed from USS *Astoria* deck logs, USS *Bunker Hill* CV-17 and USS *Wilkes-Barre* CL-103 war diaries, Commander Air Group Six War History, Narrative,

8–10, Bowman, 144–150, and 1945 History of the USS *Astoria* Aviation Unit including Somerville account.

259–263 Captain Dyer received the order...A shot of Old Grand-Dad bourbon: Constructed from USS *Astoria* deck logs, Commander Air Group Six War History, Narrative, 8–10, Bowman, 144–150, "Everything For the Boys," May 1, 1945, radio broadcast, Zdon, Duggan film, and 1945 History of the USS *Astoria* Aviation Unit including Newman, Comb, and Somerville accounts.

263 "These were anything but pleasure flights": Lind, 39.

263 "Battle of Kagoshima Bay": Constructed from USS *Astoria* deck logs and war diary and Bowman, 144–150.

263 "We got the dope today": Arrighi diary, Blodgett diary, and author interviews.

16. CASUALTIES OF WAR

264 "Giving up your pie at meal time": Lind, 26.

264 "Ho hum, the war is getting pretty mundane": Reynolds, 336.

264 Landing Day at Okinawa: Morison, *Victory in the Pacific*, 87.

265 "It was a combination of Easter Sunday for us and April Fool's Day": Lind, 39–40.

266 For Herb Blodgett, delivered mail...Blodgett would stand watch utterly alone: Blodgett diary and author interviews with Blodgett.

266 Dyer cautioned his crew about complacency: Dyer papers, LOC.

267 "Regular routine, with reveille at 4 a.m.": Lind, 40.

268–269 Dyer's predicted counterattacks began...There could be no more of this: Constructed from USS *Astoria* deck logs and action report for Operation Iceberg, USS *Cabot* CVL-28 war diary, Dyer oral history to Mason Jr., Duggan film, Schnipper photographs, Armitage, 88, Blodgett diary, and author interviews with Blodgett.

269 "We were hit in the fantail": USS *Pasadena* CL-65 Marine Carl Lewis diary, USS *Pasadena* CL-65 action report for Operation Iceberg.

271 Fred Lind wrote of *Kamikaze* patterns: Lind, 27, 48.

271 John Arrighi found a bright side: Arrighi diary.

271 The morning of April 7: Morison, *Victory in the Pacific*, 204–205.

271–273 Just after noon, with the fleet's air cover...following destroyer could retrieve the men: Constructed from USS *Astoria* deck logs, USS *Hancock* CV-19 war diary, Arrighi and Blodgett diaries, Duggan film, Schnipper photographs, and author interviews with Blodgett and Schnipper.

273–274 exhausted men remained at stations..."when the ship got hit": Constructed from USS *Astoria* deck logs and war diary, Arrighi diary, Lind, 34, and author interviews with Lind.

274 "IJN *Yamato*": IJN was the American abbreviation for Imperial Japanese Navy, the equivalent of USS for United States Ship.

274 "Japan's largest!": Arrighi diary.

274 Fred Lind's tone in his Gregg diary: Lind, 41.

275 Mitscher decided to place his remaining task groups: Constructed from Commander Task Group war diaries for 58.1, 58.3, and 58.4.

275–277 Beyond the typical spectacle…a pariah to 1,300 men: Constructed from USS *Astoria* deck logs and reports of changes, Lemon service record, NPRC, author interviews, Dyer oral history to Mason Jr., and Dyer papers, LOC.

277–278 Fully four weeks into Operation Iceberg…again set to bear the brunt: Constructed from USS *Astoria* deck logs, USS *Enterprise* CV-6, USS *South Dakota* BB-57, and USS *Bunker Hill* CV-17 war diaries, and author interviews with Lind.

278 it was *Essex's* turn yet again: Constructed from USS *Astoria* deck logs and action report for Operation Iceberg, USS *Pasadena* CL-65 war diary, and Madden and Schnipper photos.

278–279 From the searchlight platform…baseball umpire behind a catcher: Constructed from USS *Astoria* deck logs and action report for Operation Iceberg, USS *Enterprise* CV-6 war diary, Schnipper photographs, and author interviews with Schnipper.

279 "We intercepted a message": Lind, 42.

279 "two planes that got very close to the ship": Dyer oral history to Burnett Jr.

279–281 Schnipper tracked the plane…jacket whipping in the wind: Constructed from USS *Astoria* deck logs and action report for Operation Iceberg, Duggan film, Schnipper photographs, and author interviews with Schnipper.

281 At 4:16 p.m., the Zero passed low: Constructed from USS *Astoria* deck logs and action report for Operation Iceberg, US Navy photographs in records group 80-G, NARA, and author interviews with Lind.

281–282 the ship's senior medical officer…his ill-advised adventure: Constructed from USS *Astoria* action report for Operation Iceberg and Dyer oral history to Mason Jr.

282 "air-cooled thirty-caliber machine gun": Armitage, 82.

282 the next round would arrive around 7 p.m.: Constructed from USS *Astoria* deck logs and Lind, 42.

282–285 Armitage recorded one example…Mighty Ninety had racked up another plane: Armitage, 82–84.

285 Armitage watched "the radar in fascination": Constructed from Armitage, 82, Lind, 42, and Arrighi diary.

285 all four cruisers of the WASP Division had evaded near misses: Cruiser Division 17 war diaries.

286 Lavin added of his experience: Author interview with Lavin.

287 From the bridge, Captain Dyer: Constructed from USS *Astoria* deck logs and action report for Operation Iceberg, and Dyer oral history to Burnett Jr.

287 "We don't get good stuff like that": Lind, 42.

287 "It was a shock to all": Arrighi diary.

17. TETSU NO AME

288 "No news was shocking by this time": Lind, 43.

288 "The Lord plays no favorites": Dyer oral history to Mason Jr.

288–289 Men had developed tips and tricks…just as he snapped the shutter: Constructed from author interviews with Schnipper and Blodgett, Schnipper photographs, and Lind, 43.

289 six of seventeen available American fast carriers: Author construction from war diaries of fast carriers.

290 "I witnessed the largest flak barrage": Lind, 43–44.

291 "kept awake all night by air alerts": Arrighi diary.

291 "We received word that Ernie Pyle was killed": Lind, 44.

291 Rousseau Lemon voluntarily requested captain's mast: Dyer oral history to Mason Jr.

292 "another short V-mail": Schnipper V-mail letter.

292 *Franklin* was sent up east to Brooklyn Navy Yard: USS *Franklin* CV-13 war diary and US Navy photographs in records group 80-G, NARA.

292 On May 1, *Hancock* pilot Pete Somerville: Everything For the Boys" May 1, 1945, radio broadcast. Returning to action following his rescue, Somerville would go on to receive the Navy Cross for his actions over Japan.

293 "We wonder": Arrighi diary.

293 "Air attacks were unceasing": Lind, 45.

293 Goeggel took fire over Takuno Island: Constructed from USS *Astoria* deck logs and action report for Operation Iceberg, 1945 History of the USS *Astoria* Aviation Unit including Tanner account, and Schnipper photographs.

293 "Being this close to Japan": Lind, 45.

295 WASP Division was detached: Constructed from USS *Astoria* deck logs and action report for Operation Iceberg.

296–297 returning flight of Marine Corsairs…"This day made sixty days at sea": Constructed from USS *Astoria* deck logs and action report for Operation Iceberg, USS *Bunker Hill* CV-17 and USS *Wilkes-Barre* CL-103 war diaries, Schnipper photographs, Arrighi and Blodgett diaries, Lind, 46–47, and author interviews with Blodgett.

297 That same morning *Enterprise* returned: Constructed from USS *Bunker Hill* CV-17 and USS *Enterprise* CV-6 war diaries.

297–298 The next morning *Enterprise* was hit yet again…"couldn't do its job": Constructed from USS *Astoria* deck logs and action report for Operation Iceberg, USS *Enterprise* CV-6 war diary, Lind, 27, 47, author interviews with Lind, Schnipper photographs, and Arrighi diary.

298–303 *Astoria* received orders for another risky rescue mission…four-leaf clover brought luck: Constructed from USS *Astoria* deck logs and action report for Operation Iceberg, USS *Randolph* CV-15 war diary, 1945 History of the USS *Astoria* Aviation Unit including Tanner, Comb, and Morris accounts, Zdon, Bruce and Leonard, 166–174, Dyer papers, LOC, and Schnipper photographs.

303 Rousseau Lemon again requested to see the skipper: Constructed from Dyer oral history to Mason Jr., Lemon service record, NPRC, and *Mighty Ninety* newspapers.

303 "Our operations were becoming redundant": Lind, 47–48.

304 remained at two-thirds strength: Author construction from war diaries of all ships in the Fast Carrier Task Force during Operation Iceberg. Destroyers were assessed at the division level. All ships with heavier tonnage were reviewed individually.

304–305 such an uninterrupted operation...also performed at the top: Constructed from USS *Astoria*, USS *Essex* CV-9, and Cruiser Division 17 action reports from Operation Iceberg, author construction from antiaircraft action reports of all fast carriers, battleships, heavy and light cruisers involved over the period, Schnipper photographs, *Mighty Ninety* newspaper of May 17, 1945, and author interviews.

305 WASP Division as skilled *Kamikaze* killers: Delayed release in *Stars and Stripes* on August 25, 1945.

305 Fred Lind reflected on their experience": Lind, 27.

18. RELIEF

306 letter arrived from USS *Randolph*: Dyer papers, LOC.

306 Days of liberty ashore followed at Leyte: Constructed from USS *Astoria* deck logs, Arrighi diary, Schnipper photographs, and author interviews with Schnipper and Peddie.

307 "Liberty nearly did me in": Lind, 50–51.

307 "The water or something is getting the fellows sick": Arrighi diary.

307 Armitage learned that a man named Joe Broscia: Armitage, 81.

308 *LIFE* magazine arrived, men had to laugh: Constructed from "*LIFE* visits an Enchanted Isle," *LIFE*, May 7, 1945, 126–129, and *Mighty Ninety Cruise Book*.

308 "On June 1, I was sworn in": Lind, 48.

308 On June 7, men on deck were jolted: Constructed from USS *Astoria* deck logs, USS *Randolph* CV-15 war diary, Schnipper photographs, and Lind, 50.

308 The remaining fast carrier task groups steamed: Constructed from Morison, *Victory in the Pacific*, 304–307, photographs taken by *Astoria* officer John Lisle, and author interviews with Schnipper and Lind.

309–311 more somber matter to attend to...A horrified American public: Constructed from USS *Astoria* deck logs, Schnipper photographs and captions, author interviews with Schnipper, *Mighty Ninety* newspaper, "The Fleet That Came to Stay" 1945 US Navy short film, and *Astoria* junior officer John Schmitt's memoirs.

311 Additional fleet photographers were assigned aboard *Astoria*: USS *Astoria* reports of changes, author interviews with Schnipper.

19. GHOSTS OF NANSEI SHOTO

312–313 *Astoria* lost her first man...the men would learn their new mission: Constructed from USS *Astoria* deck logs, Schnipper photographs, author interviews with Schnipper and Dolci, Arrighi diary, and *Mighty Ninety* newspaper of July 21, 1945, as the previous issue had already gone to print before Ostrander's passing.

313 A popular tale that circulated among the task force: Author interviews. This term periodically showed up in action reports, including USS *Astoria* and USS *Oakland* CL-95.

313 ships were not tied to a specific invasion: Morison, *Victory in the Pacific*, 310.

313–314 "Strange things were happening at sea…it sure was impressive": Constructed from USS *Astoria* deck logs and Lind, 51.

314 caught wind of their objective: Kane, Snyder, and Arrighi diaries.

315 Flight operations for strikes: Constructed from USS *Astoria* deck logs, Morison, *Victory in the Pacific*, 310–311, Lind, 52, and Arrighi diary.

315 A second day of strikes: Constructed from USS *Astoria* deck logs and Lind, 52.

315 Beginning with July 13: Constructed from USS *Astoria* deck logs and Arrighi, Kane, and Snyder diaries.

315–316 Weather cleared the morning of the fourteenth…"I just couldn't believe it": Constructed from USS *Astoria* deck logs, Lind, 52, and Arrighi diary.

316 "Names were being submitted": Lind, 53.

318 Schnipper finally had enough: Constructed from USS *Astoria* reports of changes, author interviews with Schnipper, disciplinary entries in USS *Astoria* deck logs, and *Mighty Ninety* newspaper.

318 "They must have been serious": Lind, 53.

318 "Still waiting": Arrighi diary.

318 remarks about Ross Lemon: *Mighty Ninety* newspaper of August 5, 1945.

318 Grady Sanders was a well-liked and respected boatswain's mate: Author construction from interviews and Sanders Navy records found on www.ancestry.com.

318 The lull in fighting brought the cruiser alongside: Constructed from USS *Astoria* deck logs, USS *Wilkes-Barre* CL-103 war diary, author interviews, and Schnipper photographs.

319 786 miles to the west-southwest, the sky collapsed: Constructed from USS *Astoria* deck logs, Morison, *Victory in the Pacific*, 345, author manipulation of Google Earth, and Arrighi diary as example.

319–320 *Astoria* sailors stood in silence…Hostilities might have ceased: Constructed from USS *Astoria* deck logs, Schnipper and Rudy Guttosch photographs, and Kane and Snyder diary.

320 Further news tempered spirits: USS *Indianapolis* CA-35 DANFS entry.

320 "Aerial pictures were taken of the fleet": Lind, 55.

320 instead of confirming a return to the States: Author interviews drew out that "confirmed" became a relative term in this period; the ship's potential occupation status changed almost daily.

320–321 conducted small arms refresher…the good old US of A: Constructed from USS *Astoria* deck logs, Schnipper photographs, and author interviews with Schnipper and Peddie.

321 *Astoria* formed up: Constructed from USS *Astoria* deck logs, NARA photographs in record group 80-G, and author interviews with Schnipper.

20. UNCLE SUGAR

322 Cartoonist Joe Aman: Constructed from "Joey Fubar's Cavalcade of Humor," the *Mighty Ninety* newspaper, and a humorous memorandum on politeness that circulated the ship.

322 *Essex* detached to head into Bremerton: Constructed from USS *Astoria* deck logs and author interviews.

323 "Since I was in A Division": Author interview with Blodgett.

323 The full reception ran the length of the pier: Constructed from Schnipper photos, author interviews, and shipmate clippings from Los Angeles newspapers of September 16, 1945.

324 "While a bunch of my buddies left for home": Lind, 57.

324 Jim Peddie and 117 other men drawn: Constructed from "Blow In for a Blow-out" article and author interviews with Peddie.

324 "Reunion with the family": Lind, 57.

324 *Astoria's* crew had a 50 percent turnover: Constructed from USS *Astoria* reports of changes, Schnipper photos, and author interviews.

325 newly promoted Rear Admiral Dyer: Dyer oral histories to Burnett Jr. and Mason Jr.

325 Schnipper and his buddies did their best: Schnipper photographs, personal correspondence, and author interviews with family.

326 *Astoria* spent the rest of 1946: Constructed from USS *Astoria* DANFS entry and USS *Astoria* photos and documents in author's collection.

326 Navy experiment of the Cramp Shipbuilding Company: 1946 Cramp financial reports. (ISM)

326 Astoria remained in commission: USS *Astoria* DANFS entry.

327 destroyed an old Japanese mine: "Japanese Mine Destroyed," *New York Times*, July 17, 1948.

327 *Astoria* spent more than twenty years: Constructed from USS *Astoria* DANFS entry and 1971 Larry Coté photographs.

327 In 1972, surviving shipmates: Reunion materials in author's collection.

EPILOGUE: GUARDIANS IN THE SETTING SUN

Much of this closing covers discussions from the author with shipmates and family. Bobby Thomson's legacy stands on its own merits for this lifelong baseball fan. Other specifics are cited.

328 Reflecting in later years: Armitage, 61.

329 "life in the military service": Theaker letter.

330 "Loss of my best buddy": Lind, 6.

324 "I should like nothing better": Dyer papers, LOC.

334 "Our first skipper was a true professional": Armitage, 61.

Bibliography

PRINCIPAL ARCHIVES

J. Welles Henderson Research Center at Independence Seaport Museum, Philadelphia, Pennsylvania (ISM)

Library of Congress, Washington, DC (LOC)

National Archives and Records Administration II, College Park, Maryland (NARA)

National Archives and Records Administration, Fort Worth, Texas (NARAFW)

National Personnel Records Center, St. Louis, Missouri (NPRC)

Naval History and Heritage Command, Washington, DC (NHHC)

United States Naval Institute, Annapolis, Maryland (USNI)

COLLECTIONS

Annual Reports and records of the Cramp Shipbuilding Company, 1940–1947, ISM

Papers of George Carroll Dyer, LOC

Record Group 19-LCM, Department of the Bureau of Ships Photographs, NARA

Record Group 24, Records of the Bureau of Naval Personnel, NARA

Record Group 38, Records of the Office of the Chief of Naval Operations, NARA

Record Group 80-G, Department of the Navy Photographs, NARA

Records Group 208, Records of the Office of War Information, NARA

Records of the 8th Naval District, District Legal Officer, NARAFW

Schnipper, Herman C., Navy Photographer 1944–1946, family holdings.

PERSONAL NARRATIVES (UNPUBLISHED)

Armitage, Gerard T. "Semper Fidelis," abridged 2018. Author's collection.

Arrighi, John. Personal Diary, 1944–1945. Author's collection.

Blodgett, Herbert M. Personal Diary, 1944–1945. Author's collection.

Kane, Thomas L., and John L. Snyder. Shared Personal Diary, 1944–1945. Author's collection.

Lind, J. Fred. "Sea Attitudes: A Book of WWII Memories," undated. Author's collection.

Thomson, James H. Personal Diary, 1944–1945. Author's collection.

SERVICE RECORD

Lemon, Ross Rousseau, 1941–1945, NPRC.

INTERVIEWS AND ORAL HISTORIES

Allen, Clarence E. Interviewed by author, 2009–2010.
Blodgett, Herbert M. Interviewed by author, 2009–2012.
Brintnall, Robert L. Interviewed by author, 2009.
Comb, Donald O. Interviewed by Al Zdon, 2010.
Dolci, Deno V. Interviewed by author, 2009–2010.
Dyer, George Carroll. Interviewed by John T. Mason Jr., 1969–1971, USNI.
Dyer, George Carroll. Interviewed by Howard W. Burnett Jr., 1981–1984. Author's collection.
Lavin, Andrew J. Interviewed by author, 2009.
Lind, J. Fred. Interviewed by author, 2009.
Obuchon, Norman O. Interviewed by author, 2009.
Peddie, James. Interviewed by author, 2009–2012.
Schnipper, Herman C. Interviewed by author, 2007–2015.

US NAVY DECK LOGS (NARA RECORDS GROUP 24)

USS *Astoria* CL-90 (1944–1945)

US NAVY MUSTER ROLLS AND REPORTS OF CHANGES (NARA RECORDS GROUP 24)

USS *Astoria* CA-34 (1941–1942)
USS *Astoria* CL-90 (1944–1945)
USS *Baltimore* CA-68 (1944)
USS *Boise* CL-47 (1942–1943)
USS *Montpelier* CL-57 (1944)
USS *Santa Fe* CL-60 (1943)

US NAVY WAR DIARIES, WAR PATROL LOGS, AND ACTION REPORTS (NARA RECORDS GROUP 38)

This is a primary list, as the author also accessed the war diaries for all 122 ships that served in the Fast Carrier Task Force during Okinawa operations to create reference charts.

USS *Alaska* CB-1 (1945)
USS *Aspro* SS-309 (1945)
USS *Astoria* CA-34 (1942)
USS *Astoria* CL-90 (1944–1945)
USS *Baltimore* CA-68 (1944)

USS *Bataan* CVL-29 (1945)
USS *Biloxi* CL-80 (1944)
USS *Birmingham* CL-62 (1944)
USS *Biscayne* AVP-11 (1943)
USS *Bunker Hill* CV-17 (1945)
USS *Cabot* CVL-28 (1944–1945)
USS *Canberra* CA-70 (1944)
USS *Duluth* CL-87 (1944)
USS *Enterprise* CV-6 (1945)
USS *Essex* CV-9 (1945)
USS *Franklin* CV-13 (1945)
USS *Guam* CB-2 (1945)
USS *Halsey Powell* DD-686 (1945)
USS *Hancock* CV-19 (1945)
USS *Hickox* DD-673 (1944)
USS *Indianapolis* CA-35 (1945)
USS *Intrepid* CV-11 (1944)
USS *Lexington* CV-16 (1944)
USS *Maddox* DD-731 (1944)
USS *Miami* CL-89 (1944)
USS *Montpelier* CL-57 (1944)
USS *New Jersey* BB-62 (1944)
USS *Pasadena* CL-65 (1945)
USS *Pensacola* CA-24 (1945)
USS *Pittsburgh* CA-72 (1945)
USS *Quincy* CA-71 (1944)
USS *Randolph* CV-15 (1945)
USS *San Jacinto* CVL-30 (1945)
USS *South Dakota* BB-57 (1945)
USS *Springfield* CL-66 (1945)
USS *Tabberer* DE-418 (1944)
USS *Vincennes* CL-64 (1944–1945)
USS *Wilkes-Barre* CL-103 (1945)
USS *Wisconsin* BB-64 (1944)
USS *Wyoming* BB-32 (1944)

US NAVY WAR HISTORY (NARA RECORDS GROUP 38)

Commander Air Group Six (April 10, 1944–October 15, 1945)

ADDITIONAL USS *ASTORIA* CL-90 SOURCE DOCUMENTS

These do not exist in any archive, nor any known comprehensive collection. Many items created aboard ship were printed and circulated with few surviving copies, as the Navy had no purpose for retaining them as records. Where referenced, they are from clippings or pages that individual shipmates retained. In some cases a date was not present but could be extrapolated or estimated based on the contents.

Astoria Morning Press (printed daily). 1944–1945.
Authorized Form Letters. 1945.
History of the Aviation Unit. 1944–1945.
Holiday Cards and Menus. 1944–1945.
Joey Fubar's Cavalcade of Humor. 1945.
Mighty Ninety newspaper (printed biweekly). 1944–1945.
TBS Orders and Transcripts. 1945.
Unknown author. *Mighty Ninety Cruise Book.* 1945.

ARTICLES

Author unknown. "Blow In for a Blow-Out." *New York Times*, October 11, 1945.
Author unknown. "Solomons Island Battle." *LIFE*, October 26, 1942.
Zdon, Al. "Mission into the Heart of the Japan Inland Sea." *Minnesota Legionnaire*, November 2010, 10–12.

SECONDARY SOURCES: REFERENCE BOOKS AND PUBLICATIONS

Adcock, Al. *US Light Cruisers in Action, Warships No. 12.* Carrollton, TX: Squadron/Signals Publications, 1999.
Articles for the Government of the United States Navy. Washington, DC: United States Government Printing Office, 1932.
Bowman, Martin W. *Great American Air Battles of World War II.* Shrewsbury, England: Airlife Publishing, 1994.
Bruce, Roy W., and Charles R. Leonard. *Crommelin's Thunderbirds: Air Group 12 Strikes the Heart of Japan.* Washington, DC: United States Naval Institute Press, 1994.
Custer, Joe James. *Through the Perilous Night: The Astoria's Last Battle.* New York: MacMillan, 1944.
Eyes of the Fleet. Unites States Navy publication, circa 1944.
Frank, Richard B. *Guadalcanal: The Definitive Account of the Landmark Battle.* New York: Random House, 1990.
Friedman, Norman. *US Cruisers: An Illustrated Design History.* Washington, DC: United States Naval Institute Press, 1984.
Gilbert, Oscar E. *Marine Tank Battles in the Pacific.* Cambridge, MA: Da Capo Press, 2001.
Helpful Hints to the Navy Recruit. Washington, DC: United States Navy Recruiting and Induction Service, 1944.
King, Ernest J. "Our Navy at War: Official Report." Circulated by *United States News*, circa April 1944.
Mooney, James L. *Dictionary of American Naval Fighting Ships.* Washington, DC: Navy Department, Office of the Chief of Naval Operations, Naval History Division, 1959. (DANFS)

Morison, Samuel Eliot. *Leyte: June 1944–January 1945*. Vol. 12, *History of United States Naval Operations in World War II*. New York: Little, Brown, 1958.

———. *The Liberation of the Philippines: Luzon, Mindanao, and the Visayas, 1944–1945*. Vol. 13, *History of United States Naval Operations in World War II*. New York: Little, Brown, 1959.

———. *Victory in the Pacific, 1945*. Vol. 14, *History of United States Naval Operations in World War II*. New York: Little, Brown, 1960.

Reynolds, Clark G. *The Fast Carriers: The Forging of an Air Navy.* United States Naval Institute Press, 1968.

Talcott, Richard B. *The Making of a Sailor.* Somerville, MA: 1944.

United States Navy. *The Bluejackets' Manual.* 11th ed. Washington, DC: United States Naval Institute Press, 1943.

United States Navy. *The Bluejackets' Manual.* 12th ed. Washington, DC: United States Naval Institute Press, 1944.

Wheeler, Keith, and the editors of Time-Life Books. *The Road to Tokyo.* Chicago: Time-Life Books, 1979.

REFERENCE WEBSITES AND APPLICATION

American Battle Monuments Commission. www.abmc.gov.

Ancestry. www.ancestry.com.

Fold3. www.fold3.com.

Google Earth application.

USS Enterprise CV-6: The Most Decorated Ship of the Second World War. www.cv6.org.

Walter Duggan's 1945 film footage can be found on author's website www.mighty90.com.

Index

Page numbers in *italics* indicate illustrations.